The Pharmacologic Basis of
Psychotherapeutics

The Pharmacologic Basis of Psychotherapeutics: An Introduction for Psychologists

by

Louis A. Pagliaro, MS, PharmD, PhD
Professor, Department of Educational Psychology
University of Alberta
President, College of Alberta Psychologists
Edmonton, Alberta, Canada

and

Ann Marie Pagliaro, BSN, MSN, PhD Candidate
Professor, Faculty of Nursing
Director, Substance Abusology Research Unit
University of Alberta
Edmonton, Alberta, Canada

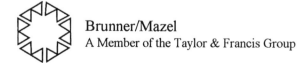
Brunner/Mazel
A Member of the Taylor & Francis Group

USA	Publishing Office:	Taylor & Francis 1101 Vermont Avenue, NW, Suite 200 Washington, DC 20005-3521 Tel: (202) 289-2174 Fax: (202) 289-3665
	Distribution Center:	Taylor & Francis 1900 Frost Road, Suite 101 Bristol, PA 19007-1598 Tel: (215) 785-5800 Fax: (215) 785-5515
UK		Taylor & Francis Ltd. 1 Gunpowder Square London EC4A 3DE Tel: 0171 583 0490 Fax: 0171 583 0581

THE PHARMACOLOGIC BASIS OF PSYCHOTHERAPEUTICS:
An Introduction for Psychologists

1 2 3 4 5 6 7 8 9 0   EBEB   9 0 9 8 7

This book was set in Times Roman. The editors were Heather Worley and Greg Edmondson. Cover design by Curtis Tow.

A CIP catalog record for this book is available from the British Library.
♾ The paper in this publication meets the requirements of the ANSI Standard Z39.48-1984 (Permanence of Paper)

Library of Congress Cataloging-in-Publication Data

Pagliaro, Louis A.
  The pharmacologic basis of psychotherapeutics: an introduction
for psychologists/by Louis A. Pagliaro and Ann Marie Pagliaro.
    p. cm.
  Includes bibliographical references.

    1. Psychopharmacology.   2. Psychotherapy—Physiological aspects.
  I. Pagliaro, Ann M.   II. Title.
  RM315.P325   1998
  615′.78—dc21   97-19994
                                                          CIP

ISBN 1-56032-677-8 (case)
ISBN 1-56032-678-6 (paper)

Dedication

This book, the first in a series of pharmacopsychology texts specifically written for psychologists and graduate psychology students, is dedicated to the advancement of the profession of psychology with the hope and trust that this advancement will be accompanied by commensurate improvements in the psychological health of those who seek, require, and receive psychotropic pharmacotherapy as an integral adjunct to their psychotherapy.

Pharmacology Texts and Reference Books by the Pagliaros

Clinical Psychopharmacotherapeutics for Psychologists. Washington, DC: Taylor & Francis, (in preparation).

Drug Reference Guide to Brand Names and Active Ingredients. St. Louis, Missouri: C. V. Mosby, (1986).

Pharmacologic Aspects of Aging. St. Louis, Missouri: C. V. Mosby, (1983).

Pharmacologic Aspects of Nursing. St. Louis, Missouri: C. V. Mosby, (1986).

The Pharmacologic Basis of Psychotherapeutics: An Introduction for Psychologists. Washington, DC: Taylor & Francis, (1998).

Problems in Pediatric Drug Therapy. Hamilton, Illinois: Drug Intelligence Publications, Washington, DC: American Pharmaceutical Association Books, (1979, 1987, 1995).

Psychologists' Psychotropic Desk Reference. Washington, DC: Taylor & Francis, (1998).

Substance Use Among Children and Adolescents: Its Nature, Extent, and Effects from Conception to Adulthood. New York, New York: John Wiley & Sons, (1996).

Contents

Special Guest Authors

Patrick H. DeLeon, PhD, JD
Recording Secretary, American Psychological Association
Administrative Assistant to U.S. Senator Daniel K. Inouye
Washington, D.C.

Morgan Sammons, PhD
Department of Defense Psychopharmacology Fellow

Editorial Advisory Committee

Rosalie J. Ackerman, PhD
Co-Chair of the Task Force on Prescription Privileges
Division 35 (Psychology of Women)
American Psychological Association
Research and Development Division
ABackans Diversified Computer Processing
Uniontown, Ohio

Robert K. Ax, PhD
Midlothian, Virginia

Martha Banks, PhD
Co-Chair of the Task Force on Prescription Privileges
Division 35 (Psychology of Women)
American Psychological Association
Research and Development Division
ABackans Diversified Computer Processing
Uniontown, Ohio

John Bolter, PhD
The Neuromedical Center
Baton Rouge, Louisiana

Ron L. Cohorn, PhD
Chairman, Prescription Privilege Committee
Texas Psychological Association
Malone & Hogan Clinic
Big Spring, Texas

Joseph E. Comaty, PhD
Director of Special Programs
East Louisiana State Hospital
Jackson, Louisiana
Adjunct Assistant Professor
Department of Psychology
Louisiana State University
Baton Rouge, Louisiana

Charles A. Faltz, PhD
San Mateo, California

Samuel A. Feldman, PhD, FAPM, FPPR
President, Board Certified Diplomate-Fellow
Prescribing Psychologists' Register Inc.
North Miami Beach, Florida

Eldridge E. Fleming, PhD, FPPR
Past President, Mississippi Psychological Association
Chair, Task Force on Psychopharmacology
Mississippi Psychological Association
Tupelo, Mississippi

Raymond A. Folen, PhD
Chief, Clinical Health Psychology Service
Department of Psychology
Tripler Regional Medical Center
Honolulu, Hawaii

Ronald E. Fox, PhD
Former President, American Psychological Association
Executive Director
Division of Organizational and Management Consulting
Human Resource Consultants
Chapel Hill, North Carolina

Alan R. Gruber, DSW, PhD
Co-Chair, Psychopharmacology Committee
Massachusetts Psychological Association
Neurobehavioral Associates
Hingham, Massachusetts

Stanley W. Sadava, PhD
Professor of Psychology
Brock University
St. Catharines, Ontario

Gary R. Schoener, PhD Candidate
Licensed Psychologist and Organizational Consultant
Executive Director
Walk In Counseling Service
Minneapolis, Minnesota

Michael Schwarzchild, PhD
Co-Chairman, Psychopharmacology Committee
Connecticut Psychological Association
Chairman, Committee on Psychopharmacology in Independent Practice
Division 42 (Independent Practice), American Psychological Association
Brookfield, Connecticut

Maxine L. Stitzer, PhD
Professor of Psychiatry and Behavioral Science
Johns Hopkins University School of Medicine
Baltimore, Maryland

Michael F. Wesner, PhD
Associate Professor of Psychology
Lakehead University
Thunder Bay, Ontario

Jack G. Wiggins, PhD
Former President, American Psychological Association
Fountain Hills, Arizona

James P. Zacny, PhD
Assistant Professor
Department of Anesthesia and Critical Care
The University of Chicago
Chicago, Illinois

List of Figures and Tables

Many informative figures and tables are used in this book. The following provides a guide to these features:

FIGURES

TABLES

Foreword

Prescription Privileges for Psychologists:
An Historical Overview

For professional psychology, the prescription privilege agenda began in earnest in the late 1980s. On November 30, 1984 U.S. Senator Daniel K. Inouye addressed the annual meeting of the Hawaii Psychological Association (HPA) and urged them to adopt: ". . . an entirely new legislative agenda which I think fits very nicely into the theme of your convention: 'Psychology in the 80's: Transcending Traditional Boundaries'. As a United States Senator, I have also been working closely during the past decade with a number of your 'natural allies'. I am particularly thinking of our nations nurse practitioners, nurse midwives, and optometrists. The members of these professions have been successful to differing degrees in amending their state practice acts to allow them to independently utilize drugs where appropriate. . . In my judgment, when you have obtained this statutory authority, you will have really made the big time. Then, you truly will be an autonomous profession and your clients will be well-served" (Inouye, 1984). Interestingly, that same year Richard Samuels, then President of the APA Division of Psychologists in Independent Practice (Division 42), called for a similar policy agenda. These futuristic "calls for action" were enthusiastically heard by many within our professional community but in retrospect, it has become evident that the vast majority of our colleagues had yet to really appreciate the monumental long-term implications for their professional identities, clinical practices, and training institutions (DeLeon, Fox, Graham, 1991).

In many ways, the maturation of the prescription privilege agenda might well be viewed as being closely related to psychology's gradual emergence over the past several decades as a bona fide health care profession. An increasing number of our colleagues no longer identify with psychology's traditional self-conceptualization of solely being a "mental health specialist". Instead, they are genuinely interested in providing "comprehensive primary care" or working as an integral element of our nation's *health care* system—effectively addressing the psychosocial and behavioral aspects of a wide range of physical ailments (DeLeon, Frank, & Wedding, 1995).

Without question, psychology's status within the health care arena has dramatically increased over the recent years. In our judgment, this evolution (maturation) has been closely related to two distinct clinical developments: the increasing appreciation by medicine of the considerable benefits of the behavioral sciences in general, and the significant successes of the other non-physician disciplines in demonstrating that they do, indeed, provide high quality and cost-effective health services. From our experiences at the national level it has become quite evident that psychology is already intimately involved in a wide range of health initiatives, including serving prominently on the university faculty of a number of professional disciplines—for example, approximately one quarter of doctoral level nursing faculty possess degrees in psychology.

Today, nearly a decade and a half since Senator Inouye's initial challenge, there has been considerable progress in the efforts of the various non-physician disciplines to obtain prescriptive authority. Optometry, for example, first obtained this clinical responsibility in the State of

Indiana in 1935. Fifty years later, Maryland became the final state in the nation to formally recognize their pharmacological expertise. Nurse practitioners began their quest with the successful passage of legislation in North Carolina in 1975. Today, 48–49 states have enacted legislation providing Advanced Practice Nursing (APN) with prescriptive authority, under various conditions; the movement clearly being towards "physician substitution" statutes (i.e., granting nursing professional autonomy). Similar progress has been made by podiatry (all states), physician assistants (40 states), and pharmacists (seven states). Not surprisingly, every step of the way (with the notable exception of physician assistants) the competing medical specialty groups strenuously opposed the granting of this particular privilege—arguing in essence that if granted, their counterparts would affirmatively "harm" their patients (i.e., that since they did not attend medical school, non-physicians represent definite "public health hazards") (DeLeon, & Wiggins, 1996).

From both a public policy and evolutionary perspective, there has also been *remarkable* progress on the prescription agenda within organized psychology (Fox, 1988; Frank, 1992; Pimental, Stout, Hoover, & Kamen, 1997). When one appreciates that the prescription agenda is being primarily advanced by the practice community, rather than by the educational community, the fact that a genuine consensus for obtaining this clinical responsibility has actually evolved, in such a relatively short period of time, is nothing short of amazing. Psychology has never really possessed "homes of its own" where psychology faculty control the day-to-day clinical experiences of their students and where truly comprehensive (including inpatient care) clinical experiences can be provided. Individual clinicians may have obtained considerable "first hand" expertise in utilizing psychopharmacological agents; however, to develop viable, not to mention credible, psychopharmacology training programs a profession must have regular access to those patients who genuinely require these services. That is, the opportunity to provide both didactic and "hands on" expertise must be readily obtainable. Without these necessary resources, it is difficult for psychology faculty who traditionally have been responsible for ensuring that graduate students are competently trained—including "signing off" on internship placements—to feel emotionally comfortable about their potential role (Fox, Schwelitz, & Barclay, 1992). Interestingly, this has not been an issue for the other disciplines.

State Legislative Experiences: During the 1989 legislative session the Hawaii House of Representatives enacted a formal Resolution (H. Res #334-90) calling on the states Center for Alternative Dispute Resolution to study the prescription issue in depth and report back the following legislative session its policy recommendations. Twenty-nine legislators had signed that resolution and extensive hearings were held in both legislative chambers. In 1993 the Indiana legislature modified its psychology licensure act to authorize prescriptive authority for those psychologists who are "participating in a federal government sponsored training or treatment program". Although this provision of the Indiana statute has not yet been implemented, the affirmative public policy stances taken by the governor (in signing the bill) and the legislature (in passing it) are clear. From our perspective the key policy lesson to be learned from these two examples is that when psychology collectively decides to become involved in the public policy/political process the prescription agenda seems not only reasonable to elected officials, it becomes substantively "doable" (DeLeon, Folen, Jennings, Willis, & Wright, 1991).

Accordingly, over the past several years we have been very pleased to witness an increasing number of prescribing bills being introduced in state legislatures across the nation—resulting in active pro and con lobbying, state association "grass roots" educational campaigns, advocacy positions taken by the popular media, and formal legislative hearings and subsequent (sub)committee votes, etc. (e.g., Hawaii, California, Florida, Louisiana, Missouri, Montana, Oregon, Tennessee). By the mid-1990s approximately 25 states had ongoing prescription privilege task forces. Viable training modules, particularly executive track initiatives targeting practicing clinicians, are actively being established. Internal psychological association surveys continue to demonstrate that initially approximately one third of the membership are supportive while another third possesses serious reservations. As the state association becomes more engaged in the policy debate, however, subsequent surveys soon find that 70–80 percent of the membership are supportive. Again, however, it is important to appreciate that, as we have indicated, even these evolving training programs are often a direct result of concerted action taken by the state psychological association elected leadership rather than spontaneous generation by our traditional training institutions.

Developments Within the APA Governance: In August 1995 the APA Council of Representatives, which is the highest governance body within the Association, formally endorsed the inclusion of prescription privileges as being appropriately within the "scope of practice" of professional psychology. This action by the Council was predicated upon a foundation carefully developed over the previous decade which involved numerous discussions between representatives from the practice, educational, and scientific communities. In many ways, the Council's action may be seen as merely reaffirming a policy first endorsed in 1986 (and authored at that time by those actively seeking policy support for the prescription privilege movement) which had expressly proclaimed that the practice of psychology was to include the use of physical, as well as purely psychological interventions (Cullen & Newman, 1997).

Five years earlier the APA 1990 Council of Representatives had voted to establish a Task Force on Psychopharmacology. This task force submitted a formal report to the Council that recommended the development of three levels of psychopharmacological training. Their report ultimately formed the basis for further action by Council in 1996 solidifying psychology's proactive stance when the Council took the additional step of formally endorsing both model prescription legislation and a model comprehensive curriculum training module.

The curriculum recommended by the Council to those interested in pursuing the prescription agenda consisted of 300 contact hours of didactic instruction in five core content areas: neurosciences; pharmacology and psychopharmacology; physiology and pathophysiology; physical and laboratory assessment; and clinical pharmacotherapeutics. A clinical practicum involving supervised medication treatment of at least 100 patients in both inpatient and outpatient settings was also recommended. The model legislation would authorize the state licensing board to deem (i.e., certify) those competent to possess independent prescribing authority. The board of medicine was not to be involved in determining psychology's clinical competence (i.e., the substitution rather than physician-extender model would be pursued).

We would note in passing that one indication of the extent to which some psychologists perceive expansion into the prescription arena as an extraordinarily significant change in psychology's history (and core definition) is the fact that to our knowledge this is the only time in our profession's history that the APA Council of Representatives ever felt it appropriate (or necessary) to expressly take a policy position on whether a particular clinical technique or modality should be considered within psychology's scope of practice. Historically, the key policy notion has always been to rely upon state licensing boards to ensure that sufficient and relevant training be available; i.e., that the particular clinical function being considered would be within the technical competence of the individual practitioner.

In informal discussions with those who have been intimately involved during this period in shaping APA's policy position on the prescriptive agenda, it would definitely appear that the seminal event which served to crystallize the underlying issues for psychology's governance leadership and ultimately galvanize the professional community behind the movement was the special retreat held by the Board of Professional Affairs (BPA) under the leadership of Norma Simon in November 1989. After extensive consultation with relevant experts, including psychologists who were intimately involved in the landmark Department of Defense (DoD) psychopharmacology training program, BPA unanimously concluded that: "BPA strongly endorses the immediate research and study intervention feasibility and curricula development in psychopharmacology for psychologists in order to provide broader service to the public and to address more effectively the public's psychological and mental health needs. And BPA strongly recommends moving to the highest APA priority a focused attention to the responsibility of preparing the profession of psychology to address the current and future needs of the public for psychologically managed psychopharmacological interventions."

The following year under future APA President Bob Resnick's leadership, BPA further recommended to the Board of Directors that a special task force on psychopharmacology be established. The APA Board of Directors concurred and recommended that the Council of Representatives fund such a task force out of its coming year's contingency funds—thus effectively setting the stage for a true policy debate at the highest level. As we have indicated, that August after extensive discussion in which at least seventeen members of Council expressed a wide range of views—including the possible impact on the homeless, women's health care, the elderly, rural America, and psychology's historical ability to develop responsive and responsible training programs—the Council voted *in favor* of establishing the historic task force 118-2. An outcome that in all candor, no one could have predicted. The actual motion adopted stated: "To determine the advisability and feasibility of psychopharmacology prescription privileges for psychologists, an APA Task Force on Psychopharmacology be formed with the following charge: 1). To involve relevant constituencies and Divisions in this process in conjunction with the Education, Science, and Practice Directorates. 2). To determine the competency criteria necessary for training of psychologists to practice the highest quality patient care without adverse consequences for patients. 3). To develop alternative curricular models necessary to achieve the above, and to consider data-based evaluation of such training and evaluate the pros & cons of each training model. This task force shall be comprised of 7 members representing a range of scientific, educational, and clinical practice expertise and should report to the APA Board of Directors and the APA Council of Representatives. . ." It should be clear from the actual language of the Council's action that throughout the process there really has been considerable involvement of all aspects of the APA governance. The Committee for the Advancement of Professional Practice (CAPP) and the Board of Educational Affairs (BEA), and particularly its Committee on Continuing Education, have also been actively and formally involved. Similarly, the leadership of the Board of Scientific Affairs (BSA) played a major role and the concerns expressed by the Board for the Advancement of Psychology in the Public Interest (BAPPI) regarding the historic over-reliance upon psychotropic medications with women and people of color were noted. We really do want to stress the extent to which throughout the associations deliberation process the widest range of views have been heard and addressed.

Health Policy Formulation—The Demonstration Approach: Very few psychologists appreciate the extent to which our nation has a rich history at both the state and federal level of systematically testing out potentially innovative and viable health care programs, including the non-traditional utilization of health professional expertise. In many ways, for example, the history of the phenomenal growth of advanced practice nursing epitomizes this notion. Under our system of constitutional "checks and balances", the various governmental entities at both the state and federal level possess the inherent authority to experiment with expanded scopes of professional practice, notwithstanding statutory limits for the private sector under the provisions of relevant licensing acts. Simply stated, unless expressly enacted into public law, there is no limit on the ability of state health departments or the various federal services to utilize their employees in whatever manner they deem appropriate. In essence, government in its role as a "provider of care" has tremendous flexibility in accomplishing that mission—government does provide a "living laboratory" for innovation.

In the mid-1970s the State of California utilized its health professions demonstration authority to explore the extent to which non-physician health care providers might properly be eventually authorized to possess prescriptive authority, and under what conditions. In November of 1982 the state issued a formal report, *Prescribing and Dispensing Pilot Projects*, in which it was noted that: "None of the projects, to date, have received the intense scrutiny that these 10 prescribing and dispensing projects have received. Over 1 million patients have been seen by these prescribing and dispensing (non-physicians) trainees over the past three years. At least 50 percent of these patients have had drugs prescribed for them or dispensed to them by these professionals" (State of California, p. i). The principle teaching methods used by project staff were lectures and seminars, varying from 16 hours to 95 hours in length. Further, only 56 percent of the trainees had graduated from an academic program with a bachelors degree or higher. Clearly these trainees possessed considerably less formal education than doctoral level psychologists. All involved in the programs (including supervising physicians) were definitely comfortable with the quality of health care provided. The state authorities found the project to be cost-effective, even when the costs of physician supervision and pharmacist consultation were considered.

The Fiscal Year 1989 Department of Defense Appropriations bill (P.L. 100-463) directed that the administration establish a demonstration pilot training project under which military psychologists could be trained and authorized to issue appropriate psychotropic medications under certain circumstances. The actual training began in August 1991 with four participants in a special 3-year postdoctoral fellowship program consisting of two years of didactic course work at the DoD Uniformed Services University of the Health Sciences, to be followed by one year of clinical "hands on" experience at Walter Reed Army Medical Center. As the training matured and began to systematically take into account the academic and clinical backgrounds of the psychologists Fellows, subsequent classes received one year of didactic work and one year of "hands on" clinical training. By the summer of 1997 ten Fellows had graduated from the program (Sammons & Brown, 1997; Sammons, Sexton, & Meredith, 1996).

It would be a tremendous understatement to suggest that the DoD initiative was controversial, particularly to organized psychiatry. From its inception, the Department contracted for an independent evaluation and two additional external evaluations were also conducted. The latter two studies conflicted as to whether the training program was fundamentally cost-effective. However, even the more critical General Accounting Office (GAO) report concluded that: "DoD has demonstrated that it can train clinical psychologists to prescribe psychotropic medication, and these psychologists have shown that they can provide this service in the MHSS [Military Health Services System] (GAO, 1997, p. 20)." At organized psychiatry's urging the National Defense Authorization Act for Fiscal Year 1996 (P.L. 104-106) had expressly prohibited the enrollment of any new Fellows in the program; however, organized psychology has been actively seeking a legislative remedy to this particular prohibition. The bottom line is that DoD did clearly demonstrate that it can train military psychologists to safely and competently provide psychotropic medications, notwithstanding the proffered and highly emotional "public health hazard" allegations of psychiatry.

Where From Here?—Although it is always difficult to predict with any sense of accuracy the future of the legislative and/or public policy process, there is no question in our minds that it is only a matter of time—and at that, a relatively brief period of time—before psychology attains its first legislative prescriptive privilege success at the state level. Over the years various federal psychologists have reported that even without formal training they have personally made the clinical decisions as to which psychopharmacological drugs should be taken by their patients; that is, our colleagues within the federal system have, and do, functionally and legally prescribe, notwithstanding psychiatry's objections and protestations to the contrary. In at least one agency, the Indian Health Service (IHS) hospital bylaws and central office policy memorandums formally recognized this practice.

Not surprisingly, the DoD psychopharmacology training program objectively demonstrated that it is possible to train psychologists to utilize psychopharmacological agents responsibly. Each of the ten Fellows has expressed to us their confidence that the quality of their clinical services has been excellent and that possessing this clinical expertise has opened up entirely new clinical responsibilities. The concern expressed by some of our psychology colleagues that possessing prescription privileges would cause psychology's clinicians to lose their fundamental behavioral science (and psychology) identity simply has not happened. Instead, the Fellows all enthusiastically describe the clinical advantages to their patients of their fundamental psychological orientation to the use of psychotropic medications. And, we would again reiterate that psychiatry's proffered "public health hazard" allegations have had no basis in fact (DeLeon, Sammons, & Fox, 1995)!

In our judgment, an important historical aspect to the prescription privilege movement has been the necessity to date of developing post-doctoral training modules, targeted towards practicing clinicians. These colleagues are already licensed to independently "diagnose and treat" patients and the additional psychopharmacology training has essentially enhanced their clinical capacities while allowing them to retain their fundamental behavioral science and psychology identity. What will be the long term effect on the profession, if eventually, the decision is made to incorporate prescription training at the predoctoral level is admittedly unclear and only time will tell (DeLeon, Sammons, & Sexton, 1995).

Today there are a number of different training programs being established across the country, some of which interestingly rely considerably upon professional nursing's expertise. As our nation's educational institutions become more attuned to the implications of the rapidly evolving advances within the communications field and as the health care industry itself becomes more responsive to the advances evolving within computer technology, one must expect that these will have a major impact upon prescribing practices. How these changes will affect psychology's presence can not be known at this time. For example, will the ready availability of telemedicine services provide psychology with a greater capacity to obtain supervision experiences for its rural practitioners, or will this technology instead serve to undercut psychology's increased access argument before state legislatures? Or perchance, will technological advances instead open up new markets for psychopharmacological consultation services with prescribing rural primary care physicians and nurse practitioners (DeLeon, et al. 1996)?

There are many public and professional policy issues for professional psychology to systematically address as we continue to expand into the prescription arena. What will be the probable impact on interdisciplinary relationships, how (if at all) should our ethical standards be modified, etc? We are confident that as long as the profession ensures that providing high quality patient care remains the highest priority, that our educational and professional institutions will in the long run be able to address these new challenges with distinction (Lorion, Iscoe, DeLeon, & VandenBos, 1996).

The views expressed in this Foreword are those of the individual authors and not those of the APA, the U.S. Navy, or the Department of Defense.

Pat DeLeon
APA Recording Secretary
and
Morgan Sammons
DoD Psychopharmacology Fellow

References

Cullen, E. A., & Newman, R. (1997). In pursuit of prescription privileges. *Professional Psychology: Research and Practice, 28*(2), 101–106.

DeLeon, P. H., Folen, R. A., Jennings, F. L., Willis, D. J., & Wright, R. H. (1991). The case for prescription privileges: A logical evolution of professional practice. *Journal of Clinical Child Psychology, 20*(3), 254–267.

DeLeon, P. H., Fox, R. E., & Graham, S. R. (1991). Prescription privileges: Psychology's next frontier? *American Psychologist, 46,* 384–393.

DeLeon, P. H., Frank, R. G., & Wedding, D. (1995). Health psychology and public policy: The political process. *Health Psychology, 14*(6), 493–499.

DeLeon, P. H., Howell, W. C., Newman, R. S., Brown, A. B., Keita, G. P., & Sexton, J. L. (1996). Expanding roles in the twenty-first century. In R. J. Resnick & R. H. Rozensky (Eds.), *Health psychology through the life span: Practice and research opportunities* (pp. 427–453). Washington, DC: American Psychological Association.

DeLeon, P. H., Sammons, M. T., & Fox, R. E. (1995, November). A commentary: Canada is not that far north. *Canadian Psychology, 36*(4), 320–326.

DeLeon, P. H., Sammons, M. T., & Sexton, J. L. (1995). Focusing on society's real needs: Responsibility and prescription privileges? *American Psychologist, 50*(12), 1022–1032.

DeLeon, P. H., & Wiggins, J. G. (1996). Prescription privileges for psychologists. *American Psychologist, 51*(3), 225–229.

Fox, R. E. (1988). Prescription privileges: Their implications for the practice of psychology. *Psychotherapy, 25*(4), 501–507.

Fox, R. E., Schwelitz, F. D., & Barclay, A. G. (1992). A proposed curriculum for psychopharmacology training for professional psychologists. *Professional Psychology: Research and Practice, 23*(3), 216–219.

Frank, R. G. (1992). Prescription privileges for psychologists: Now is the time. *Physical Medicine and Rehabilitation: State of the Art Reviews. 6*(3), 565–571.

Inouye, D. K. (1984, November). Invited address at the Hawaii Psychological Association Annual Convention, Honolulu.

Lorion, R. P., Iscoe, I., DeLeon, P. H., & VandenBos, G. R. (Eds.). (1996). *Psychology and public policy: Balancing public service and professional need.* Washington, DC: American Psychological Association.

Pimental, P. A., Stout, C. E., Hoover, M. C., & Kamen, G. B. (1997). Changing psychologists' opinions about prescriptive authority: A little information goes a long way. *Professional Psychology: Research and Practice, 28*(2), 123–127.

Sammons, M. T., & Brown, A. B. (1997). The department of defense psychopharmacology demonstration project: An evolving program for postdoctoral education in psychology. *Professional Psychology: Research and Practice, 28*(2), 107–112.

Sammons, M. T., Sexton, J. L., & Meredith, J. M. (1996). Science-based training in psychopharmacology: How much is enough? *American Psychologist, 51,* 230–234.

State of California, Office of Statewide Health Planning and Development, Division of Health Professions Development. (1982, November). *Prescribing and dispensing pilot projects* (Final report to the legislature and to the healing arts licensing boards). Sacramento, CA: Author.

U.S. General Accounting Office (GAO) (1997). *Defense health care: Need for more prescribing psychologists is not adequately justified.* (GAO/HEHS-97-83). Washington, DC: U.S. Government Printing Office.

Preface

We are in a time of significant economic, political, and social change. This time of change is affecting the professional practice of psychology in a variety of ways as traditional disciplinary lines are dissolving and new boundaries are being drawn. Major practice issues, such as prescription and hospital admitting privileges for psychologists, need to be expediently and adequately addressed. Naturally, it is to be expected that some psychologists, perhaps because they are content with the status quo or because they are fearful of change, may wish that things be left as they are. Unfortunately, things cannot be left as they are. As noted by Chesterton almost 90 years ago, "If you leave a thing alone you leave it to a torrent of change" (*Orthodoxy*, 1908). Thus, our only logical and rational alternative is to become involved with the changes and to view the process of change not as a threat but as an opportunity to broaden the professional practice of psychology and, in so doing, improve the health and well-being of people who require psychological services.

As many psychologists have come to realize, appropriate pharmacotherapy can be a useful adjunct to appropriate psychotherapy and, as such, is a welcome tool for psychologists. Certainly, the optimal professional practice of psychology requires, if not prescription privileges for psychologists, at least a minimum significant degree of specialized knowledge about the propensity for psychotropics to affect behavior, cognition, learning, memory, and psychological health. Even those psychologists who choose not to prescribe psychotropics as part of their professional practice require an understanding of the use and effects of these drugs.

Such understanding is essential in order for all psychologists to meet more competently and comprehensively the needs of their patients, many of whom will be prescribed a psychotropic by a family physician or another prescriber (e.g., advanced practice nurse, cardiologist, clinical pharmacist, dentist, or psychiatrist). For example, even psychologists considered to be the best *psychotherapists* in the world would more than likely be unsuccessful in the treatment of a depression if they were unaware that the clinical depression was a direct adverse result of the use of a benzodiazepine (e.g., Ativan®, Halcion®, Valium®) with the adverse drug reaction of depression. In another example, school psychologists, considered to be the best learning specialists in the world, would be unable to plan optimal programs for learning disabled children if they were unaware that the children's learning problems were a direct result of anticonvulsant drug therapy, which some children require for the treatment of seizure disorders, or too high a dosage of methylphenidate (Ritalin®), which is commonly prescribed to children for the treatment of attention-deficit/hyperactivity disorder (ADHD). This argument becomes even more relevant when it is recognized that virtually every psychological disorder, whether characterized by DSM-IV or other relevant criteria (e.g., ICD), can have its signs and symptoms mimicked by the adverse drug reactions of the various psychotropics.

Prescription privileges and related issues are being actively addressed by the profession of psychology in several countries, including Canada, South Africa, New Zealand, and the United Kingdom. In these countries, professional practice acts are increasingly being rewritten to incorporate a *nonexclusive* scope of practice for all of the health professions. By providing "nonexclusive" scopes of practice, these acts appropriately and correctly recognize that no one individual or group "owns" exclusively knowledge of a particular area of mental health practice (e.g., prescription authority). However, nowhere has this issue received more scrutiny and active debate within the profession of psychology than in the United States, where it has received the official endorsement of the American Psychological Association, the largest psychological association in the world. The Foreword of this text, written by Patrick DeLeon and Morgan Sammons, provides a historical overview of the debate and progress surrounding this crucial issue for psychologists.

The Ad Hoc Task Force on Psychopharmacology of the American Psychological Association has recommended three levels of psychopharmacology education. Level 1, "basic psychopharmacology education," would provide a minimal level of psychopharmacology education for all psychologists in clinical practice. Level 2, "collaborative practice," would provide additional education to enable psychologists to participate actively as partners with physicians and other prescribers in determining the need for and the monitoring of psychotropic therapy for patients they "share." Level 3, "prescription privileges," would provide the education necessary for psychologists to have independent psychotropic prescription privileges.

In accordance with these developments in psychology and the need for related formal advanced education, the authors of this text developed, at the University of Alberta, the "Hierarchical Integrated Series of Graduate/Postgraduate Courses in Pharmacopsychology," which they have taught since 1990 to both graduate psychology students and postgraduate psychologists in private practice.[1,2] The development of the "hierarchical series" was based on three basic assumptions: (1) that no single profession or group "owns" exclusively any given knowledge; (2) that psychologists, who as a group are the highest academically prepared health care professionals, are able to comprehend and to apply appropriately in clinical contexts the information and concepts of clinical pharmacology relevant to the promotion of mental health; and (3) that appropriate pharmacotherapy, when prescribed by psychologists, should be used only as an adjunct to appropriate psychotherapy.[3,4]

The current series of textbooks, of which this text is the first, is based on the authors' experience in teaching the hierarchical series of pharmacopsychology courses to a variety of graduate students in psychology and postgraduate psychologists in independent practice in many different settings. The development of this series of textbooks also reflects the authors' concern that psychologists be provided with reference texts that are pharmacologically correct and that specifically reflect the expanded professional practice of psychology. Although each of the three initial textbooks in the series can be used alone, they have been developed as a complementary set to delineate the pharmacopsychologic knowledge required for the optimal professional practice of psychology (i.e., basic principles of pharmacotherapy, synopses of psychotropic drugs, and clinical psychopharmacotherapeutics).

---

[1] Interested readers can contact the authors for a copy of the syllabus "A Hierarchical Integrated Series of Graduate/Postgraduate Courses in Pharmacopsychology."

[2] The "Hierarchical Integrated Series of Graduate/Postgraduate Courses in Pharmacopsychology" was also developed to help psychologists and graduate psychology students become better prepared to more competently perform research in the area of pharmacopsychology. In this regard, the series has become a foundational component of the research program of most of the authors' own doctoral students.

[3] For example, when treating a depressed patient, a psychologist would use appropriate pharmacotherapy to complement or augment established psychotherapy (e.g., cognitive therapy). In this example, if the psychologist believed that psychotherapy was unnecessary and that only pharmacotherapy was required, then the patient should be referred to another prescriber (e.g., advanced practice nurse; family physician; psychiatrist).

[4] The third assumption is predicated upon the following rationale. First, psychotherapy is the core foundational aspect of clinical psychology treatment services (i.e., while psychologists may provide additional forms of treatment, such as biofeedback and hypnotherapy, psychotherapy remains the *raison d'etre* for the existence of clinical psychology as a distinct treatment-providing health care profession). Second, although research studies examining the relative therapeutic benefits of pharmacotherapy and psychotherapy have provided mixed results, a growing consensus is that the appropriate combination of these psychotherapeutic modalities in the treatment of amenable mental disorders leads, overall, to greater success (i.e., better therapeutic outcome) than the use of either modality alone.

The first volume in the series, *The Pharmacologic Basis of Psychotherapeutics: An Introduction for Psychologists*, introduces psychology students and psychologists to the basic principles and concepts of pharmacotherapy. As such, it assumes no prior knowledge of the principles and concepts of pharmacotherapy and should be readily amenable for use by the graduate psychology student or postgraduate psychologist in clinical practice. The second volume in the series, *Psychologists' Psychotropic Desk Reference*, provides psychologists with a valuable synopsis of all of the clinically relevant data currently available for each of the psychotropics marketed in North America. These data have been subsumed and arranged within individual drug monographs in order to facilitate the conceptualization and rapid retrieval of desired information when needed. The optimal use of this text requires a knowledge of the basic principles and concepts of psychotherapeutics, discussed in the first volume in the series. The third and last volume in the series, *Clinical Psychopharmacotherapeutics for Psychologists*, in preparation, will critically discuss each of the major psychological disorders that is amenable to pharmacotherapy as an adjunct to psychotherapy. Thus, emphasis is on the validated effectiveness of these combined therapeutic approaches and related issues, including their empirical validation.[5] The optimal use of this text requires mastery of the information presented in the first and second volumes in the series, which have been designed to facilitate retrieval and review of required material.

Thus, the present volume is the foundational text that provides the pharmacologic basis of psychotherapeutics that is required for optimal use of the second and third volumes in this series. Together, these three volumes reflect all three levels of pharmacopsychology education. *The Pharmacologic Basis of Psychotherapeutics: An Introduction for Psychologists* is divided into six chapters. The Foreword, "Prescription Privileges for Psychologists: An Historical Overview," written by Patrick DeLeon, a champion of prescription drug privileges for psychologists, and Morgan Sammons, one of the first graduates of the Department of Defense Psychopharmacology Fellowship Program, provides a brief history of the major events leading to prescription privileges for psychologists. It also provides a precis of the arguments that have been made both for and against this expanded role for psychologists.[6] Chapter 1, "Introduction to the Basic Principles of Pharmacotherapy," describes and discusses the various purported mechanisms by which psychotropic drugs elicit their effects in the human body. Chapter 2, "The Psychotropics," introduces readers to the psychotropic drugs, including their differentiation according to abuse liability and pharmacologic classification. In addition, an overview of the remaining chapters in the textbook, in terms of their relevance to the central theme of the text and their application to clinical practice, is presented. Chapter 3, "Pharmacokinetics and Pharmacodynamics," deals with the processes of absorption, distribution, and elimination (i.e., metabolism and excretion) of psychotropic drugs from the human body. In addition, the concept of therapeutic drug monitoring (TDM) and the influences of age and disease states on pharmacokinetic and pharmacodynamic processes are presented and discussed. Related mathematical modeling, including graphical representations and formulas, is included. Chapter 4, "Administration of Psychotropics," provides an overview of the various formulations of psychotropic drugs (e.g., injectables, tablets, transdermal delivery systems) and their methods of administration (e.g., intramuscular injection, oral ingestion). Attention is given to optimizing drug delivery and therapeutic response.

---

[5] The three-volume series of texts focuses exclusively on the therapeutic uses of the psychotropics. Psychologists who require additional specific information regarding the problematic patterns of abusable psychotropic use (i.e., those patterns associated with addiction and habituation) are referred to *Substance Use Among Children and Adolescents: Its Nature, Extent, and Consequences From Conception to Adulthood* (Pagliaro & Pagliaro, 1996) and *Substance Use Among Women* (Pagliaro & Pagliaro, in press).

[6] We are extremely grateful to Patrick DeLeon and Morgan Sammons, who took time from extremely busy schedules to write the Foreword for this first text in the "Series."

Chapter 5, "Adverse Drug Reactions," discusses the nature and extent of adverse drug reactions involving the psychotropic drugs. Adverse drug reactions that mimic the various psychological disorders, including those related to the use of nonpsychotropic drugs (e.g., antibiotics, antiulcer drugs), also are discussed. Several comprehensive tables have been included to facilitate retrieval of relevant information. Chapter 6, "Drug Interactions," discusses the general mechanisms and sites of drug interactions that are known to occur in the human body. Individual monographs for each clinically significant drug interaction known to involve the psychotropics are provided, with attention to the specific nature, mechanisms, and clinical consequences of the drug interactions. Methods used to prevent or manage each of these interactions also are discussed.

As a means for ensuring that each chapter is as comprehensive, well written, and up to date as humanly possible, the chapters have been subjected to a rigorous process of writing and revision. This has been done by the authors taking into consideration their extensive academic and clinical backgrounds, in terms of both clinical pharmacology and psychology, and the related, relevant published literature. In addition, an Editorial Advisory Committee, composed of distinguished academics, researchers, and clinical psychologists from across North America, was established to help to ensure that the focus and leveling of the series of textbooks was appropriately directed to the needs and abilities of graduate psychology students and psychologists.[7] Each chapter has been independently reviewed by several members of the Editorial Advisory Committee, who have given freely of their time and expertise in order to help produce a series of textbooks that should become a proud standard for psychologists. The authors, and all psychology students and psychologists who use these texts, owe a profound debt of gratitude to these advisory committee members.[8]

It is hoped that, by using the information presented in this specially developed three-volume series of pharmacopsychology texts, psychologists will be better able to provide their patients who have various psychological disorders with optimal psychotropic pharmacotherapy as an appropriate adjunct to psychotherapy and, thus, optimize the benefit derived by all patients who seek professional treatment from psychologists. In our earnest attempt to provide the best possible series of pharmacopsychology texts for psychologists, we are humbly reminded of the following words and sentiment paraphrased from Adlai Stevenson:

We have not done as well as we would have liked to have done,
But we have done our best, honestly and forthrightly.
No one can do more and you (our colleague psychologists)
are entitled to no less.

LAP/AMP
1998

---

[7] For example, in order to assist with this goal, the Editorial Advisory Committee (EAC) identified terms with which psychologists might not be readily familiar. The most common terms were then defined and arranged in a glossary that can be found in Appendix 2 at the end of this text.

In relation to leveling, it should be noted that the three-volume series, although in many regards introductory to the subject matter, was written for psychologists at a graduate level of education. Therefore, the "series" is significantly more comprehensive and at a higher scholarly level than will be found in related undergraduate texts, including those generally written for medical students.

[8] The responsibility for the completeness and accuracy of all information provided within this text remains with the authors.

Acknowledgments

The authors gratefully acknowledge the assistance of a number of people whose hard and diligent work made this text and this series of texts possible. First, Herb Reich, for bringing us together with the publisher, Taylor & Francis. What began as a working relationship several books ago, has developed into a wonderful friendship. Next, we would again like to thank the members of the Editorial Advisory Committee for their help and encouragement throughout this entire process. A deep expression of gratitude is extended both to the Dean of Nursing, Marilynn J. Wood, for her continuing support of our textbook writing, particularly in an era of diminishing academic resources, and to Lynn Szoo for her typing of seemingly countless revisions. Last, but certainly not least, we would like to formally acknowledge the assistance of all at Taylor & Francis, and extend our sincerest thanks to Mac Fancher, Bernadette Capelle, Alex Schwartz, and Heather Worley, for both their faith in us and this new project and for their continuing assistance and support at every phase of this project.

1

Introduction to the Basic Principles of Pharmacotherapy

Introduction

An understanding of four basic principles of pharmacotherapy (i.e., structure–activity relationship, dose–response relationship, variability in dose response, and therapeutic index) is necessary for psychologists to understand how a variety of factors influence prescribed pharmacotherapy. For example, understanding of these basic principles enables psychologists to appreciate how slight modifications to the chemical (molecular) structure of a psychotropic drug molecule can give rise to a new drug in the same class or family that has different physiochemical properties and causes different pharmacologic effects. This concept of drug structure modification and resultant influence on pharmacologic activity is known as the "structure–activity relationship" (SAR).

Many examples of the application of the concept of SAR can be found among the psychotropics. Consider, for example, the group of drugs known collectively as the benzodiazepines (see Chapter 2, "The Psychotropics").[1] Slight changes in the molecular structure of the benzodiazepine molecule (see Figure 1-1) result in physiochemical (e.g., lipid solubility, pK_a) changes and resultant differences in pharmacologic activity (e.g., fewer adverse drug reactions; longer duration of action). Pharmacologic activity also is affected by the concentration of a drug at its site of action.

The relationship between drug concentration over time and observed pharmacologic effect is often referred to as the "pharmacodynamics" of the drug (see also Chapter 3, "Pharmacokinetics and Pharmacodynamics"). The pharmacodynamic relationship of drug concentration to effect is probably best conceptualized by examining the dose–response curve (Figure 1-2). For most drugs, if the log of an administered dose is plotted against the percentage of observed pharmacologic response in a single subject, an "S"-shaped, or sigmoidal, "dose–response" curve is typically obtained.[2] The curve indicates that a graded response is achieved from differing doses of the drug. The upper and lower ends of the curve usually are reciprocal of each other, although the lower end of the curve may be absent or difficult to observe in some cases (e.g., in the presence of dose-dependent kinetics; see Chapter 3, "Pharmacokinetics and Pharmacodynamics"). Figure 1-2 is an example of a typical sigmoidal dose–response curve. However, the slope of the curve (i.e., whether or not the "S" is flattened) depends on which drug and which specific pharmacologic

---

[1] Although chlordiazepoxide (Librium®) was the original member of the benzodiazepine family introduced for clinical use in North America, the next introduced member of the benzodiazepine family, diazepam (Valium®), is generally considered the standard or prototype against which all other members of this drug class are compared.

[2] The same type of curve is obtained if dose is plotted on a rectilinear graph against response. However, the use of the log of the dose creates a more standardized "S"-shaped curve with a steeper slope.

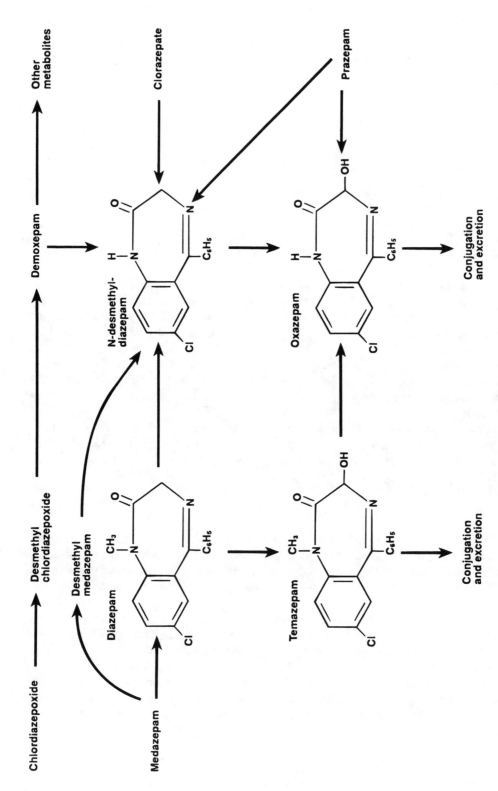

Figure 1-1. The molecular structure and metabolic relationship among several of the benzodiazepines.

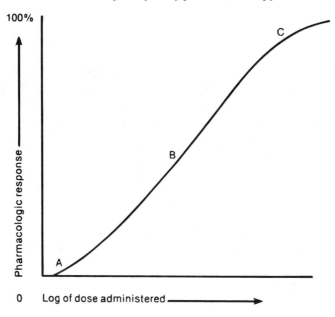

Figure 1-2. Dose–response curve illustrating the typical relationship between dose and response.

response are plotted. The steeper the slope, the smaller the difference in dose from minimum to maximum obtainable response.

The curve in Figure 1-2 is divided into three portions: A, B, and C. An examination of the lower portion of the curve (A) indicates a minimal or threshold dose of the drug (i.e., a pharmacologic or therapeutic quantity) that must be administered before a pharmacologic effect is observed.[3] The middle or linear segment of the curve (B) is the portion that is most often encountered in clinical practice. This portion of the curve is responsible for the *law of conservation of dose*, according to which a dose of a drug is directly proportional to its blood, plasma, or serum concentration and, thus, its observed effect. Under this law, when the dose of a drug is increased or decreased, the expected effect is proportionately increased or decreased. This law accounts for the prescriber's ability to successfully modify the dose of a drug on the basis of a patient's response. However, an examination of Figure 1-2 reveals that the law of conservation of dose clearly does not apply when the dose and response are at either of the extreme ends of the curve (i.e., "A" or "C"). The law also does not apply for certain psychotropic drugs (e.g., phenytoin [Dilantin®]) that exhibit what is known as capacity-limited, or dose-dependent, kinetics (see Chapter 3, "Pharmacokinetics and Pharmacodynamics").

An examination of the upper portion of the dose–response curve ("C") indicates that, as 100% of the pharmacologic response is achieved, the curve tapers off or becomes more horizontal. Thus, a "ceiling effect" is obtained. In other words, once a maximal effect is achieved, increasing the dose of a drug will not increase its desired effect. However, increasing the dose may increase adverse drug reactions or toxic effects that may not yet have reached their own maximal, or ceiling, effect.

A curve that may help conceptualize the variability of psychotropic drug response in a

---

[3] The use of doses below this minimal therapeutic threshold is common in the practice of homeopathic medicine. Any observed effects, by definition, are not directly caused by the drug but may be mediated psychologically (see later discussion of "placebo effect" in this chapter).

population of patients is shown in Figure 1-3. When the minimum dose necessary to achieve a certain pharmacologic effect is plotted against the number of patients who respond to that particular dose, a bell-shaped, or Gaussian (normal) distribution, curve is obtained. This curve indicates the wide range of variability in response that can be expected when a certain dose of a psychotropic drug is administered to a number of different patients.[4] Although most patients display the desired pharmacologic response when an average dose (A) of a particular psychotropic drug is ingested, inhaled, inserted, or injected, some patients do not display these effects. For approximately 15% of the patients at either extreme of the curve shown in Figure 1-3, the average dose that is effective for 50% of the population (i.e., ED_{50}) will be either too small or too large. The ED_{50} is calculated to produce a pharmacologic effect with a relatively low incidence of adverse drug reactions and toxic effects in the "average" patient. Thus, the average dose for a particular drug should be used as a *guide only* for prescribing safe and effective dosages for most patients.

The safety of the average dose varies from drug to drug. The margin of safety[5] can be defined as the difference between the maximum therapeutic dose and the minimum toxic dose.[6] Drugs that have a wide margin of safety can usually be prescribed more safely than those that do not. However, drugs that have a narrow margin of safety (e.g., where the difference between

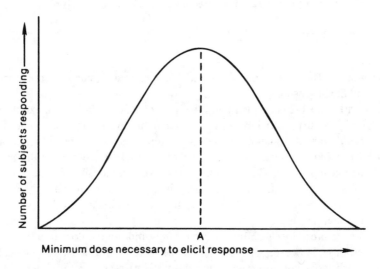

Figure 1-3. Normal distribution of subjects pharmacologically responding to a minimum effective dose of drug.

[4] Individual variability in drug response among the sample population can be explained, for the most part, by differences in age, health status, psychologic status, environmental status, and genetic predisposition.

[5] The margin of drug safety also is measured by the "therapeutic index" (TI). The TI is the ratio of the minimum therapeutic drug concentration to the minimum toxic drug concentration. The higher the TI, the "safer" the drug. Conversely, the lower the TI, the less "safe" the drug. For example, the benzodiazepines (e.g., diazepam) have a high TI, while the antimanic lithium has a low TI. In experimental preclinical research, the TI is sometimes calculated, with animal data, as the ratio of the ED_{50} (i.e., the dose that is effective for 50% of the population) to the LD_{50} (i.e., the dose that is lethal for 50% of the population).

It should be noted that animal data can provide, at best, only an approximation of what occurs in humans because of species differences. It also is difficult to establish comparable human doses, environmental conditions, ages, and health status under experimental conditions in laboratory animals. These difficulties are particularly apparent in relation to the psychotropics. In this regard, there is *no* adequate animal model of the human brain and its higher order functions. For these reasons, the information presented in this text, as well as the other two texts in this series, is based solely on human data.

[6] Toxicity in this context is defined differently for various drugs depending, among other factors, on their use and the availability of alternative drugs. Thus, the minimum toxic dose may refer to the dose at which adverse drug reactions of any type are first noted, the dose at which major adverse drug reactions are noted, or the minimum lethal dose.

the therapeutic and toxic doses may be only a few micrograms per milliliter of blood concentration) must be prescribed more precisely for a particular patient, often with the assistance of monitored blood levels (see Chapter 3, "Pharmacokinetics and Pharmacodynamics," for additional discussion).

Psychologists must keep these basic principles in mind when interpreting the results of pharmacologic studies, prescribing pharmacotherapy, and predicting the effects of specific drugs in specific patients. A basic understanding of the general mechanisms of drug action also is of assistance in this regard.

Mechanisms of drug action

Drugs act through a variety of mechanisms in order to elicit their pharmacologic effects.[7] These mechanisms have been divided into five categories: (1) binding at a receptor site, (2) chemical reaction, (3) physical action, (4) functional disruption, and (5) psychologic action. The psychotropic drugs, for reasons that will become apparent upon examination of these mechanisms, appear to elicit their effects primarily by Mechanisms 1 and 5.

Binding at a receptor site

Most drugs appear to act at a molecular level by binding (attaching) to specific macromolecules in the body. These macromolecules are known as drug receptors. Early evidence for this mechanism of action was provided by observation of the selectivity and specificity of drug action.[8] According to this mechanism of action, a drug must be attracted to a receptor to which it binds.[9] These events start a series of biochemical reactions that ultimately result in the observed pharmacologic action of the drug. An interesting corollary associated with this proposed mechanism of drug action is that a drug cannot create a biologically new action;[10] rather, it simply begins or regulates an endogenous action.[11] Another corollary of this mechanism of action is that the free or unbound portion of a drug molecule, but not the protein-bound (or complexed) portion, can interact with a drug receptor and, subsequently, elicit a pharmacologic effect (see Chapter 3, "Pharmacokinetics and Pharmacodynamics," and Chapter 6, "Drug Interactions").

The concept of receptors dates back to the beginning of the 20th century and the work of

---

[7] The mechanisms of drug action presented here are general mechanisms. For additional detailed information and precise molecular mechanisms of action for each of the various psychotropics, interested readers are referred to the companion volume to this text, *Psychologists' Psychotropic Desk Reference* (Pagliaro & Pagliaro, 1998). See also related discussion in Chapter 2, "The Psychotropics."

[8] How the drug gets to the receptor site is discussed in Chapter 3, "Pharmacokinetics and Pharmacodynamics," and Chapter 4, "Administration of Psychotropics."

[9] The term *affinity* is commonly used to denote the degree of a drug's attraction to and ability to bind to a specific receptor.

[10] Although the drug may be a "new" chemical entity (or be "new" to the body), it must act on *existing* receptors. This line of reasoning contributed significantly to the discovery of the various endorphin receptors within the body. Previous to this discovery, the receptors to which the opiate analgesics (see Chapter 2, "The Psychotropics") bind were commonly known as the "opiate receptors." Recognition that the opiate analgesics did not create the receptor to which they bind encouraged the search for the endogenous receptors. The search, to date, has resulted in the identification of several receptors (i.e., *mu*, *kappa*, *delta*) and receptor subtypes (e.g., *mu*-1, *mu*-2) to which endogenous "morphine-like" substances bind. These endogenous substances are the endorphins and enkephalins. Hence, the "opiate receptor" also is referred to as the "endorphin receptor."

[11] The endogenous chemical that binds to the receptor is commonly known as a "ligand."

Paul Ehrlich, a pharmacologist. In 1905, Ehrlich introduced the term *receptor*. Receptors, or receptor sites, have since been empirically established for several psychotropic drugs, including the benzodiazepines, nicotine, and opiate analgesics. However, for most drugs, this mechanism of action remains speculative.

The mechanism of binding to a receptor site was originally thought of in terms of a lock-and-key model. Although this representation is not entirely accurate, it provides a useful way to conceptualize a drug and its receptor site. The three-dimensional structure of a receptor determines its spatial relationship (physical compatibility) to a drug and its physiochemical properties (i.e., polarity or charge). In turn, these characteristics determine its affinity (binding or attraction) toward a drug and work in unison to determine whether the drug will cause a certain action. They also determine how strong the action will be in relation to a specific dose (i.e., potency). Thus, different drugs in the same pharmacologic class or family may differ in both efficacy (maximum obtainable pharmacologic effect) and potency (the dose necessary to elicit a specific pharmacologic effect).

Figure 1-4 is a stylized model of a drug and its receptor illustrating the various types of attracting forces (bonds) that function to hold the drug and receptor in place. The figure also illustrates how the chemical structure of the drug is compatible with the physical structure (i.e., cavities and flat surfaces) of the receptor. This physical compatibility allows the drug to get close enough to the receptor to bind to it and, thus, elicit its pharmacologic effects.[12] It also prevents other drugs from binding to the receptor. Of course, other factors, such as the number of functioning receptors[13] and drug concentration at the receptor sites, also play major roles in determining patient response.

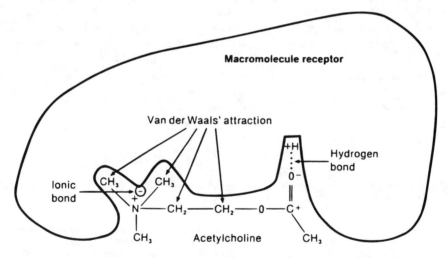

Figure 1-4. Stylized illustration of acetylcholine interacting at its receptor site.

[12] Using the previously noted representation of a lock and key for a receptor and drugs that attempt to bind to the receptor, the notion of "physical compatibility" can be visualized by looking at a set of keys and noting that specific keys only work on specific locks for which they are physically compatible (i.e., an office key will not start a car, nor will a car key open the front door to an office). By the same token, opiate analgesics will not bind or cause an effect at the benzodiazepine receptor, and benzodiazepines will not bind or cause an effect at the opiate receptor.

[13] An area of increased interest and research in the 1990s, although largely limited to animal models and the postmortem study of human tissues, is the effect of disease states (e.g., heart failure) and drugs (e.g., antidepressants) on the functioning of receptors. For example, it has been postulated that various diseases and drug therapy can affect physiologic responses and other drug actions by influencing the nature and extent of drug–receptor binding. This may occur as a result, for example, of an effect on enzymes required for the facilitation of drug–receptor binding or by directly modifying the physical–chemical structure of the receptor. In these cases, it appears that "modifying the receptor" (i.e., in terms of the suggested lock-and-key model; "changing the lock") generally decreases the affinity of the drug for the receptor. Thus, these processes are commonly referred to as "receptor down regulation."

For most drugs, binding to a receptor site is a reversible process, and, thus, the primary action of a drug may be terminated by simply separating the drug from the receptor. This reversible process is one way by which drug interactions can occur (i.e., those interactions that involve competition between drugs for binding sites on the receptor molecule) (see Chapter 6, "Drug Interactions").[14]

The study of drug–receptor binding and competition for binding sites has given rise to two terms: agonist and antagonist. These terms are widely used in relation to discussing the mechanism of drug action. An agonist is a drug that binds to the receptor site and causes a direct action by activating the receptor. An antagonist is a drug that binds to the receptor site but produces no direct pharmacologic action. However, an antagonist produces an indirect action in the presence of an agonist by successfully competing for the agonist's available binding sites and, thus, reducing its pharmacologic action. Thus, if naloxone (Narcan®), an opiate antagonist, is administered alone, it elicits virtually no pharmacologic action; however, if it is administered with the opiate analgesic oxymorphone or any other opiate analgesic, it effectively antagonizes (blocks) the pharmacologic action of the opiate analgesic.[15] Obviously, given the previous discussion of physical compatibility with receptor sites, the chemical structure of agonists and antagonists must be closely related (Figure 1-5), and some antagonists (e.g., nalorphine [Nalline®]) often possess some agonist action (i.e., function as partial agonist–antagonists). In fact, some drugs work as either an agonist or antagonist as a function of dose. Figure 1-5 compares the chemical structures of the agonist oxymorphone (Numorphan®) and the antagonist naloxone (Narcan®) (see also related discussion in Chapter 2, "The Psychotropics").

Chemical reaction

Chemical reactions involve typically the binding, or recombining, of two ions or chemical groups, one positively charged and one negatively charged. This mechanism of action is easily conceptualized by the following simple equation:[16]

$$X^{(+)} + Y^{(-)} \rightleftharpoons XY.$$

Examples of drugs that act by chemical reactions include antacids, many antidotes, and acid-base regulators, such as those used to modify blood or urine pH. Antacids neutralize the hydrochloric acid that is secreted into the stomach by a simple chemical reaction. Antacids, which are basic compounds, combine with hydrochloric acid, a weak acid, to form carbon dioxide, water, and a chloride salt (e.g., calcium chloride if the antacid contains calcium, such as calcium carbonate [Tums®], or sodium chloride if the antacid contains sodium, such as sodium bicarbonate [baking soda]).

Many antidotes, such as the metal chelator, or binder, edetate calcium disodium (Versene®) and the heparin (Liquaemin®) antidote protamine sulfate, also act by chemical binding and neutralizing. Edetate calcium disodium has a high affinity or attraction for lead (Pb^{++}). Thus, the calcium (Ca^{++}) in the molecule is readily displaced by lead. The lead, no longer in a free

---

[14] In competitive situations, the drug with the higher affinity for the receptor will preferentially bind to it and also will be capable of displacing, from already occupied receptor sites, drug molecules that have a lower affinity.

[15] For people addicted to opiate analgesics, the administration of naloxone would immediately precipitate the opiate withdrawal syndrome.

[16] If X is considered to be the drug and Y the receptor, then the mechanism of chemical reactions would be subsumed under the mechanism of "binding at a receptor site." Either conceptualization of the mechanism of action is acceptable; however, a clearer understanding of mechanisms of drug action is provided by using a separate classification for chemical reactions.

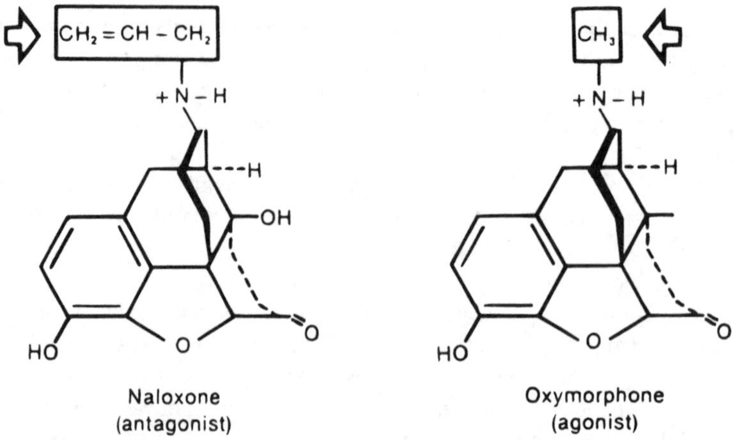

Figure 1-5. Structural similarity between antagonist (naloxone) and agonist (oxymorphone). Note that the only chemical and structural difference is in the attachment to the nitrogen (N) atom, indicated by a box and arrow.

(active) form, is subsequently excreted as the soluble lead–edetate complex. Protamine sulfate (a strong base) combines with heparin (a strong acid) to form a physiologically inert complex and, thus, acts as an antidote for heparin overdosage. Antitoxins provide passive immunity by binding to specific toxins and, thereby, neutralizing their effects.[17]

Acid-base regulators can acidify or alkalinize blood or urine. Acidifers (e.g., ammonium chloride) increase free hydrogen ion concentration, whereas alkalinizers (e.g., sodium bicarbonate) decrease free hydrogen ion concentration. Thus, these regulators lower or raise, respectively, the pH of the blood or urine.

Another way in which drugs act by chemical reactions can be demonstrated by observing the mechanism of action of vitamins. The B vitamins (e.g., nicotinic acid, pyridoxine, riboflavin, and thiamine) act as *coenzymes* to permit or enhance the efficiency of various chemical (metabolic) reactions in the body.

Physical action

Some drugs act by a direct physical action. A common example of this mechanism of drug action is the bulk-forming and lubricant laxatives. Bulk-forming laxatives, such as methylcellulose and plantago seed, absorb fluid from the gastrointestinal tract, increasing their bulk and facilitating peristalsis of the colon by means of direct physical pressure on the receptors in the bowel (Figure 1-6). Lubricant laxatives, such as mineral oil, form a barrier between the wall of the colon and feces to prevent reabsorption of water from the feces, thus facilitating fecal formation and passage.

Osmotic diuretics (e.g., mannitol and urea) increase urine volume by a simple physical mechanism of action. By their presence in the renal tubules, they cause the concentration of the tubular solution to increase. Water then passes through the membrane of the proximal convoluted tubules of the nephron from a region of low concentration to a region of high concentration in an attempt to equalize the concentration on both sides of the membrane (osmotic effect). The end result is an increased rate of urine flow. Certain laxatives (e.g., magnesium

---

[17] This particular example of chemical reactions can also be thought of as a "false receptor" because the antitoxin binds with the toxin and, thus, prevents the toxin from binding with its physiologic receptor.

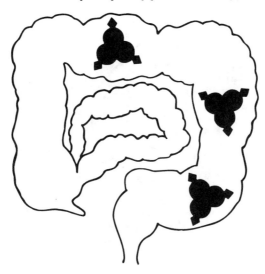

Figure 1-6. Schematic representation of bulk-forming laxatives (e.g., psyllium [Metamucil®]) placing direct physical pressure on the receptors in the wall of the colon, thereby eliciting their pharmacologic action.

sulfate [Epsom salts]) work by the same osmotic principle; however, instead of drawing water into the renal tubules, they draw water into the colon.

Some drugs act by direct physical action on the exterior skin surface. These drugs include those such as zinc oxide, which, when applied to the skin as a paste, forms a physical barrier. This physical barrier protects the skin from the irritating effects of overexposure to the sun (when it is used, for example, as a sunscreen applied to the face) or urine (when it is used on infants to prevent diaper rash). Rapidly evaporating solutions (e.g., isopropyl alcohol) cool the skin simply by means of evaporation. Another interesting physical mechanism of action involves the use of petroleum jelly (petrolatum) to treat infestation of pediculi on the eyelashes. When applied to the eyelashes, petroleum jelly physically suffocates the pediculi without causing irritation to the eye.

Functional disruption

The mechanism of drug action, functional disruption, can occur on several different levels, including molecular, cellular, and organic levels. At the molecular level, disruption, or alteration, of deoxyribonucleic acid (DNA) generally results in loss of function for the affected cells. For example, the anticancer drugs (e.g., cisplatin [Platinol®], mitomycin [Mutamycin®]) act by directly cross linking or binding together DNA strands or chains (Figure 1-7), which in turn results in improper DNA replication and cell death. The antineoplastic antimetabolites also act at the molecular level. Methotrexate (Mexate®), for example, binds to the enzyme dihydrofolate reductase and prevents the reduction of folic acid to tetrahydrofolate (a precursor compound necessary for DNA synthesis in the cell). The immunosuppressant azathioprine (Imuran®) acts in a similar manner by inhibiting the synthesis of the amino acid purine, which is necessary for DNA synthesis.

Griseofulvin (Fulvicin®), an antifungal, binds with the microtubule protein of fungal cells, disrupting the mitotic spindle, and prevents cell division and growth of the fungus. Paraaminobenzoic acid (PABA) is chemically converted to folic acid in bacteria and then further to tetrahydrofolic acid, an enzyme necessary for cell growth. Antibacterial sulfonamides have a chemical

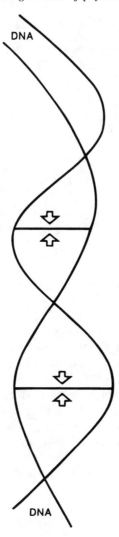

Figure 1-7. Disruption of DNA function by the inappropriate binding together (cross linking) of the DNA strands (arrows) caused by anticancer drugs such as cisplatin (Platinol®) and mitomycin (Mutamycin®).

structure similar to that of PABA. They act by inhibiting the incorporation of PABA into folic acid. This action prevents the production of tetrahydrofolic acid and, thus, inhibits bacterial cell growth. Humans, because they use preformed folic acid, are not affected by the PABA inhibitory action of the sulfonamides.

Psychologic action

The mechanism of psychologic action is mediated through the central nervous system (CNS), which can activate body systems to actually cause physical effects.[18] It also can make a person

---

[18] These effects can be either positive or negative. They can result in healing, such as the disappearance of warts or the alleviation of a headache. However, they also can cause adverse effects such as nausea or vomiting.

think that a drug is causing an effect that it is not. Common examples of psychologic drug action include the habituation associated with the use of some of the abusable psychotropics, such as cocaine. This mechanism explains the placebo effect as well (i.e., any observed effect attributed to a drug that has no direct pharmacologic relationship to the drug).

Placebos are pharmacologically inert substances (e.g., subtherapeutic injections of normal saline, sugar pills) that are predominantly used in double-blind, placebo-controlled research studies to identify drug effects among a sample of naive subjects. However, the placebo effect is also a psychologic mechanism that applies to all drugs, whether directly pharmacologically active or not.[19,20]

Every drug is capable of eliciting a placebo effect. Thus, the effect may be modified by the patient's expectations and also by the suggestions and expectations of the psychologists who prescribe the drug. This mechanism of action has important implications for clinical psychologists who prescribe psychotropic drugs. A commonly occurring example of the placebo response is observed when one or two aspirin tablets are ingested for a simple tension headache and, reportedly, almost immediate relief is obtained, even though the aspirins have not yet been substantially absorbed from the gastrointestinal tract, nor have they yet achieved a "pharmacologically" significant blood level.[21]

Age-dependent drug selection and response

Pharmacotherapy must be tailored to meet the individual needs of each patient, taking into consideration such unique variables as general state of health, concurrent medical disorders, psychologic status, past medical history, genetic predisposition, current physical condition (including body organ functions), known allergies, and other prescription and nonprescription pharmacotherapy the patient may be receiving. The psychologist uses this information to devise pharmacotherapy that will provide the patient with optimal therapeutic benefits with minimal adverse drug reactions. Whereas pharmacotherapy always should be individualized to the needs of each patient, it is well recognized that two groups in particular, the very young and the very old, require special attention in relation to drug selection and dosage.

There are many similarities in the manner in which the young and old respond to pharmacotherapy. For example, kidney dysfunction in both of these groups increases the half-life of elimination for drugs that are eliminated primarily in unchanged form (i.e., as parent drug) in the urine. In general, however, as in the case of kidney dysfunction, the reasons for the similar responses for the young and the old are quite different. Among the young, immature body systems are still developing to their full capacity, whereas, among the elderly, aging body systems, in response to the normal physiologic process of aging, are losing their functional capacity (see Chapter 3, "Pharmacokinetics and Pharmacodynamics," for additional discussion).

Special considerations when prescribing pharmacotherapy for the young

Pharmacotherapy must be specially tailored and monitored for the young because of the variety of factors involved in human physiologic development (see Chapter 3, "Pharmacokinetics and

---

[19] Placebo and other drug actions are *not* mutually exclusive. In fact, they generally occur together with the use of most drugs. Only the percentage of response due to either placebo or drug differs depending on other variables related to the patient, the prescriber, and the context of use.

[20] It could be argued that the placebo response should not even be included in this discussion because it does not involve a direct drug action. However, it does involve, at least, an indirect drug action because, if the drug (i.e., the "placebo") had not been administered, the effect would not have been observed.

[21] For more details on drug absorption and the relationship of blood levels to drug action, see Chapter 3, "Pharmacokinetics and Pharmacodynamics."

Pharmacodynamics," for additional discussion). This process begins before birth, because of the teratogenic potential of many drugs, and it continues through adolescence when the young complete physiologic maturation and become adults.

Teratogenesis

Special considerations for pharmacotherapy among the young must begin before birth to minimize the risk of a teratogenic drug insult. A teratogen may be defined as a substance or factor that causes the production of physical or developmental abnormalities in the developing embryo or fetus. Birth defects caused by drugs that the mother consumes have been fairly well documented and can be prevented if clinical psychologists working with the mother are aware of their occurrence and effectively advise their patients of these possible effects.

The developing embryo or fetus is most susceptible to a teratogenic drug effect during the first trimester of pregnancy because of the sequence of human development (Figure 1-8). Following this period, the next most troublesome period is usually at birth, when the drug may exhibit its pharmacologic effect in the neonate. For example, heroin-addicted mothers may deliver neonates suffering from heroin withdrawal symptoms, and mothers treated with thiopental during labor may have neonates who exhibit neurobehavioral depression. Fortunately, the adverse drug reactions noted at birth that are an extension of the normal or expected pharmacologic effects of a particular drug are usually reversible with proper recognition and care. Birth defects, such as cleft lip, congenital heart defects, fetal alcohol syndrome, and other multiple congenital anomalies, are not as easily or as successfully dealt with. For these other, more serious effects, the best "treatment" is prevention.

The placenta, previously referred to as the placental barrier, is physiologically similar to a sieve that allows the passage of most substances but restricts the passage of others. The major mechanisms by which drugs cross the placenta are active transport, breaks in the placental villi, facilitated diffusion, pinocytosis, simple diffusion, and ultrafiltration. Drug transfer across the placenta is governed by the concentration gradient between the maternal and fetal sides. It also is governed by the characteristics of the drug, including degree of ionization, lipid solubility, and molecular weight (i.e., size of the molecules). In general, nonionized drugs, which are lipid soluble and have a low molecular weight, have the best chance of crossing the placenta to the fetus. Drug transfer and the relationship between a drug bound to tissue or plasma protein are illustrated in Figure 1-9.

Most drugs can cross the placenta, but not all are dangerous or harmful to the fetus. Those that are most likely to cause a teratogenic effect and that should generally be avoided among women who are, or who may become, pregnant include alcohol, chlorpropamide (Diabinese®), danazol (Danocrine®), diethylstilbestrol (Honvol®), disulfiram (Antabuse®), heroin, isotretinoin (Accutane®), lithium (Eskalith®, Lithane®, Lithobid®), mephenytoin (Mesantoin®), methotrexate (Mexate®), methyltestosterone (Android®), norethindrone (Norlutin®), phenobarbital (Luminal®), phenytoin (Dilantin®), primidone (Mysoline®), progestogens, quinine, testosterone, tetracycline (Achromycin®), thalidomide (Kevadon®), trimethadione (Tridione®), and warfarin (Coumadin®).

Drugs excreted in breast milk

Unless information to the contrary exists for a particular drug, it can be assumed that any drug taken by a mother who is breast-feeding will be excreted in her breast milk. However, the concentration in breast milk for the vast majority of drugs will be insufficient to cause any pharmacologic action or elicit any clinical symptoms among nursing infants.

The excretion of drugs into breast milk depends on many factors, including the maternal

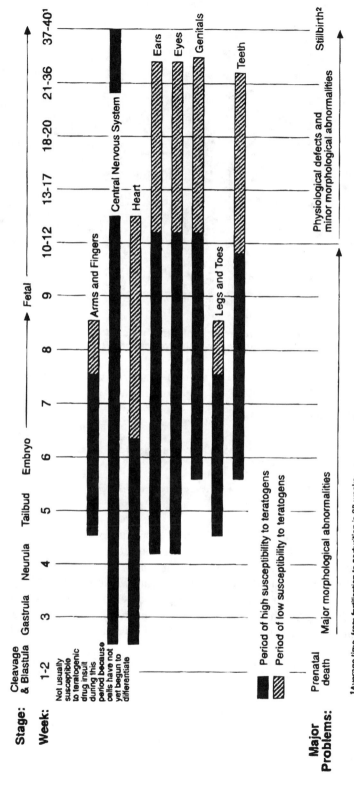

Figure 1-8. *Sequences and timing of human organogenesis indicating variation in teratogenic susceptibility.*

13

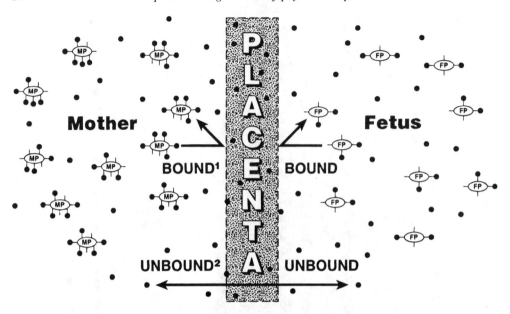

1 The portion of drug bound to plasma protein or ionized which does not cross the placenta
2 The portion of unionized or unbound drug which crosses the placenta

● unbound drug (note that the unbound drug concentration generally is in equilibrium across the placenta unless the drug is too large to cross)

MP   maternal protein with bound drug

FP   fetal protein with bound drug

Note that the concentration of plasma protein as well as the protein-binding capacity may differ significantly between mother and fetus

Figure 1-9. Process of drug transfer across the human placenta with particular reference to free and protein-bound drug.

blood concentration of the drug, the physiochemical properties of the drug (e.g., molecular weight, lipid solubility, and degree of ionization), composition of the breast milk, and the nursing behavior of the infant (i.e., frequency and amount of feeding). If a mother requires pharmacotherapy, the best time in relation to breast-feeding would be about 15 minutes after breast-feeding or 3 to 4 hours before the next feeding. This schedule generally minimizes the amount of drug excreted in the breast milk. However, it should be noted that this general rule will not apply to all drugs (e.g., the milk concentration of salicylate is maximal 4 hours after maternal administration).

Although most drugs do not cause a problem for the nursing infant, the psychologist should be alert to the drugs that may cause associated pharmacologic effects among nursing infants. These drugs include amphetamine (Benzedrine®), cascara sagrada, chloral hydrate (Noctec®), chloramphenicol (Chloromycetin®), cyclophosphamide (Cytoxan®), cyclosporine (Sandimmune®), diazepam (Valium®), doxorubicin (Adriamycin®), ergot alkaloids, heroin, lithium (Eskalith®, Lithane®, Lithobid®), methadone (Dolophine®, Methadose®), methotrexate (Mexate®), metronidazole (Flagyl®), tetracycline (Sumycin®), and tetrahydrocannabinol (marijuana).[22] If

---

[22] All of the listed psychotropics, if ingested in sufficient quantities, can adversely affect performance on neurobehavioral and developmental and psychometric tests that may be administered to nursing neonates and infants.

these or other drugs present a problem for the nursing infant and the mother is not able to discontinue pharmacotherapy, then breast-feeding probably should be discontinued.

Childhood poisonings

Accidental childhood poisoning is a major health problem. As soon as an infant can crawl (about 6 months of age), an accidental poisoning can occur. However, drug poisonings usually occur among children between 2 and 5 years of age. These poisonings occur primarily as a result of the child's curiosity, a tendency to put most objects in the mouth, greater mobility (starting with the toddler stage), and lack of sufficient cognitive development to appreciate danger.

The majority of accidental poisoning deaths related to drug ingestion result from ingesting analgesics (particularly aspirin), antidepressants, antipsychotics, iron supplements, and sedative-hypnotics. To minimize accidental drug poisoning, parents and others caring for young children should be informed about the seriousness of the problem, and they should be advised to have all of their drugs provided in containers with child-resistant caps and to store these containers in a locked cabinet or drawer safely out of the reach of children. It should be stressed that nonprescription drugs, such as aspirin and iron tablets, can be just as hazardous to young children as the prescription psychotropics.

Adverse drug reactions

Children, because of their immature drug receptors and mechanisms of metabolism and excretion, are particularly sensitive to some drugs, even if adjustments to dosage are made on the basis of body surface area. Examples of drugs that may cause specific adverse drug reactions among children include the following: corticosteroids, which, when administered to children, may inhibit both normal epiphyseal development and growth hormone effects, resulting in growth suppression; aspirin, there being a possible association between aspirin use among children who have chickenpox or influenza and Reye's syndrome; chloramphenicol (Chloromycetin®), an antibiotic, which, when administered to newborn infants, may cause the gray baby syndrome because of an immature metabolic pathway (e.g., glucuronide conjugation) present during the first few days of life; hexachlorophene, which, when applied as a soap to the scalps of neonates, can be significantly absorbed and cause neurotoxicity; succinylcholine (Anectine®), which, when administered to children, may cause myoglobinemia significantly more often than when administered to adults; and tetracycline, which, if administered to children under 8 years of age, may become incorporated in developing teeth and cause permanent staining and enamel hypoplasia (see Chapter 5, "Adverse Drug Reactions," for additional discussion).

Kidney function

Kidney blood flow is lower in the neonate, and the glomerular filtration rate of the infant is approximately 50% of the normal adult rate. The kidney matures relatively rapidly, however, and by the 6th to 12th month of life should reach the adult rate. Until this time, however, drugs that are primarily excreted unchanged in the urine (e.g., lithium [Eskalith®, Lithane®, Lithobid®]) will have a much longer half-life of elimination than would normally be expected, and their dose or dosage schedules must be adjusted accordingly (see Chapter 3, "Pharmacokinetics and Pharmacodynamics").

Liver function

Liver function is not fully developed at birth, so some enzymes produced in the liver that are responsible for drug metabolism (e.g., glucuronyl transferase, which is needed to conjugate chloramphenicol) are not available in the neonate, and administering even reduced doses of some drugs may cause severe unexpected reactions, such as the gray syndrome (see earlier discussion). Several drugs, including amphetamines, diazepam (Valium®), nalidixic acid (Neg-Gram®), phenytoin (Dilantin®), and phenylbutazone (Azolid®), are more slowly metabolized by neonates and, therefore, have a longer half-life of elimination, which must be considered when devising a dosing schedule. Fortunately, by the end of the neonatal period, most drug metabolizing enzymes are fully functioning.[23]

Another important factor in relation to liver function is protein binding. Protein binding of drugs is important in determining their volume of distribution and pharmacologic effect.[24] The major serum or plasma protein to which drugs bind is albumin, which is produced by the liver. Until a child is about 2 years of age, the mechanism for producing albumin is not fully developed. Thus, younger children may have a higher percentage of free (active) drug circulating in their blood from a given dose of a drug. This mechanism may result in significant effects, even though the dosage was reduced according to the weight, age, or body surface area of the child.

Volume of distribution
Fluid constitutes approximately 80% of the body weight of an infant. This percentage of body weight gradually decreases to the adult percentage of body weight (55%) by 2 years of age. The volume of distribution of some drugs (e.g., the cardiac glycoside digoxin [Lanoxin®] and the antibiotic gentamicin [Garamycin®]) that are highly water soluble will, thus, be expected to be larger among neonates and infants as opposed to adults because of the differences in percentage of total body water and its associated fluid spaces (i.e., intracellular and extracellular). Therefore, alterations in dose or dosage schedule may need to be made to reflect the altered volume of distribution.[25]

Drug receptors
Health care professionals have observed for some time that some drugs demonstrate either a remarkably strong (e.g., atropine, kanamycin [Kantrex®]) or weak (e.g., halothane [Fluothane®], succinylcholine [Anectine®]) effect when administered to children.[26] Although most of these effects can be explained by the factors previously discussed (e.g., liver function, volume of distribution), it has been postulated that some drug receptors may not be fully developed among children. Altered or "immature" receptors (see earlier discussion in the "mechanisms of drug action" section) also may help account for the majority of seemingly paradoxical drug actions (e.g., the calming effect of the CNS stimulant methylphenidate [Ritalin®]) that are observed among children.[27]

Childhood dosing and drug administration
Several dosing formulas (e.g., Clark's rule, Fried's rule, Young's rule) have been developed to estimate dosages for infants and children as a fraction of the normal adult dose. Body surface

---

[23] The neonatal period is generally defined as the first month of life, beginning at birth for full-term infants (i.e., Days 1 to 30).

[24] Recall that the free drug, but not the protein-bound drug, elicits a pharmacologic effect (see earlier discussion in this chapter).

[25] See Chapter 3, "Pharmacokinetics and Pharmacodynamics," for a definition and discussion of the concept of "volume of distribution."

[26] Some authors refer to this phenomenon simply as children being particularly sensitive or resistant to the effects of certain drugs.

[27] Other theories can also account for this observed phenomenon. For example, another theory suggests that (1) certain areas of the CNS of children with ADHD are understimulated, (2) behavioral problems noted among children with ADHD are primarily reflective of maladaptive attempts by these children to self-stimulate the CNS, and (3) CNS stimulants, such as methylphenidate, stimulate the understimulated areas of the CNS of these children with ADHD and, thus, ameliorate the need for the observed behavioral problems. Note that this theory can also be interpreted as supportive of the presence of altered or "immature" receptors.

area, which uses two measures, height and weight (Figure 1-10), is generally believed to provide better estimates for dosing of infants and children than the formulas based on age or weight alone. In some cases, the dose calculated for infants and children by means of the body surface area nomogram (or other dosing formulas) may exceed the maximal recommended adult dose. However, this dose should generally *not* be prescribed. Doses for infants and children should

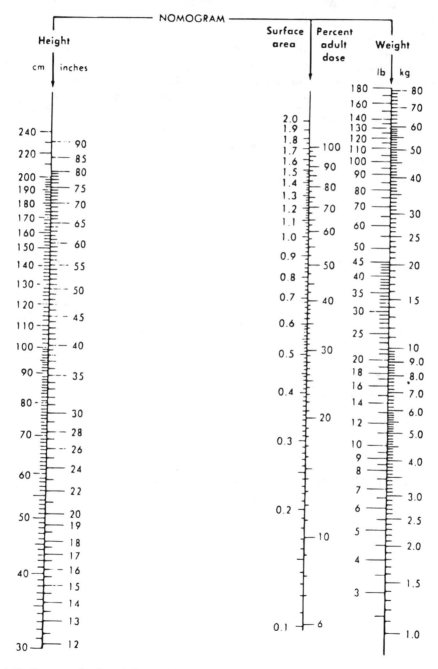

Figure 1-10. Nomogram for the calculation of body surface area among children based upon a knowledge of their height and weight.

not exceed the maximal recommended adult dose, except in rare cases in which the dosage guidelines specifically recommend this. A specific case involves the bronchodilator theophylline. Its dosage may at times exceed the normal adult dosage because of its shorter half-life of elimination in children.

It should be emphasized that formulas or nomograms are used to calculate approximate doses for infants and children. However, only by means of careful titration and adjustment will the optimal dosage be arrived at for each individual patient because of the influence of the factors previously discussed.

When administering drugs to infants and young children, or when instructing a parent to do so, try to administer the entire dose at once, avoid administering drugs with essential foods (e.g., milk or formula) because the infant or child may begin to associate the unpleasant drug taste with the food, avoid making drugs so flavorful or treated in such a manner that they may later be sought out as candy, advise parents and others responsible for the care of young children always to keep all drugs (prescription and nonprescription) in child-resistant containers and stored out of children's reach, and remember that administering drugs to young infants and small children always requires tact and skill. For additional details and specific information in relation to psychotropic drug administration, see Chapter 4, "Administration of Psychotropics."

Special considerations when prescribing pharmacotherapy for the elderly

Elderly people suffer two to five times the frequency of adverse drug reactions from pharmacotherapy than younger adults, and from 5% to 30% of admissions of elderly people to hospitals may be associated with inappropriate pharmacotherapy.[28] These problems often are not recognized because of the following factors: a low level of suspicion, ascribing signs and symptoms to old age, more than one health care provider prescribing pharmacotherapy, a failure to inquire about nonprescription drug use, atypical presentation of signs and symptoms among the elderly (e.g., higher pain threshold, more referred pain), a difficulty in communication (e.g., poor vision and hearing), and a lack of time necessary to adequately assess elderly patients, particularly among clinicians paid by the visit or patient. In addition, physiologic changes that are a natural result of aging profoundly influence pharmacotherapy for the elderly, even in the absence of disease.[29]

Kidney function

Kidney (renal) blood flow and the dependent mechanisms of glomerular filtration and tubular secretion are decreased among the elderly. There also is a reduction in the number of functioning nephrons. Consequently, drugs that are eliminated predominantly in unchanged form by the kidneys (e.g., digoxin [Lanoxin®], gentamicin [Garamycin®], kanamycin [Kantrex®], lithium [Eskalith®, Lithane®], penicillin [Bicillin A-P®], sulfamethizole [Thiosulfil®]) will remain in the body longer (i.e., will have a longer half-life of elimination).[30] If dosages are not reduced,

---

[28] See Chapter 5, "Adverse Drug Reactions," for additional information and discussion.

[29] Before proceeding, so as not to inadvertently contribute to the stereotype of ageism, it should be noted that these physiologic changes occur in the *average* elderly patient (i.e., aging is a unique and individual process that occurs at different rates among different people). However, whereas the occasional elderly person may be found who is in better health than a person half his or her age, for the vast majority of elderly people, the physiologic changes noted here will be an accurate representation of their particular individual clinical condition.

[30] See Chapter 3, "Pharmacokinetics and Pharmacodynamics," for more details concerning the effect of kidney function on pharmacokinetics.

overdosage will result at an increased frequency, as will the incidence and the severity of adverse drug reactions.

Composition of body mass
Several changes occur in the composition of the body mass as a natural consequence of aging. These changes include increased fat (as opposed to lean) body tissue that can cause delayed onset of pharmacologic effects followed by accumulation on repeated dosing with fat-soluble drugs (e.g., barbiturates [Seconal®, Nembutal®], diazepam [Valium®], lidocaine [Xylocaine®]). Reduction of heart, kidney, and muscle mass also occurs and can cause toxic blood or tissue levels of a drug when a usually recommended adult dose is prescribed. Total body fluid also decreases as a percentage of total body weight, from 55% among younger adults to 45% among elderly adults.

Volume of distribution
Among patients who have congestive heart failure, the volume of distribution of many drugs (e.g., digoxin [Lanoxin®], furosemide [Lasix®], lidocaine [Xylocaine®]) is reduced so that a usual adult dose may result in toxic blood levels (see Chapter 3, "Pharmacokinetics and Pharmacodynamics," for further details).

Another factor affecting the volume of distribution among elderly patients is a significantly reduced albumin concentration. Thus, as noted previously for young children, the concentration of a free (active) drug can be significantly higher than expected if a usual adult dose of a highly protein-bound drug (e.g., meperidine [Demerol®], phenytoin [Dilantin®], phenylbutazone [Novo-Butazone®], warfarin [Coumadin®]) is prescribed to an elderly patient. Greater competition of drugs for protein-binding sites also exists among elderly patients, and the potential for drug interactions mediated by a protein-binding mechanism is significantly increased (see Chapter 6, "Drug Interactions").

Liver function
The rate of some forms of liver (hepatic) metabolism (i.e., hydroxylation and conjugation reactions) for several drugs (e.g., acetaminophen [Tylenol®], antipyrine) has been demonstrated to be significantly decreased (on average) among the elderly. This decrease is associated with longer half-lives of elimination for these drugs among elderly patients. These findings, however, are *not* generalizable to all other drugs, and it appears that most drugs are normally metabolized by elderly patients. However, it should be noted that elderly patients may be more susceptible to drug-induced liver toxicity (e.g., hepatitis caused by isoniazid [Nydrazid®]) than are younger adults.

Drug receptors
As was the case for infants and young children, health care professionals have observed for some time that elderly patients appear to be particularly susceptible or resistant to the effects of certain drugs (e.g., barbiturates). Most of these effects can be explained by the age-related factors previously discussed. However, it has been postulated, at least for drugs that operate at drug receptors, that these effects may be the result, at least in part, of decreased numbers or responsiveness (i.e., sensitivity) of drug receptors among elderly patients (e.g., down regulation of beta-1 adrenoreceptors in the heart and beta-2 adrenoreceptors in the lungs).

Aging body systems
Elderly patients may experience more seemingly paradoxic drug responses and adverse drug reactions than patients in other age groups because of their decreased functional reserve in a

variety of body systems (e.g., cardiovascular, nervous, renal) and the resultant lack of a safety margin with which to cope with drug effects (see also previous discussion of "drug receptors").

Interactions with multiple disease states

Multiple disease states and polypharmacy, involving both prescription and nonprescription drugs, are common among elderly patients. Therefore, drug–drug and drug–disease state interactions are much more frequently observed in this age group. Interactions involving the psychotropics that additively or synergistically depress the sensorium are particularly problematic for elderly patients. These effects contribute to poor self-esteem among elderly patients and to the significant number of elderly patients who are inappropriately classified as suffering from senile dementia (see Chapter 6, "Drug Interactions," for additional discussion).

Dosing and drug administration for the elderly

Special consideration for dosing and monitoring the effects of pharmacotherapy for elderly patients are particularly important because of the factors previously discussed. These factors generally have not been given wide attention in the past. Thus, dosing for elderly adults is not as exact as for infants, children, and younger adults. For other age groups, specific dosages and general formulas have been extensively determined. However, only for a very few drugs has an exact dosage been determined for elderly adults, and, because of the multitude of factors affecting pharmacotherapy for the elderly, the only equations that have been devised are as yet necessarily complex and laborious to use.

Principles of pharmacotherapy for elderly patients

Psychologists should be aware of the following principles in relation to prescribing pharmacotherapy for elderly patients. The major factors that necessitate special considerations for this age group are polypharmacy, multiple coexistent disease states, and the natural physiologic changes associated with aging. In dealing with these factors, the following points must be kept in mind: (1) Is pharmacotherapy necessary? (2) What is the therapeutic end point of pharmacotherapy? (3) Is the drug correct? (4) Is the dosage correct? (5) Is the dosage form correct? (6) What adverse drug reactions or toxic effects may occur? (7) What drug interactions may occur? (8) Is the drug correctly labeled and packaged? (9) Who is responsible for drug administration? (10) Is the patient capable and willing to follow his or her planned pharmacotherapy? and (11) Can any of the patient's other pharmacotherapy be discontinued?

Each of these questions is briefly discussed, and examples that may make the relevance of the questions more apparent are presented.

Is pharmacotherapy required? Often, pharmacotherapy is not the therapy of choice. This is particularly true for elderly patients, who, because of the natural consequences of aging, are more likely to have multiple medical conditions, each of which necessitates some form of therapy. In this regard, psychologists must use their knowledge and skills to determine whether an alternate therapy may be used to treat the patient's problem. Can a sedative-hypnotic drug be avoided if the patient engages in increased physical activity, avoids caffeinated beverages in the evening, avoids large volumes of fluids near bedtime, or drinks a warm glass of milk at bedtime?[31] Can antidepressant pharmacotherapy be avoided if voluntary visiting is arranged to decrease the patient's loneliness, the drugs causing the depression (e.g., cimetidine [Tagamet®], reserpine [Serpasil®]) are discontinued, or appropriate psychotherapy is used? Old age should

---

[31] It should be noted that milk contains the amino acid tryptophan, which may have a sedating effect on the central nervous system.

not, however, be used as a criterion to withhold rationally formulated pharmacotherapy that may improve the dignity of an elderly person and the quality of his or her life.

What is the therapeutic end point of pharmacotherapy? Rational pharmacotherapy always should be associated with a general goal (e.g., curing a condition, relieving symptoms, improving the quality of life) and a predefined end point that can indicate whether the goal has been (or is being) achieved. Quantitative measures (e.g., improved memory) should be established to serve as indicators of the success or failure of pharmacotherapy. Other measures also may serve as indicators that the pharmacotherapy should be reevaluated, or a time frame (e.g., every 6 months) may be associated with this variable. Pharmacotherapy should never be "as needed" for an indefinite period without a definite time frame for reevaluation.

Is the drug correct? Misdiagnosis is particularly common among elderly patients. Ideally, as more educational programs are designed that focus specifically on the psychology of aging and on preparing psychologists with specialized training, the problem of misdiagnosis will decrease. A commonly encountered example of misdiagnosis and misprescription among elderly patients involves using antipsychotics for elderly people when their confusion is the result of other pharmacotherapy that they are receiving. Another commonly encountered example is the use of sedative-hypnotics to treat the anxiety associated with depression. In this situation, the sedative-hypnotic often significantly exacerbates the patient's depression. A better therapeutic choice in this situation would be to select an effective antidepressant that also possesses some anxiolytic properties (see Chapter 2, "The Psychotropics").

Is the dosage correct? As previously noted, specific dosages for most psychotropics (and other drugs) have not yet been generally determined for elderly patients. However, loading doses (see Chapter 3, "Pharmacokinetics and Pharmacodynamics") are not generally needed, and lower than usual adult dosages are usually required to prevent toxicity because of age-related physiologic changes (e.g., decreased kidney function, decreased volume of distribution). Some drugs (e.g., antibiotics, diuretics) may need to be prescribed in higher than normal doses if the desired therapeutic response is not obtained. Thus, elderly patients initially require more monitoring and reevaluation than younger patients in order to properly adjust and titrate drug dosage regimens to meet their individual needs.

Is the dosage form correct? Some elderly patients find liquid dosage forms easier to swallow than capsules or tablets, and changing to liquid forms may significantly increase their ability to participate actively in their pharmacotherapy. Sometimes suppositories may be preferred (see Chapter 4, "Administration of Psychotropics"). Prescribing psychologists must ensure that the bioavailability (see Chapter 3, "Pharmacokinetics and Pharmacodynamics") is not significantly changed by changing the dosage form (or that the dose and dosage are adjusted accordingly) (see also related discussion in Chapter 4, "Administration of Psychotropics").

What adverse drug reactions may occur? The psychologist should know which adverse drug reactions to look for and should also ensure that the patient is properly instructed in regard to the occurrence and management of adverse drug reactions. The patient should be made aware of both minor adverse drug reactions to expect (this generally significantly increases compliance) and major adverse drug reactions that require discontinuation of the psychotropic, notification of the prescribing psychologist, and other required actions such as accessing emergency medical services (see Chapter 5, "Adverse Drug Reactions").

Postural (orthostatic) hypotension is a particularly troublesome adverse drug reaction for elderly patients. Associated falls may often lead to a fractured hip or hospitalization that would not otherwise have been required. Several antipsychotic drugs, including chlorpromazine (Thorazine®) and the tricyclic antidepressants (TCAs), may cause this effect. Psychologists should caution their patients about such problematic adverse drug reactions and provide instruction in regard to measures that may minimize their occurrence (e.g., arising slowly from bed).

What drug interactions may occur? Elderly patients are at particular risk for experiencing drug interactions because of a variety of factors, including polypharmacy and decreased plasma albumin concentration. In addition, because of their decreased functional reserve capacity (as previously noted), the probability of such interactions resulting in adverse drug reactions is significantly increased. It always is necessary to be aware of possible drug interactions and of their potential severity (e.g., Does the interaction necessitate a change in pharmacotherapy, and, if so, which drug is a safe alternative?). Patients must also be carefully informed about which drugs and foods may interact with their prescribed pharmacotherapy and how to prevent or manage such interactions (see Chapter 6, "Drug Interactions").

Is the drug correctly labeled and packaged? In addition to the usually required information (i.e., name of drug, strength, quantity, dosage, name of patient, and name of prescriber) and auxiliary information (i.e., major potential adverse drug reactions and toxic effects; activities, foods, and drugs to avoid), elderly patients often have other special drug labeling and packaging needs. For example, is the print on the labels large enough for the patient to read? Does the patient read English? If not, are directions available in his or her preferred language, or is a responsible person available to provide required assistance? Can the elderly patient open child-resistant containers or special packaging (e.g., unit dose containers, bubble packages)?

Who is responsible for administering the drug? Can the patient administer his or her own drug, or do factors such as blindness or arthritis prevent safe administration without assistance? Can the patient follow complicated multidrug regimens, or is he or she too confused or forgetful to do so? Possible solutions to these common problems may include assistance from family members or developing memory aids (e.g., dosing cards, calendars, or containers) to assist the patient to remember when the drug should be administered. The community health or home care nurse also can assist with administering drugs in the home. Finally, patients may find it helpful to use longer acting dosage forms that require only twice daily (e.g., lithium extended release tablets [Eskalith CR®, Lithobid®]) or once monthly (e.g., haloperidol decanoate injection [Haldol LA®]) administration.

Is the patient compliant? Estimates of noncompliance rates among elderly patients range from 20% to 80%. If psychologists attend to the basic questions presented here, the major reasons for noncompliance among their elderly patients will, more than likely, have been effectively dealt with. In addition, psychologists should ensure that their patients are provided with both oral and written instructions in relation to their pharmacotherapy and explain to their patients the importance of compliance.[32] Elderly patients should be asked to repeat the instructions in their own words to assess comprehension of the directions (i.e., the appropriate directions may have been correctly given, but this does not ensure that the patient correctly understood them). They also should be asked to read any written instructions and be provided with the opportunity to ask questions or clarify any information that may be unclear to them.

Can any of the patient's other pharmacotherapy be discontinued? Take advantage of the opportunity, whenever evaluating a patient for the need for new or additional pharmacotherapy, to reevaluate thoroughly the previous or current pharmacotherapy and to discontinue any unnecessary pharmacotherapy (both prescription and nonprescription). Not only will this reevaluation of pharmacotherapy save the patient the time, money, and trouble of continuing unnecessary pharmacotherapy; it also may improve his or her quality of life by perhaps eliminating an

---

[32] In accordance with their individual mental abilities, personalities, and clinical conditions, patients should be actively involved in the planning and selection of their pharmacotherapy. For example, a patient may be told that an antidepressant would be a useful adjunct to his or her psychotherapy for depression. After discussion, the patient could either consent to or decline antidepressant pharmacotherapy. If he or she agrees to pharmacotherapy, subsequent discussion could briefly outline the rationale for choosing a specific antidepressant for that particular patient.

unnecessary adverse drug reaction (e.g., mental confusion) or decreasing the potential for a drug interaction.

Whenever a change is made in pharmacotherapy, the prescribing psychologist should ascertain whether a change in dosage of the remaining drugs is required. For example, if a drug that induces drug metabolism[33] (e.g., phenobarbital [Luminal®]) is added to or discontinued from a patient's pharmacotherapeutic regimen, the dosage of concurrently prescribed drugs (e.g., the anticoagulant warfarin [Coumadin®]) may need to be increased or decreased to prevent toxicity because these drugs will not continue to be metabolized at the same rate. Collaboration with the patient's other prescribers (in this case, the prescriber of the anticoagulant) is required.

Summary

This chapter has presented an overview of four basic principles of pharmacotherapy: structure-activity relationship, dose-response relationship, variability in dose response, and therapeutic index. An understanding of these basic principles can assist prescribing psychologists to better interpret pharmacologic studies and prescribe optimal psychotropic pharmacotherapy for their patients. Five general mechanisms of drug action also were discussed, including binding at a receptor site, chemical reaction, physical action, functional disruption, and psychological action.

The exact mechanism of action for most drugs remains unknown. However, several theories have been advanced to explain specific types of drug action. An awareness of a drug's mechanism of action enables psychologists to better understand why different drugs in the same pharmacologic class have similar actions. Psychologists should more fully appreciate that, because of slight chemical or structural modifications, related drugs may be more (or less) potent and may produce more (or fewer) adverse drug reactions. A knowledge of the mechanisms of drug action also enables psychologists to predict drug interactions. Further information on the specific mechanisms of action for various classes of drugs can be found in the following chapter, "The Psychotropics."

This chapter also has focused on two special groups of patients, the young and the old, who have special needs and considerations in relation to pharmacotherapy. Special mechanisms responsible for altered pharmacologic response among these patient groups have been summarized. The pharmacologic principles for effectively dealing with these age-related effects so that therapeutic drug response can be optimized among these patients also have been presented. Psychologists should keep in mind that many of these principles can be generalized to prescribing pharmacotherapy for other patient groups and, thus, can assist in optimizing therapeutic response with a minimum of adverse drug reactions.

---

[33] See Chapter 6, "Drug Interactions," for other examples and for a comprehensive discussion of drugs that both stimulate (induce) and decrease (inhibit) metabolism.

2

The Psychotropics

Introduction

The term *psychotropic* refers to all exogenous chemicals, drugs, and xenobiotics whose major direct action on the central nervous system (CNS) results in changes in cognition, learning, memory, behavior, perception, or affect.[1] The psychotropics can be conveniently further classified as either "abusable" or "nonabusable" depending on their propensity to produce addiction and habituation (see Figure 2-1). This classification has been found to be both accurate and parsimonious.

Only those categories of psychotropics that are currently approved for therapeutic use in North America for the symptomatic management of mental disorders are discussed in this reference text (see Table 2-1). Depending on theoretical or disciplinary orientation, these disorders also can be variably referred to as "emotional disorders," "psychiatric disorders," or "psychological disorders." For additional details regarding the "abuse" of these psychotropics and for discussion of the other psychotropics (e.g., the psychedelics) that are not currently approved for therapeutic use,[2] readers are referred to the comprehensive text *Substance Use Among Children and Adolescents: Its Nature, Extent, and Effects From Conception to Adulthood* (Pagliaro & Pagliaro, 1996). For additional clinical therapeutic data and information regarding nonapproved uses[3] of the psychotropics, readers are referred to the companion volume to this text, *Clinical Psychopharmacotherapeutics for Psychologists* (Pagliaro & Pagliaro, in press).

To familiarize readers with the psychotropics that are of most relevance to prescribing psychologists, this chapter presents an in-depth overview of the indications, mechanisms of action, therapeutics, adverse drug reactions (ADRs), and other clinically relevant data concerning the following classifications of psychotropics: antidepressants and antimanics; antipsychotics; sedative-hypnotics; opiate analgesics and antagonists; and amphetamines and other CNS stimulants.

---

[1] Anticonvulsants and anti-parkinsonians, although producing actions that could qualify them to be included in this classification, have been deliberately excluded because their prescription and use are considered, at this time, to be primarily outside of the area of practice and expertise of clinical psychologists (i.e., they are used primarily by physicians to treat neurological disorders, and it is not anticipated that psychologists generally will be prescribing these particular psychotropics). The centrally acting skeletal muscle relaxants and general anesthetics also have been excluded for similar reasons. However, when relevant, exceptions (e.g., the use of anticonvulsants, such as carbamazepine and valproic acid, to treat mental disorders) have been included in the discussion.

[2] A noted exception to this rule involves the principal active cannabinoid in *Cannabis sativa* (i.e., marijuana, hashish, hashish oil), delta-9-tetrahydrocannabinol (THC). THC also is known as dronabinol and is available in Canada under the trade name of Marinol®. It is available for the treatment of severe nausea and vomiting associated with cancer chemotherapy.

[3] Approval of specific drugs for use in the treatment of specific disorders is determined by the FDA or HPB and is generally based on the results obtained from controlled clinical studies.

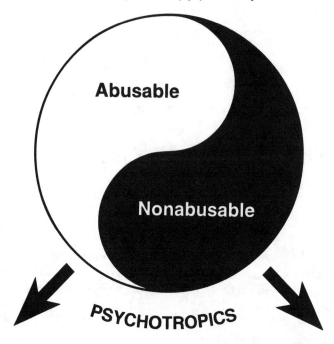

PSYCHOTROPICS

Central Nervous System Depressants:
OPIATES (Codeine, Heroin, Meperidine, Morphine, Pentazocine)
SEDATIVE HYPNOTICS (Alcohol [Beer, Wine, Distilled Liquor], Barbiturates, Benzodiazepines, Miscellaneous)
VOLATILE SOLVENTS & INHALANTS (Gasoline, Glue)

Central Nervous System Stimulants:
AMPHETAMINES, CAFFEINE, COCAINE, NICOTINE (Tobacco)

Psychedelics:
LSD, MESCALINE (Peyote), PCP, PSILOCYBIN, THC (Marijuana, Hashish, Hash Oil),

Anticonvulsants:
(Carbamazepine, Phenytoin, Primidone, Valproic Acid)

Antidepressants:
MONOAMINE OXIDASE INHIBITORS (Moclobemide, Phenelzine, Tranylcypromine)
SELECTIVE SEROTONIN REUPTAKE INHIBITORS (Fluoxetine, Paroxetine, Sertraline)
TRICYCLIC ANTIDEPRESSANTS (Amitriptyline, Desipramine, Imipramine, Nortriptyline)
MISCELLANEOUS (Amoxapine, Bupropion, Maprotiline, Trazodone)

Antiparkinsonians:
(Levodopa)

Antipsychotics:
(Chlorpromazine, Clozapine, Haloperidol)

Figure 2-1. Abusable and nonabusable psychotropics.

Antidepressants and antimanics

The antidepressants comprise a diverse group pf psychotropics, which includes the monoamine oxidase inhibitors (MAOIs), selective serotonin reuptake inhibitors (SSRIs), tricyclic antidepressants (TCAs), miscellaneous antidepressants, and the antimanics (see box). This section discusses the indications, mechanisms of action, therapeutics, and ADRs of these psychotropics.

Table 2-1. Classification of the psychotropics currently approved for clinical use in North America.

Antidepressants and antimanics
    Monoamine oxidase inhibitors (MAOIs)
    Selective serotonin reuptake inhibitors (SSRIs)
    Tricyclic antidepressants (TCAs)
    Miscellaneous antidepressants
    Antimanics
Antipsychotics
    Butyrophenones
    Dibenzoxazepines
    Dihydroindolones
    Diphenylbutylpiperidines
    Phenothiazines
    Thioxanthenes
    Miscellaneous (atypical) antipsychotics
CNS depressants
    Opiate analgesics
        Opiate agonists
        Opiate agonists/antagonists (mixed)
    Sedative-hypnotics
        Barbiturates
        Benzodiazepines
        Miscellaneous sedative-hypnotics
CNS stimulants
    Amphetamines
    Amphetamine-like CNS stimulants
    Miscellaneous (anorexiants) CNS stimulants

Antidepressants and Antimanics Generally Available for Use in North America[4]

Monoamine oxidase inhibitors (MAOIs)
    Moclobemide (Manerix®) (🍁)
    Phenelzine (Nardil®)
    Tranylcypromine (Parnate®)

Selective serotonin reuptake inhibitors (SSRIs)[5]
    Fluoxetine (Prozac®)
    Fluvoxamine (Luvox®)
    Paroxetine (Paxil®)
    Sertraline (Zoloft®)

Tricyclic antidepressants (TCAs)
    Amitriptyline (Elavil®)
    Clomipramine (Anafranil®)[6]

continued. . .

[4] While most of these antidepressants and antimanics are available for use throughout North America, some are available *only* in either Canada or the United States at the time of publication, as indicated by the maple leaf (🍁) and star (⋆), respectively.

[5] Note that clomipramine and fluvoxamine are used primarily for their anti-obsessional actions for the treatment of patients who have obsessive–compulsive disorder.

[6] Although structurally a TCA, clomipramine is a potent inhibitor of serotonin and, thus, shares many pharmacologic properties with the SSRIs. Some taxonomies classify clomipramine as an SSRI because of its potent serotonin inhibitory activity. Similarly, some taxonomies also classify venlafaxine as an SSRI because of its potent serotonin inhibitory activity.

Desipramine (Norpramin®, Pertofrane®)
Doxepin (Adapin®, Sinequan®)
Imipramine (Tofranil®)
Nortriptyline (Aventyl®, Pamelor®)
Protriptyline (Triptil®, Vivactil®)
Trimipramine (Surmontil®)

Miscellaneous antidepressants
Amoxapine (Asendin®)
Bupropion (Wellbutrin®) (★)
Maprotiline (Ludiomil®)
Mirtazapine (Remeron®) (★)
Nefazodone (Serzone®)
Trazodone (Desyrel®)
Venlafaxine (Effexor®)

Antimanics
Carbamazepine (Tegretol®)
Lithium (Eskalith®, Lithane®, Lithobid®)
Valproic acid (Depakene®, Depakote®, Epival®)

Indications

Antidepressants and antimanics are drugs used to treat various mood disorders, which generally can be defined as pathological disturbances of mood that can be organized along a continuum from depression to elation (e.g., mania). Mood disorders differ from normal fluctuations of mood in that they are profound and prolonged and seriously affect a person's life whether he or she is at work, school, home, or leisure. Mood disorders are divided into two broad classes: the depressive disorders and the bipolar disorders. The depressive disorders, in particular, have been subdivided in various ways according to (1) supposed etiology (e.g., reactive or exogenous as opposed to endogenous, implying that one group of disorders is caused by something in the environment while another group is caused by some factor in a person's biology), (2) severity (e.g., mild as opposed to severe, generally equating with neuroses and psychoses), and (3) the period of life at which time they occur (e.g., adolescent depression, postpartum depression).

For the purposes of this chapter, the depressive disorders can be best regarded as presenting a common syndrome with causes that should be regarded as multifactorial. In other words, depressive disorders are neither solely reactive nor solely endogenous; rather, they depend on the interaction of the biologic, psychologic, and sociologic variables composing the personal context of individual patients. The bipolar disorders are characterized by major depressive episodes and various combinations of manic, mixed, and hypomanic episodes. For many patients, these episodes can be pharmacologically managed with the antidepressants and antimanics because of the proposed relationship of these psychotropics to endogenous neurotransmitters involved in the etiology of mood disorders.

Antidepressants: Mechanisms of action and therapeutics

Major neurotransmitters presently implicated etiologically with major depressive episodes include acetylcholine, dopamine, gamma-aminobutyric acid, norepinephrine, and serotonin.

Evidence that implicates these neurotransmitters includes measures of their concentration levels in the blood, cerebral spinal fluid, and urine. Reflective of these and other clinical data is the biogenic amine (catecholamine) theory of depression and mania. According to the biogenic amine theory, a deficiency in biogenic amines is responsible for depression, and a surplus is responsible for mania. However, controversy remains over which specific amines are most important: the major amine neurotransmitters, such as dopamine, norepinephrine (noradrenaline), and serotonin, or the trace amines, such as phenylethylamine and tryptamine.

Figure 2-2 depicts a metabolic map showing the formation of two of the amines considered relevant to the etiology of depression, tryptamine and serotonin. Central to this map is an essential amino acid, L-tryptophan (essential because it has to be ingested and cannot be synthesized by the human body). L-tryptophan is decarboxylated to tryptamine, one of the trace amines noted previously. It also is hydroxylated to 5-hydroxytryptophan (5-HTP), which, in turn, is decarboxylated to 5-hydroxytryptamine (5-HT) (serotonin). With this simple scheme in mind, and also taking into account that a deficiency of amines, in general, may underlie depression, perhaps the etiology and treatment of depression can be better understood.

Estrogens are depicted in the upper right area of the metabolic map (Figure 2-2) with a dotted line descending to the base. Estrogens, in fact, cause a relative deficiency of vitamin B_6 (pyridoxine), which is the essential cofactor for the decarboxylase enzyme. Consequently, as the same decarboxylase is involved in the formation of tryptamine, serotonin, and dopamine (and, therefore, norepinephrine) from various amino acids, it is apparent that a deficiency of pyridoxine will cause a deficiency in biogenic amines.

The middle part of the chart indicates the effect of the thyroid hormones. In general, thyroxine and its congeners are catabolic substances liberating amino acids from proteins and

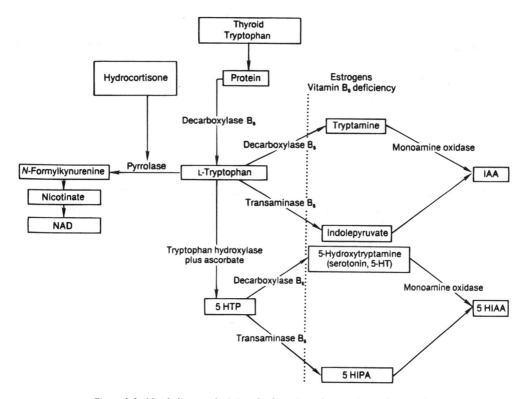

Figure 2-2. Metabolic map depicting the formation of tryptamine and serotonin.

amines from amino acids. Measuring the amines in the urine of a patient who has hyperthyroidism with associated thyrotoxicosis (i.e., toxicity associated with hyperactivity of the thyroid gland) is almost comparable to measuring the amines in the urine of a patient who is receiving monoamine oxidase inhibitors (MAOIs). In both cases, the urine contains high levels of amines. In addition, the patient who has thyrotoxicosis is usually anxious. This state of anxiety is almost entirely the result of large amounts of circulating norepinephrine in the bloodstream, reflecting peripheral metabolism. Within the brain, a variety of conditions can occur. During the early stages, liberation of stored amine may lead to excessive amounts of cerebral amines and, perhaps, a state of mania. During the later stages, the inevitable depletion of amine stores will occur, leading to a state of depression. Thus, the biogenic amine theory provides one possible explanation of the various mental disorders that may occur among patients who have thyroid disease.

The effects of cortisone (i.e., glucocorticosteroids) are depicted on the left of the diagram. The administration of cortisone can produce euphoria, which is probably associated with the liberation of biogenic amines. Among patients who require long-term cortisone pharmacotherapy resulting in Cushing's syndrome, the most common mental complication is depression. It is thought that cortisone acts (as estrogen may) by inducing an enzyme called tryptophan pyrrolase that results in an increase in tryptophan. This reaction depletes the source of amine production and causes a relative deficiency in pyridoxine. Some interesting characteristics of cortisone levels are that (1) they show a diurnal variation, (2) they are higher among women, and (3) they increase in old age. These characteristics of cortisone levels, in part, provide a biochemical basis for the following observations: (1) Mood shows a diurnal variation; (2) depression is more common among women; and (3) depression is more common during old age.

Figure 2-3 is a highly stylized representation of a synapse between a presynaptic neuron and a postsynaptic neuron common to the hypothalamus or the reticular activating system in the upper brain stem. This diagram is designed to show the normal cycle of biogenic amine formation and destruction (catabolism). The formation of the amine from the essential amino acid tryptophan is on the left. Tryptophan, which is present in the cell cytoplasm, is decarboxylated to the amine (1) and is almost immediately bound (2a) in a storage vesicle by combination with adenosine triphosphate (ATP). This binding with ATP in storage vesicles seems to be biologically necessary for at least two reasons: (1) Without binding, free amine would be susceptible to degradation by monoamine oxidase, and, (2) in emergency situations, the rate of formation of biogenic amines is too slow to provide a massive and instantaneous release of required amines.

After being stored in the vesicle, the amine is normally released by a nerve impulse. After its egress into the synaptic cleft (3), it acts on the postsynaptic receptor, which is stereospecific, and thus activates the postsynaptic neuron. Thereafter, the amine is normally reabsorbed into the presynaptic neuron and is either restored in the vesicle (4a → 2a) or destroyed by the monoamine oxidase (5) found in the mitochondria. The end product is the production of an aldehyde acid or glycol, which is then excreted in the urine. It is argued that the various antidepressants act by similar mechanisms. The TCAs inhibit the reuptake of the biogenic amines into the presynaptic neuron and, thus, increase synaptic levels of these neurotransmitters, particularly norepinephrine.[7] The SSRIs act, as their name implies, primarily by blocking presynaptic reuptake of serotonin and, thus, increase its concentration in the synaptic cleft. The MAOIs inhibit monoamine oxidase and, therefore, potentiate the effects of all of the biogenic

---

[7] Research suggests that the reduction in the number of postsynaptic receptors (i.e., down regulation) of α_2- and β-adrenergic receptors also may significantly contribute to the action of the TCAs and the other antidepressants. Down regulation of the serotonergic receptors, particularly the 1A and 2 subtypes of 5-HT, also appears to be integrally involved in the mechanism of action of several of the antidepressants.

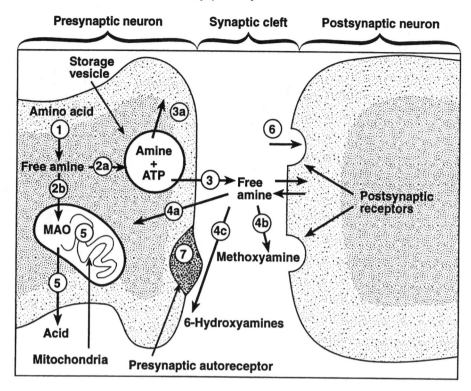

Stage/Activity

(1) Neurotransmitter formation

(2a) Binding/Storage

(2b) Oxidation

(3) Liberation/Release into the synaptic cleft

(3a) False neurotransmitter

(4a) Reuptake of neurotransmitter into presynaptic neuron

(4b) O-methylation by catechol-o-methyltransferase (COMT)

(4c) 6-hydroxylation

(5) Oxidation by monoamine oxidase (MAO)

(6) Postsynaptic receptor interaction

(7) Presynaptic autoreceptor interaction

Intervention/Drug Action

1. **Levodopa, Tryptophan:** enhance catecholamine neurotransmitter synthesis

2a. **Reserpine:** blocks norepinephrine uptake and storage in vesicles

3. **Amphetamines:** promote release of neurotransmitter from storage vesicles into the synaptic cleft
   Lithium: interferes with release of neurotransmitter from storage vesicles

3a. **Methyldopa:** formation of a false neurotransmitter

4a. **TCAs, Cocaine:** block reuptake of neurotransmitters from the synaptic cleft into the presynaptic neuron

5. **MAOIs:** inhibition of monoamine oxidase

6. **Antipsychotics:** antagonize (block) dopamine receptors
   Atropine: antagonizes (blocks) muscarine receptors
   Bromocriptine: agonist activity at dopamine receptors (i.e., mimics endogenous neurotransmitter)
   Nicotine: agonist activity at cholinergic (nicotinic) receptors (i.e., mimics endogenous neurotransmitter)

7. **Clonidine:** Interaction at presynaptic α_2-adrenergic autoreceptor
   LSD: disruption of autoreceptor function

Figure 2-3. Normal cycle of amine formation and destruction and associated proposed sites of action for several psychotropics.

amines (i.e., dopamine, norepinephrine, and serotonin) by inhibiting their metabolic destruction or degradation (i.e., conversion to aldehydes and acids).[8]

A primary precept in therapeutics is to remove the cause of the condition, but this may be difficult to achieve with the depressive syndromes. For example, an environmental cause may be known and yet nothing can be done about it, as occurs in the case of bereavement reactions in which depressive responses are generally not pathological. Or the cause may be known, as in a cimetidine-induced depression (see box for a list of drugs implicated in causing or aggravating depression). However, the removal of the cause (cimetidine [Tagamet®]) may not always alleviate the depression because some depressions may continue an autonomous course once they have been initiated, even if the cause is removed.[9]

Examples of Drugs That Can Aggravate or Cause Depression[10,11]	
Alcohol	Indomethacin
Amantadine	**Levodopa**
Antipsychotics	Methyldopa
Cimetidine	**Opiate analgesics**
Corticosteroids	Propranolol
Fenfluramine	**Sedative-hypnotics**
Guanethidine	

Antidepressants: ADRs

Many of the antidepressants can cause drowsiness, and safety precautions should be implemented as indicated. Patients should be warned of this reaction and cautioned against performing activities that require alertness, judgment, or coordination (e.g. driving an automobile; operating dangerous or hazardous machinery; supervising children) until they become familiar with their individual response to the antidepressant pharmacotherapy. Many depressed patients are either suicidal or have the potential for suicide; thus, suicide precautions should be implemented as required.[12]

The ADRs most often cited are those associated with the anticholinergic actions of the TCAs. These ADRs may be particularly troublesome for elderly patients and may precipitate acute glaucoma, urinary retention, or paralytic ileus among susceptible patients. However, the SSRIs are discontinued in approximately 10% of patients as a result of ADRs (most frequently headache, insomnia, and nausea). They also appear to cause more sexual dysfunction (e.g., anorgasmia) than do the other classes of antidepressants. The MAOIs actually possess the best (lowest) ADR profile of all of the antidepressants. However, their associated clinically significant

---

[8] The correlation between the ability to inhibit monoamine oxidase and antidepressant activity is low. This low correlation suggests that other additional mechanisms (e.g., down regulation; see Footnote 7) may play a significant role in this regard.

[9] Brief general guidelines are provided in the following discussion. For a comprehensive overview of the clinical treatment of depression, including pharmacotherapy, psychotherapy, and electroconvulsive therapy, the reader is referred to the companion volume to this text, *Clinical Psychopharmacotherapeutics for Psychologists* (Pagliaro & Pagliaro, in press).

[10] See Chapter 5, "Adverse Drug Reactions," for further examples and discussion.

[11] Psychotropics are listed in boldface.

[12] In this regard, it is prudent to prescribe for dispensing the *minimum* quantity of an antidepressant that will suffice until the patient's next scheduled appointment. Initially, depending on individual patient assessment, the supply may need to be limited to 2 weeks. In all cases, a 30-day supply should *not* be exceeded.

drug interactions tend to limit their clinical use (see Chapter 5, "Adverse Drug Reactions," and Chapter 6, "Drug Interactions," for further discussion).

A thorough knowledge of the ADRs associated both with the various classes of antidepressants and with the individual members (drugs) within each class will significantly assist prescribing psychologists in terms of knowing which antidepressants to select and avoid for a particular patient. Prescribing psychologists can safely assume that *all* of the listed antidepressants possess approximately equal efficacy (at least in terms of a *population* of depressed patients) because they have been labeled and approved for marketing in North America as antidepressants (see Chapter 1, "Introduction to the Basic Principles of Pharmacotherapy"). Knowing which antidepressant to select will, therefore, focus not so much on choosing an effective antidepressant (i.e., they are all relatively equally effective) but on choosing the antidepressant that causes a minimum of ADRs for a specific patient, unless the ADRs are therapeutically beneficial (e.g., the ADR of nighttime sedation for a depressed patient who has insomnia) (see Table 5-10 in Chapter 5, "Adverse Drug Reactions").

Antidepressants: Therapeutics

After the most appropriate antidepressant has been chosen, the next consideration must be the dosage schedule.[13] Many clinicians advocate prescribing the total daily dosage for ingestion before retiring for bed in the evening in the case of the soporific (sleep-inducing) antidepressants (e.g., amitriptyline [Elavil®] and doxepin [Sinequan®]), using the argument that a one-dose-at-night regimen ensures maximal patient compliance and allows the patient to sleep away most of the troublesome ADRs. While this dosing protocol may be beneficial for many patients, it should be realized that when the maximum impact of these ADRs occurs at night, patients, particularly those who are elderly, who must get up to use the bathroom may feel dizzy, fall down, and break a hip. The dosage must, therefore, be individualized to meet the requirements of each patient, and there must always be an attempt to maximize therapeutic effects while minimizing ADRs.

Usually, a minimum of 2 to 3 weeks of antidepressant pharmacotherapy is required before adequate patient response can be determined. For this reason, patients must be advised to wait out the ADRs for the therapeutic benefits of antidepressant pharmacotherapy. Ideally, most patients will improve at or before 3 weeks. However, because there is no usual maintenance dosage for the antidepressants, the initially satisfactory dosage must be maintained as long as the patient requires pharmacotherapy, sometimes for as long as several years to prevent relapse and the recurrence of depression.

In general, it may be expected that for most patients the typical depressive episode will last at least 3 months. Therefore, antidepressants should be continued at therapeutic dosage levels for a *minimal* 3-month period. Many clinicians prefer long-term (e.g., 6 to 24 months) maintenance pharmacotherapy with the initial satisfactory dosage. Thereafter, the dosage may be halved and the patient monitored for 3 or 4 weeks for the return of the signs and symptoms of depression. If these signs and symptoms return, the initial satisfactory dosage level must be resumed while the patient is monitored for another 3 months (or longer), and the process of dosage reduction can again be attempted. If the dosage can be halved without any return of the signs and symptoms of depression during the ensuing 3 or 4 weeks, then pharmacotherapy generally can be safely discontinued.

---

[13] *Dose* refers to a specific amount of drug administered at one time (e.g., "30 mg"), whereas *dosage* refers to a specific amount of drug *and* how frequently it is to be administered (e.g., "30 mg every evening one-half hour before bedtime;" "60 mg orally daily in two individual doses").

If patients do not achieve therapeutic benefit despite achieving appropriate blood concentration levels, they should be referred for electroconvulsive therapy (ECT) if their depression is severe. For patients who appear refractory to pharmacotherapy with a single antidepressant, concurrent tricyclic antidepressant and MAOI pharmacotherapy may be required. This combination of pharmacotherapy should be initially prescribed with caution and only when patients are hospitalized (see Chapter 6, "Drug Interactions," for a detailed discussion of possible adverse reactions associated with concurrent TCA and MAOI pharmacotherapy).

Patients who have recurrent depression may benefit from long-term antidepressant pharmacotherapy or long-term antimanic pharmacotherapy. In choosing one or the other, the etiology of the depression must be used as a guide. For patients who have a family history of episodes of mood elevation (i.e., mania or bipolar disorder), lithium is generally considered to be the pharmacotherapy of choice.[14]

Antimanics

The antimanics include lithium, carbamazepine, and valproic acid. Lithium has been generally regarded as the drug of choice for the symptomatic management of bipolar disorder. More recently, the anticonvulsants carbamazepine and valproic acid have been used with therapeutic benefit for the management of this mood disorder.

Lithium: Mechanism of action and therapeutics

Lithium, an element discovered in 1817, has been used in the treatment of various physical and mental disorders for the last 150 years. Lithium (Eskalith®, Lithane®, Lithobid®) is currently approved for the treatment of acute mania and bipolar disorders. It is a monovalent cation that competes at cellular sites with other cations in the body, particularly sodium. Lithium alters sodium transport by inhibiting the sodium pump. This action, in turn, appears to affect the synthesis, storage, release, and reuptake of neurotransmitters, particularly norepinephrine and serotonin. Lithium also inhibits the intracellular formation of cyclic AMP. However, its exact mechanism of action in the control of mania is unknown.[15]

ADRs. Lithium has a low therapeutic index (i.e., ~2), and, thus, ADRs are experienced by most patients prescribed lithium pharmacotherapy. However, the ADRs are usually not severe and rarely necessitate the discontinuation of pharmacotherapy. The ADRs that occur during the first 2 weeks of lithium pharmacotherapy are the most bothersome, but these reactions disappear generally with continued pharmacotherapy and rarely recur. They may recur, however, if the tissue concentration increases for any reason, such as if patients inadvertently increase their dosage or experience sodium depletion caused by excessive sweating, vomiting, or concurrent diuretic pharmacotherapy. Occasionally ADRs may persist. However, lithium pharmacotherapy is generally well tolerated among patients. It is important for clinical psychologists to inform and reassure patients and their families, as appropriate, about the following ADRs and assist them with their management.

---

[14] This has been traditionally true and in large part continues as the norm. However, as increased clinical experience is gained with valproic acid, many clinicians are beginning to prescribe it as their first-line choice in the treatment of mania or bipolar disorder because it is associated with fewer ADRs and less toxicity.

[15] For example, one theory purports that the dysregulation of affect noted in bipolar (manic-depressive) disorders is due to a disturbance in biological rhythms. Correspondingly, because it has been noted that lithium can slow and stabilize the oscillations of circadian rhythms, this action has been advanced as the mechanism by which lithium produces its antimanic effect. Note that an alternative interpretation is that disturbances in circadian rhythms and mood may both be related to a common underlying condition or mechanism.

ADRs that occur during early pharmacotherapy include abdominal pain, diarrhea, nausea, and vomiting. It is helpful to have patients ingest each oral dose (i.e., tablets or capsules) with meals and at least 30 minutes before bedtime. This procedure also assists patients to manage their lithium pharmacotherapy. Fine tremor of the hands, fatigue, and muscle weakness are other bothersome reactions. Patients can be encouraged to perform gross rather than fine motor activities and plan needed rest periods during the day. Patient complaints of sleepiness, light-headedness, feeling dazed or restrained, and memory impairment are important to monitor. Safety precautions may be indicated, including the restriction of activities that require alertness, judgment, or physical coordination. Excessive urination (polyuria), usually accompanied by excessive thirst (polydipsia), also can be bothersome. Ensure that patients drink at least eight glasses of water or other beverages a day and schedule daily activities so that they have adequate access to bathroom facilities. Other ADRs include edema and weight gain. Persistent hand tremors may require a reduction in dosage, particularly among elderly patients.

In regard to ADRs:

1. All ADRs appear to be fully reversible with discontinuation of the lithium pharmacotherapy.
2. The occurrence of ADRs is not necessarily related to dosage. However, frequency and severity of the ADRs is usually related to dosage.
3. ADRs are similar to the early signs of lithium toxicity. However, they differ in regard to the following: ADRs are not disabling; ADRs do not progressively worsen; and ADRs are not associated with toxic lithium blood levels.

Lithium toxicity. Lithium toxicity is a dose-related phenomenon that occurs when more lithium is ingested than can be eliminated. Signs and symptoms of acute lithium toxicity include abnormal constant involuntary cyclical movement of the eyeball (nystagmus), confusion, diarrhea, disorientation, hyperreflexia, incoordination (ataxia), seizures, tremor, and vomiting. These signs and symptoms are usually associated with lithium blood concentrations in excess of 2 mmol/L (2 mEq/L). If not corrected, coma and death may ensue. Lithium toxicity never occurs instantaneously, even when large doses are ingested. Generally, several hours elapse before signs and symptoms of toxicity appear. In the usual clinical situations, signs of impending toxicity are visible 1 to 3 days before the clinical picture of toxicity becomes fully developed. At this point, it can often be interrupted by discontinuing the drug or reducing the dosage.[16] See Chapter 3, "Pharmacokinetics and Pharmacodynamics," and Chapter 5, "Adverse Drug Reactions," for additional discussion.

Carbamazepine: Mechanism of action and therapeutics
Carbamazepine (Tegretol®) is an iminostilbene derivative that is structurally related to the tricyclic antidepressants. It is used *primarily* as an anticonvulsant for the treatment of a wide range of seizure disorders,[17] but it also has been approved for the treatment of pain associated with trigeminal neuralgia and for the treatment of both acute mania and bipolar (i.e., manic-depressive) disorders. The use of carbamazepine for the treatment of acute mania and bipolar disorder is generally reserved for patients who are resistant to, or cannot tolerate, lithium

---

[16] In cases of suicide attempts and when signs and symptoms are severe, patients should be hospitalized for appropriate medical management of lithium toxicity. There is no specific antidote for lithium toxicity and medical support of body systems may be required. In cases of severe toxicity, hemodialysis, which is the most effective means of removing lithium from the body, should be considered.

[17] Carbamazepine has been effectively used to treat patients who have generalized tonic–clonic seizures and both simple and complex partial seizures.

pharmacotherapy. Although carbamazepine shares many similar anticonvulsant actions with phenytoin (Dilantin®), its mechanism of action for the control of bipolar disorder is unknown.
ADRs.   ADRs reported frequently during the initiation of carbamazepine pharmacotherapy include allergic skin reactions (e.g., skin rashes), and double vision (diplopia), dizziness, drowsiness, headache, nausea, and vomiting. These ADRs can usually be managed by reducing the dosage and rarely require the discontinuation of pharmacotherapy.

Rare, serious, and potentially fatal ADRs have been associated with carbamazepine pharmacotherapy. These ADRs include agranulocytosis, aplastic anemia, and the Stevens–Johnson syndrome (see Chapter 5, "Adverse Drug Reactions," for additional details and discussion).

Valproic Acid: Mechanism of action and therapeutics
Valproic acid (Depakene®, Epival®) is *primarily* prescribed as an anticonvulsant for the treatment of various seizure disorders, including simple and complex absence seizures and primary generalized seizures with tonic–clonic manifestations. It also has been approved for the treatment of acute manic episodes associated with bipolar (i.e., manic-depressive) disorders. An inactive prodrug form of valproic acid (i.e., divalproex sodium) has been marketed for the treatment of acute mania. Divalproex sodium dissociates into valproic acid in the gastrointestinal tract after oral ingestion; thus, the observed pharmacologic actions, including ADRs and toxicity, are those associated with valproic acid.

The use of valproic acid for the treatment of acute mania is generally reserved for patients who are resistant to, or cannot tolerate, lithium pharmacotherapy (although this is starting to change; see Footnote 14).
ADRs.   The ADRs observed commonly with valproic acid pharmacotherapy include asthenia, diarrhea, dizziness, headache, nausea, pain, somnolence, tremor, and vomiting. Although rare, liver failure resulting in death has been associated with valproic acid pharmacotherapy. Young children and patients who have preexisting liver dysfunction appear to be at particular risk for this ADR.

Antidepressant and antimanic section summary

This section has examined the various types and uses of the antidepressants and antimanics. Their mechanisms of action were considered in regard to the biogenic amine theory of depression and mania. The depressive syndrome has been related to the modification or alteration of the level of various amines within the central nervous system. With an understanding of the various antidepressants and antimanics, including their mechanisms of action and ADRs, prescribing psychologists will be better able to provide optimal pharmacotherapy to patients who require adjunctive pharmacotherapy for the symptomatic management of depressive disorders.

Antipsychotics

The antipsychotics comprise a diverse group of psychotropics, which includes the butyrophenones, dibenzoxazepines, dihydroindolones, diphenylbutylpiperidines, phenothiazines, thioxanthenes, and miscellaneous, or atypical, antipsychotics (see box). This section discusses the indications, mechanisms of action, therapeutics, and ADRs of these psychotropics.

Antipsychotics Generally Available for Use in North America[18,19]

Butyrophenones
        Droperidol (Inapsine®)
        Haloperidol (Haldol®)

Dibenzoxazepines
        Loxapine (Loxapac®, Loxitane®)

Dihydroindolones
        Molindone (Moban®) (★)

Diphenylbutylpiperidines
        Fluspirilene (Imap®) (✤)
        Pimozide (Orap®)

Phenothiazines
        Chlorpromazine (Largactil®, Thorazine®)
        Fluphenazine (Moditen®, Permitil®, Prolixin®)
        Mesoridazine (Serentil®)
        Methotrimeprazine (Nozinan®) (✤)
        Pericyazine (Neuleptil®) (✤)
        Perphenazine (Trilafon®)
        Pipotiazine (Piportil L4®) (✤)
        Prochlorperazine (Compazine®, Stemetil®)
        Promazine (Sparine®) (★)
        Thioproperazine (Majeptil®) (✤)
        Thioridazine (Mellaril®)
        Trifluoperazine (Stelazine®)
        Triflupromazine (Vesprin®) (★)

Thioxanthenes
        Flupenthixol (Fluanxol®)
        Thiothixene (Navane®)
        Zuclopenthixol (Clopixol®) (✤)

Miscellaneous (atypical) antipsychotics
        Clozapine (Clozaril®)
        Olanzapine (Zyprexa®) (★)
        Risperidone (Risperdal®)

Indications

The antipsychotics are generally indicated for the symptomatic management of schizophrenia and other psychotic disorders. Traditionally, psychotic disorders, or psychoses, were differentiated from neuroses on the basis of the severity of signs and symptoms and patient response

---

[18] While most of these antipsychotics are available for use throughout North America, some are available *only* in either Canada or the United States at the time of publication, as indicated by the maple leaf (✤) and star (★), respectively.

[19] Note that both droperidol and prochlorperazine are used *primarily* for their antiemetic actions for the prevention or control of nausea and vomiting associated with the stimulation of the chemoreceptor trigger zone (CTZ).

to psychotropic pharmacotherapy.[20] Neuroses, defined as *emotional disorders* caused by an unresolved, unconscious conflict, are characterized by several general signs and symptoms. These general signs and symptoms include usually specific avoidance behavior, change in behavior (e.g., increase or decrease in eating or smoking), lack of interest in the environment (i.e., anhedonia), sexual disturbances (e.g., frigidity or impotence), emotional discharges to relieve tension (e.g., fighting, shouting), and sleep disturbances. The neuroses are varied in type and include a variety of specific conditions, including anxiety neurosis, depersonalization neurosis, depressive neurosis, hypochondrial neurosis, hysteric neurosis, neurasthenic neurosis, obsessive–compulsive neurosis, and phobic neurosis. Psychoses have been defined as major mental disorders of physical or psychological origin and are generally characterized by a severe impairment in the ability to think, to respond emotionally, and to relate to reality. The characteristics of psychoses frequently include regressive behavior, inappropriate mood, diminished impulse control, disordered thought, delusions (e.g., of grandeur or persecution), and hallucinations.[21]

It is important for prescribing psychologists to be able to differentiate between these two types of mental disorders because psychoses usually respond well to pharmacotherapy with the antipsychotics, whereas neuroses do not. Typically, the characteristics of these two disorders are the opposite, or converse, of each other. Following is a summary of the general differentiation between psychoses and neuroses.

Psychoses	Neuroses
Generally a hereditary predisposition	Generally no hereditary predisposition[22]
Probably a biochemical abnormality of the central nervous system	Probably a learned maladaptive response to stress
Severe inability to function in society	Mild to moderate inability to function in society
Often no recognizable precipitating stress	Usually a recognizable precipitating stress
Person usually considers his or her behavior to be normal	Person often realizes that his or her behavior is abnormal
Often severely out of contact with reality	Usually no loss of contact with reality
Psychotherapy is usually of no benefit	Psychotherapy may be the best treatment
Person often responds to antipsychotic pharmacotherapy and can tolerate well large dosages	Antipsychotics are usually of no benefit, and large dosages are not well tolerated

It should be noted that some patients simultaneously display characteristics of both neuroses and psychoses. Mental disorders are no more exclusive than are physical disorders. Just as people can concurrently suffer from both hypertension and diabetes, so too can people concurrently suffer from more than one type of mental disorder.[23]

---

[20] It should be noted that some taxonomies of mental disorders (e.g., DSM-IV) do not use the term *neurosis* (although earlier versions of the DSM had used this term). Psychologists using the DSM-IV would tend to organize or classify these disorders listed according to Axis I or Axis II criteria. The taxonomy presented provides an *example* of a theoretical alternative to the "atheoretical" DSM-IV taxonomy and also provides a conceptual pharmacologic advantage by clearly differentiating between those disorders that are generally amenable to antipsychotic pharmacotherapy and those that are not.

[21] Schizophrenia is generally regarded as the prototype for psychotic disorders. It also is regarded as one of the most severe and potentially debilitating of mental disorders. Schizophrenia occurs in approximately 1% of people worldwide, without a particular predisposition among people of various racial or ethnic groups. Of all of the mental disorders, schizophrenia remains one of the most resistant to all forms of currently available therapy.

[22] This may not be accurate for some of the more severe neuroses. In addition, research has suggested that some "personality disorders" (defined according to DSM-IV criteria) appear to have a hereditary predisposition.

[23] Depressive disorders, for example, commonly occur among schizophrenic patients and are associated, in this context, with a poorer prognosis in relation to the therapeutic outcome for schizophrenia and a higher rate of suicide.

Mechanism of action

The antipsychotics, also known as antipsychotic tranquilizers, major tranquilizers, or neuroleptics, are derived from a number of different chemical families. These families include the butyrophenones, dibenzoxazepines, dihydroindolones, diphenylbutylpiperidines, phenothiazines, thioxanthenes, and the atypical antipsychotics.[24] Although chemically diverse, the antipsychotics share generally a number of common pharmacologic actions, including antipsychotic activity, ataraxia, sedation, potentiation of other drugs that produce CNS depressant actions, reduction in operant behavior, selective inhibition of conditioned avoidance behaviors, antiemetic activity, adrenergic and cholinergic blocking activity, impaired vigilance, increased secretion of prolactin, and production of extrapyramidal reactions. None of the antipsychotics have been associated with addiction or habituation. The degree of pharmacologic action, including ADRs, varies with chemical classification, dosage, and individual patient factors.

The antipsychotics appear to interact with dopamine-containing neurons. Specifically, they appear to block the dopamine (D_2) receptors and inhibit dopamine-stimulated cAMP production. However, the exact mechanism of their action is complex and remains incompletely understood. For example, the blockade or interaction of antipsychotics at other receptors (e.g., serotonin receptor [5-HT_2]) also may play a role.[25] Research in this area currently includes development and testing of various new psychotropics, including antagonists of different serotonin (i.e., 5-HT) receptor subtypes, antagonists of different dopamine receptor subtypes, modifiers of CNS microtransmitters (i.e., amino acids, peptides), and mixed-function drugs.

Therapeutics

All of the antipsychotics have demonstrated clinical efficacy for the symptomatic management of psychotic disorders. Thus, the choice of a particular antipsychotic for a particular patient is generally based on its associated ADRs. For example, if a patient has cardiovascular dysfunction, then an antipsychotic with relatively few cardiovascular effects should be prescribed. Likewise, if a patient is agitated and has difficulty sleeping, an antipsychotic with sedating actions would be a likely choice. However, in all cases in which the data are available, the patient's response to previous antipsychotic pharmacotherapy should be used as a guide. If a patient has previously responded favorably to a particular antipsychotic, it should generally, unless contraindicated, be tried again. Lower dosages should be initially prescribed and the dosage should be gradually increased, if needed, according to individual patient response.

The antipsychotics can generally be dosed once daily because of their long half-lives of elimination (greater than 24 hours). Single daily dosing is usually prescribed for administration 30 minutes before bedtime so that patients can benefit from associated sedative actions while also sleeping through other minor, but troublesome, ADRs. Antipsychotics are metabolized in the liver. Their metabolites, including active metabolites (see Chapter 3, "Pharmacokinetics and Pharmacodynamics;" Table 3-6) and varying amounts of unchanged (unmetabolized) drug, are

---

[24] Before a discussion of the various classifications of the antipsychotics, a common misconception should be clarified. Contrary to what has been presented in many other pharmacology texts, the term *minor tranquilizer* is a misnomer that has led to considerable confusion. Pharmacologically, the only tranquilizers are the major, or antipsychotic, tranquilizers. The term *minor tranquilizer* was developed as an advertising gimmick by the pharmaceutical manufacturers when the benzodiazepines were introduced to the marketplace during the early 1960s. However, the benzodiazepines do not possess any tranquilizing activity. They are, pharmacologically, members of the sedative-hypnotic group of psychotropic drugs (see related discussion later in this chapter).

[25] Several of the newer atypical antipsychotics (see later discussion), including clozapine (Clorazil®) and risperidone (Risperdal®), have a high affinity for the 5-HT_{2A} receptor subtype. It is postulated that blockade of this receptor is associated with their efficacy against the negative signs and symptoms of schizophrenia.

eliminated in the urine and feces. Thus, their dosages generally require modification for patients who are elderly, frail, or debilitated and those who have significant kidney or liver dysfunction. Whereas patients who have psychosis can tolerate high dosages of antipsychotics, antipsychotics are generally not well tolerated by people who are not psychotic. The antipsychotics can actually precipitate symptoms of psychoses among these patients.

Patients who have a history of *severe* cardiovascular dysfunction should be evaluated by a cardiologist and undergo an electrocardiogram (ECG) before antipsychotic pharmacotherapy is prescribed. The antipsychotics are associated with potentially serious adverse cardiovascular ADRs (e.g., tachycardia).

Most available antipsychotics appear to be able to lower the seizure threshold and, consequently, may induce seizures among susceptible patients (e.g., patients who have histories of epilepsy). This effect may be most pronounced with the less potent antipsychotics (e.g., aliphatic phenothiazines). In general, patients who have histories of seizure disorders and are not receiving anticonvulsant pharmacotherapy should *not* receive antipsychotic pharmacotherapy.

The antipsychotics should be prescribed cautiously, particularly the butyrophenones, for patients who have Parkinson's disease. The increased dopamine blockade associated with their mechanism of action may cause a resumption of parkinsonian signs and symptoms, even when patients are stabilized on their anti-parkinsonian drugs.

Women who are or who may become pregnant should be prescribed antipsychotics only when necessary, particularly during the first trimester of pregnancy. Although not conclusively teratogenic, many antipsychotics can cross the placental barrier to the fetal circulation. The use of antipsychotic pharmacotherapy during pregnancy has been shown to result in a neonatal depression syndrome followed by agitation. Antipsychotics also are excreted in breast milk in small quantities. The benefits associated with the prescription of these drugs to pregnant or breast-feeding women must be weighed against the possible risks to the mother and fetus or infant.[26]

Antipsychotics, particularly chlorpromazine (Largactil®, Thorazine®) and thioridazine (Mellaril®), should be prescribed cautiously for elderly, frail, or debilitated patients because they are generally more sensitive to the *anticholinergic actions* of these drugs. Elderly patients also experience ADRs at lower dosages and more quickly develop toxic reactions. In addition, elderly patients are prone to more severe sedative effects and postural (orthostatic) hypotension, which can result in serious falls and related injuries. Elderly men, particularly those who have prostatic hypertrophy, are prone to urinary hesitancy or retention. Elderly women experience generally more constipation and bowel obstruction.

When antipsychotics are prescribed in combination with anticholinergics (e.g., atropine) or other drugs that have anticholinergic actions (e.g., anti-parkinsonian drugs), anticholinergic actions can be potentiated. Patients who are receiving combined pharmacotherapy should be carefully monitored for agitation, confusion, constipation, dilated pupils, disorientation, dry mouth, dysarthria, memory impairment, and tachycardia. If these signs and symptoms are observed, antipsychotic pharmacotherapy should be discontinued. Severe cases of anticholinergic toxicity require emergency medical evaluation and treatment. Physostigmine, a cholinergic agonist, may be required.

Antipsychotics have revolutionalized the treatment of severe mental disorders since their introduction in France during the early 1950s. However, the antipsychotics are no panacea. Approximately 15% of treated patients fail to respond, and another 35% respond only marginally. Although not usually effecting a cure, the judicious use of the antipsychotics has permitted the

---

[26] For additional discussion, the reader is referred to *Problems in Pediatric Drug Therapy* (3rd ed.; Pagliaro & Pagliaro, 1995).

majority of patients who have psychoses to be managed on an outpatient basis and, thus, be free from a totally institutionalized life.

ADRs

The antipsychotics have been associated with a variety of ADRs affecting most body systems (see Chapter 5, "Adverse Drug Reactions"). However, extrapyramidal reactions, tardive dyskinesia, and the neuroleptic (antipsychotic) malignant syndrome are primarily associated with this group of psychotropics.

Extrapyramidal reactions
About 30% of patients who are prescribed antipsychotics will develop some sort of extrapyramidal reaction.[27] The extrapyramidal reactions include akathisia (i.e., motor restlessness marked by an inability to sit quietly or to sleep), dyskinesia (i.e., impairment of voluntary muscle movements), dystonia (i.e., abrupt onset muscular spasms, particularly affecting the head and neck, including oculogyric crisis [i.e., prolonged fixation of eyeballs in one position, usually sideways or upward] and torticollis [i.e., shortening of the neck muscles, which results in the head being tilted to the affected side with the chin pointing to the opposite side]), slurring of speech, hypersalivation, and parkinsonism (i.e., bradykinesia, masked facies, rigidity [stiffness of the cogwheel type], shuffling gait, and variable tremor). These reactions may range from minor reactions, which resolve with continued pharmacotherapy or a reduction of dosage, to severe reactions, such as potentially irreversible tardive dyskinesia, which generally requires a discontinuation of pharmacotherapy.

Tardive dyskinesia
Tardive dyskinesia is a late occurring neurologic syndrome characterized by involuntary sucking and smacking of the lips, jaw movements, darting of the tongue, oral–facial dyskinesias, and widespread choreoathetosis.[28] In some cases, the severe effects of tardive dyskinesia may be *irreversible* even after discontinuation of antipsychotic pharmacotherapy. Tardive dyskinesia remains one of the most distressing ADRs associated with antipsychotic pharmacotherapy and can be caused by any of the antipsychotics. The incidence of tardive dyskinesia increases with the age of the patient and the total cumulative antipsychotic dosage.

Various drugs have been used to treat tardive dyskinesia (e.g., baclofen [Lioresal®], clonazepam [Klonopin®, Rivotril®], levodopa [Dopar®, Larodopa®], and manganese). However, results have been mixed, and the efficacy of these drugs remains unproven and unsatisfactory. Thus, optimal pharmacotherapy requires attention to prevention and the following recommendations: (1) Prescribe the lowest effective antipsychotic dose; (2) reevaluate patients at regular intervals; (3) minimize, where possible, the long-term, regular use of anticholinergics (e.g., trihexyphenidyl [Artane®, Tremin®]) for the prophylactic treatment of extrapyramidal reactions; (4) closely monitor patients; and, (5) whenever possible, discontinue antipsychotic pharmacotherapy at the first signs and symptoms of tardive dyskinesia.[29] Following the discontinuation of antipsychotic

---

[27] This percentage is a general percentage that will vary depending on the antipsychotic prescribed, its dosage, and the duration of antipsychotic pharmacotherapy. For example, the use of clozapine (Clorazil®) and olanzapine (Zyprexa®) has been associated with a relatively low incidence of extrapyramidal reactions. See the discussion of the various classes of antipsychotics later in this chapter and in Chapter 5, "Adverse Drug Reactions."

[28] Choreoathetosis is characterized by extreme range of motion, jerky involuntary movement, and fluctuating muscle tone (from hypotonia to hypertonia). In addition to being associated with tardive dyskinesia, choreoathetosis is also commonly noted in patients with cerebral palsy.

[29] When antipsychotic and anti-parkinsonian drugs are discontinued, they should be gradually tapered off simultaneously or the antipsychotic tapered off first, over 1 to 2 weeks, with close monitoring of patients in order to avoid the return, or exacerbation, of extrapyramidal reactions.

pharmacotherapy, the tardive dyskinesia may initially worsen. However, the worsening of tardive dyskinesia is usually for only a short time. Tardive dyskinesia remits totally and spontaneously for many patients.

Neuroleptic (antipsychotic) malignant syndrome

Neuroleptic malignant syndrome (NMS) is a relatively rare, but sometimes fatal, ADR associated with antipsychotic pharmacotherapy. It is presumably related to low dopamine levels, but the exact mechanism is yet to be determined. The NMS is characterized by catatonia, dysarthria, fever, fluctuating blood pressure, muscle rigidity, stupor, and tachycardia. Its occurrence is considered to be a medical emergency. Mortality rates associated with NMS are approximately 20% for severe untreated cases. In the event of suspected NMS, antipsychotic pharmacotherapy should be immediately discontinued and the patient referred for medical evaluation and confirmation of NMS. Emergency medical treatment may be required and may include the administration of bromocriptine (Parlodel®), a dopamine agonist, and dantrolene (Dantrium®), a skeletal muscle relaxant (see also related discussion in Chapter 5, "Adverse Drug Reactions").

Therapeutics and ADRs associated with specific chemical families

Following is a brief discussion of the antipsychotics according to chemical family. Familiarity with these groupings should enable psychologists to appreciate the similarities between chemically related antipsychotics and to be aware of the ADRs to be expected from any related new drugs that may be developed. It should be readily apparent that prescribing more than one antipsychotic from the same chemical family would be expected to offer no additional therapeutic benefit because of their similarities in action; thus, this practice is not recommended. The ADRs listed for each group are meant to highlight some of the major similarities and differences among the various antipsychotics. For additional detailed discussion, see Chapter 5, "Adverse Drug Reactions."

Butyrophenones

Therapeutics.   The butyrophenones are similar to the phenothiazines; however, they may have a more rapid onset of action and are associated with fewer anticholinergic and autonomic ADRs. The two members of this class currently approved for use in North America are droperidol (Inapsine®) and haloperidol (Haldol®). Droperidol also is used for its antiemetic effect, particularly in relation to anesthesia (because of its significant sedative effect). Haloperidol is available as a long-acting depot injectable formulation that can be administered once monthly (see Chapter 4, "Administration of Psychotropics," for additional details and discussion).
ADRs.   Butyrophenone pharmacotherapy has been frequently associated with extrapyramidal reactions, including akathisia and dystonia. Other ADRs include occasional blood disorders, abnormal lactation (galactorrhea), menstrual changes, postural hypotension, sedation, and tardive dyskinesias.

Dibenzoxazepines

Therapeutics.   Dibenzoxazepines are similar to the phenothiazines. Loxapine (Loxapac®, Loxitane®) is the only drug in this class currently approved for use in North America.
ADRs.   Loxapine pharmacotherapy has been frequently associated with extrapyramidal reactions, including akathisia. Drowsiness also is common. Loxapine also has been occasionally associated with anticholinergic effects (e.g., blurred vision, dry mouth, decreased gastrointestinal

[GI] motility, urinary retention, and tachycardia), convulsions (particularly among patients who have seizure disorders), dystonia, hypotension or hypertension, and tardive dyskinesia.

Dihydroindolones

Therapeutics. Molindone (Moban®) is the only drug in this chemical family that is currently approved for use in North America. The anorexia and weight loss associated with molindone pharmacotherapy may have clinical benefit for patients who require antipsychotic pharmacotherapy and for whom weight gain is a real or perceived concern.

ADRs. Molindone has been frequently associated with extrapyramidal reactions, including akathisia. Anticholinergic effects (e.g., blurred vision, dry mouth, decreased GI motility, urinary retention, and tachycardia) also are common. Molindone may occasionally cause anorexia, drowsiness, dysphoria, menstrual changes, postural hypotension, and skin rashes.

Diphenylbutylpiperidines

Therapeutics. Fluspirilene (Imap®) and pimozide (Orap®) are the only diphenylbutylpiperidines currently manufactured and approved for the symptomatic management of psychotic disorders in North America. Pimozide also is approved for the symptomatic management of Gilles de la Tourette's syndrome.

ADRs. The diphenylbutylpiperidines frequently cause extrapyramidal reactions, including akathisia, dystonia (particularly torticollis), and parkinsonism. They may occasionally cause convulsions (particularly among patients who have seizure disorders), headache, hypotension, and tachycardia.

Phenothiazines

The phenothiazines are considered to be the prototype antipsychotics against which other antipsychotics are compared and contrasted because they were the first class of antipsychotics to be synthesized and introduced into clinical practice in the early 1950s. There are more individual drugs in this chemical family than in all of the other antipsychotic chemical families combined.

The phenothiazines are usually well tolerated by patients who have psychoses. Although their sedative effects are rapidly prominent, their full therapeutic benefit may not be observed for several weeks depending on their individual half-lives of elimination (see Chapter 3, "Pharmacokinetics and Pharmacodynamics," for additional discussion). This lag period between the appearance of ADRs and therapeutic benefit may need to be explained to patients, as appropriate to their individual clinical circumstances.

The phenothiazines have been subdivided into three groups (i.e., aliphatic, piperazine, piperidine) according to the chemistry of the phenothiazine side-chain (see Figure 2-4). The individual drugs within these groups share specific therapeutic actions and ADRs because of their chemical similarity (see "mechanisms of drug action" section in Chapter 1, "Introduction to the Basic Principles of Pharmacotherapy").

Aliphatics. The aliphatic phenothiazines include chlorpromazine (Largactil®, Thorazine®), methotrimeprazine (Nozinan®), promazine (Sparine®), and triflupromazine (Vesprin®).

Therapeutics. This group includes the prototype phenothiazine, *chlorpromazine*. The aliphatics are the most commonly used group of the phenothiazine antipsychotics because of their lower incidence of extrapyramidal reactions. In addition, their strong sedative actions can be of benefit for patients who are agitated or for inducing sleep when dosed before retiring for bed. Although possessing equivalent efficacy to the other phenothiazines, they are relatively lower in potency (i.e., a higher milligram dosage is required to achieve comparable actions).

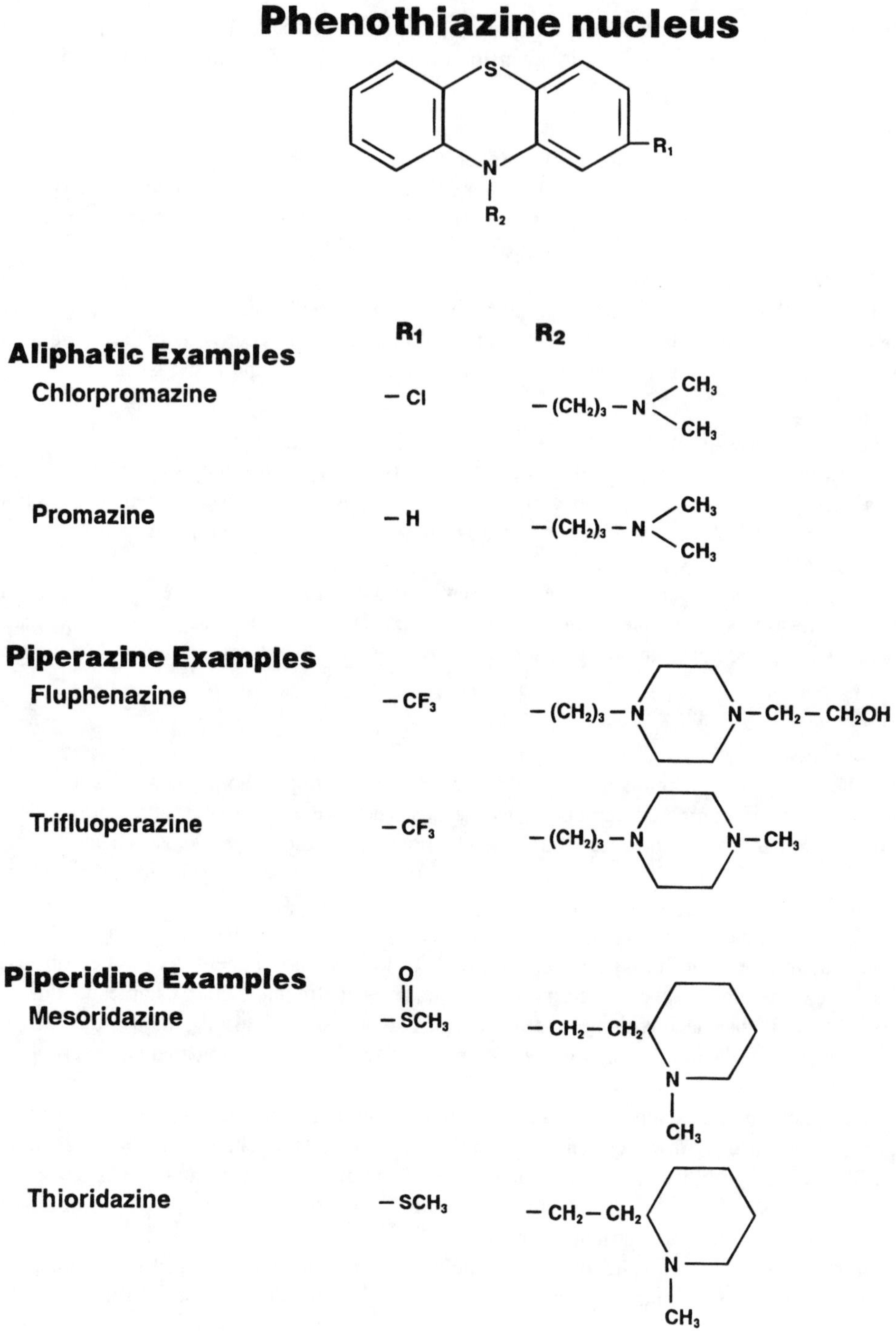

Phenothiazine nucleus

	R_1	R_2
Aliphatic Examples		
Chlorpromazine	$-Cl$	$-(CH_2)_3-N\begin{smallmatrix}CH_3\\CH_3\end{smallmatrix}$
Promazine	$-H$	$-(CH_2)_3-N\begin{smallmatrix}CH_3\\CH_3\end{smallmatrix}$
Piperazine Examples		
Fluphenazine	$-CF_3$	$-(CH_2)_3-N\bigcirc N-CH_2-CH_2OH$
Trifluoperazine	$-CF_3$	$-(CH_2)_3-N\bigcirc N-CH_3$
Piperidine Examples		
Mesoridazine	$-\overset{O}{\overset{\|}{S}}CH_3$	$-CH_2-CH_2\bigcirc N-CH_3$
Thioridazine	$-SCH_3$	$-CH_2-CH_2\bigcirc N-CH_3$

Figure 2-4. Phenothiazine molecule nucleus with examples of various side-chain configurations for the three subgroups: aliphatic, piperazine, and piperidine.

ADRs. Aliphatics frequently cause anticholinergic actions (e.g., blurred vision, confusion, constipation, dry mouth, decreased GI motility, drowsiness, tachycardia, urinary retention, and postural [orthostatic] hypotension). They may occasionally cause cholestatic jaundice; convulsions (at high doses); ECG changes, including prolongation of the Q-T and P-R intervals, S-T depression, and blunting of the T wave; extrapyramidal reactions, including dystonia and tardive dyskinesia (incidence is less than that associated with the piperazine derivatives); menstrual changes; photosensitivity; skin rashes; and weight gain.

Piperazines. The piperazine phenothiazines include acetophenazine (Tindal®), fluphenazine (Moditen®, Permitil®, Prolixin®), perphenazine (Trilafon®), prochlorperazine (Compazine®), thioproperazine (Majeptil®), and trifluoperazine (Stelazine®).

Therapeutics. Piperazines generally have a higher potency on a milligram per milligram basis than the other phenothiazines. Therefore, they require generally lower dosages. They also have a relatively greater antiemetic action than the other phenothiazines. This antiemetic action is elicited by means of a direct central action upon the chemoreceptor trigger zone (CTZ) in the medulla. One member of this group, prochlorperazine, is actually prescribed more often for the medical treatment of nausea and vomiting than for the symptomatic management of psychotic disorders.

Fluphenazine injectable pharmacotherapy (decanoate or enanthate salts) is indicated for patients who require long-term antipsychotic pharmacotherapy and would benefit from once or twice monthly dosing (see Chapter 4, "Administration of Psychotropics," for additional discussion).

ADRs. Piperazines often cause extrapyramidal reactions, including akathisia and dystonia. They may occasionally cause anticholinergic reactions (e.g., blurred vision, drowsiness, dry mouth, decreased GI motility, tachycardia, and urinary retention), abnormal lactation (galactorrhea), anorexia, menstrual changes, postural (orthostatic) hypotension, photosensitivity, tardive dyskinesia, and weight gain. Long-term, high-dosage pharmacotherapy has been associated with lens opacity. Overall, the piperazines cause less sedation and postural (orthostatic) hypotension than do the other phenothiazines. However, their use has been associated with a significantly higher incidence of extrapyramidal reactions.

Piperidines. The piperidine phenothiazines include mesoridazine (Serentil®), pericyazine (Neuleptil®), pipotiazine (Piportil L4®), and thioridazine (Mellaril®).

Therapeutics. The piperidines are similar to the aliphatic phenothiazines in many regards, but they produce less sedation. They also appear to cause a lower incidence of extrapyramidal reactions.

ADRs. Piperidine pharmacotherapy has been frequently associated with anticholinergic effects (e.g., blurred vision, drowsiness, dry mouth, decreased GI motility, tachycardia, and urinary retention), inhibition of ejaculation among males, postural (orthostatic) hypotension, and weight gain. They may occasionally cause abnormal lactation (galactorrhea), extrapyramidal reactions including akathisia and tardive dyskinesia, ECG changes, menstrual changes, and photosensitivity. Long-term, high-dosage pharmacotherapy may cause ocular lens opacity and retinal pigmentation. These reactions may result in visual impairment or blindness, particularly with thioridazine.

Thioxanthenes

Therapeutics. Flupenthixol (Fluanxol®), thiothixene (Navane®), and zuclopenthixol (Clopixol®) are the members of the thioxanthenes currently in therapeutic use. They are structurally similar to the phenothiazines, but also possess some antidepressant activity that may be beneficial when treating psychotic patients who have depressed affect.

ADRs.   Thioxanthenes frequently cause anticholinergic effects (e.g., blurred vision, constipation, dry mouth, decreased GI motility, tachycardia, and urinary retention), drowsiness, and extrapyramidal reactions (e.g., akathisia, dystonia, and tremor [more common with thiothixene and zuclopenthixol]). They may occasionally cause abnormal lactation (galactorrhea), menstrual changes, postural (orthostatic) hypotension, and skin rash. Long-term, high-dosage pharmacotherapy with thioxanthenes may cause lens opacity.

Atypical antipsychotics

The miscellaneous, or "atypical," antipsychotics available for use in North America include clozapine (Clozaril®), olanzapine (Zyprexa®), and risperidone (Risperdal®).[30] Several significant therapeutic advantages have been purported for the newer "atypical" antipsychotics, over the older "conventional" antipsychotics. These advantages include therapeutic response among some schizophrenic patients who are otherwise treatment resistant, equivalent efficacy in relation to the amelioration of the positive signs and symptoms of psychoses (e.g., delusions, hallucinations), apparently greater efficacy in relation to the amelioration of negative signs and symptoms of psychoses (e.g., amotivation, blunted affect, social withdrawal), and a lower incidence and severity of extrapyramidal reactions. Clozapine is discussed because it has been in clinical use for a much longer period of time than the other two atypical antipsychotics.

Therapeutics.   Clozapine, an atypical antipsychotic introduced in the early 1990s, was the first new antipsychotic introduced following a hiatus of over 20 years. Clozapine has demonstrated effectiveness and is indicated for patients who have treatment-resistant schizophrenia and who are nonresponsive, or intolerant to, the other antipsychotics.[31]

ADRs.   Clozapine produces potent adrenolytic, anticholinergic, antihistaminic, and antiserotonergic actions. The most common ADRs include constipation, dizziness, drowsiness, headache, hypersalivation, hypotension, and tachycardia. These ADRs occur alone or in combination in 10% to 40% of patients. The incidence of extrapyramidal reactions is among the lowest of all of the antipsychotics and are limited primarily to mild akathisia, rigidity, and tremor. However, potentially fatal neutropenia (agranulocytosis or granulocytopenia) (i.e., a reduction in blood neutrophil count often resulting in an increased susceptibility to bacterial and fungal infections; severe neutropenia may be fatal) (~2% of patients) and seizures (~5% of patients) have limited the more widespread use of clozapine.

Antipsychotic section summary

This section has presented an overview of the antipsychotics, including their general indications, mechanisms of action, therapeutics, and ADRs. Attention was given to the various similarities and differences among the major chemical families of antipsychotics.

Sedative-hypnotics

The sedative-hypnotics comprise a diverse group of psychotropics, which includes the barbiturates, benzodiazepines, and miscellaneous sedative-hypnotics (see box). This section discusses the indications, mechanisms of action, therapeutics, and ADRs of these psychotropics.

---

[30] Olanzapine and risperidone are similar in pharmacology and are generally subclassified as the serotonin–dopamine antagonists (SDAs).

[31] Approximately one third of patients who are resistant to other antipsychotics also fail to respond significantly to clozapine pharmacotherapy.

Sedative-Hypnotics Generally Available for Use in North America[32,33,34,35,36]

Barbiturates

       Amobarbital (Amytal®)

       Butabarbital (Butisol®)

       Mephobarbital (Mebaral®) (★)

       Pentobarbital (Nembutal®)

       Phenobarbital (Luminal®)

       Secobarbital (Seconal®)

Benzodiazepines

       Alprazolam (Xanax®)

       Bromazepam (Lectopam®) (♣)

       Chlordiazepoxide (Librium®)

       Clorazepate (Tranxene®)

       Diazepam (Valium®)

       Estazolam (ProSom®)

       Flurazepam (Dalmane®)

       Ketazolam (Loftran®) (♣)

       Lorazepam (Ativan®)

       Midazolam (Versed®)[37]

       Nitrazepam (Mogadon®) (♣)

       Oxazepam (Serax®)

       Quazepam (Doral®) (★)

       Temazepam (Restoril®)

       Triazolam (Halcion®)

continued. . .

[32] Some other drugs are commonly used to induce sleep but do not truly belong in the pharmacologic classification of sedative-hypnotics. For example, diphenhydramine (Benadryl®) is actually an antihistamine that is indicated for the treatment of allergic conditions and motion sickness. However, because of its significant anticholinergic and sedative "side-effects," diphenhydramine has been used to induce sleep. Doxylamine (Unisom®) is a similar-acting antihistamine that also has been used to induce sleep. Both diphenhydramine and doxylamine are generally available without prescription.

[33] While most of these sedative-hypnotics are available for use throughout North America, some are available *only* in either Canada or the United States at the time of publication, as indicated by the maple leaf (♣) and star (★), respectively.

[34] During the late 1970s and early 1980s, methaqualone (Quaalude®) was widely abused. The abuse of this drug (known on the streets as "ludes") resulted in significant morbidity and mortality. Methaqualone was removed from *legal* use in North America during the mid-1980s. However, illicit supplies from foreign countries (e.g., China, Mexico) continued the abuse of methaqualone into the late 1990s. Although touted as an aphrodisiac, methaqualone possesses no such pharmacologic activity. However, similar to *all* sedative-hypnotics (including alcohol), its use can decrease social inhibitions and thus, indirectly contribute to increased sexual activity.

[35] Buspirone belongs to a unique class of drugs known chemically as azaspirodecanediones. Although sharing some of the properties of the benzodiazepines, it does not bind to the benzodiazepine–GABA receptor complex. It is *not* a true sedative-hypnotic, but it has been included here because of its pharmacologic activity and promotion as an anxiolytic. However, it appears to have lower efficacy than the benzodiapezines in this regard, and its use, therefore, is not generally recommended over the benzodiazepines.

[36] Alcohol (ethanol, ethyl alcohol) is pharmacologically classified as a sedative-hypnotic and shares the general pharmacologic properties of the members of this classification. Until earlier this century, it was still commonly prescribed for its sedative-hypnotic actions. For a comprehensive review and discussion of the pharmacology of alcohol, the reader is referred to *Substance Use Among Children and Adolescents: Its Nature, Extent, and Consequences From Conception to Adulthood* (Pagliaro & Pagliaro, 1996).

[37] Midazolam is a short-acting benzodiazepine that is administered by injection to provide sedation for brief diagnostic procedures and anesthesia.

Miscellaneous sedative-hypnotics
> Buspirone (BuSpar®)
> Chloral Hydrate (Noctec®)
> Chlormezanone (Trancopal®) (★)
> Ethchlorvynol (Placidyl®)
> Meprobamate (Equanil®, Miltown®)
> Methaqualone (Quaalude®)
> Paraldehyde (Paral®)
> Zolpidem (Ambien®) (★)

Sedative-hypnotics are psychotropic drugs that produce a depression of the central nervous system (CNS) leading to sedation or anxiolytic actions and, upon increasing dosage, to a loss of consciousness or hypnosis. Sedation, hypnosis, and general anesthesia are extensions of CNS depression. With the exception of some of the benzodiazepines and buspirone, these actions can be produced by virtually all of the members of this pharmacologic drug class. In terms of clinical importance and pharmacologic actions, the sedative-hypnotics can be conveniently divided into three categories: the barbiturates, the benzodiazepines, and other miscellaneous sedative-hypnotics.

Indications

The sedative-hypnotics are generally indicated for the short-term symptomatic management of anxiety disorders. They also are indicated for the short-term symptomatic management of sleep disorders (i.e., insomnia).

Anxiety

Anxiety may be defined as a feeling of apprehension, dread, uneasiness, or worry (apprehensive expectation). Signs and symptoms include difficulty concentrating, easy distractibility, irritability, restlessness, and sleep disturbances (generally in relation to falling and/or staying asleep) (see also discussion of "neurosis" earlier in this chapter). Severity of anxiety can range from mild, which often serves psychosociobiologic adaptive functions and requires no treatment, to severe, such as panic attacks that may be totally incapacitating.

Anxiety can be symptomatically managed with sedative, or anxiolytic, pharmacotherapy, particularly benzodiazepine pharmacotherapy; whenever possible, however, the underlying cause should be determined and treated. Pharmacotherapy should be used only when psychotherapy alone is found to be inadequate. In addition, anxiety associated with depression should *not* be treated with a sedative-hypnotic anxiolytic but with an appropriate antidepressant (see discussion of "antidepressants" earlier in this chapter). Likewise, anxiety associated with the use of a CNS stimulant should be treated by reducing the dosage or discontinuing the CNS stimulant (see discussion of "CNS stimulants" later in this chapter).

Sleep

Natural sleep is composed of two basic stages that occur cyclically: (1) rapid eye movement sleep (REM sleep) and (2) non–rapid eye movement sleep (N-REM sleep). During a normal sleep episode, people progress through four stages from wakefulness to an N-REM stage of deep sleep that is followed by a lighter REM stage. It is during this latter stage that dreaming occurs. As the sleep episode continues, people cycle back and forth from N-REM to REM sleep until wakefulness is again experienced. Each of the sleep stages is associated with various physiological changes. For example, postural immobility and cerebral deactivation occur during N-REM sleep; postural changes and dreaming occur during REM sleep. Gastric acid secretion and nocturnal angina attacks occur during REM sleep, whereas night terrors and sleepwalking have been most often associated with deep N-REM sleep. The physiologic value of each of the sleep stages has not been fully determined. However, it is well recognized that the sedative-hypnotics affect differently the various stages of sleep (see later discussion in this section).

Table 2-2 presents various clinical disorders and related sleep laboratory findings. Such disorders should be considered before initiating sedative-hypnotic pharmacotherapy for the symptomatic management of sleep disorders.[38] Patients who have duodenal ulcers are often prescribed hypnotic drugs if insomnia also exists. For these patients, it might at first seem desirable to prescribe a sedative-hypnotic that suppresses REM sleep and avoid excess gastric acid production during REM sleep. However, the suppression of REM sleep may later lead to a phenomenon known as REM rebound. REM rebound is a situation in which REM sleep, often associated with increased dreaming, nightmares, and insomnia, is sharply increased. If REM rebound occurs, patients who have a medical disorder affected by sleep may notice an acute exacerbation of their disorder during sleep episodes. REM rebound may occur when (1) patients use a sedative-hypnotic that suppresses REM sleep for an extended period of time and experience REM "breakthrough" or (2) patients sleep past the clinical effects of a sedative-hypnotic that suppresses REM sleep.

When prescribing a particular sedative-hypnotic to induce sleep, the following ideal qualities should be considered: (1) The sedative-hypnotic should cause effective induction and maintenance of sleep (this effectiveness should not diminish quickly or necessitate an increased dose); (2) it should have a rapid onset of action; (3) it should have little or no interference with REM sleep or other stages of sleep; (4) it should not cause a hangover effect (i.e., there should be no drug accumulation when used as recommended); (5) it should not interact with other concurrent pharmacotherapy; and (6) it should be inexpensive.

Table 2-2. Clinical disorders related to sleep.

Clinical condition	Sleep laboratory finding
Medical disorders	
Bronchial asthma	Attacks occur at all sleep stages except Stage 4, particularly among children
Coronary arteriosclerosis	Anginal attacks and ECG changes increase during REM sleep
Duodenal ulcer	Gastric acid secretion is markedly increased during REM sleep
Hypothyroidism	Stage 4 or deep N-REM sleep is markedly decreased with substantial increase after treatment when patient is euthyroid
Sleep disorders	
Insomnia (primary)	Autonomic activity is high during sleep as compared with normal sleepers, for whom it is low
Nocturnal enuresis	Most episodes occur during N-REM sleep
Sleep apnea (breathing-related sleep disorder)	Attacks occur at all sleep stages; signs and symptoms are exacerbated by the use of sedative-hypnotics, including alcohol, before bedtime
Sleepwalking and night terrors	Virtually all episodes occur during N-REM sleep

[38] Psychologists need to be aware of these related medical disorders but need not to be the ones to confirm or rule out these disorders. In this situation referral to, and collaboration with, an appropriately trained health care professional (e.g., advanced practice nurse, physician) would be in order.

Specific chemical families

Barbiturates

The barbiturates are among the oldest sedative-hypnotics in use today. Their use dates from the introduction of barbital in 1903. The barbiturates also represent the entry of the modern era of pharmacotherapy for anxiety and insomnia. Before their introduction, the only drugs available for the treatment of anxiety and insomnia were alcohol, the bromides, chloral hydrate, paraldehyde, sulfonal, and urethane. More than 2,500 different barbiturates have been synthesized. Approximately 50 have been commercially marketed and were the mainstay for the treatment of anxiety and insomnia until being displaced by the benzodiazepines in the 1960s and 1970s. Of these, only about 10 remain on the market. The reasons for the decline in the use of the barbiturates are related to (1) abuse potential, (2) significantly lower therapeutic index relative to the benzodiazepines, (3) increased Drug Enforcement Administration (DEA) controls, and (4) the increased availability, marketing, and clinical use of the benzodiazepines.

Mechanism of action.   Barbiturates vary greatly in their potencies and pharmacokinetic properties. These variations are explained in part by their differences in lipid solubility (see Table 2-3). Thiopental (Pentothal®), the most lipid soluble, has the most rapid onset and shortest duration of action.[39] Thus, it has long been postulated that barbiturates penetrate the CNS lipid membrane and alter ion channels or enzymes to cause specific physiologic changes. However, pharmacologic actions, other than the induction of sleep, do not correlate well with lipid solubility theories. Additional factors are also relevant.

A popular current theory helpful for explaining the mechanism(s) of action of the barbiturates is the theory arguing that they bind to receptor sites adjacent to the gamma-aminobutyric acid (GABA) receptor. This binding results in the retention of GABA at its receptor and an increased influx of chloride through the associated chloride channels, which produces neuronal inhibition. This proposed mechanism is similar to the one proposed to explain the action of the benzodiazepines (see later discussion) with the exception that the two classes of sedative-hypnotics act at distinct receptor sites (which also are probably adjacent to the GABA receptor sites and surround the chloride ion channel) (see Figure 2-5).

Therapeutics and ADRs.   All of the barbiturates exhibit CNS depressant activity, and, depending on the specific barbiturate, dose, and method of administration, a variety of related actions may

Table 2-3. *Selected properties of the barbiturates when orally ingested.*

Drug	Adult serum half-life (hours)	Duration of action	Relative lipid solubility	Comments
Amobarbital (Amytal®)	8–42	Intermediate	113	
Butabarbital (Butisol®)	34–42	Intermediate	1	
Mephobarbital (Mebaral®)	12–24	Long	56	75% converted to phenobarbital
Pentobarbital (Nembutal®)	15–48	Intermediate	106	
Phenobarbital (Luminal®)	72–144	Long	34	
Secobarbital (Seconal®)	19–34	Intermediate	—	
Thiopental[a] (Pentothal®)	3–8	Short	1000	

[a] Thiopental is used as an intravenous anesthetic only because of its high lipid solubility, rapid onset of action, and short duration of action. In the lay popular press, thiopental is commonly referred to as "truth serum."

[39] Because of its high lipid solubility, rapid onset of action, and short duration of action, thiopental is used solely as an intravenous anesthetic. In the lay popular press, thiopental has commonly been referred to as "truth serum."

GABA$_A$ Receptor Complex

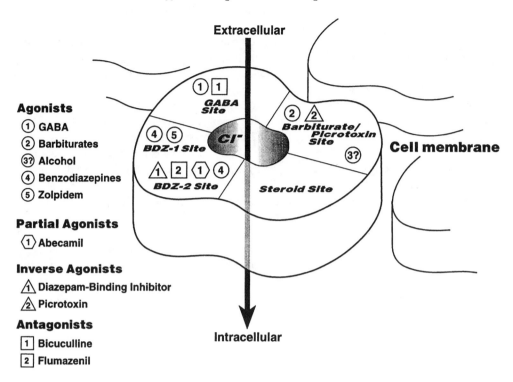

Figure 2-5. Schematic model of the GABA$_A$ receptor complex indicating sites of related psychotropic action.

be seen. Useful clinical applications include the induction of sleep and general anesthesia. Potentially lethal extensions of these actions include respiratory depression, coma, and death. These actions may also may occur in cases of overdosage. Barbiturates, notably phenobarbital (Luminal®) and mephobarbital (Mebaral®), also are useful adjuncts in the treatment of epilepsy. However, there is little evidence to suggest any antianxiety action other than sedation among the barbiturates, and the benzodiazepines remain the anxiolytics of choice (see discussion of "benzodiazepines" later in this chapter).

Effects on sleep. The barbiturates have been shown to interfere with REM sleep and Stages 3 and 4 of N-REM sleep. Regular long-term use of barbiturates has resulted in REM rebound characterized by insomnia and more frequent and intense dreams, including nightmares. As mentioned previously, physiologic changes, such as angina and exacerbation of gastric ulcers, can occur during episodes of REM rebound.

Tolerance. Tolerance to the CNS actions of the barbiturates may occur, depending on the regularity with which they are used. With regular long-term use, a decrease in therapeutic effectiveness by the second week of use has been demonstrated in sleep laboratories (see the section on "liver effects" for a possible explanation).

Paradoxic excitation. Barbiturates may produce a paradoxic excitement, particularly among children and elderly patients. Such effects also have been observed among chronically ill and debilitated patients. For this reason, the use of barbiturates, particularly phenobarbital and mephobarbital, is best avoided among these groups of patients.

Respiratory depression. The barbiturates produce a dose-related respiratory depression (i.e., the higher the dose, the greater the degree of respiratory depression). Lower doses, such as those used to induce and maintain sleep, may decrease respirations to the level of normal sleep. However, higher doses cause a decrease in the rate, depth, and volume of respirations. Overdosage may result in respiratory arrest.

Cardiovascular effects.   Normal therapeutic doses of the barbiturates are associated with few cardiovascular effects other than a transient hypotension and a decrease in heart rate. However, an overdosage may cause a profound hypotension resulting in kidney failure and cardiovascular collapse.

Liver metabolism.   Barbiturates do not have a direct adverse effect on the liver. However, they are metabolized by the liver, and, thus, patients who have liver dysfunction may show an increased sensitivity to usual barbiturate doses. For this reason, the use of barbiturates is best avoided among patients who have active liver disease (e.g., cirrhosis, hepatitis). Barbiturates also alter the metabolic functions of the liver by stimulating the hepatic microsomal enzyme system. Barbiturates stimulate this metabolizing mechanism to the extent that other drugs metabolized by the liver may be metabolized and eliminated from the body at a much faster rate than usual and their effectiveness significantly decreased. Probably the best-known example of this effect is the concurrent use of barbiturates and oral anticoagulants, such as warfarin (Coumadin®, Panwarfin®). In this situation, the blood concentration of warfarin may be decreased to the point where it is ineffective. On the other hand, when patients who have been on concurrent pharmacotherapy *discontinue* the barbiturate without appropriately decreasing the anticoagulant dosage, they may experience a tremendous increase in the level of anticoagulant activity and resultant bleeding as the hepatic microsomal enzyme system returns to normal (see Chapter 3, "Pharmacokinetics and Pharmacodynamics," and Chapter 6, "Drug Interactions," for additional discussion).

Benzodiazepines

Since the introduction in 1960 of the first benzodiazepine, chlordiazepoxide (Librium®), a large number of chemically similar formulations have been developed and marketed. A plethora of clinical data also have accumulated concerning the use of this class of sedative-hypnotics. Benzodiazepines, as a drug class, show remarkable structural and metabolic similarities (see discussion of the structure–activity relationship [SAR] in Chapter 1, "Introduction to the Basic Principles of Pharmacotherapy" and Figure 1-1). The primary differences among class members exist in (1) the duration of action, as determined by the rate of metabolism, and (2) the presence or lack of active metabolites (see Table 2-4). It is interesting that, despite the seeming similarities among benzodiazepines, they have been promoted for different indications. Flurazepam (Dalmane®) and temazepam (Restoril®) are promoted strictly as hypnotics, whereas chlordiazepoxide (Librium®), clorazepate (Tranxene®), lorazepam (Ativan®), and prazepam (Centrax®) are promoted primarily as anxiolytics. At least one benzodiazepine, clonazepam (Klonopin®, Rivotril®), is used primarily as an anticonvulsant. Another, diazepam (Valium®), is used to treat insomnia and status epilepticus, while alprazolam (Xanax®) has been approved for the treatment of panic disorder. Although dissimilarities do exist among members of this class of sedative-hypnotics, enough similarities exist to permit a discussion of the class as a group.

Mechanism of action.   Like all sedative-hypnotics, the benzodiazepines have marked CNS depressant activity. This CNS depressant activity may be manifested by an attenuation of aggressive behavior, an induction of sleep, a reduction of anxiety, seizure control, and a reduction of muscle spasms.

Even though benzodiazepines have been commercially available for almost 40 years, the precise site and mechanism of their action are not completely understood. It is currently postulated that benzodiazepines act in concert with gamma-aminobutyric acid (GABA) to inhibit neurotransmission, particularly in the cerebral cortex and the limbic system, including the amygdala and

Table 2-4. Selected pharmacokinetic and pharmacodynamic properties of the benzodiazepines following oral administration.

Benzodiazepine	Onset of action	Adult serum half-life (hours) (range) (parent drug)	Duration of action (including metabolites)	Active metabolites
Alprazolam (Xanax®)	Intermediate	7–16	Intermediate	Yes: alphahydroxyalprazolam demethylalprazolam
Bromazepam (Lectopam®)	Rapid	8–19	Intermediate	No
Chlordiazepoxide (Librium®)	Intermediate	5–30	Intermediate	Yes: desmethylchlordiazepoxide demoxepam, N-methyldiazepam (nordiazepam) (desmethyldiazepam) oxazepam
Clorazepate (Tranxene®)	Intermediate	1–2	Long	Yes: N-methyldiazepam (nordiazepam) (desmethyldiazepam)
Diazepam (Valium®)	Rapid	14–90	Long	Yes: N-methyldiazepam (nordiazepam) (desmethyldiazepam), N-methyloxazepam, oxazepam, temazepam
Estazolam (ProSom®)	Rapid	10–24	Intermediate	No
Flurazepam (Dalmane®)	Rapid	1–2	Long	Yes: desalkylflurazepam, flurazepam aldehyde, hydroxyethylflurazepam
Ketazolam (Loftran®)	Rapid	1–2	Long	Yes: diazepam N-methyldiazepam (N-demethylketazolam)
Lorazepam (Ativan®)	Intermediate	12–15	Intermediate	No
Nitrazepam (Mogadon®)	Rapid	18–57	Long	No
N-methyldiazepam	Slow	50–99	Long	Yes: oxazepam
Oxazepam (Serax®)	Intermediate	6–11	Intermediate	No
Quazepam (Doral®)	Rapid	34–44	Long	Yes: 2-oxoquazepam, N-desalkyl-2-oxoquazepam
Temazepam (Restoril®)	Rapid	3–18	Intermediate	No
Triazolam (Halcion®)	Intermediate	2–5	Short	No

Note that the half-life of elimination remains constant regardless of the method of administration. See Chapter 3, "Pharmacokinetics and Pharmacodynamics," for discussion.

the thalamus. A GABA receptor complex has been identified at which benzodiazepines appear to enhance GABA-mediated chloride influx through chloride ion channels (see Figure 2-5).[40]

In the absence of GABA, the benzodiazepines do not appear to be able to open the chloride channels and elicit their CNS depressant action. However, the precise and complete mechanism(s) of their action remains unknown. Even though high affinity binding of the benzodiazepines at the GABA receptor complex has been clearly demonstrated, it has yet to be proven that this interaction is directly and solely responsible for the various pharmacologic actions of the benzodiazepines in humans.

[40] Two GABA complexes have been identified, $GABA_A$ and $GABA_B$. The benzodiazepines, as well as the benzodiazepine antagonist flumazenil, bind to benzodiazepine receptors (i.e., BZD-1 and BZD-2) primarily within the $GABA_A$ complex. Likewise, barbiturates appear to bind preferentially to barbiturate receptors within the $GABA_A$ complex. The $GABA_A$ complex is composed of several subunits (i.e., alpha, beta, gamma, delta, and rho).

Therapeutics.

Effects on anxiety.   The benzodiazepines possess the best anxiolytic activity of all of the currently available sedative-hypnotics. Therapeutic efficacy in this regard appears to be roughly equivalent among the various benzodiazepines. Thus, choice of a specific benzodiazepine to treat anxiety is based on other characteristics such as individual pharmacokinetic characteristics[41] and familiarity or accumulated experience with use.[42]

Effects on sleep.   The benzodiazepines, unlike other sedative-hypnotics, do not cause a dose-related progressive depression past the lighter stages of sleep from which patients can be easily aroused. The benzodiazepines also do not affect normal physiologic sleep stages when used at usual doses. Both REM and N-REM sleep occur with no REM rebound following discontinuation of use. However, at higher doses, REM suppression may occur. Research has suggested that the benzodiazepines that have short durations of action (e.g., estazolam [ProSom®] and triazolam [Halcion®]) are much more likely to cause rebound insomnia than are those with longer durations of action (e.g., clorazepate [Tranxene®] and diazepam [Valium®]) (see Table 2-4).

ADRs.   The benzodiazepines, when used in recommended doses, are generally well tolerated by most patients. The ADRs that most commonly occur are generally an extension of CNS depressant actions and include confusion, diminished motor coordination, disorientation, lethargy, and oversedation. The incidence of these ADRs appears to be higher among elderly patients who have used moderate to high doses. Other ADRs reported infrequently with the benzodiazepines include a variety of reactions that affect most body organ systems.

Respiratory effects.   The benzodiazepines cause only a slight degree of respiratory depression, even with overdosage.[43] Thus, they generally do not require respiratory supportive measures in such circumstances. An exception to this rule may be the rapid intravenous injection of diazepam (Valium®), which has resulted in apnea. However, it is not clear whether diazepam or propylene glycol, which is used as a solvent for diazepam injection, is responsible for this effect.

Cardiovascular effects.   The benzodiazepines do not appear to produce clinically significant cardiovascular effects among the majority of patients. However, hypotension and tachycardia have been reported.

Other body system effects.   The effects of the benzodiazepines on other organ systems appear to be clinically insignificant for most patients.

Addiction and habituation.   As with other sedative-hypnotics, addiction may develop with regular long-term use of the benzodiazepines. Although the potential for addiction exists for all of the benzodiazepines, the associated withdrawal phenomena generally are much less severe with this class of sedative-hypnotics than with the other classes (i.e., alcohol, barbiturates, miscellaneous sedative-hypnotics).[44] Habituation also occurs with regular long-term use.

---

[41] As an example, oxazepam (Serax®) is often chosen to treat elderly patients because its elimination is relatively unaffected by liver dysfunction. See Chapter 1, "Introduction to the Basic Principles of Pharmacotherapy," Figure 1-1, and Chapter 3, "Pharmacokinetics and Pharmacodynamics."

[42] As an example, diazepam (Valium®) has been widely used among children. This experience and available related data would dictate its preferred use to treat anxiety among children.

[43] This "slight degree" of respiratory depression applies *only* when the benzodiazepines have been used alone. Concurrent use of benzodiazepines and, for example, alcohol can result, and frequently has resulted, in overdose deaths due to *severe* respiratory depression.

[44] Addiction to the benzodiazepines is often an insidious process, particularly because of the less severe pathology involved and the social acceptance of use by both users and prescribers. Thus, it is not surprising that estimates of the number of individuals, from all levels of society, addicted to the benzodiazepines in North America generally are well in excess of 1 million. Discontinuation of long-term benzodiazepine pharmacotherapy or personal use is advised because of concerns regarding questionable continued therapeutic efficacy; development of ADRs, including addiction and neuropsychological impairment; and associated social and economic costs of continued use. Successful withdrawal strategies should combine gradual benzodiazepine dosage reduction and appropriate psychotherapy.

The benzodiazepine withdrawal syndrome can be characterized as consisting of three parts or phases. Phase 1 includes symptoms of "rebound" anxiety and insomnia beginning within 1 to 4 days of discontinuation of benzodiazepine use and lasting for several days (depending on the half-life of elimination). This is followed by Phase 2 of the withdrawal syndrome, which is characterized by symptoms of anxiety, difficulty concentrating, headache, irritability, and sleep disturbances. It is during this phase, which generally lasts for 1 to 3 weeks, that patients will approach the prescriber requesting (and often pleading or demanding) that their benzodiazepine prescription be renewed. The last phase follows usually with a return of anxiety, which may persist for several months.

Overdosage.   As with all of the sedative-hypnotics, benzodiazepine overdosage requires emergency symptomatic medical support of body systems with increasing attention to benzodiazepine elimination. The effects of benzodiazepines on the cardiovascular and respiratory systems are significantly less severe than those observed with the other sedative-hypnotics. Benzodiazepine overdosage also can be treated with the benzodiazepine antagonist flumazenil.

Flumazenil (Anexate®, Romazicon®) antagonizes the pharmacologic effects of the benzodiazepines by means of competitively blocking (binding to) the benzodiazepine receptor. This benzodiazepine antagonist has a short half-life of elimination (i.e., approximately 1 hour). Therefore, overdosages with long-acting benzodiazepines must be carefully monitored and the flumazenil readministered as needed. In addition, patients, particularly those who have histories of regular long-term, high-dosage benzodiazepine use, should be monitored for signs and symptoms of benzodiazepine withdrawal (i.e., anxiety, dizziness, sweating, tachycardia) that can be precipitated by flumazenil antagonist action.

Miscellaneous sedative-hypnotics

Several other sedative-hypnotics have been used to promote sleep or manage the signs and symptoms of anxiety. These sedative-hypnotics include chloral hydrate, meprobamate, paraldehyde, and several other sedative-hypnotics that fall between classification categories. These sedative-hypnotics have been grouped together in the miscellaneous category.

Chloral hydrate.   Chloral hydrate (Noctec®) is the oldest member of the sedative-hypnotic drug class that is still in clinical use, having been introduced in 1869. Like other members of the sedative-hypnotics, chloral hydrate, at usual therapeutic doses, produces CNS depression resulting in sleep. It is most often used as a hypnotic, either as chloral hydrate or as the monosodium salt of the phosphate ester of trichloroethanol, triclofos sodium (Triclos®). Once ingested, both forms are quickly converted to the active metabolite trichloroethanol.

Drug interactions.   Chloral hydrate's active metabolite, trichloroethanol, appears to displace several drugs from their plasma protein-binding sites. This interaction results in the increased metabolism of the displaced drugs and, thus, variable clinical actions (e.g., potentiation or antagonism of the action of oral anticoagulants may be observed, depending on the dose of each drug and the frequency of dosing) (see Chapter 3, "Pharmacokinetics and Pharmacodynamics," and Chapter 6, "Drug Interactions," for further discussion).

Effects on sleep.   Unlike the barbiturates, chloral hydrate does not appreciably affect REM sleep, at least in the usual therapeutic doses. Higher doses reportedly cause REM suppression upon the initiation of pharmacotherapy. A return to normal sleep patterns is usually observed within 2 weeks. The discontinuation of chloral hydrate has not been generally associated with REM rebound.

ADRs: Addiction and habituation.   Continued regular long-term use of chloral hydrate may result in addiction and habituation. The amount of trichloroethanol formed from chloral hydrate decreases with regular use and, for patients who require long-term pharmacotherapy, may necessitate an increase in dosage or the selection of an alternative sedative-hypnotic.

ADRs: Respiratory and cardiovascular effects.   Chloral hydrate does not produce a noticeable effect on respiratory or cardiac function at recommended doses. However, an overdosage produces serious respiratory depression and hypotension. In addition, patients who have preexisting cardiac dysfunction appear to be at risk for developing cardiac complications when high doses of chloral hydrate are used.

ADRs: GI effects.   Chloral hydrate and, to a lesser extent, triclofos sodium are irritating to the gastric mucosa and may cause various associated ADRs, including nausea, stomach pain, and occasional vomiting. These effects can be minimized by ingesting each dose of chloral hydrate with meals (see Chapter 4, "Administration of Psychotropics").

Meprobamate.   Meprobamate (Equanil®, Miltown®) predates the benzodiazepines, having been introduced into clinical practice in 1950. The pharmacologic profile of this sedative-hypnotic falls between the barbiturates and benzodiazepines, and it quickly gained widespread popularity for both licit and illicit use. The use of meprobamate, much like the barbiturates, significantly decreased with the introduction of the benzodiazepines (see earlier discussion in this chapter). Currently, meprobamate is approved for use only as an anxiolytic and should be reserved for patients who cannot tolerate, or are refractory to, the benzodiazepines.

Paraldehyde.   Paraldehyde (Paral®) also is worthy of note, not because it is a superior sedative-hypnotic but because its use may lead to serious clinical sequelae. Paraldehyde is a liquid formulation that, in years past, was widely used in the treatment of alcoholic delirium tremens. This use was based on the mistaken belief that a major portion of the dose of paraldehyde was excreted through the lungs and, thus, would spare the alcohol impaired liver the work of metabolizing an additional drug. However, although a small percentage of a paraldehyde dose is excreted by the lungs, between 70% and 80% of the dose is metabolized in the liver to acetaldehyde and then to carbon dioxide and water. A patient who has a history of alcoholism, with associated liver dysfunction, may be unable to manage this increased metabolic demand and may experience toxic effects of the drug that are similar to those seen with chronic alcoholism. Thus, overdosage or mismanagement of pharmacotherapy may easily occur. In addition, paraldehyde, once opened and exposed to the air, readily decomposes to acetic acid.

Other miscellaneous sedative-hypnotics.   A number of other nonbarbiturate, nonbenzodiazepine sedative-hypnotics have been developed during the last 20 years. Drugs in this miscellaneous subclass of sedative-hypnotics all cause CNS depression to varying degrees. For example, chlormezanone (Trancopal®) and buspirone (BuSpar®) are mildly sedating and, therefore, are not suitable for hypnosis. Others, such as methyprylon (Noludar®), are rapidly absorbed and metabolized and are, therefore, not useful for daytime sedation or for treating anxiety. For all practical purposes, these sedative-hypnotics have been, or could be, largely replaced clinically by the benzodiazepines, both for treating anxiety and for inducing sleep.

Drug interactions.   Ethchlorvynol, glutethimide, and methyprylon stimulate the hepatic microsomal enzyme system much like the barbiturates and, thus, may interfere with the action of other drugs metabolized by the liver. See Chapter 6, "Drug Interactions," for additional details and discussion.

Effects on sleep.   Virtually all drugs in the miscellaneous subclass of sedative-hypnotics cause a decrease in REM sleep, an increase in N-REM sleep, and an REM rebound following their discontinuation. Exceptions include chloral hydrate, as previously discussed, and methaqualone. Methaqualone increases REM sleep at low doses and suppresses REM sleep at higher doses.

ADRs.   The primary ADRs seen with this group of drugs are related to their CNS activity. Confusion, disorientation, drug hangover, mental clouding, or paradoxic excitement may occur, particularly with regular long-term use. Respiratory depression and hypotensive effects similar to those seen with the barbiturates may occur in cases of overdosage.[45] All drugs in this group may produce a tolerance to their clinical effects with continued use. Sudden discontinuation after regular long-term use will produce signs and symptoms of withdrawal similar to those seen with the barbiturates.

Whereas drugs of this group show similar pharmacologic actions, some unique differences exist, particularly related to ADRs. Buspirone (BuSpar®), for example, can cause nasal congestion and skin rash. Ethchlorvynol (Placidyl®) can produce a facial numbness, giddiness, and a mintlike aftertaste. Methaqualone (Quaalude®) may cause transient paresthesia and a peripheral neuropathy that may persist after its discontinuation. Methaqualone, incidentally, has been subject to a high degree of abuse, purportedly because of the mistaken belief that it has aphrodisiac actions. However, these actions are more likely due to a dissociative state that can be seen with high doses without the sedative effects observed with the barbiturates.

Sedative-hypnotic section summary

A variety of sedative-hypnotics are available for the effective induction of sleep or the reduction of anxiety. These drugs should be prescribed for specific indications for no longer than *30* consecutive days in order to minimize the potential for habituation or addiction.[46]

Whereas the barbiturates are effective CNS depressants, their associated ADRs bring into question their continued use for inducing sleep. Respiratory depression, interference with REM sleep, potential drug interactions, the REM rebound phenomenon, decreased effectiveness with regular long-term use, and drug accumulation are all potentially serious enough to dissuade their use for the treatment of insomnia. Chloral hydrate, although an older hypnotic, remains effective. It does not suppress REM sleep or cause REM rebound when its use is discontinued. At usual doses, it does not suppress respirations or cause alterations in blood pressure. However, an overdosage may affect both of these body systems. Chloral hydrate also may be of therapeutic usefulness for elderly and other patients who have liver dysfunction because it is metabolized outside of the hepatic microsomal enzyme system.

Since the introduction of the benzodiazepines for the treatment of anxiety and the induction of sleep, other sedative-hypnotics are approaching obsolescence. That the benzodiazepines are as effective as barbiturates, yet have fewer ADRs, speaks strongly in favor of their use when a sedative-hypnotic is required. In addition, the benzodiazepines (1) do not interfere with REM sleep at usual doses, (2) do not interfere with hepatic metabolism to the extent that barbiturates do, (3) do not produce an appreciable tolerance (although addiction and habituation occur with regular long-term use), (4) have a high therapeutic index, and (5) possess significant anxiolytic activity.

Opiate analgesics and opiate antagonists

The opiate analgesics and antagonists comprise a group of psychotropics that includes the pure opiate agonists, mixed agonist/antagonists, and pure opiate antagonists (see box). This section

---

[45] Although buspirone (BuSpar®) frequently causes nasal congestion and may cause shortness of breath, respiratory depression has not been reported.

[46] Appropriate attention must also be given to effective adjunctive measures to treat both sleep and anxiety disorders. In this regard, appropriate psychotherapy is often of paramount clinical importance. For additional discussion regarding the clinical treatment of these and related disorders, the reader is referred to the companion volume, *Clinical Psychopharmacotherapeutics for Psychologists* (Pagliaro & Pagliaro, in press).

discusses the indications, mechanisms of action, therapeutics, and ADRs associated with these psychotropics.

Opiate Analgesics and Antagonists Generally Available for Use in North America[47]

Opiate agonists
        Anileridine (Leritine®) (♣)
        Codeine [methylmorphine]
        Diacetylmorphine [diamorphine, heroin] (♣)
        Fentanyl (Duragesic®, Sublimaze®)
        Hydromorphone (Dilaudid®)
        Levorphanol (Levo-Dromoran®)
        Meperidine [pethidine] (Demerol®)
        Methadone (Dolophine®)
        Morphine (M.O.S.®, Morphitec®, Oramorph-SR®)
        Oxycodone (OxyContin®, Supeudol®)
        Oxymorphone (Numorphan®)
        Propoxyphene (Darvon®)

Opiate agonists/antagonists (mixed)
        Butorphanol (Stadol®)
        Dezocine (Dalgan®) (★)
        Nalbuphine (Nubain®)
        Pentazocine (Talwin®)

Opiate antagonists (pure)
        Naloxone (Narcan®)
        Naltrexone (ReVia®, Trexan®)

Opiate analgesics

Indications

Opiate analgesics have been both a blessing and a curse for humanity over the centuries as they have been used to both relieve pain and provide escape from "life's pains, disappointments, and impossible tasks." Despite a long history of use and an increasing amount of scientific knowledge, significant therapeutic problems remain regarding the use of opiate analgesics for the symptomatic treatment of pain. The first problem concerns the management of acute pain, such as postoperative pain, when all too often insufficient amounts of analgesics are prescribed in terms of dose or frequency of administration. A similar problem is often observed among many patients who are suffering from severe cancer pain.[48] In a rather contradictory manner, patients who have chronic benign pain are often prescribed high doses of opiate analgesics when there is evidence that these psychotropics have limited use for the safe and effective treatment of long-term benign pain problems.

An encouraging factor is the burgeoning field of pain research that has emerged over the

---

[47] While most of these opiate analgesics are available for use throughout North America, some are available *only* in either Canada or the United States at the time of publication, as indicated by the maple leaf (♣) and star (★), respectively.

[48] A very positive and increasing trend in this area has been the use of patient-controlled analgesia (PCA). See Chapter 4, "Administration of Psychotropics," for additional discussion of PCA.

last three decades. This field of research has been aimed at the study of endogenous opiate-like substances (e.g., endorphins and enkephalins), specific sites of action of the opiate analgesics in the nervous system, complex interactions of various nerve pathways that transmit and control pain, and the response of the human organism to the sensations and emotions produced by any stimulus perceived as painful or pleasurable. With new knowledge, some of the myths, fears, and confusion about opiate analgesic pharmacotherapy can be dispelled, allowing more rational and effective pharmacotherapy for a wide variety of pain problems or disorders.[49]

Mechanism of action

The opiate analgesics act to "relieve pain" in a complex manner in the central nervous system (CNS). Basically, the opiate analgesics can be classified as: (1) neurotransmitter chemicals (e.g., morphine) naturally derived from the poppy plant, *Papavera somniferum*;[50] (2) a modification of these neurochemicals (e.g., diacetylmorphine [heroin]); or (3) synthesized neurochemicals (e.g., methylmorphine [codeine]) that mimic endogenous nervous system neurotransmitters or neuromodulating compounds (i.e., endorphins and enkephalins) that are naturally present in the human body. All of the opiate analgesics elicit their effects by binding to opiate receptors. Three major subtypes of opiate receptors have been identified to which the opiate analgesics bind (i.e., mu, kappa, and delta).

In the brain, the analgesic action of the endogenous neuromodulating compounds and the exogenous opiate analgesics occurs primarily in the periaqueductal gray area, the amygdala, the hypothalamus, the medial parts of the thalamus, the frontal (cerebral) cortex, and the basal ganglia, where they increase message transfers.[51] This increased neuroactivity tends to lower the number of nociceptive messages received from the peripheral nervous system (PNS), which would have been perceived (interpreted) as pain in the conscious areas of the brain. Opiate antagonists (e.g., naloxone [Narcan®]) have the opposite action. They allow more nociceptive messages to pass through the pain-modulating system and to register as pain in the conscious brain. Opiate analgesics and opiate antagonists also act in the dorsal horn of the spinal cord (Figure 2-6). Some opiate analgesics act as both agonists and antagonists (e.g., pentazocine [Talwin®]). By themselves, they can produce analgesia in the event of nociceptive input; however, if used at the same time as a pure opiate agonist, they will block its action. Analgesia generally is not observed unless nociceptive messages are received from the PNS. The pure antagonists of opiates include naltrexone (ReVia®) and naloxone (Narcan®) (see later discussion in this chapter).

As previously noted, high concentrations of opiate receptors and enkephalin innervation have been identified in the dorsal horn of the spinal cord, the periaqueductal gray area, and the thalamus. The paleospinothalamic tract connects through these areas (Figure 2-7). It conducts dull, poorly localized pain messages, such as the tenderness experienced when a bruise is touched, rather than the localized, sharp pain that was felt when the area was initially injured. Opiate analgesics decrease the pain messages within this system.

High concentrations of opiate receptors and enkephalins also are found in the amygdala, hypothalamus, and frontal cortex (Figure 2-7). These areas of the brain are associated with the perception and expression of emotion, as well as other functions (e.g., learning, memory). The opiate analgesics are thought to decrease the severity of pain as an emotional, conscious

---

[49] For a detailed discussion of the therapeutic management and treatment of pain, including the use of alternative and adjunctive measures (e.g., acupuncture, biofeedback, TENS), the interested reader is referred to the companion volume to this text, *Clinical Psychopharmacotherapeutics for Psychologists* (Pagliaro & Pagliaro, in press).

[50] *Papavera somniferum* literally translates from Latin to "the poppy that induces sleep."

[51] Although not confined to particular regions of the CNS, opiate receptor subtypes are found to be highly concentrated within specific regions: the mu subtype within the periaquaductal gray matter and the thalamus, the kappa subtype within the amygdala and frontal (cerebral) cortex, and the delta subtype within the basal ganglia.

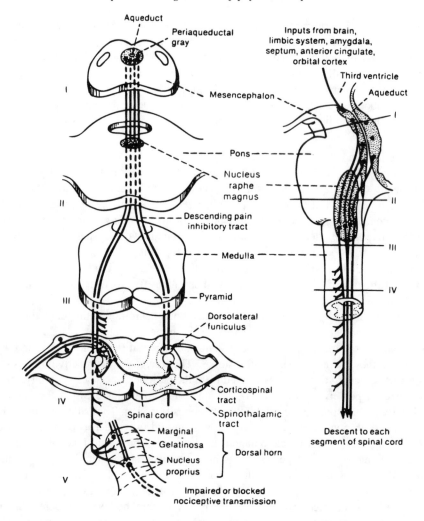

Figure 2-6. Representation of pain transmission and pain modulation systems of the spinal cord and brain stem.

experience by their activity in these areas.[52] The euphoria experienced with the use of some opiate analgesics (e.g., heroin) probably also is produced or moderated through activity within these areas, as is the craving associated with opiate habituation.

Some areas of the brain stem and medulla also have high concentrations of opiate receptors and enkephalins. Some of the ADRs associated with the opiate analgesics, such as respiratory depression and nausea, are produced here. The desirable suppression of cough when the opiates (e.g., codeine, hydrocodone) are used as antitussives also appears to be associated with their activity in this region (i.e., suppression of the cough reflex center in the medulla). Opiate analgesics also act on the intestines to slow smooth muscle contraction. This action results in constipation, an ADR commonly associated with opiate analgesic pharmacotherapy. However, this action also is used therapeutically to counteract diarrhea.

---

[52] Note that the opiate analgesics do *not* block *all* pain sensation (i.e., they do not "cure" pain but, rather, diminish its perception). Therefore, adjunctive pain relief measures, including appropriate psychotherapy, are generally required, particularly in the management of chronic, severe pain.

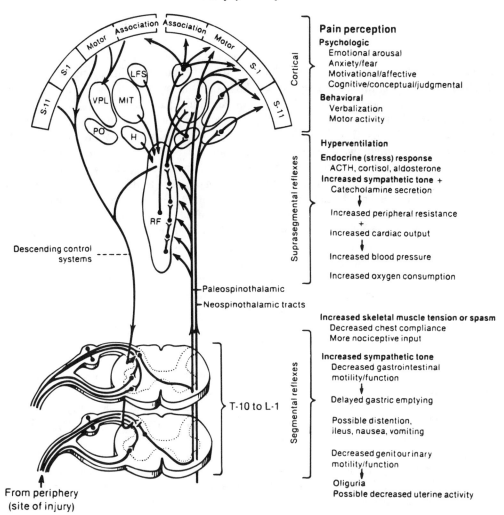

Figure 2-7. The ascending pain pathways (paleospinothalamic and neospinothalamic tracts) and the descending pain inhibitory systems.

Therapeutics and ADRs

When opiate analgesics are prescribed, a common concern is the possibility of the development of addiction and habituation. Addiction is generally associated with the development of both tolerance (i.e., the gradual increase in drug dose required to produce the same physiologic action) and a withdrawal syndrome, which occurs upon abrupt discontinuation of the drug. The signs and symptoms of the withdrawal syndrome are immediately relieved upon resumed use of the drug. The signs and symptoms of the opiate withdrawal syndrome include abdominal cramps, diarrhea, muscle pains, nausea, and sweating.[53]

[53] The opiate withdrawal syndrome often has been characterized as being equivalent to a "bad case of the flu." While this characterization is relatively accurate, the subjective perception among people who are addicted to opiates and who are undergoing withdrawal is that it is considerably more severe. However, the risk of serious morbidity and mortality associated with untreated (i.e., "cold turkey") opiate withdrawal is very low, unless: (1) extremely high dosages have been used for long periods of time; (2) a long-acting opiate analgesic, such as methadone, has been used; or (3) the user has a preexisting compromising disorder, such as a seizure disorder.

Opiate analgesics are used primarily for the treatment of acute, moderate to severe pain.[54] However, they also may be required for the management of chronic cancer pain. When opiate analgesics are prescribed for the long-term management of cancer pain, the risks for addiction and habituation should be weighed against a potentially better quality of life for the patient, who often may have a rather limited life expectancy. Addiction and habituation can be problematic in regard to the management of chronic benign (noncancerous) pain. It is known that, for most chronic pain problems, opiate analgesics are seldom appropriate because their effectiveness in altering pain levels is significantly diminished when they are prescribed over prolonged periods of time. Although withdrawal from opiate analgesics can be completed over 1 to 2 weeks without producing life-threatening signs and symptoms, habituation generally is more difficult to manage. With these thoughts in mind, the prescription of opiate analgesics should be tailored to the patient's requirements in relation to either acute pain or chronic cancer pain management. Opiate analgesics should not be used for the treatment of other types of chronic pain.

Opiate analgesics should be prescribed cautiously for elderly, frail, or debilitated patients and those who are sedated or have severe kidney or liver dysfunction. Opiate analgesics also should be used cautiously among patients who have acute head injuries or other medical disorders that may be associated with increased intracranial pressure (e.g., brain tumor). The respiratory depression produced by the opiate analgesics leads to an increase in blood carbon dioxide levels that increase blood flow to the brain with resultant increased intracranial pressure. If intracranial pressure is already increased, as occurs with head injuries or other medical conditions, then damage to the brain can be increased. Extremely close medical monitoring of these patients is required. Opiate analgesic pharmacotherapy also may mask the clinical course of these patients.

When opiate analgesics are prescribed intravenously, they should be injected with care. Too rapid injection may cause sudden apnea, bronchoconstriction, drowsiness, and hypotension. Therefore, slow injection (i.e., over 3 to 5 minutes) is the general rule. Emergency equipment and personnel should be immediately available whenever opiates are intravenously injected (see Chapter 4, "Administration of Psychotropics," for additional details).

Opiate analgesics should be cautiously prescribed to patients who have respiratory dysfunction (e.g., asthma, emphysema, pneumonia). Opiate analgesics decrease respiratory drive, predominantly decreasing the rate of respirations. They also cause an increase in airway resistance by stimulating smooth muscle contraction in the airways.[55] This combination of actions may be fatal for a patient who has incipient respiratory failure from an acute or chronic respiratory condition. Therefore, if opiate analgesics are prescribed for such patients, frequent monitoring of body systems, particularly respiratory function is imperative. In this regard, it is important to note that the duration of respiratory depressant actions associated with opiate analgesic pharmacotherapy may be longer than the duration of analgesic actions.

When prescribing opiate analgesics, clinical psychologists also must be concerned about hypotension. Postural (orthostatic) hypotension is commonly observed among elderly and debilitated patients who are prescribed opiate analgesics. Clinical psychologists must ensure that these patients are closely monitored for pronounced hypotension. Patients who have experienced recent blood or fluid loss, such as occurs in cases of severe trauma and hemorrhage, also require cautious prescription of opiate analgesics and close monitoring.[56]

---

[54] A noted exception to this rule is the use of methadone in opiate addiction maintenance programs.

[55] The respiratory effects of the opiate analgesics appear to be primarily modulated by interaction with the mu-2 receptor subtype. Because all currently available opiate analgesics bind, to varying degrees, to both mu-1 and mu-2 receptor subtypes, *all* cause varying degrees of respiratory impairment.

[56] It should again be emphasized that in these and all similar cases involving medical conditions or other disorders, the prescribing psychologist should, whenever necessary, collaborate with (or refer to) an appropriate health care provider (e.g., advanced practice nurse, physician, etc.).

Any activity requiring attention, judgment, or psychomotor coordination (e.g., driving a motor vehicle, operating dangerous equipment, supervising children) should be avoided, particularly when high dosages are prescribed, because opiate analgesics may adversely affect these mental and physical functions. In addition, learning, memory, and performance on psychometric tests may be significantly impaired. Patients and their family members as appropriate need to be advised about these effects. The tendency for postural (orthostatic) hypotension among patients who are prescribed high dosages of opiate analgesics, as previously noted, also will adversely affect these mental and physical functions.

Opiate antagonists

Opiate antagonists reversibly block opiate receptors. The opiate antagonists have little, if any, pharmacologic activity among patients who are opiate free, although they will rapidly reverse all of the opiate's analgesic and other actions, including respiratory depression and coma, among patients who have opiates in their bloodstreams. When an opiate antagonist is required, such as in the case of opiate overdosage, a pure opiate antagonist (e.g., naloxone [Narcan®]) should be used. The use of opiate antagonists is not associated with the development of addiction or habituation. However, they can precipitate the opiate withdrawal syndrome among patients who are addicted to opiate analgesics.

Naltrexone (ReVia®) is pharmacologically identical to naloxone (Narcan®) except that: (1) it has a significantly longer half-life of elimination (i.e., 4 hours versus 1 hour); (2) it has an active metabolite with a half-life of elimination of approximately 13 hours; and (3) it is effective when orally ingested. Therefore, naltrexone can be orally dosed significantly less frequently than the injectable naloxone formulation while retaining equivalent therapeutic effect.

The longer duration of action of naltrexone also has led to its use as adjunctive pharmacotherapy in the treatment of opiate addiction. In this regard, it is used to maintain the opiate-free state among detoxified, formerly opiate-addicted patients because it blocks the effects of opiate analgesics that may be subsequently used. Adjunctive naltrexone pharmacotherapy has been found to be particularly useful for the treatment of formerly opiate-addicted health care professionals (e.g., nurses, pharmacists, physicians) who are highly motivated to remain opiate free but who must continue to work in professional environments where opiate analgesics are commonly used and readily available. Naltrexone also has, more recently, been advocated for use as an *adjunct* to psychotherapy for the treatment of alcohol use disorders.

Opiate analgesics and antagonists section summary

This section has examined the various types and uses of the pure opiate agonist analgesics, as well as the mixed opiate agonists/antagonists and the pure opiate antagonists. Opiate analgesics are one of the most frequently prescribed classes of psychotropics. For a comparison of the opiate and weaker analgesics, including the opiate agonists/antagonists, see Tables 2-5, 2-6, and 2-7. With an understanding of the various opiate analgesics, including their actions, indications, and ADRs, clinical psychologists will be better able to prescribe optimal pharmacotherapy for their patients who require these psychotropic drugs.

Table 2-5. Selected pharmacodynamic parameters and relative potency of common injectable opiate analgesics.

Opiate analgesic	Method of administration[a] Subcutaneous (SC) Intramuscular (IM)	Onset (minutes)	Peak action (hours)	Duration (hours)	Approximate equivalent dose (mg)[b]
Alphaprodine (Nisentil®)	SC or IM	5 to 10	Within 0.5	1 to 2	50
Anileridine (Leritine®)	SC or IM	Within 15	0.5 to 1	2 to 3	30
Butorphanol (Stadol®)	SC or IM	Within 30	Within 1	5 to 7	2
Codeine	SC or IM	15 to 30	1 to 1.5	4 to 6	120
Dezocine (Dalgan®)	SC or IM	Within 30	Within 1.5	2 to 4	10
Diacetylmorphine (Heroin)	SC or IM	Within 30	Within 1.5	4 to 6	5
Fentanyl (Duragesic®)	SC or IM	5 to 15	Within 0.5	Up to 2	0.1
Hydromorphone (Dilaudid®)	SC or IM	15 to 30	0.5 to 1.5	4 to 5	1.5
Levorphanol (Levo-Dromoran®)	SC or IM	Within 60	1 to 1.5	5 to 8	3
Meperidine (Demerol®)	SC or IM	10 to 15	0.5 to 1	2 to 4	75
Methadone (Dolophine®)	SC or IM	10 to 15	1 to 2	4 to 8	10
Morphine (MS-Contin®)	SC or IM	Within 30	0.5 to 1.5	Up to 7	10
Nalbuphine (Nubain®)	SC or IM	Within 15	Within 0.5	3 to 6	10
Oxymorphone (Numorphan®)	SC or IM	5 to 10	Within 0.5	3 to 6	1

[a] These opiate analgesics may be administered by other methods. However, the data listed are derived from studies in which the drugs were administered intramuscularly or subcutaneously.
[b] This column lists the doses that should provide *approximately* the same amount of analgesia (e.g., it would take approximately 120 mg of *codeine* to provide the same amount of analgesia as 10 mg of *morphine*).

Table 2-6. Relative potency of common oral analgesics.

Drug	Method of administration Oral (PO)	Onset (minutes)	Peak action (hours)	Duration (hours)	Approximate equivalent dose (mg)[a]
Acetaminophen[b] (Tempra®, Tylenol®)	PO	10 to 20	0.5 to 1	4 to 6	650
Aspirin[b] (Bayer®, Bufferin®)	PO	15 to 30	2	4 to 6	650
Codeine[c]	PO	15 to 30	1 to 1.5	4 to 6	32
Pentazocine (Talwin®)	PO	15 to 30	1	4	30
Propoxyphene (Darvon®)	PO	Within 30	2	6 to 12	65 to 100

[a] This column lists the doses that should provide approximately the same amount of analgesia (e.g., it would take approximately 650 mg of *aspirin* to provide the same amount of analgesia as 32 mg of *codeine*).
[b] Acetaminophen and aspirin are nonopiate analgesics.
[c] Codeine appears in the previous table and can be used as a reference when comparing the weaker and stronger analgesics or the opiate and nonopiate analgesics.

Table 2-7. Comparison of higher potency opiate and nonopiate analgesics.

	Higher potency opiate analgesics[a]	Nonopiate analgesics
Indications	Moderate to severe pain of an acute nature (e.g., major surgery, trauma, myocardial infarction, renal stones)	Mild to moderate pain
Generally *inappropriate* indications for use	Chronic pain with the exception of those associated with some cancers	Severe pain
Method of administration	Injection (i.e., intramuscular, intravenous, subcutaneous), usually	Oral, usually
Adverse drug reactions	Primarily associated with CNS depression; direct effects on smooth muscle of the gastrointestinal tract	Primarily associated with local reactions in the gastrointestinal tract or excretory organ (e.g., kidney, liver)
Recipients	Primarily hospitalized patients, particularly when administered by injection	Hospitalized and nonhospitalized patients

[a] Codeine, pentazocine, and propoxyphene are *not* included among the higher potency opiate analgesics.

Amphetamines and other central nervous system stimulants[57]

The amphetamines and other CNS stimulants comprise a group of psychotropics that includes the amphetamines, amphetamine-like stimulants, and miscellaneous (anorexiant) CNS stimulants (see box). This section discusses the indications, mechanisms of action, therapeutics, and ADRs of these psychotropics.

CNS Stimulants Generally Available for Use in North America[58,59]

Amphetamines
> Amphetamine (Adderall®)[60]
> Benzphetamine (Didrex®) (★)
> Dextroamphetamine [dexamphetamine] (Dexedrine®)
> Methamphetamine [desoxyephedrine] (Desoxyn®) (★)

Amphetamine-like stimulants
> Methylphenidate (Ritalin®)
> Pemoline (Cylert®)

Miscellaneous (anorexiant) CNS stimulants
> Dexfenfluramine (Redux®)
> Diethylpropion (Tenuate®)

continued. . .

---

[57] These drugs also are referred to as behavioral stimulants, psychostimulants, and psychomotor stimulants.

[58] Caffeine, cocaine, and nicotine are other CNS stimulants that are generally available for use in North America, but they are not addressed here. Interested readers are referred to *Substance Use Among Children and Adolescents: Its Nature, Extent, and Consequences from Conception to Adulthood* (Pagliaro & Pagliaro, 1996) for a comprehensive discussion of these drugs.

[59] While most of these CNS stimulants are available for use throughout North America, some are available *only* in either Canada or the United States at the time of publication, as indicated by the maple leaf (♣) and star (★), respectively.

[60] Available as a mixed amphetamine salts combination product containing amphetamine aspartate, amphetamine sulfate, dextroamphetamine saccharate, and dextroamphetamine sulfate and prescribed as a single-ingredient product.

Fenfluramine (Ponderal®, Pondimin®)
Mazindol (Sanorex®)
Phendimetrazine (Prelu-2®) (★)
Phenmetrazine (Preludin®) (★)
Phentermine (Ionamin®)

Many drugs from various chemical families have the ability to stimulate the central nervous system (CNS) both directly (e.g., caffeine) and indirectly (e.g., cocaine). The psychotropics discussed in this section can all be classified as indirect-acting sympathomimetic amines with predominantly CNS stimulant and anorexiant activity.

Mechanism of action

The amphetamines and amphetamine-like CNS stimulants act primarily by an indirect mechanism. They inhibit the reuptake and/or stimulate the release of biogenic amines (e.g., dopamine, norepinephrine, and serotonin) from presynaptic storage vesicles. This action elicits their biologic effects (e.g., CNS stimulation, decreased appetite, decreased sense of fatigue, increased blood pressure). These psychotropics do not elicit a direct effect at the receptor site.[61] Repeated use at short intervals leads to a progressive reduction and eventual absence of response as the biogenic amines (which were initially present in the nerve terminals) are depleted.

Indications

Amphetamine was first synthesized in the late 1800s. However, it was not used clinically until the early 1930s, when it was introduced as a nasal decongestant (i.e., "Benzedrine Inhaler"). Recognition of its ability to increase blood pressure and cause CNS stimulation resulted in other clinical and nonclinical interest. For example, during World War II, amphetamines were widely distributed to both Allied and Axis servicemen to fight fatigue and enhance performance.[62] At that time, the amphetamines also started to become popular as "diet pills" and were beginning to be used by college students (i.e., GIs returning to study after the war) to stay awake to study for their examinations. During the postwar years, the amphetamines, known commonly as "wake-amines," were widely abused in Japan as well as Sweden and other European countries.

The CNS stimulants are generally indicated for the symptomatic management of attention-deficit/hyperactivity disorder and exogenous obesity. The CNS stimulants should *not* be used to hasten a patient's recovery from anesthesia or CNS depressant drug overdosage. In these latter cases, proper emergency symptomatic medical support of body systems dictates ventilatory and circulatory support until recovery occurs, particularly because CNS stimulants may complicate recovery by inducing cardiac dysrhythmias, hypertension, or violent behavior. In addition, the action of the CNS stimulant may diminish before the action of the sedative, resulting in

---

[61] This depletion of biogenic amines may help explain the phenomenon of amphetamine tolerance and the well-recognized poststimulation depression or fatigue commonly observed following an "amphetamine run." This phenomena is similar to the cocaine "blues" or dysphoria.

[62] The still-in-use street names "bombs" and "bomber pilot" for the amphetamines date from this usage during World War II. They are also commonly known as "truck drivers."

respiratory arrest or hypotensive crises. These latter effects may go unnoticed if monitoring was discontinued during the time of stimulant effectiveness.

Attention-deficit/hyperactivity disorder[63]

Children who have attention-deficit/hyperactivity disorder (ADHD) pose diagnostic and therapeutic challenges. The main clinical features manifested by these children are hyperactive behavior, impulsivity, easy distractibility, and a limited attention span. Thus, these children display an incessant shifting of attention and wandering activity that becomes problematic when they are obliged to function in a classroom or other restrictive setting. The disorder makes it difficult for children to learn in the traditional classroom setting, and their increased activity is generally considered to be distracting and disrupting to both their teachers and the other students in their classrooms. ADHD is one of the most frequently encountered mental disorders in childhood, with incidence estimates ranging from 5% to 10%. It is also significantly more frequently diagnosed among boys than girls, respective ratios reportedly ranging from 5:1 to 10:1.

There are several conditions that have been associated with ADHD. These conditions include childhood autism, conduct disorder, environmental stresses (e.g., dysfunctional family, child abuse or neglect), fetal alcohol syndrome, mental retardation, seizure disorder, and Tourette's disorder. It is important to arrive at a definite diagnosis, because the therapeutic implications vary with each cause. In this regard, it is important that a comprehensive psychological assessment, including appropriate psychological testing, be performed to rule out or confirm the presence of associated concurrent mental disorders.[64]

Apart from pharmacotherapy, the management of children who have been diagnosed with ADHD requires appropriate family counseling and modified educational management. The psychotropic drugs that are most commonly prescribed for the pharmacotherapy of ADHD are methylphenidate (Ritalin®), pemoline (Cylert®), dextroamphetamine (Dexedrine®), and mixed amphetamine salts (Adderall®).[65] Unfortunately, learning improves at lower doses than does behavior, and as higher doses increasingly control objectionable behavior, learning suffers.[66] Dextroamphetamine is alleged to be twice as potent as methylphenidate and has been suggested as a possible drug of choice for the treatment of adults who have "residual" ADHD. However, methylphenidate is generally considered superior, particularly among children, because its use is associated with fewer ADRs.

Long-term use of CNS stimulants may cause a delay in linear growth among children. This ADR appears to be more of a problem with dextroamphetamine but may occur with methylphenidate when higher dosages are used. This ADR is primarily a result of the anorexiant actions generally associated with the CNS stimulants. A significant number of children who are prescribed CNS stimulants for the symptomatic management of ADHD appear to develop

---

[63] This disorder also has been referred to as "hyperactivity," "hyperkinesis," and "minimal brain dysfunction."

[64] Readers are referred to the companion volume to this text, *Clinical Psychopharmacotherapeutics for Psychologists* (Pagliaro & Pagliaro, in press), for a comprehensive review and discussion of the assessment, diagnosis, and treatment of ADHD and related concomitant disorders.

[65] The frequency of use is in the order listed, with the overwhelming majority of children who have ADHD being prescribed methylphenidate.

[66] This is an example of a potential therapeutic dilemma for prescribing psychologists, particularly school psychologists. At lower dosages, learning is optimized among children who have ADHD, but their behavior may still prove disruptive to classmates, teachers and parents. At high CNS stimulant dosages, behavior is much better controlled (i.e., generally children who have ADHD are much more acceptable to classmates, teachers, and parents), but learning has been compromised. We would recommend the former line of action.

problematic patterns of CNS stimulant (e.g., cocaine) use following discontinuation of stimulant pharmacotherapy during adolescence.[67]

Central nervous system stimulant pharmacotherapy is not universally successful in treating ADHD. Some children may not respond to pharmacotherapy and their behavior may, in fact, worsen. Therapeutic benefit must be carefully monitored and the drug dosage adjusted individually after careful observation of the child and appropriate psychological testing by clinical psychologists in conjunction with the child's pediatrician, teachers, parents, and others involved in his or her health promotion (e.g., social worker). Anorexia and insomnia are rarely a problem if CNS stimulants are prescribed in a single dose in the morning before a child leaves for school. A repeat dose at noon may be required depending on the child's observed individual response. Late afternoon or evening doses may result in insomnia. Children under 6 years of age are generally not treated with stimulant pharmacotherapy. Hallucinations, a syndrome resembling Gilles de la Tourette's syndrome, depression, and apathy are less common ADRs but may occur, particularly with methylphenidate pharmacotherapy. Acute liver failure, which can result in death or the need for a liver transplant, has been associated with the use of pemoline. See Chapter 5, "Adverse Drug Reactions," for further information regarding this ADR and a comprehensive discussion of the ADRs associated with all of the CNS stimulants.

Although other drugs, such as tricyclic antidepressants, are sometimes used for the treatment of childhood ADHD, opinions vary about their value, and they are generally reserved for cases that prove refractory to CNS stimulant pharmacotherapy. Central nervous system stimulant pharmacotherapy continues to be the mainstay for the treatment of ADHD among children (and increasingly among adolescents and adults). Dosages must be individualized and carefully selected and adjusted in consideration of *both* behavioral symptoms and effects on learning.

Exogenous obesity

Apart from being a national preoccupation, obesity represents a major public health problem. It is well established that obesity increases the risk for developing diabetes mellitus, coronary and cerebrovascular diseases, hypertension, osteoarthritis, thrombophlebitis, and stasis ulcers. Reducing excess body weight is a desirable therapeutic goal. However, treatment is often extremely frustrating for both patients and clinical psychologists. Grossly obese patients usually have hypercellular and hypertrophic fat cells, limb and trunk fat accumulation, a history of an obese childhood, and refractoriness to therapy. Although body weight can be reduced, these patients almost universally reaccumulate fat. In contrast, adult-onset obesity is generally associated with hypertrophic, rather than hypercellular, fat cells; truncal obesity (middle-age spread); no history of childhood obesity; and a better response to therapy.

Various CNS stimulants are used in weight reduction programs to capitalize on their appetite-suppressing actions. Most authorities do not recommend the use of CNS stimulants as a component of weight reduction programs because their anorexian actions are exhausted long before weight reduction goals are achieved. The risk of addiction and habituation to these drugs also is high.[68] A medically managed exercise and dietary program continue to be the major factors in a successful weight reduction program.

---

[67] Although strongly suggested, available data do not conclusively confirm this association. If the association actually does exist, it is interesting to speculate that the "cause" of problematic patterns of CNS stimulant use, at least for some people, might involve "self-medication" for the treatment of ADHD that has continued (undiagnosed) through adolescence and into early adulthood. For further discussion, readers are referred to *Substance Use Among Children and Adolescents: Its Nature, Extent, and Consequences from Conception to Adulthood* (Pagliaro & Pagliaro, 1996).

[68] For a detailed discussion of the abuse of the amphetamines, interested readers are referred to *Substance Use Among Children and Adolescents: Its Nature, Extent, and Consequences from Conception to Adulthood* (Pagliaro & Pagliaro, 1996).

More recently marketed drugs for symptomatic management of obesity (e.g., dexfenflura-mine [Redux®]) are generally referred to by their manufacturers not as CNS stimulants but, rather, as anorectics, anorexiants, anorexigenics, or appetite suppressants. However, because they act primarily by increasing serotonin, share a close chemical structure to the amphetamines, and frequently cause symptoms commonly associated with CNS stimulation (e.g., anxiety, decreased appetite, increased blood pressure, insomnia, nervousness), these drugs have been categorized together with the miscellaneous CNS stimulants. Although data concerning their abuse potential are not yet available, it is expected that these drugs will be subject to significant abuse, as have virtually all previously introduced "appetite suppressants" (see Chapter 5, "Adverse Drug Reactions").

Narcolepsy

Narcolepsy is a relatively common sleep disorder among adults. It is reported, by some estimates, to be more common than epilepsy, with a prevalence four times greater among men than women. The two types of narcolepsy, simple and compound, are characterized by excessive daytime drowsiness and sleep attacks. In compound narcolepsy, cataplexy (i.e., sudden, generalized weakness or paralysis in response to an emotional stimulus), sleep paralysis (i.e., awakening from sleep unable to move but still able to breathe), and hypnagogic hallucinations (i.e., vivid, often unpleasant dreams upon falling asleep) occur along with the daytime drowsiness and sleep attacks that characterize simple narcolepsy. Narcolepsy must be differentiated from other causes of daytime sleepiness, principally those conditions characterized by sleep apnea, which, by interrupting normal sleep, cause daytime drowsiness.

Narcoleptic patients have a restless sleep interrupted by movements and periods of wake-fulness. Night sleep is abnormally fragmented and is often reduced in total duration. In both simple and compound narcolepsy, it is important for patients to maintain a regular and adequate night sleep because disruption of the usual sleep schedule worsens symptoms.

Simple narcolepsy is treated with CNS stimulant pharmacotherapy (e.g., methylphenidate or dextroamphetamine). The dosage and dosing schedule must be individualized. Insomnia may complicate therapy if the last dose is prescribed near bedtime. Anorexia with significant weight loss or addiction and habituation may require discontinuation of CNS stimulant pharmacotherapy.

Compound narcolepsy is treated with tricyclic antidepressants, which control the cataplexy and the sleep paralysis. However, the CNS stimulants are still required in individualized dosages to control daytime drowsiness and sleep attacks.

Amphetamines and other CNS stimulant section summary

The CNS stimulants come from a wide variety of chemical families. The use of these psychotrop-ics has been limited to a few clinical conditions, in large part because of their association with addiction and habituation.[69] These clinical conditions include ADHD, exogenous obesity, and narcolepsy.

Summary

The psychotropics are defined as drugs whose major, direct action within the central nervous system results in changes in cognition, learning, memory, behavior, perception, or affect. The

---

[69] The use of CNS stimulants in the treatment of various neurological conditions (e.g., brain-injured patients with abulia or amotivational syndrome) is increasing but requires further evaluation, particularly in relation to long-term efficacy and sequelae.

psychotropics that are available for use in North America include the following classifications: antidepressants and antimanics, antipsychotics, central nervous system depressants (i.e., opiate analgesics, sedative-hypnotics), and central nervous system stimulants, including anorexiants. Knowledge of and familiarity with these groups and their specific pharmacologic actions assist prescribing psychologists in prescribing appropriate psychotropic pharmacotherapy for their patients when it is required as an adjunct to psychotherapy.

3

Pharmacokinetics and Pharmacodynamics

Introduction

The ultimate goal of psychologists who prescribe psychotropic drugs for their patients as an adjunct to psychotherapy is to obtain therapeutic efficacy with a minimum of adverse and toxic effects. Three major factors—input (absorption), distribution, and output (elimination)—must be considered and clearly understood if this goal is to be met (see Figure 3-1). Pharmacokinetics involves the mathematical modeling of these three factors, thus enabling description and prediction of the time course of drug concentrations in various body fluids (e.g., blood, plasma, serum, urine).[1,2] Thus, pharmacokinetics contributes to drug selection and dosing by interposing quantitative measurements relating drug dosage and concentrations in various body fluids with respective pharmacologic effects. Appropriate application of pharmacokinetic principles when

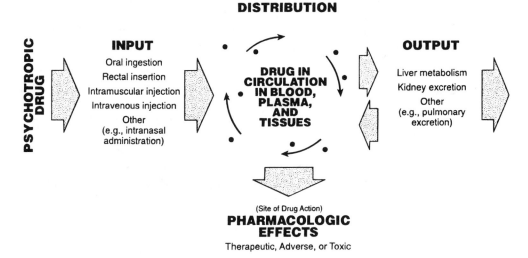

Figure 3-1. The process of input, distribution, and output of psychotropics in the human body and the corresponding pharmacologic effect(s).

[1] Blood, plasma, and serum are defined as follows: blood—the corpuscles and platelets suspended in plasma; plasma—the fluid portion of the blood and lymph, consisting of serum, protein, and chemicals in aqueous solution; and serum—the fluid portion of the blood after coagulation (i.e., after the removal of coagulation factors and products).

[2] The designation of drug concentration as blood, plasma, or serum concentration is a factor of the analytical laboratory procedures used in the chemical extraction and analysis of specific drug samples. All such samples are initially obtained from the patient in the form of whole blood samples. Thus, the designation as blood, plasma, or serum concentrations has no significant clinical or pharmacokinetic importance other than in relation to the procedures used for laboratory analysis.

Table 3-1. Factors that may influence pharmacokinetic parameters.

Drug factors
    Physicochemical properties
    Product formulation
Patient-specific factors
    Age
    Cardiac function[a]
    Ethnicity
    Gender
    Genetics
    Health state (physical, psychological)
    Kidney (Renal) function[a]
    Liver (Hepatic) function[a]
    Pregnancy
    Race
    Weight
Drug interactions
    Drug–drug
    Drug–disease
    Drug–food

[a] Dysfunction can be a result of disease or other factors, such as age. For example, in both neonates and elderly people, kidney function is significantly reduced, but for different reasons (i.e., immature body organ function among neonates versus decreased body organ function as a result of aging among the elderly).

prescribing pharmacotherapy for patients results in improved therapeutic response with a minimum of adverse drug reactions and toxic effects (see Table 3-1). Note that modeling, such as depicted in Figure 3-2, is often used to facilitate these pharmacokinetic "predictions." The use of pharmacokinetic principles also enables psychologists to consider other factors (e.g., age, genetics, medical disorders, concomitant drug therapy) that can affect input, distribution, and output and, thus, affect the efficacy of pharmacotherapy (see Table 3-2).

Input: The serum concentration–time curve

The "input" of psychotropic drugs depends generally on their methods of administration, including oral ingestion, buccal or sublingual placement, rectal insertion, and intramuscular or intravenous injection (see Chapter 4, "Administration of Psychotropics"). The relationship between input and resultant therapeutic effects or adverse drug reactions is reflected by the blood concentration–time curve. This curve, for a specific psychotropic drug after input, is representative of a function of the drug's corresponding distribution and output for a particular patient. In most cases, the blood, plasma, or serum concentration of a psychotropic drug (see Chapter 1, "Introduction to the Basic Principles of Pharmacotherapy") at its site of action can elicit a number of pharmacologic effects in a particular patient. These effects include the desired therapeutic effect, an adverse drug reaction, or a toxic effect (see Chapter 5, "Adverse Drug Reactions").

Psychotropic drug input, or absorption, is affected by a number of drug and patient factors (see Tables 3-3 and 3-4). These factors can affect both the extent (i.e., how much) and the rate (i.e., how fast or slow) by which a drug is absorbed into the bloodstream (i.e., systemic circulation).[3,4] The process of drug absorption and its measurement can have significant clinical implications that may be best illustrated by a brief discussion of the concept of "bioavailability."

---

[3] The extent of drug absorption is denoted by F, the fraction of drug available to the systemic circulation. F values can range from 0 to 1. For example, if a patient ingests a 40-mg oral antidepressant tablet and if, because of the factors noted in Tables 3-3 and 3-4, only half of this amount (i.e., 20 mg) is absorbed from the GI tract into the systemic circulation, then the F value is 0.5.

[4] The rate of drug absorption is denoted by Ka, the rate constant for absorption.

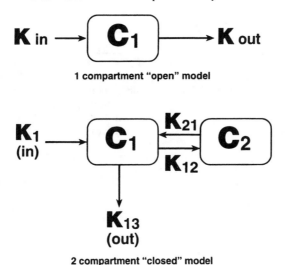

Figure 3-2. Pharmacokinetic modeling illustrating the one-compartment open model and the two-compartment closed model.

Table 3-2. Clinical uses of pharmacokinetic data.

- Predict blood, tissue, and urine *drug levels* with any drug dosage
- Calculate the optimum *dosage* for each individual patient
- Estimate adverse and toxic drug effects related to the possible *accumulation* of drugs and their metabolites
- Explain *drug interactions* involving other drugs or foods and beverages
- Evaluate differences in *bioavailability* among different manufacturers' formulations of the same drug
- Explain how changes in *physiology* (e.g., kidney and liver function) associated with age, gender, genetics, and disease affect the input, distribution, and output of psychotropic drugs
- Correlate *drug concentration* with therapeutic effect

Bioavailability

Bioavailability, as the term implies, is directly concerned with how much of a drug is absorbed into the systemic circulation after its administration. By definition, 100% of a drug is absorbed into the systemic circulation when it is intravenously injected.[5] When other methods of drug administration are used (e.g., oral ingestion, buccal or sublingual placement, rectal insertion, or intramuscular injection) (see Table 3-5), the bioavailability is equal to or less than 100% (i.e., $F \leq 1.0$). These concepts have direct clinical application when, for example, a patient continues to "input" the same drug at the same dosage but by different methods of administration.[6] When the dose and method of administration are kept constant but the manufacturer of the drug product changes the formulation,[7] clinical psychologists should be concerned about "bioequivalence."

---

[5] In terms of the F value discussed earlier, for drugs injected intravenously, $F = 1.0$ (by definition).

[6] This situation is typically encountered among hospitalized patients who have been receiving psychotropic pharmacotherapy by intravenous injection and are discharged with oral dosage forms for economy and ease of administration. This situation also occurs when patients who usually use oral dosage forms for their psychotropics require an injectable form because of nausea or vomiting related to an acute illness (e.g., the "flu").

[7] This situation occurs commonly, for example, when "generic" psychotropic drugs are used in place of "brand name" psychotropic drugs in order to decrease cost.

Table 3-3. Factors influencing drug absorption.

Drug factors	Patient factors	Other factors
Active ingredient(s)	Age	Gastric emptying time
Chemical stability (to water, light, and oxygen)	Gender	Timing of dose relative to meals
Chemical structure	Health state (physical & mental)	Method of administration
Crystal form	Intestinal motility	Fluids available to dissolve the drug
Degree of hydration	Physical activity	pH of gastric fluids
Lipid solubility		Size of dose that can be delivered
Molecular weight		Potential for first-pass metabolism
Particle size		Blood flow to site of absorption (e.g., intestine, muscle)
Physical stability (vapor pressure, melting or boiling point)		Effects of other drugs (or food) ingested concurrently
pK_a[a]		
Salt form		
Water solubility		
Dosage formulation		
Inert ingredients[b]		
Topical formulations[c]		
spreadability (lotions, gels)		
Adherence (transdermal delivery systems)		
Oral formulations		
Solid dosage forms[c]		
Order of mixing, method and size of granulation		
Compression pressure or packing density		
Special coatings including their water solubility and the pH dependence of solubility		
Liquid dosage forms		
Suspensions[c]		
viscosity		
solubility		
pourability		

Note. See also Tables 3-4 and 3-5 and Chapter 4, "Administration of Psychotropics."
[a] pK_a is the pH at which 50% of a drug is in the ionized form (i.e., the form that is much less likely to cross biologic membranes).
[b] These same factors also apply to each inert ingredient found in a drug formulation.
[c] Only those factors distinctive for a particular dosage formulation are listed. For each formulation, all factors listed under inert ingredients apply.

Bioequivalence

Bioequivalence, as the term implies, is directly concerned with how much and how fast the same dose of a drug is absorbed into the systemic circulation when input is different (e.g., oral ingestion of 50 mg of Drug A versus intramuscular injection of 50 mg of Drug A) or when input is the same but the drugs are from different manufacturers (e.g., a 50-mg tablet of Brand X versus a 50-mg tablet of Brand Y). To state that different methods of administration or different brands of a particular drug are bioequivalent implies that the *amount* and *rate* of absorption from the site of input (i.e., bioavailability) are equivalent (see Figures 3-3 and 3-4).

Table 3-4. Factors affecting gastric emptying, intestinal motility, and gastrointestinal blood flow.

Factor	Effect on gastric emptying
Volume ingested	As volume increases, there is initially an increase followed by a decrease in rate of emptying; bulky meals tend to empty more slowly than liquids
Type of meal	
Bulky	Decrease rate of emptying
Fats	Decrease rate of emptying
Carbohydrates	Decrease rate of emptying
Liquid	Increase rate of emptying
Osmotic pressure of ingested material	As osmotic pressure increases, rate of emptying decreases
Temperature of ingested material	As temperature increases to body temperature, rate of emptying increases
Viscosity of ingested material	As viscosity increases, rate of emptying decreases
Body positioning	When a person lies on the left side, rate of emptying decreases
Psychologic state	Aggressive emotional states tend to increase rate of emptying
	Depressive states tend to decrease rate of emptying
Drugs	
Anticholinergics (e.g., atropine) and drugs that produce anticholinergic actions (e.g., **phenothiazines, tricyclic antidepressants**)	Decrease rate of emptying
Opiate analgesics (e.g., **morphine, meperidine**)	Decrease rate of emptying
Medical disorders	
Stomach neoplasm	Decreases rate of emptying
Gastric ulcer	No effect
Ulcer of pyloric antrum or associated with duodenal ulcer	Decreases rate of emptying
Uncomplicated duodenal ulcer	Increases rate of emptying
Miscellaneous factors	
Acidification (e.g., HCl, H_2SO_4, tartaric acid, citric acid)	Decreases rate of emptying
$NaHCO_3$ (sodium bicarbonate) 1 hour after a meal	Decreases rate of emptying
Alcohol ingestion before a meal	Decreases rate of emptying

Factor	Effect on intestinal motility
Food	Decreased rate of transit
Increased viscosity of meal	Tends to retard transit rate; decreases diffusion as well as decreasing dissolution rate, and, thus, also decreases absorption
Medical disorders	
Constipation	Decreases rate of transit
Diarrhea	Increases rate of transit
Lack of digestive juices	Decreases rate of transit
Insulin, hypoglycemia	Increases intestinal motility and increases rate of transit
Lack of thyroxine secretion	Decreases rate of transit

continued. . .

Table 3-4. Factors affecting gastric emptying, intestinal motility, and gastrointestinal blood flow—Continued.

Factor	Effect on intestinal motility, continued
Drugs	
Morphine, tricyclic antidepressants	Decreases intestinal motility and, thus, decreases rate of transit
Miscellaneous factors	
Pregnancy	Decreases transit rate (probably because of smooth muscle relaxation)
Bile secretion	Increases transit rate

Factor	Effect on gastrointestinal blood flow
Food	Increases blood flow to the gastrointestinal tract
Physical exercise	Decreases blood flow to the gastrointestinal tract
Hypotensive conditions and syncope	Decreases blood flow to the gastrointestinal tract

Note. Modified from Hoener (1986).

Table 3-5. Comparison of drug absorption from various sites of the gastrointestinal tract.

Buccal, sublingual	Stomach and intestine	Rectum
Examples of psychotropics absorbed buccally and sublingually: nicotine chewing gum (Nicorette®) and lorazepam (Ativan®)	Examples of psychotropics ingested (oral dosage forms [solid, liquid]): most psychotropics	Examples of psychotropics absorbed from the rectum: barbiturates and opiate analgesics (suppositories, enemas)
Independent of gastric emptying	Absorption depends upon gastric emptying and intestinal transit time	Independent of gastric emptying
Small area for absorption	Large area of absorption	Small area for absorption
Acceptable to most patients	Acceptable to most patients	Poor patient acceptability
A small amount of drug is likely to be swallowed and lost through GI degradation or, if absorped, hepatic metabolism	Concurrent food ingestion may affect absorption[a]	Dose lost with defecation
After placement (buccal or sublingual), drug enters systemic circulation directly and avoids first-pass hepatic metabolism	Drug enters systemic circulation from hepatic (portal) circulation and, thus, is subject to first-pass hepatic metabolism	Drug may enter portal or systemic circulation depending on placement site in rectum (i.e., high or low)

[a] Absorption may increase or decrease depending on the nature of the food ingested (e.g., alkaline versus acidic) and the particular drug involved. (See Tables 3-3 and 3-4 for additional information. See also Chapter 4, "Administration of Psychotropics".)

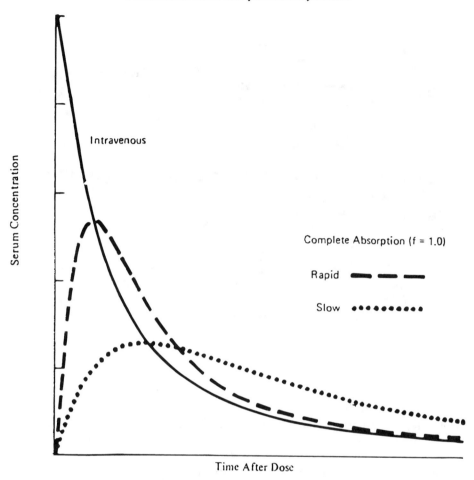

Figure 3-3. Graphical illustration of bioavailability.

This concept is particularly relevant when various methods of administration are used or when "generic brands" are selected, perhaps for cost factors, over "name brands" of the various psychotropic drugs.[8]

Distribution

The volume of distribution (Vd) relates a given *drug concentration* in body fluids to a given *amount of drug* in body fluids. Thus, when the amount of drug in body fluids is divided by the

[8] In this situation, the prescribing psychologist should be concerned about whether the "generic" drug product is identical in bioequivalence to the "name brand" drug product, *not* whether the "generic" is better or worse. A classic example involving this situation occurred several years ago in North America when several patients with congestive heart failure, who had been receiving long-term, chronic drug therapy, suddenly developed toxicity to their heart medication. It was discovered that all of these patients had been switched by their physicians or pharmacists from the name brand of digoxin (i.e., Lanoxin®) tablets to a generic brand of digoxin tablets in order to decrease prescription costs for the patient. As it turned out in these cases, the generic product actually had greater bioavailability (i.e., was a superior pharmaceutical formulation), but, because the patients' dosages had been stabilized with the Lanoxin® brand, all of the patients had experienced an overdosage when switched to the "same" dosage of the generic brand.

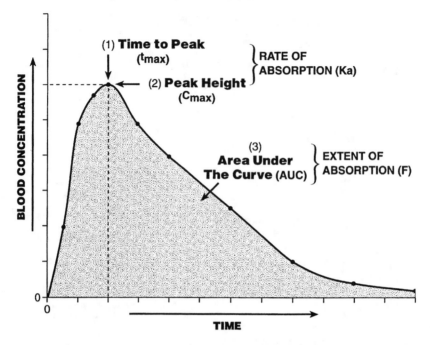

Figure 3-4. Graphical illustration of bioequivalence.

volume of distribution, the measured drug concentration is obtained, assuming that the drug is *equally* distributed throughout all body fluids[9] (e.g., blood, total body water). The volume of distribution represents not a real physiological volume, such as the blood volume or total body water, but rather a theoretical or "apparent" volume of body fluids. Thus, the volume of distribution is often referred to as an "apparent" volume of distribution.

Depending on a number of factors, including a drug's acid dissociation constant (pK_a), degree of plasma protein binding, the partition coefficient into fatty tissues, and the degree of binding to other tissues, the volume of distribution may vary widely. For example, the affinity that a psychotropic drug has for water or fat (i.e., whether it is hydrophilic or lipophilic) can affect distribution in a variety of ways. For example, women at equal body weights generally have proportionately more body fat than men. Therefore, when they consume alcohol, they generally display greater effects with smaller amounts (i.e., at an equal mg/kg dose). This is explained, in part, by the observation that alcohol is relatively hydrophilic and readily distributes into water. Thus, after absorption, the amount of alcohol remaining in the blood of women is relatively large (i.e., the low apparent volume of distribution results in higher blood concentrations), resulting in greater pharmacologic effect.

Output

The output, or elimination, of psychotropic drugs from the body involves *metabolism* and *excretion*. Metabolism occurs primarily within the liver, whereas excretion occurs primarily through the kidneys. The major two kinetic measures for these processes are the *half-life of*

---

[9] Equal distribution of drug throughout all body fluids generally does not occur because of differences in blood flow to various tissues and other related factors such as plasma protein binding and lipid solubility.

elimination and *clearance*, respectively. Before proceeding to a discussion of these measures, the process of metabolism is briefly discussed.

Metabolism

Drug metabolism, the chemical modification of a drug in the body, is commonly referred to as drug biotransformation or drug detoxification. Drug metabolism has two principal functions: (1) to convert drugs to less pharmacologically active metabolites, a homeostatic mechanism that prevents a pharmacologic reaction from continuing indefinitely, and (2) to convert drugs to more water-soluble metabolites (i.e., more polar or ionized compounds) that can be more readily and rapidly excreted.[10] Although most psychotropic drugs undergo significant metabolism, some (e.g., barbital, psilocybin) are excreted by the kidney almost entirely in unchanged form. The psychotropic drugs that undergo hepatic metabolism (e.g., alcohol, benzodiazepines, phenothiazines) may be converted to one or more products (i.e., metabolites). Although most metabolites are less pharmacologically active and more polarized (i.e., possess a greater net electrical charge) than their parent drugs, "active metabolites" (e.g., nordiazepam) possess generally a pharmacologic activity that is equal to, greater than, or different from the parent drug itself (see later discussion in this chapter and Table 3-6; see also Chapter 2, "The Psychotropics," Table 2-4).

Sites of metabolism

Drug metabolism occurs in many tissues and organs, including the blood, brain, gastrointestinal (GI) tract, kidneys, lungs, and skin. However, the most important metabolic reaction, drug oxidation, occurs primarily in the liver. Drug oxidation is mediated through the cytochrome P_{450} hepatic microsomal enzyme system and its subfamilies, P450-2D6 and P450-3A (3A3 and 3A4).[11,12] See related discussion in Chapter 6, "Drug Interactions."

Rates of metabolism

Generally, the rates of metabolism for therapeutic doses of psychotropic drugs are directly proportional to their plasma concentrations. Therefore, their rates of metabolism decrease as plasma drug concentrations decrease. In this situation, Equation 1 applies:

$$\text{Rate of metabolism} = k_m C_p, \tag{1}$$

where k_m = metabolic rate constant in reciprocal time units (e.g., hr^{-1}) and C_p = plasma concentration of drug (e.g., in $\mu g/ml$).

However, Equation 1 is a simplified form of a more complex equation, Equation 2. This equation describes the rate of metabolism more accurately:

---

[10] For example, most metabolites do not undergo tubular reabsorption in the kidney to any great extent because of their polarity and, thus, are excreted in the urine.

[11] The enzyme cytochrome P450 is found in the endoplasmic reticulum (microsomal fraction) of liver cells.

[12] Examples of psychotropics metabolized through the cytochrome P450-3A subfamily include the benzodiazepines, alprazolam (Xanax®), midazolam (Versed®), and triazolam (Halcion®). Examples of psychotropics metabolized through the cytochrome P450-2D6 subfamily include the opiate analgesic codeine and the tricyclic antidepressants desipramine (Norpramin®, Pertofrane®) and nortriptyline (Aventyl®, Pamelor®). The P450-2D6 subfamily possesses genetic polymorphism; the majority of the human population falls into the group of "normal" metabolizers, with a minority falling into a smaller group of "slow" metabolizers.

Table 3-6. Metabolic activation of psychotropics.

Psychotropic	Active metabolite(s)	Pharmacologic action(s) of metabolite and comments
Amitriptyline (Elavil®)	Nortriptyline	Antidepressant
Bupropion (Wellbutrin®)	Hydroxybupropion	Antidepressant
Chloral hydrate (Noctec®)	Trichloroethanol	Hypnotic
Chlordiazepoxide (Librium®)	Desmethylchlordiazepoxide	Anxiolytic; sedative
Chlorpromazine (Thorazine®)	7-hydroxychlorpromazine	Antipsychotic
Codeine	Morphine	Analgesic
Desipramine (Norpamin®)	10-hydroxy-desipramine	Antidepressant
Diazepam (Valium®)	N-desmethyldiazepam	Anxiolytic; sedative
Dopamine (Intropin®)	Norepinephrine	Endogenous amine
Fenfluramine (Pondimin®)	Norfenfluramine	Anorexiant
Fluoxetine (Prozac®)	Norfluoxetine	Antidepressant
Flurazepam (Dalmane®)	Desethyl- and didesethyl-flurazepam	Hypnotic
Glutethimide (Doriden®)	4-hydroxyglutethimide	Hypnotic
Imipramine (Tofranil®)	Desipramine	Antidepressant
Meperidine (Demerol®)	Normeperidine	Analgesic
Mephobarbital (Mebaral®)	Phenobarbital	Sedative; anticonvulsant
Methamphetamine (Desoxyn®)	Amphetamine	CNS stimulant; anorexiant
Methsuximide (Celontin®)	N-desmethylsuximide	Anticonvulsant
Nefazodone (Serzone®)	Hydroxynefazodone	Antidepressant
Nortriptyline (Aventyl®)	10-hydroxy-nortriptyline	Antidepressant
Phendimetrazine (Prelu-2®)	Phenmetrazine	CNS stimulant; anorexiant
Primidone (Mysoline®)	Phenobarbital	Anticonvulsant; sedative
Risperidone (Risperdal®)	9-hydroxy-risperidone	Antipsychotic
Thioridazine (Mellaril®)	Mesoridazine	Antipsychotic
Trimethadione (Tridione®)	Dimethadione	Anticonvulsant

Note. See Chapter 2, "The Psychotropics," Table 2-4, for additional related data regarding the metabolic activation of the benzodiazepines.

$$\text{Rate of metabolism} = \frac{V_{max}C_p}{K_m + C_p}, \qquad (2)$$

where V_{max} is the maximum possible rate of metabolism for a drug, depending on the amount of metabolizing enzyme available, and K_m is a Michaelis constant representing the drug concentration at which the rate of metabolism is half that of the maximum rate. The plasma concentrations (C_p) at therapeutic dose levels of most drugs are much less than the concentration at which K_m occurs, and the enzyme systems are never exhausted. Thus, the value of $K_m + C_p$ approximates that of K_m alone, and Equation 2 can be simplified to Equation 1:

$$\text{Rate of metabolism} = \frac{V_{max}C_p}{K_m} = k_m C_p. \qquad (3)$$

When drugs display this pattern of metabolism, they are said to obey first-order kinetics. Their elimination from the plasma also is first order. In other words, regardless of dose, a certain percentage of the drug present in the body is eliminated per unit time interval (i.e., $\times$ % hr^{-1}).

However, the rate of metabolism of some drugs, including phenytoin (Dilantin®) and other psychotropics (e.g., fluvoxamine [Luvox®], moclobemide [Manerix®]), is dose dependent. These drugs obey what is referred to as dose-dependent, Michaelis–Menten, nonlinear, or zero-order kinetics. When a drug follows zero-order kinetics, a certain amount (as opposed to percentage) of drug is eliminated from the body per unit time (i.e., $\times$ mg hr^{-1}). If blood concentrations of these drugs are high (such as in an acute overdosage), then Equation 2 is applicable. At high blood concentrations of drugs, metabolism is not a first-order process, and observed rates of metabolism and excretion from blood are slower than when blood drug concentrations are in the therapeutic range. The half-life (i.e., the time it takes a drug to fall to one half of its blood concentration) of these drugs also increases because both K_m and C_p, as denoted in Equation 2, are increased at high plasma drug concentrations. The combination of a high blood concentration and a slow rate of drug metabolism and excretion often results in drug toxicity. Some properties of zero- and first-order metabolic processes are listed in Table 3-7.

Metabolic processes affecting the availability of a psychotropic drug
Several processes affect the availability to the systemic circulation of orally ingested drugs, including gastrointestinal metabolism and first-pass (hepatic) metabolism. Each of these processes is discussed.
Gastrointestinal metabolism. Orally ingested drugs may be metabolized during their absorption phase by an enzyme system present in the gastrointestinal epithelium. Gastrointestinal metabolism results in significant quantities of an inactive metabolite and a much reduced amount of the parent drug being made available to the systemic circulation. Sulfate formation is of particular importance. Some drugs are conjugated with sulfate in significant amounts in the intestinal wall. The sulfate conjugate is absorbed but quickly eliminated in the urine.

This process explains why comparatively larger amounts of certain psychotropic drugs, including chlorpromazine (Largactil®, Thorazine®), levodopa (Dopar®), and morphine (MS Contin®), are excreted as pharmacologically inactive sulfate conjugates when they are orally ingested but not when they are intravenously injected. Thus, when comparing the dose of these drugs on a milligram per milligram basis, they are found to be less effective orally than when injected. Intestinal sulfate formation can be reduced significantly if another substance that is sulfated is ingested concomitantly with the drug. For example, vitamin C is sulfated in the GI tract and is, therefore, a competitive inhibitor of intestinal drug sulfation. Significant amounts of various esterases, decarboxylases, and digestive enzymes also are present in the GI tract and contribute to intestinal metabolism.

Table 3-7. Comparison of some properties of zero- and first-order metabolism.

Zero order	First order
$T_{1/2}$ is dependent on dose	$T_{1/2}$ is independent of dose
Metabolic pattern may be influenced by dosage form	Metabolic patterns are independent of dosage form
Drug decline in the body is nonexponential (i.e., decline is at a constant rate, x mg hr^{-1})	Drug decline in the body is exponential (i.e., percentage decline is constant, x % hr^{-1})
Percentage of dose recovered as a particular metabolite changes with respect to dose	Percentage of dose recovered as a particular metabolite is constant for an individual
Competitive inhibition of metabolism is present	Competitive inhibition of metabolism is absent
An abnormal (i.e., curvilinear) dose–response relationship may be observed	A normal (i.e., linear) dose–response relationship is observed

Note. Zero-order kinetics also is referred to as dose-dependent, Michaelis–Menten, or nonlinear kinetics.

Hepatic first-pass effect.   Psychotropic drugs may be absorbed intact from the GI tract. However, immediately after absorption, these drugs are transported to the liver by the portal vein
prior to reaching the systemic circulation. During their passage through the liver, some drugs
are extensively metabolized (and, occasionally, completely metabolized) to pharmacologically
inactive, or significantly less active, products. Thus, for these drugs, significantly reduced
amounts of the active drug reach the systemic circulation for transport to their sites of action.
This process is called the first-pass effect (i.e., the effect of the first pass of the drug through
the liver). The first-pass effect provides one explanation for the observed differences in the
fraction of drug available to the systemic circulation when the same amount of drug is ingested
orally or injected intravenously directly into the general (i.e., systemic) circulation. Examples
of drugs that are subject to extensive first-pass metabolism in humans include lidocaine (Xylo-
caine®), an antidysrhythmic; propranolol (Inderal®), a beta-adrenergic blocker; and sertraline
(Zoloft®), an antidepressant. The first-pass effect can be completely avoided by the intravenous
injection of a drug. Drugs that are administered buccally or sublingually, rectally, transdermally,
or by inhalation, also significantly avoid the hepatic first-pass effect (see Chapter 4, "Administration of Psychotropics").

Metabolic activation.   Some drugs are metabolized to other products that retain the pharmacologic actions of the parent drug. For a few other drugs, it is the metabolite that is pharmacologically active. In some instances (e.g., vitamin D), a metabolic activation reaction is required.
Psychotropics that are metabolized to pharmacologically active products in humans are listed
in Table 3-6.

Toxigenesis.   Some drugs are metabolized in humans to products that are extremely toxic. One
example, in particular, is worthy of comment. Acetaminophen (Tylenol®), a commonly used
nonprescription analgesic/antipyretic, is normally excreted primarily as glucuronide and sulfate
salts. N-hydroxyacetaminophen is a minor metabolite that dehydrates to a quinonoid compound
(N-acetyl-benzoquinoneimine) in the body. This product is normally inactivated by reacting
with liver glutathione. When excessive amounts of acetaminophen are ingested, glutathione stores
become depleted, and the intermediate metabolite then reacts with vital liver cell constituents and
forms coordinate covalent bonds, resulting in cell necrosis. Thus, hepatotoxicity is one of the
dangers of acetaminophen overdosage. The cautious use of acetaminophen, therefore, is advised
for patients who have liver dysfunction, including that associated with chronic alcoholism or
infectious hepatitis.

Excretion

Active drugs and metabolites are excreted from the systemic circulation by different processes
(e.g., excretion in bile, breast milk, expired air, feces, saliva, sweat, and urine) (see Table
3-8). Of these processes, excretion in the urine is by far the most important and is discussed first.

Excretion in the urine

The kidneys are implicated in the elimination of virtually all drugs or drug metabolites among
humans. Four distinct processes appear to be involved in drug excretion into the urine: glomerular
filtration, active tubular secretion, and active and passive reabsorption. These processes are
illustrated in Figure 3-5.

Glomerular filtration.   Arterial blood flows into the glomeruli of the kidneys through an afferent
arteriole. In the glomeruli, plasma fluid and low molecular weight molecules are filtered from
the blood by perfusing across the fenestrated capillaries of Bowman's Capsule. Blood cells and

Table 3-8. Drug excretion.

Excretion pathway	Mechanism	Examples
Bile	Active transport and passive diffusion from blood into the bile	Organic carboxylic and sulfonic acids, other acids (e.g., chlorothiazide [Diuril®]), quaternary bases, ouabain, cardiac glycosides (e.g., digoxin [Lanoxin®]), numerous glucuronides
Breast milk	Active and passive diffusion	Numerous acidic and basic drugs
Expired air	Passive diffusion	Drugs and metabolites with high vapor pressures (e.g., alcohol, guaiacol), gaseous metabolites (e.g., carbon dioxide)
Feces	Biliary excretion	Drugs that are excreted into the bile
Saliva	Active and passive secretory processes	Numerous drugs including the penicillin and tetracycline antibiotics (see also Table 3-9)
Sweat	Passive diffusion	Numerous drugs including the sulfonamide antibiotics
Urine	Glomerular filtration and active tubular secretion	Virtually all non-protein-bound ("free") drugs undergo tubular filtration. "Bound" drugs may undergo tubular secretion (e.g., the antibiotic, dicloxacillin [Dycil®])

large molecules (i.e., those with a molecular weight in excess of 50,000) are not filtered in the normal, undamaged glomerulus. Thus, the urine is virtually protein free, and only free drug (i.e., drug that is not bound to plasma protein) is filtered. The total glomerular filtration for a healthy adult approaches 200 L of fluid per day. However, approximately 99% of this fluid is reabsorbed in the tubular portion of the kidney. The remainder, approximately 1.5 L (or 1 ml/min), is excreted as urine. This fluid reabsorption mechanism results in high urinary concentrations of solutes, including drugs and metabolites, which are less efficiently reabsorbed.

Active tubular secretion. Some drugs (e.g., penicillins, salicylates, thiazide diuretics) and metabolites undergo tubular secretion. This physiological process is termed an active transport process. The drug diffuses against a concentration gradient from efferent arterioles through the tubular membrane into the kidney tubule. Plasma protein binding does not interfere with tubular secretion. However, the process has limited capacity, and drugs may therefore compete with one another for the active carrier (see Chapter 6, "Drug Interactions," for additional discussion).

Active and passive reabsorption. Active and passive reabsorption of drugs and metabolites also occurs in the renal tubules. The former process requires a carrier transport system, whereas the latter depends on the principles of diffusion: concentration gradient between the concentrated urine and blood, pH of urine, and pK_a of drug or metabolite. Lipid-soluble drugs are efficiently reabsorbed by a process of passive reabsorption. Drugs and metabolites that are not lipid soluble, including those that are in ionized form in the urine, are poorly reabsorbed. However, urinary pH can be pharmacologically modified to affect the degree of reabsorption of specific drugs.

Urine pH. The renal clearance of weak acids and bases is significantly influenced by urinary pH. For example, the renal clearance of weak acids (e.g., barbiturates) can be increased if the urine is made alkaline. An alkaline urine results in more of the drug (i.e., weak acids) being

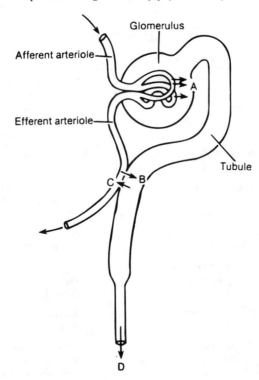

Figure 3-5. Diagrammatic representation of drug excretion by the kidneys. The illustrated functional and structural unit of the kidney composed of the glomerulus and the tubule is known as the nephron. The sites and processes involved are indicated by: A, glomerular filtration; B, active tubular secretion; C, active or passive reabsorption; and D, urinary excretion.

in ionized form. Conversely, the renal clearance of weak acids is decreased in acidic urine because more drug is in the nonionized form. The opposite is true of weak bases (e.g., amphetamine, codeine, imipramine [Tofranil®], meperidine [Demerol®], morphine [M.O.S.®]). Thus, the renal clearance of some drugs can be significantly modified depending on the urine pH. In the clinical context of overdosages (e.g., amphetamine overdosage), changes in urinary pH can be used to promote drug excretion. Common compounds used to alter urinary pH follow.

Manipulation of Urinary pH:
    The following compounds render the urine acidic:

- Ammonium chloride
- Amino acid hydrochloride (HCl) salts (e.g., arginine HCl, lysine HCl)

The following compounds render the urine basic:

- Antacids (e.g., calcium carbonate, sodium bicarbonate)
- Sodium glutamate

Biliary excretion

The liver continually produces bile,[13] which is transported by the bile duct to the gall bladder for storage. Up to 1 L of bile is produced and emptied daily into the duodenum. During the passage of the bile through the bile duct, free exchange of drugs and metabolites to and from the blood occurs. Thus, the bile can be a pathway for the elimination of some psychotropic drugs (e.g., morphine) and their metabolites (e.g., 5-hydroxyphenyl-5-phenylhydantoin [HPPH], the inactive metabolite of phenytoin [Dilantin®]). These drugs and metabolites enter the small intestine and are either reabsorbed into the systemic circulation or excreted in the feces. The former situation is referred to as enterohepatic reabsorption, or recycling. Enterohepatic recycling may continue until metabolism and renal and fecal excretion eventually eliminate the drug completely from the body. Drugs that exhibit enterohepatic recycling may persist in the body for lengthy periods of time.

Salivary excretion

Salivary excretion is not an important route of elimination because most drugs that are present in the saliva are swallowed and pass through to the GI tract, where they are reabsorbed or excreted in the feces. Examples of drugs that are excreted in the saliva are the penicillin and tetracycline antibiotics. However, saliva/plasma drug concentration ratios for some psychotropic drugs (e.g., lithium [Eskalith®, Lithane®], phenytoin [Dilantin®]) are relatively constant. In these instances, drug concentrations in saliva can be used to estimate drug concentrations in plasma. Saliva/plasma ratios have been determined for several drugs. Psychotropics with ratios in excess of 0.1 are identified in Table 3-9.

Excretion in breast milk

Almost all of the drugs that are present in a mother's blood also will be present in her breast milk. However, breast milk concentrations of these drugs will depend on several factors, including the drug's lipid solubility, maternal blood concentration, degree of plasma protein binding, degree of ionization, and molecular weight. Examples of psychotropic drugs excreted in breast milk include alcohol, amphetamines, carbamazepine (Tegretol®), chloral hydrate (Noctec®), and nicotine (Nicoderm®). (For a comprehensive review of this topic and detailed discussion of involved drugs, readers are referred to O'Mara and Nahata [1995] and Pagliaro and Pagliaro [1996].)

Table 3-9. Psychotropics excreted in the saliva.

Psychotropic	Saliva/plasma ratio
Amobarbital (Amytal®)	0.35
Caffeine	0.55
Carbamazepine (Tegretol®)	0.26
Ethosuximide (Zarontin®)	1.04
Lithium (Eskalith®, Lithane®)	2.85
Pentobarbital (Nembutal®)	0.42
Phenobarbital (Luminal®)	0.32
Phenytoin (Dilantin®)	0.11
Primidone (Mysoline®)	0.97

[13] Bile is a thick, viscid fluid secretion of the liver. It contains bilirubin, cholesterol, and other organic and inorganic substances. Bile both aids digestion of nutrients and stimulates peristalsis of the intestines.

Excretion through perspiration
Numerous drugs and other substances have been detected in perspiration. Examples are arsenic, benzoic acid, iron, lead, mercury, salicylic acid, sulfonamides, thiamine, and urea. However, this process of excretion is not a significant mechanism of elimination for any of the psychotropic drugs.

Excretion through the lungs
Volatile solvents and inhalants (e.g., gasoline, model airplane glue) and their metabolites (carbon dioxide) are excreted into expired air. A few drugs, such as some anesthetic gases and alcohol,[14] are also eliminated, at least in part, through the lungs.

Related pharmacokinetic concepts

Two pharmacokinetic concepts, elimination half-life and clearance, are used to mathematically model the factors of input, distribution, and output. These two concepts are briefly discussed.

Elimination half-life
The elimination half-life ($T_{1/2}$) can be simply defined as the amount of time it takes a drug concentration to "fall" to one half of its initial or current blood level (Figure 3-6).[15] The concept of half-life of elimination is particularly useful in determining (1) how long it will take to achieve steady-state blood levels, and, therefore, optimal therapeutic (or toxic) effect at a constant dosage, and (2) how long a drug remains in the body following its discontinuation. For example,

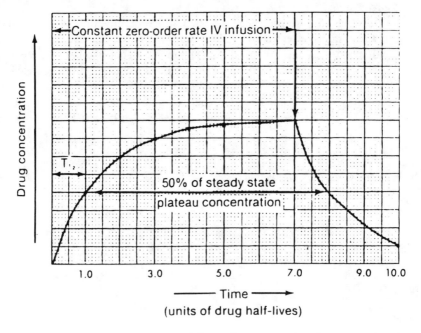

Figure 3-6. Relationship between $T_{1/2}$ and time to drug concentration plateau at steady state.

[14] This is the basis for operation of the "breathalyzer."
[15] It should be noted that the discussion here and throughout the remainder of this chapter may not always apply to drugs that display dose-dependent or capacity-limited kinetics. See earlier discussion.

if a drug were discontinued, it would take one half-life of elimination, by definition, for the blood level (plasma or serum concentration) of the drug to decrease to 50%. During the time period of an additional half-life of elimination, the blood level would again fall by 50% (i.e., 50% of the 50% remaining, or a total of 25%). During the time period of the third half-life of elimination, the blood level would continue to fall by 50% (i.e., 50% of the 25% remaining, or a total of 12.5%). During the time period equivalent to these three half-lives, the total blood concentration of the drug would have decreased by 87.5% (i.e., 50% + [50% of the remaining 50%] + [50% of the remaining 25%] = 87.5%). Continuing with this process, it becomes apparent that virtually 100% of the drug will be eliminated from the body after approximately *five* half-lives of elimination.[16] Most of the antipsychotics have long half-lives of elimination (more than 24 hours) and, thus, can be dosed once daily. However, other psychotropics do not (e.g., methylphenidate [Ritalin®]), and they require dosing throughout the day in order to maintain therapeutic serum concentrations and associated psychotropic effects (see Chapter 2, "The Psychotropics").

Although a knowledge of the half-life of elimination is necessary for prescribing dosing regimens, it is rarely a good measure of changes in blood concentration and efficacy of psychotropic pharmacotherapy. For example, the half-life of elimination of a drug may remain unchanged for patients who have congestive heart failure. However, the volume of distribution often decreases (see "effect of disease") and, consequently, the blood concentration of the drug increases in proportion to the decrease in volume of distribution (unless the dose is appropriately decreased). The pharmacokinetic concept of clearance has been found to be more clinically useful in this and similar situations.

Clearance
Clearance[17] essentially represents the product of the volume of distribution and the rate constant of elimination, where the rate constant of elimination is defined as 0.693 (i.e., the natural logarithm of 2) divided by the half-life of elimination. Changes in clearance and volume of distribution appear to be the independent variables in the relationship and can be correlated to specific physiologic conditions in the body. Changes in the rate constant of elimination or half-life appear to be dependent variables influenced by changes in independent variables.

Whereas, as previously noted, the volume of distribution does not have an actual physiologic correlate, clearance is a measure that is much more clearly related to actual physiologic processes. For example, for a psychotropic drug for which the renal clearance approximates the glomerular filtration rate (GFR), the kidney has, at every minute, the ability to completely remove the drug, in essence, from 100 ml of plasma (i.e., as represented by the dotted area in Figure 3-7).
Renal clearance. Renal clearance (CL_R) is usually calculated by the top equation in Figure 3-7, that is, the rate of drug elimination in the urine, $\Delta U/\Delta t$ (i.e., the amount excreted unchanged in the urine over any given time period), divided by the midpoint plasma concentration (Cp_{mid}) during that time period. This midpoint plasma concentration is, in fact, supposed to represent the average plasma concentration during the time of drug elimination. The average plasma concentration may be more accurately represented as the area under the plasma concentration time curve, AUC (i.e., the amount of drug available to the systemic circulation), during the time interval divided by the time interval (Δt), as represented in the second equation in Figure 3-7. Eliminating the change in time (i.e., Δt) from the numerator and denominator of the second

---

[16] Correspondingly, it can be shown that at a *constant* dosage regimen, it takes approximately *five* half-lives to achieve steady state (see related discussion for additional details).

[17] Clearance has been defined as a hypothetical volume of blood from which a drug is completely cleared per unit of time (e.g., "x ml/min").

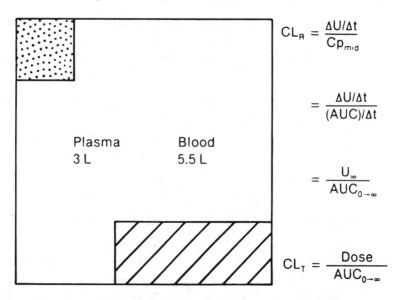

$$CL_R = \frac{\Delta U / \Delta t}{Cp_{mid}}$$

$$= \frac{\Delta U / \Delta t}{(AUC) / \Delta t}$$

$$= \frac{U_\infty}{AUC_{0 \to \infty}}$$

$$CL_T = \frac{Dose}{AUC_{0 \to \infty}}$$

Figure 3-7. Hypothetical plasma or blood volume, where dotted area represents fraction of volume cleared of drug per minute by renal mechanisms (e.g., 100 ml/min for renal clearance measured with respect to drug concentrations in plasma) and the area containing diagonal lines represents fraction of volume cleared of drug per minute by all elimination mechanisms (e.g., 300 ml/min). Equations demonstrate the relationship between renal and total body clearances.

equation yields the result that the renal clearance is, in fact, the amount of drug eliminated over any time period divided by the area under the plasma concentration time curve during that time period. The third equation in Figure 3-7 allows the time period discussed to be the entire time necessary to describe the course of drug disposition, the total amount of drug excreted unchanged in the urine (U_x) divided by the total area under the plasma concentration time curve ($AUC_{0 \to \infty}$).

Total plasma clearance. Whereas renal clearance represents that fraction of the total plasma (or blood) pool that is cleared by the kidney per unit time, the total plasma (or blood) clearance represents a hypothetical volume of the plasma (or blood) pool that is cleared per unit time by all elimination mechanisms.[18] Thus, it may readily be seen that total clearance (CL_T) differs from renal clearance (CL_R) only in that the total dose appears in the numerator of the equation rather than simply the amount eliminated by renal excretion.

Relationship between clearance and physiologic processes. In Figure 3-7, the total plasma clearance is 300 ml/min (i.e., the portion of the figure represented by diagonal lines). In this example, renal clearance would represent 100 ml/min, while other processes of elimination, most likely hepatic metabolism, would be responsible for 200 ml/min. Now it is possible to see that clearance measurements, unlike volumes of distribution, have real limitations related to physiologic parameters.

Hepatic clearance can never be any faster than blood flow to the liver, because the drug must be delivered to the liver before it can be metabolized and eliminated. Thus, if blood levels were measured, the maximum hepatic clearance rate would be approximately 1.5 L/min. Likewise, the maximum renal clearance would be approximately 1.2 L/min, the average rate of blood flow to the kidneys. For a drug that is eliminated only by renal excretion, the maximum

---

[18] Sometimes referred to as total body clearance (TBC), this process is the resultant sum of renal clearance and nonrenal clearance. Although some (generally small) amounts of drugs can be eliminated from various body organs (e.g., skin, lungs) in unchanged form (see earlier discussion), nonrenal clearance is predominantly accounted for by metabolic clearance (which, in turn, is predominantly accounted for by hepatic clearance).

clearance would be equal to the kidneys' glomerular filtration rate (i.e., approximately 120 ml/min).[19]

Table 3-10 presents clearance values for hepatic metabolism and renal excretion for four representative psychotropics.[20] Naloxone (Narcan®) and chlordiazepoxide (Librium®) represent psychotropics that are cleared almost exclusively by hepatic metabolism. However, there is a large difference in their clearance values that, in fact, represents different mechanisms. The total body clearance of naloxone (~1,400 ml/min) approaches the maximum clearance possible (i.e., naloxone clearance is a function of blood flow to the liver), whereas the total body clearance of chlordiazepoxide (~35 ml/min) would probably be independent of blood flow and is generally designated as a drug showing capacity-limited metabolism. Increases in metabolic enzymes by means of induction (see Chapter 6, "Drug Interactions") can be expected to lead to changes in chlordiazepoxide clearance but not necessarily to changes in naloxone clearance because naloxone's total body clearance is already much closer to its physiologic maximum. However, changes in blood flow rate, as occurs in various medical disorders (e.g., congestive heart failure), may lead to changes in naloxone clearance but not changes in chlordiazepoxide clearance. In contrast, lithium (Eskalith®, Lithane®) is a psychotropic cleared predominantly by renal excretion. Thus, changes in renal function have a marked effect on lithium clearance. Primidone (Mysoline®) is intermediate, with approximately half of its total body clearance mediated by hepatic metabolism and half by renal excretion.

Relationship between clearance and half-life

Elimination half-lives are not good predictors of clearance. It is important to consider the differences between clearance and half-life when attempting to understand the underlying mechanisms for the effect of a medical disorder (or other factors) on drug disposition (distribution and elimination). For example, the half-life of diazepam (Valium®) appears to increase with the age of the patient. Therefore, it could be speculated that the ability of the liver to metabolize diazepam decreases as a function of age. However, when clearance is plotted versus age, it becomes readily apparent that there is no significant age effect on hepatic metabolism (as denoted by the virtually horizontal line through the data points). The increased half-lives actually result from an age effect on the volume of distribution. The hepatic processes responsible for

Table 3-10. Selected hepatic, renal, and total body clearances and half-lives for four representative psychotropics in a healthy 70-kg adult male.

Psychotropic	Hepatic clearance (ml/min)	Renal clearance (ml/min)	Total body clearance (ml/min)	Half-life (average)
Chlordiazepoxide (Librium®)	35	Negligible	35	10 hr
Lithium (Lithane®)	Negligible	22	22	2 hr
Naloxone (Narcan®)	1,400	Negligible	1,400	1 hr
Primidone (Mysoline®)	35	35	70	8 hr

[19] When we discuss actual physiologic clearances and attempt to relate them to body processes, it is important to deal with blood clearances. Plasma clearances may be converted to blood clearances when the hematocrit and the partition of the drug between the red blood cells and the plasma are known.

[20] Recall that other body organs also can contribute to clearance. For example, many of the anesthetic gases are eliminated, generally in unchanged form, through the lungs. Alcohol, to a much lesser extent, is another example of a drug cleared through the lungs (note that this is the basis for determining blood alcohol concentration levels as measured by the Breathalyzer® test among possibly impaired motorists).

metabolizing diazepam are fairly constant over the age ranges studied (see later discussion concerning "effect of age" and Table 3-15).

Application

With a basic understanding of pharmacokinetic principles, psychologists can better prescribe and monitor psychotropic pharmacotherapy for their patients. In regard to dosing selected psychotropics, most pharmacokinetic adjustments for a patient can be made according to one simple relationship, rate in = rate out, and related equations.

Calculations at steady state:

$$\text{Rate in} = \text{Rate out} \tag{4}$$

When this simple equation is applied to the clinical situation for a particular patient for whom a clinical psychologist wants to maintain a certain average plasma level ($C_{p\ ave}$), Equation 4 may be converted to Equation 5.

$$\frac{F \times \text{Dose}}{\tau} = \text{Clearance} \times C_{p\ ave}, \tag{5}$$

where F (availability) is the fraction of a dose available to the systemic circulation, τ (tau) is the dosing interval, and $C_{p\ ave}$ is the average desired plasma drug concentration.

For Drug A, assume that the desired $C_{p\ ave} = 8$ µg/ml, and assume clearance = 60 ml/min.

$$\frac{F \times \text{Dose}}{\tau} = 60 \text{ ml/min} \times 8 \text{ µg/ml}$$

$$= 480 \text{ µg/min} = 28.8 \text{ mg/hr.}$$

The example calculation given in Equation 5 could be for a patient who has normal renal function and for whom an average Drug A plasma level of 8 µg/ml is desired. The "rate in" will equal clearance multiplied by this steady-state level, that is, 480 µg/min, or 28.8 mg/hr. Because the availability (F) of intravenous Drug A is, by definition, equal to 1.0, the clinical psychologist then may choose the dosing scheme at multiples of approximately 30 mg/hr. Thus, the clinical psychologist may choose to dose the psychotropic drug six times a day and, therefore, would prescribe 120 mg every 4 hours or dose the drug three times a day and prescribe 240 mg every 8 hours depending on such factors as the indication for use and half-life.

Although these equations are most useful for reaching a given average plasma level,[21] it is important to realize that the change in the dosing interval will cause the plasma level time curve at steady state (i.e., after five half-lives at the same dosage) to have *different* maximum (peak) and minimum (trough) values depending on the dosing interval, even though the *average*

---

[21] In their simplest form, these equations can be converted to provide the following equation indicating that the average plasma concentration at steady state is equal to the dose per interval of time divided by total clearance:

$$\text{i.e.,} \left[C_{p\ ave}^{ss} = \frac{(F \times \text{Dose})/\tau}{CL_T} \right].$$

level will always be 8 μg/ml. If the prescribing psychologist chose to infuse Drug A at a continuous rate of 480 μg/min, then the level of 8 μg/ml would be maintained continuously. However, if one of the other dosing schedules suggested (e.g., 4- or 8-hour intervals) were chosen, then the maximum and minimum levels would differ.

A simplified way of calculating these maximum ($C_{p\,max}^{ss}$) and minimum ($C_{p\,min}^{ss}$) values is given in Equations 6 and 7.[22]

Maximum and minimum levels at steady state (assuming absorption is much faster than elimination, or input>>output):

$$C_{p\,max}^{ss} = \frac{F \times Dose/Vd}{\text{Fraction lost in a dosing interval}} \tag{6}$$

$$= \frac{240 \text{ mg}/14 \text{ L}}{0.94} = 18.3 \text{ μg/ml}$$

$$C_{p\,min}^{ss} = C_{p\,max}^{ss} \times \text{Fraction remaining after dosing interval} \tag{7}$$

$$= 18.3 \text{ μg/ml} \times 0.06 = 1.1 \text{ μg/ml}.$$

The denominator of Equation 6, the fraction lost in a dosing interval, may be easily calculated when the half-life is known. For example, an 8-hour dosing interval was chosen for Drug A. Assuming a half-life of 2 hours, 50% of the amount of drug in the body would be lost in the first 2 hours after the last dose, 75% in 4 hours, 88% in 6 hours, 94% in 8 hours, and 97% in 10 hours. Correspondingly, only 6% of the total amount of drug in the body would remain at the end of the 8-hour dosing interval. Thus, with this dosing regimen, a maximum level of 18.3 μg/ml and a minimum level of 1.1 μg/ml would be achieved. This dosing schedule would probably not be a good one for this patient because, during each 8-hour dosing interval, high, potentially toxic levels would be maintained for more than 1 hour, and levels possibly below the minimum effective concentration would be expected over 4 hours. A possibly better choice might be to dose 120 mg every 4 hours. In this dosing schedule, the fraction of drug lost in a dosing interval would be $\frac{3}{4}$, and maximum and minimum levels at steady state would be 11.4 and 2.9 μg/ml, respectively.[23] However, in either case, it is important to note that the *average* level is still 8 μg/ml.

In this example, the fraction of drug eliminated from the body was derived from the simple algorithm that 50% of the amount of drug remaining to be eliminated is eliminated within the time frame of each successive half-life. Thus, as previously noted, it takes approximately five half-lives after the discontinuation of pharmacotherapy for a drug to be virtually entirely (i.e., 97%) eliminated from the body.[24] The same algorithm also applies to drug accumulation within

---

[22] These equations assume that absorption is much faster than elimination and that the system comes quickly into distribution equilibrium. These assumptions are readily met for intravenously administered psychotropics.

[23] The rational selection of dosing intervals requires a knowledge not only of the maximum (i.e., peak) and minimum (i.e., trough) blood levels to be obtained but also of the minimum therapeutic and minimum toxic blood levels associated with the particular drug (see later discussion regarding "therapeutic drug monitoring").

[24] This observation has significant clinical application in cases of drug overdosage or when a more rapid therapeutic effect is desired. For example, when the SSRIs (see Table 3-11) are compared, it is clear that fluoxetine takes the longest amount of time to reach steady state and to be eliminated from the body upon discontinuation of pharmacotherapy. Thus, if these factors were a concern for a particular patient, a different SSRI might be selected, *not* on the basis of efficacy or toxicity but on the basis of its significantly shorter half-life of elimination.

Table 3-11. Comparative pharmacokinetic parameters of the SSRIs.

SSRI	F (oral)	Urinary excretion[a] (%)	Active metabolite	T_{max} (hr)	Protein binding (%)	Clearance (ml/min/ kg)	$T_{1/2}$ (average) (hr)
Fluoxetine (Prozac®)	0.8	<2	Norfluoxe-tine ($T_{1/2}$ = 9 *days*)	6–8	94	10	48
Fluvoxamine (Luvox®)[b]	0.94	<5	None	2–8	77		20
Paroxetine (Paxil®)	0.64	<2	None	4–5	95	10	24
Sertraline (Zoloft®)	0.44[c]	<5	None	6–8	>98	38	26
Venlafaxine (Effexor®)	0.9	5	0-desmethyl-venlafaxine ($T_{1/2}$ = 11 hours)	2	<35	22	5

Note. Average values and ranges are provided for comparative purposes. These data are based on population studies. Thus, parameters for individual patients *may* be significantly different, particularly if they happen to be among the population outliers.
[a] Urinary excretion, in this context, is the amount of parent drug eliminated in unchanged form in the urine.
[b] Fluvoxamine is subject to zero-order kinetics. See Table 3-7.
[c] Food increases the oral bioavailability of sertraline by approximately 40%.

the body and a plateau that occurs with constant rates of IV infusion or multiple dosing by oral and other methods of administration.

The relationship between frequency of dosing and minimum/maximum plasma concentrations is illustrated in Figure 3-8. In this figure, it can be seen that, after five half-lives, all three curves (i.e., dosing regimens) yield the *same* average plasma concentration (i.e., the steady-state plasma concentration). However, these curves differ significantly from one another in relation to their observed minimum and maximum plasma concentrations.

Whereas constant IV infusion of a drug provides a constant plasma concentration once the steady-state level has been achieved, less frequent dosing intervals (i.e., Curve 2) have the

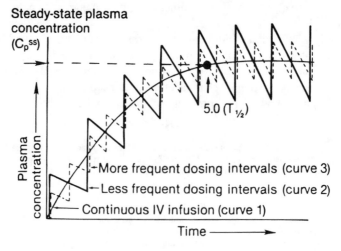

Figure 3-8. Relationship between frequency of dosing interval, tau (τ), and minimum/maximum plasma concentrations.

greatest variability in minimum and maximum plasma concentrations. As dosing intervals become more frequent (i.e., Curve 3), this variability decreases geometrically. For example, if the dosing interval for Curve 3 is half of that for Curve 2 (i.e., 120 mg every 4 hours versus 240 mg every 8 hours for the Drug A example given earlier), then the average minimum and maximum plasma concentrations would be closer to the actual steady-state concentration.

As noted, it generally takes approximately five half-lives to reach steady-state drug concentration. However, when full, rapid pharmacologic action is required, such as occurs in emergency situations (e.g., calming a violent schizophrenic patient, controlling seizures), a "loading" dose (e.g., of an antipsychotic or anticonvulsant, respectively) also can be prescribed to rapidly achieve steady-state levels.[25]

Therapeutic drug monitoring

Pharmacodynamics is concerned with the time course and intensity of drug response in relation to blood levels (concentrations) (see Chapter 1, "Introduction to the Basic Principles of Pharmacotherapy"). With the basic equations presented in this chapter, clinical psychologists can determine appropriate drug dosing schedules for their patients using the concept of therapeutic drug monitoring (TDM) (i.e., a specific steady-state concentration that is believed to be effective would be the objective of the dosage regimen suggested).[26] Therapeutic drug monitoring has many relevant clinical applications (see Table 3-12).

While a powerful concept for clinical psychologists, the clinical application of TDM is limited to those drugs that show a significant positive correlation between serum concentration and pharmacologic or toxicologic response. TDM has been demonstrated to be particularly useful and to provide valuable therapeutic data in conditions that do *not* have well-defined and easily measured clinical end points and when drugs have a narrow therapeutic index, possess a large degree of interindividual variability, and can be assayed and have their blood levels

Table 3-12. Indications for a drug blood concentration assay in clinical context.

Absence of therapeutic response
• Altered absorption
• Altered clearance ⎫
• Altered elimination ⎬ assist in the "rule out" of
• Patient's inability to manage his or her ⎭ possible causes
  pharmacotherapy
Drug overdosage/suspected toxicity
• Monitor blood levels for toxicity and observe
  for efficacy of overdosage treatment measures
Suspected drug interactions
• Confirmation of interaction and mechanism
Therapeutic confirmation
• To confirm that dosage selected has resulted in
  concentrations within the established therapeutic
  blood concentration range (see Table 3-13)

---

[25] A loading dose is simply a higher, generally two to three times higher, than normal dose that is administered once upon the initiation of pharmacotherapy. It is used in order to achieve the desired pharmacologic effect more rapidly without having to wait the time interval equivalent of five half-lives at a constant dosage.

[26] Note that steady state must be achieved (i.e., the drug absorption and distribution phases are complete) for the TDM concept to be appropriately applied.

determined in a rapid and reliable manner. Table 3-13 lists those psychotropics that meet these TDM criteria and presents their desired corresponding concentration ranges.

Effect of age

Age affects pharmacokinetics and pharmacodynamics as a result of associated physiologic changes. While these changes can be considered as occurring along a continuum, they are most readily apparent at either end of the age continuum (i.e., among the very young and the very old).

Several age-dependent physiologic changes have been identified that influence pharmacokinetic parameters among neonates, infants, and young children. These include changes to the following: bile acids, enzyme capacity, extracellular water, rate of gastric emptying, gastric pH, glomerular filtration rate, intestinal motility, protein binding, renal tubular secretion, and total body water. The exact nature of these changes, the specific pediatric age group(s) affected, the pharmacokinetic consequences, and examples of affected drugs can be found in Table 3-14.

Similarly, for those individuals at the opposite end of the age continuum (i.e., the elderly), many of the same physiologic changes also affect pharmacokinetic parameters and, consequently, drug dosage and effect.[27] See Table 3-15 for a detailed list of age-dependent physiologic changes among elderly people and related pharmacokinetic consequences. It is both interesting and clinically significant that, although liver mass and enzyme metabolizing activity are generally

Table 3-13. Therapeutic drug monitoring: Therapeutic blood concentration range for selected psychotropics.

Drug	Therapeutic blood concentration range[a]	
Amitriptyline (Elavil®)	60–220 ng/ml	(250–900 nmol/L)[b]
Carbamazepine (Tegretol®)	4–12 µg/ml	(17–50 µmol/L)
Clomipramine (Anafranil®)		(300–1,000 nmol/L)
Desipramine (Norpramine®, Pertofrane®)		(430–800 nmol/L)
Doxepin (Sinequan®)		(500–900 nmol/L)
Ethosuximide (Zarontin®)	40–100 µg/ml	(280–710 µmol/L)
Imipramine (Tofranil®)	175–350 ng/ml	(550–1,015 nmol/L)[c]
Lithium (Lithane®)	0.3–1.5 mEq/L	(0.3–1.5 mmol/L)
Maprotiline (Ludiomil®)		(200–800 nmol/L)
Nortriptyline (Aventyl®, Pamelor®)	50–150 ng/ml	(150–495 nmol/L)
Phenobarbital (Luminal®)	15–40 µg/ml	(65–172 µmol/L)
Phenytoin (Dilantin®)	10–20 µg/ml	(40–80 µmol/L)
Primidone (Mysoline®)	6–12 µg/ml	(27–55 µmol/L)[d]
Protriptyline (Triptil®, Vivactil®)	100–200 ng/ml	(350–700 nmol/L)
Trimipramine (Surmontil®)		(500–800 nmol/L)
Valproic Acid (Depakene®)	50–100 µg/ml	(350–700 µmol/L)

[a] Optimal assaying time for these psychotropics is during steady state and immediately before the next dose (i.e., at "trough" concentrations).
[b] Concentration range for amitriptyline plus its active metabolite, nortriptyline.
[c] This concentration range includes parent drug and active metabolite.
[d] Primidone is metabolized, in part, to phenobarbital.

[27] Although the involved physiologic parameters (e.g., kidney function) may have similar appearing changes (e.g., decreased function) and consequences (e.g., increased half-life of elimination) among the young and the old, the reasons for the changes are usually quite different. Among neonates, infants, and young children, the noted changes are due primarily to immaturity of body organ systems, while, among elderly individuals, the noted changes are due primarily to loss of functional capacity of the body organ systems that is a consequence of the normal aging process (a process that can be further exacerbated by injury or disease).

Table 3-14. Age-dependent physiologic changes among neonates, infants, and young children *and related pharmacokinetic consequences.*

Physiologic change	Age group(s) affected	Pharmacokinetic consequence(s)	Example drugs[a]
Absorption			
↑ gastric pH (i.e., ↓ acid secretion)	Neonates and infants	↑ F of basic drugs;	Basic drug: penicillin G
		↓ F of acidic drugs	Acidic drug: **phenobarbital**
↓ gastric emptying; ↓ intestinal motility	Neonates and infants to 8 months of age	Variable effects depending on the drug	↑ F: ampicillin ↑ F: penicillin G ↓ F: acetaminophen ↓ F: **phenobarbital** ↓ F: **phenytoin**
↓ bile acids	Neonates	↓ F	Vitamin E
Distribution			
↑ total body water (TBW); ↑ extracellular water (ECW)	Neonates and infants	↑ Vd	Aminoglycosides Ampicillin Theophylline Ticarcillin
↓ protein binding	Neonates	↑ Vd ↑ free drug concentration	**Phenobarbital** **Phenytoin** Theophylline Warfarin
Metabolism			
↓ hepatic enzyme activity (capacity)	Neonates and infants (to 3 months of age)	↑ $T_{1/2}$ elimination ↓ Cl	↓ glucoronidation: chloramphenicol ↓ hydroxylation: **amobarbital** lidocaine **phenytoin**
↑ hepatic enzyme activity (capacity)	Children (1 to 12 years of age)	↓ $T_{1/2}$ elimination ↑ Cl	Theophylline (increased rate of methylation to caffeine)
Excretion			
↓ glomerular filtration rate (GFR)	Neonates and infants (to 6 months of age)	↓ Renal clearance; ↑ $T_{1/2}$ elimination	Aminoglycosides Ampicillin Digoxin
↓ renal tubular secretion	Neonates and infants	↓ Renal clearance; ↑ $T_{1/2}$ elimination	Furosemide Penicillins Sulfonamides

[a] Psychotropics are indicated in boldface.
[b] Protein binding is decreased as a result of the reduced binding capacity of albumin among neonates. Albumin is the principal plasma protein to which drugs bind.

reduced among elderly people, the capacity of the aged liver to metabolize most drugs does *not* significantly change.

Effect of disease

Studies in pharmacokinetics have been concerned with the changes brought about in drug input, distribution, and output among patients who have been diagnosed with particular medical

Table 3-15. Age-dependent physiologic changes among elderly people *and related* pharmacokinetic consequences.

Physiologic change	Pharmacokinetic consequences	Example drugs
Absorption		
↑ gastric pH (i.e., ↓ acid secretion)	↑ F of basic drugs; ↓ F of acidic drugs	Basic drug: penicillin G Acidic drug: **phenobarbital**
↓ gastric emptying; ↓ intestinal motility	Variable effects depending on the drug	↑ F: ampicillin ↑ F: penicillin G ↓ F: acetaminophen ↓ F: **phenobarbital** F: **phenytoin**
Distribution		
↓ total body water (TBW); ↓ intracellular water (ICW)	↓ Vd	Lithium
↓ body weight, including vital organs	↓ Vd	Most drugs, including the **psychotropics**
↓ lean body mass;	↑ Vd for fat soluble drugs;	Fat soluble drugs: **sedative hypnotics**
↑ adipose tissue	↓ Vd for water soluble drugs	Water soluble drugs: **Lithium**
↓ cardiac output	↓ Vd	Furosemide Lidocaine
↓ protein binding[a]	↑ Vd ↑ free drug concentration	**Phenobarbital** **Phenytoin** Theophylline Warfarin
Excretion		
↓ glomerular filtration rate (GFR) ↓ renal blood flow (RBF)	↓ renal clearance; ↑ $T_{1/2}$ elimination	Aminoglycosides Ampicillin Digoxin **Lithium** Procainamide
↓ renal tubular secretion	↓ renal clearance; ↑ $T_{1/2}$ elimination	Furosemide Penicillins Sulfonamides

Note. Modified from Ritschel (1983). Psychotropics are indicated in boldface.
[a] Protein binding is decreased as a result of reduced albumin production by the liver. Albumin is the principal plasma protein to which drugs bind.

disorders. One of the initial well-controlled studies in this area was carried out by Thomson and coworkers (1973), who studied the disposition of lidocaine in normal people and those who had congestive heart failure, renal failure, or liver failure (alcoholic cirrhosis). Figure 3-9 depicts the plasma concentration time curves for lidocaine following 50-mg doses by rapid intravenous injection (i.e., less than 5 minutes) among seven patients who had heart failure. These values are compared with average values found for normal subjects who did not have heart failure and who were administered the same dose. The plasma concentration levels of lidocaine among the heart failure patients are significantly greater than those for the normal subjects. The volume of distribution among the heart failure patients is significantly less than that found among the normal subjects. Both of these effects are probably related to the decreased cardiac output associated with congestive heart failure. That is, the drug distributes less readily to remote

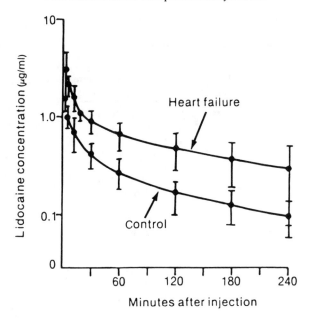

Figure 3-9. Blood concentrations of lidocaine following a 50-mg IV injection of lidocaine among subjects who have, and do not have, heart failure.

portions of the body when the cardiac output is decreased, thereby decreasing the volume available for drug disposition.

It is important to realize that when the volume of distribution decreases by approximately 40%, as in cases of heart failure, the blood levels will increase by that percentage. In addition, the clearance of the drug, which apparently approaches blood flow rate, is decreased because the blood flow to the clearing organs, the liver or kidneys, is decreased in heart failure. The decrease in volume of distribution and the decrease in clearance appear to counteract each other for this particular drug so that the apparent half-life of lidocaine is the same for patients who have heart failure and for those who do not. In contrast, the volume of distribution for the patients with liver failure is greater than that found for patients who do not. However, in spite of the increased volume, clearance decreases, probably because of a decrease in the ability of the liver to metabolize the drug. Although there is an increase in volume of distribution, the decrease in clearance is more substantial. Thus, the half-life increases for lidocaine among the patients who have liver failure.[28]

Examples of medical disorders that may affect the relationship of dosage schedules to the effects seen with particular psychotropics are presented in Table 3-16. An awareness of the effects of listed medical disorders will enable clinical psychologists, on the basis of clearance concepts, to predict the dosage regimens for attaining the target blood levels listed in Table 3-13.

[28] The relationship between clearance and half-life of elimination may be clarified by considering the following equation:

$$T_{1/2} = \frac{0.693 \times Vd}{CL_T}$$

Thus, if the volume of distribution remains constant, the half-life of elimination and total body clearance are inversely related to each other (i.e., as one increases, the other decreases).

Table 3-16. Examples of medical disorders that may affect the pharmacokinetics of some psychotropics.

	Medical disorder		
Psychotropic	Renal failure (e.g., uremia)	Hepatic failure (e.g., cirrhosis)	Hypoalbuminemia (e.g., nephrotic syndrome)
Alprazolam (Xanax®)		↑ protein binding ↓ clearance ↑ half-life	
Chlordiazepoxide (Librium®)		↓ protein binding ↓ clearance ↑ volume of distribution ↑ half-life	
Fluoxetine (Prozac®)		↓ clearance ↑ half-life	
Meperidine (Demerol®)	↓ protein binding ↓ clearance ↑ half-life	↓ clearance ↑ half-life	
Nordiazepam[a]	↓ protein binding	↓ clearance ↓ half-life	
Phenytoin (Dilantin®)	↓ protein binding ↑ volume of distribution ↑ clearance	↓ clearance	↓ protein binding ↑ volume of distribution ↑ clearance
Triazolam (Halcion®)		↓ clearance ↑ half-life	
Valproic acid (Depakene®)	↓ protein binding	↓ protein binding ↑ volume of distribution ↑ half-life	

Note. This table is not meant to be exhaustive but, rather, illustrative. Other conditions (e.g., obesity, pregnancy) also may cause variability in the kinetics of the psychotropics.
[a] Nordiazepam (desmethyldiazepam) is an active metabolite of chlordiazepoxide (Librium®), clorazepate (Tranxene®), diazepam (Valium®), and prazepam (Centrex®).

Summary

An overview of the mathematic modeling and use of pharmacokinetics for determining dosage schedules for prescribing and monitoring psychotropic pharmacotherapy has been presented. Realizing that a target blood level can be maintained if the rate of "drug in" equals the rate of "drug out," clinical psychologists may readily prescribe the appropriate dosage regimen for a particular drug for a particular patient. Using the concepts presented here, and with a knowledge of the changes in the physiologic processes affecting drug clearance as a function of age, gender, genetics, disease, and other factors, clinical psychologists will be able to prescribe therapeutic dosage schedules and make appropriate dosage adjustments that will help to maintain target blood levels appropriate for their patients. With these abilities, clinical psychologists can expect to provide optimal pharmacotherapy as an adjunct to psychotherapy with a minimum of adverse and toxic effects.

4

Administration of Psychotropics

Introduction

Adjunctive pharmacotherapy for the symptomatic management of psychological disorders may not be required by all patients who access psychological services. However, it will be required by selected patients, including those who have been diagnosed with anxiety disorders; attention-deficit/hyperactivity disorder (ADHD); depressive disorders, including bipolar disorders; eating disorders (i.e., obesity); schizophrenia or other psychotic disorders; sleep disorders (insomnia); and substance-related disorders, including alcohol and opiate withdrawal, maintenance of abstinence from alcohol use, and tobacco smoking cessation. Prescribing and monitoring appropriate adjunctive pharmacotherapy, including the monitoring of therapeutic response and adverse drug reactions, are essential aspects of the provision of optimal adjunctive pharmacotherapy for individual patients.

Prescribing psychologists also are responsible for ensuring that their patients, or others who may be involved with a patient's mental health care (e.g., family members, residential staff, school personnel), understand the correct administration of prescribed pharmacotherapy, including the safe care and storage of dosage forms. Attention to these aspects of adjunctive pharmacotherapy will help to ensure the achievement of optimal therapeutic benefit with a minimum of adverse drug reactions and overdosages or accidental poisonings. Patients who require short-term or long-term pharmacotherapy must have an adequate understanding of the administration and storage of their psychotropic drugs and be involved as much as possible in the monitoring of response. This chapter presents an overview of the major dosage forms available for the psychotropic drugs and their associated method(s) of administration (see Table 4-1).[1,2] Particular attention is given to the various factors that may affect the prescription and use of these major dosage forms.

The correct prescription of psychotropic pharmacotherapy requires careful product and dosage selection with attention to the best method of administration for a particular patient. While some patients, particularly those who are hospitalized or who are in residential care, may have assistance from nurses or others involved with their care, most patients will be responsible for their own pharmacotherapy. These patients require careful instruction regarding the correct use of their prescribed dosage forms in order to achieve optimum therapeutic benefit with a minimum of adverse drug reactions. This chapter provides guidelines that can assist psychologists

---

[1] The appropriate use of universal precautions (i.e., treating all patients as if they have been infected with the human immunodeficiency virus) is recommended for drug administration procedures that expose psychologists, or others involved with the administration of prescribed psychotropic pharmacotherapy, to blood and other body fluids. The use of protective gloves, gowns, and masks may be required for selected patients depending on their prescribed pharmacotherapy and clinical condition. Psychologists also are reminded that basic hand washing remains an essential aspect of all drug administration.

[2] For more detailed information and specific guidelines for administering psychotropic drugs to infants, children, and adolescents, readers are referred to "Administering Drugs to Infants, Children, and Adolescents" (Pagliaro, 1995).

Table 4-1. *Major methods of psychotropic drug administration and associated dosage forms.*

Method of administration	Dosage form
Oral	Liquid dosage forms: elixir, solution, spray, suspension, syrup
	Solid dosage forms: capsule (hard, soft), tablet
Rectal	Suppository
Nasal	Spray
Transmucosal	
Buccal	Chewing gum
Sublingual	Tablet
Transdermal	Transdermal delivery system
Injectable	
Intramuscular	Aqueous solutions, suspensions
Intravenous	Aqueous solutions
Subcutaneous	Aqueous solutions, suspensions

with this task. Although the correct administration of psychotropic drugs is important, it constitutes only one aspect of the provision of optimal adjunctive psychotropic pharmacotherapy. Pharmacokinetics, clinically significant drug interactions, and adverse drug reactions are other major areas of concern for prescribing psychologists. These and other aspects of psychotropic pharmacotherapy are discussed in the other chapters of this textbook.

Oral dosage forms

Psychotropic drugs are generally available in a variety of liquid and solid oral dosage forms (see Table 4-1). Although oral dosage forms offer several advantages, including stability, portability, and convenience of use, they have several disadvantages. For example, liquid and solid oral dosage forms can cause a variety of adverse drug reactions (ADRs) involving the gastrointestinal system, such as constipation, diarrhea, gastric irritation and bleeding, nausea, stomach upset, and vomiting. These ADRs are usually associated with their local irritating effects but also can be the result of their direct pharmacologic action (e.g., opiate analgesics affect directly the smooth muscle of the intestines and slow intestinal motility, causing constipation). In addition, the willingness of patients to follow their prescribed psychotropic pharmacotherapy may be adversely affected by such factors as the unpleasant taste (e.g., chloral hydrate [Noctec®]), smell (e.g., phenytoin [Dilantin®]), or texture of the dosage form or the need for frequent dosing throughout the day (e.g., methylphenidate [Ritalin®]).

    The absorption of oral dosage forms can be variable because of the influence of such factors as the rate of gastric emptying, transit time through the gastrointestinal tract, and the pH of gastric and intestinal fluids. These factors, in turn, can be influenced by the presence of food or liquids in the gastrointestinal tract or the actions of other drugs that a patient may be concurrently receiving (e.g., phenothiazines, because of their anticholinergic action, may increase intestinal transit time by slowing bowel motility) (see Table 4-2). In addition, the type of oral dosage form selected (e.g., capsule versus tablet) and the differences between "identical" dosage forms produced by different manufacturers may significantly affect drug absorption and the resultant pharmacotherapeutic effects (see Chapter 3, "Pharmacokinetics and Pharmacodynamics"). However, in spite of these limitations, oral dosage forms continue to be the most commonly used of the dosage forms available for the psychotropic drugs. Attention to the factors affecting the prescription and use of oral dosage forms is required to help to ensure optimal pharmacotherapy.

Table 4-2. Factors that influence the rate of gastric emptying.

Factor	Effect on gastric emptying
Body positioning	Lying on the left side decreases rate of emptying
	Lying on the right side enhances rate of emptying
Disease states	
Diabetic diarrhea	Decreases rate of emptying
Stomach neoplasm	Decreases rate of emptying
Ulcer of pyloric antrum or associated with duodenal ulcer	Decreases rate of emptying
Uncomplicated duodenal ulcer	Increases rate of emptying
Drugs	
Alcohol before a meal	Decreases rate of emptying
Anticholinergics (e.g., atropine, TCAs)	Decrease rate of emptying
Bile salts	Decrease rate of emptying
Opiate analgesics (e.g., meperidine, [Demerol®] morphine [M.O.S.®])	Decrease rate of emptying
Potassium chloride	Decreases rate of emptying
Sodium chloride, sodium bicarbonate	Increase rate of emptying up to a maximum concentration and thereafter decrease rate of emptying
Sodium bicarbonate 1 hour after a meal	Decreases rate of emptying
Stimulants (e.g., amphetamines, caffeine)	Increase rate of emptying
Osmotic pressure of ingested material	As osmotic pressure increases, rate of emptying decreases
Psychological state	Aggressive emotional states tend to increase rate of emptying; depressive states tend to decrease rate of emptying
Temperature of ingested food or beverage	As temperature increases to body temperature, rate of emptying increases
Type of meal	
Acid (e.g., increased acidification by hydrochloric acid)	Decreases rate of emptying
Caloric level	Higher calorie meal decreases rate of emptying more so than carbohydrates
Carbohydrates	Decrease rate of emptying
Fasting state	Increases rate of emptying
Fats	Decrease rate of emptying
Large meal	Prolonged delay in emptying
Small meal or snack	Delays rate of emptying
Viscosity of ingested material	As viscosity increases, rate of emptying decreases
Volume of ingested material	As volume increases, there is initially an increase followed by a decrease in rate of emptying; bulky meals tend to empty more slowly than liquid meals (see Viscosity)

Generally, oral dosage forms should be prescribed so that the dosing schedule is as simple as possible (e.g., once-daily dosing) without compromising therapeutic efficacy. In addition, prescribing psychologists should be attentive to individual patient preferences for taste, odor, and texture and accommodate to these preferences whenever possible. For example, chlorpromazine (Largactil®, Thorazine®) is formulated in a variety of oral dosage forms, including capsules, tablets, oral suspension, flavored or unflavored syrups, or concentrated oral solution, that can be selected according to individual patient needs and preferences.

Although oral dosage forms are convenient and offer a variety of options for individualizing psychotropic pharmacotherapy, they are *contraindicated* for patients who are sedated, struggling, vomiting, undergoing gastric or intestinal suction, unconscious, or unable for any other reason to ingest foods or liquids by mouth (e.g., fasting for laboratory tests, religious reasons, or surgery).

All oral dosage forms should be stored safely so that they cannot be accessed by young children, confused family members, or others residing in the home or residence. Expiration dates should be periodically checked and any expired drugs safely deposed (e.g., returned to the dispensing pharmacy for safe and appropriate disposal). The manufacturer's storage recommendations (e.g., protect from moisture and light, store under controlled room temperature)[3] should be followed to avoid drug deterioration, which can negate the therapeutic benefits of pharmacotherapy.

Liquid dosage forms

Liquid oral dosage forms, including elixirs, oils, solutions, suspensions, and syrups, are commonly available for most of the psychotropic drugs. Liquid dosage forms are generally prescribed for patients who have difficulty swallowing solid oral dosage forms, such as capsules and tablets. All liquid oral dosage forms are, by their very nature, less portable and less convenient to ingest than solid oral dosage forms (e.g., they require generally the use of some form of measuring device). In addition, solutions and elixirs can be particularly irritating to the gastric mucosa and, thus, are commonly associated with such ADRs as nausea and vomiting. Syrups and some elixirs are sweetened to increase their palatability. These formulations may present a potential problem for patients who require dietary regulation of sugar (e.g., patients who have diabetes mellitus) when chronic, long-term pharmacotherapy is required. The alcohol content of elixirs and some syrups (e.g., butabarbital elixir, which contains 7% alcohol; morphine oral syrup [M.O.S.®], which contains 5% alcohol; and phenobarbital elixir, which contains 10% alcohol) also may preclude their use for patients who have histories of problematic patterns of alcohol use, are receiving disulfiram (Antabuse®) pharmacotherapy, or cannot tolerate the additional central nervous system depression that would be associated with use of these substances.

The alcohol, sodium, and sugar content of liquid oral dosage forms has received increased attention, and recent changes have been made to some formulations. For example, Dilaudid® Oral Liquid (hydromorphone) has been formulated as an unflavored, clear, alcohol-free liquid that can be mixed with fruit juice according to individual taste preferences. Prescribing psychologists should be aware of the alcohol, sodium, and sugar content of liquid oral dosage forms. These formulation ingredients (i.e., nonmedicinal ingredients) should be carefully considered when making product selections for particular patients, particularly when long-term pharmacotherapy is required.

Oral suspensions (e.g., amitriptyline [Elavil®]), including those that are formulated as powders or granules for reconstitution with purified water prior to dispensing, are often made available for psychotropic drugs that are insoluble, unstable, or unpalatable when in solution. Other suspension products are formulated as ready-to-use liquids. Oral suspensions, because they tend to precipitate out of solution, must be well shaken to ensure that the correct dose is measured and ingested. Syrups should be ingested with an appropriate amount of water or other compatible liquid chaser to ensure that the entire dose has been swallowed. The oral syrup

---

[3] The bathroom is one of the most common places used by patients to store drugs in the home. Advise patients to avoid storing their psychotropic drugs in the bathroom because of the high temperature and humidity, which can contribute to the decomposition of the drugs. Instruct them to safely store their psychotropic drugs according to manufacturer recommendations in a locked cabinet or drawer in a cool, dry room.

formulation of meperidine (Demerol®) also should be ingested with sufficient water (30 to 60 ml) to lessen its associated topical anesthetic effect.

Unpleasant-tasting liquid dosage forms can be made more palatable by diluting them in a small amount of water or other compatible beverage (e.g., cold fruit juices and soft drinks) or soft food (e.g., cold applesauce or pudding). For example, haloperidol (Haldol®) solution can be mixed in apple, orange, or tomato juice or cola drinks before ingestion. Psychologists also must ensure that patients are aware of the beverages and soft foods that should be avoided when diluting their liquid dosage forms, because pH incompatibilities or the formation of precipitates may affect drug potency. For example, patients should be advised *not* to dilute their dose of haloperidol with coffee or tea. Patients who require chlorpromazine (Largactil®, Thorazine®) pharmacotherapy may prefer ingesting their dose diluted in grapefruit, prune, tomato, or V-8 juice. However, these patients should be advised *not* to dilute their dose with apple juice, coffee, cola, diet ginger ale, root beer, or tea. Although fluphenazine oral concentrate can be diluted with tomato or fruit juices, milk, and noncaffeinated soft drinks, it should *not* be diluted with beverages that contain caffeine (e.g., coffee, cola drinks), tanis (e.g., tea), or pectinates (e.g., apple juice) because of physical incompatibility. When assisting patients in making their liquid oral dosage forms more palatable, always consult product labeling for beverage and food compatibilities.

Several psychotropic drugs are becoming available as concentrated oral liquid formulations (e.g., concentrated oral solutions, Intensols®) (Table 4-3). These products are highly concentrated oral liquid dosage forms and, thus, are dosed in small volumes. They are relatively tasteless and compatible when mixed with most beverages and soft foods. The Intensols® can be ingested with small amounts of juices, soft drinks, applesauce, or pudding. Thus, the Intensols® and other concentrated oral liquid dosage forms are well suited for patients who are elderly, confused, frail, or debilitated; require fluid restriction; or require nutritional formulas by gastric or nasogastric feeding tubes. They also may be helpful for patients who have difficulty ingesting solid oral dosage forms because of drug-induced extrapyramidal reactions (e.g., dysphagia) and tardive dyskinesia affecting the face and mouth (e.g., lip smacking, tongue darting).

Administering liquid dosage forms

There are several types of devices that have been developed to facilitate both the measurement and administration of oral liquid dosage forms. These devices include plastic calibrated drug cups, spill-proof liquid drug spoons, and oral syringes and droppers. Plastic drug cups are usually calibrated in 5-ml increments, teaspoons, tablespoons, and ounces, and they accommodate up to 30 ml. Plastic oral syringes are calibrated in 1-ml increments, usually accommodate up to 10 ml, and have no needle. They are commonly used in inpatient settings and clinics. Oral drug syringes (e.g., Monoject Oral Drug Syringe®) are manufactured by various drug or medical supply companies and are sold in many community pharmacies for home use. They are available

Table 4-3. Commonly used psychotropics available as concentrated oral Intensol® formulations.

Psychotopic	Available concentrations
Chlorpromazine	30 mg/ml
	100 mg/ml
Morphine sulfate (concentrated immediate release oral solution)	20 mg/ml
Thioridazine	30 mg/ml
	100 mg/ml

with both clear plastic and amber-colored barrels for non-light-sensitive and light-sensitive drugs, respectively.

Some concentrated oral liquid dosage forms, including those for chlorpromazine (Largactil®, Thorazine®), diazepam (Valium®), morphine (M.O.S.®), and thioridazine (Mellaril®), are supplied with their own measuring devices in the form of calibrated droppers. The calibrated dropper supplied with a drug product *always* should be used to measure accurately the required dose of the drug. However, these devices should not be used interchangeably among liquid drug products because their viscosities may vary and significantly affect the accuracy of the amount of drug measured and ingested. Patients, and others who may be responsible for their drug administration, should be taught to use measuring devices correctly. This instruction is particularly important when measuring doses of the highly concentrated oral liquid dosage forms or drugs that have a narrow therapeutic index.

The standard household teaspoon, commonly thought to hold 5 ml of liquid drug, is *not* recommended for measuring oral liquid dosage forms because of the variability in measured volume associated with such factors as the style of the teaspoon, the viscosity of the liquid measured, and the person measuring the volume. Generally, the oral drug syringe should be used for measuring liquid dosage forms when drugs have a narrow therapeutic index (e.g., chlorpromazine [Largactil®, Thorazine®], lithium [Eskalith®, Lithane®]) or when several different people are preparing the drug for administration (e.g., family members, residential care personnel). The oral drug syringe is the most accurate liquid measuring device and ensures a more correct and consistent dosage of liquid formulations. Thus, patients, or those who will be involved with their pharmacotherapy, should be instructed regarding the correct use of the oral drug syringe. In addition, they should be taught to routinely check expiration dates on liquid formulations to ensure that drugs are not outdated and to safely store liquid formulations in a cool, dark place, preferably in a locked drawer or cabinet, to prevent inadvertent ingestion of the drug by another family member or resident.

Psychologists must be alert to the fact that all of the measuring devices for liquid oral dosage forms have the potential for measurement error. In order to prevent such errors, psychologists should be familiar with the drug products they prescribe, particularly those dispensed with droppers or other special measuring devices. Psychologists should have a sample drug container available for demonstrating correct drug measurement and administration techniques for their patients.

The accuracy of the dose of an oral liquid form delivered from a unit dose container has received attention because of the substantial volume of residual liquid left remaining in the unit dose container after the dose has been ingested. Questions regarding the need to compensate for drug loss have been raised. However, unit dose products are customarily overfilled to achieve delivery of the proper dose. For this reason, patients should be instructed to ingest their dose directly from the liquid unit dose container. They should be advised not to fill the container with water and ingest the residual drug in an attempt to ensure a full dose. They also should be instructed not to transfer the drug to other containers or devices (e.g., oral drug syringe) for ingestion.

Solid dosage forms

Solid oral dosage forms include various types of tablets and capsules that generally offer greater drug stability and dosing accuracy than oral liquid dosage forms. However, these solid oral dosage forms have some disadvantages, including esophageal irritation or injury associated with "pill-induced esophageal injury" or "pill sticking" to the mucosa of the esophagus. In addition, the bioavailability of a solid oral dosage form may be less than that obtained from an equivalent dose of a liquid oral dosage form (see Chapter 3, "Pharmacokinetics and Pharmacodynamics"). Solid oral dosage forms also may present problems for some patients (e.g., those who have arthritis or low frustration tolerance) who have difficulty opening containers that have child-resistant lids or have difficulty removing small tablets or capsules from plastic blister packs.

Tablets

Tablets are the most widely used oral dosage form because of their convenience, compactness, dosing accuracy, ease of administration, economy, portability, and stability. There are a wide variety of tablets generally differentiated by color, flavor, shape (e.g., oval, rectangular, round, square, triangular), type of coating (e.g., enteric, film, thin sugar), and size, which usually depends on the amount of drug, binders, excipients, fillers, and other nonmedicinal ingredients. Some tablets have been reformulated as caplets, which are capsule-shaped tablets (e.g., meprobamate [Miltown®-600]), to facilitate drug transit through the esophagus. Extended-release (i.e., controlled-release, prolonged-release, sustained-release) tablets (e.g., codeine [codeine Contin®]; methylphenidate [Ritalin SR®]) and chewable tablets (e.g., carbamazepine [Tegretol Chewtabs®]) also are available and are designed to gradually release their active drug ingredient into the gastrointestinal tract over a period of up to 24 hours.[4]

Tablets that have no coating (e.g., diethylpropion [Tenuate®]), film coatings (e.g., amitriptyline [Elavil®]), or thin sugar coatings (e.g., mesoridazine [Serentil®]) dissolve readily in the stomach when ingested. Enteric coatings can either (1) protect the stomach from the irritating effects of some drugs (e.g., aspirin [Entrophen®, Novasen®]) or (2) protect the drug (e.g., divalproate sodium [Epival®]) from being degraded by the acidic secretions of the stomach. Enteric-coated tablets should *not* be cut in half, chewed, crushed, or dissolved in the mouth. Also, enteric-coated tablets generally should *not* be ingested with antacids or milk, which can theoretically destroy the enteric coating.

In order to obtain the desired maximum benefit from these various tablet formulations, they must be ingested according to their specific design, intended use, and pharmacologic action. For example, in order to dissolve at the correct rate, extended-release tablets should not be chewed or crushed. On the other hand, chewable tablets (e.g., chewable acetaminophen [Children's Anacin-3®], chewable pemoline [Cylert Chewable®]) require thorough chewing before swallowing to ensure complete disintegration and proper drug absorption. If they are not chewed completely before swallowing, some chewable tablets (e.g., calcium carbonate antacids [Tums®]) will not have maximum effectiveness and can cause serious adverse drug reactions, such as gastrointestinal obstruction requiring surgical intervention. Other tablets (e.g., enteric-coated valproic acid tablets [i.e., Depakote®]) should be swallowed whole without being broken, chewed, or allowed to dissolve in the mouth because they can irritate the mouth and throat.

In an effort to simplify drug dosing schedules, several drugs (e.g., clorazepate [Tranxene-SD®], methamphetamine [Gradumet Sustained-Release Desoxyn®], methylphenidate [Ritalin® SR], oxycodone [OxyContin®]) have been formulated as sustained- or extended-release tablets.

---

[4] Buccal and sublingual tablets and some lozenges (e.g., Fentanyl Oralet®) are actually not orally ingested but are placed inside the cheek, under the tongue, and sucked (not chewed), respectively, for dissolution and transmucosal absorption.

These tablets deliver the drug over a prolonged period and, thus, reduce the need for frequent dosing throughout the day. In order to ensure that these tablets dissolve at the correct rate and to prevent dangerous adverse drug reactions associated with "dumping" the full dose, sustained- and extended-release tablets should *not* be chewed or crushed.[5,6]

When a patient cannot swallow a tablet that should not be broken, chewed, crushed, or dissolved in the mouth, an alternative oral dosage form (i.e., oral liquid dosage form) or other method of administration (i.e., intramuscular injection, rectal insertion) should be used. This recommendation also applies when unscored tablets must be cut in halves or quarters to obtain the correct dose, particularly for drugs that have a narrow therapeutic index (e.g., lithium [Eskalith®, Lithane®, Lithobid®]).

Capsules

Many psychotropic drugs are formulated for oral administration as hard (e.g., secobarbital [Seconal®]) or soft (e.g., chloral hydrate [Noctec®]) gelatin capsules, Gelcaps®, gelatin-filled capsules (temazepam [Restoril®]), and soluble elastic capsules (e.g., ethchlorvynol [Placidyl®]). If patients have difficulty swallowing capsules, the capsules can be prepared in various ways so that their drug contents can be ingested more easily. For example, hard gelatin capsules generally can be taken apart and their contents (e.g., powder or time-release beads) gently mixed in a small amount (teaspoonful) of soft food, such as cold applesauce or pudding. Patients should be cautioned against ingesting powder contents without adequately mixing them because of the danger of inhaling the powder into the lungs and resultant lung irritation or toxicity (e.g., aspiration pneumonia). They also should be cautioned against chewing time-release beads (e.g., divalproex [Depakote® Sprinkle]) that have been sprinkled on or gently mixed into soft foods. Such drug–food mixtures should be ingested immediately and not prepared for future use. They also should be followed with a glassful of cool water or compatible juice or other beverage to ensure that the *entire* dose is swallowed.

Soft gelatin capsules contain liquid forms of drug (e.g., chloral hydrate [Noctec®]). These capsules generally cannot be taken apart. However, most soft gelatin capsules can be dissolved in a small amount of water and ingested as a liquid dosage form. This procedure helps to ensure that the entire dose is ingested. However, some soft gelatin capsules (e.g., valproic acid [Depakene® 500 mg]) are enteric coated and should not be dissolved. Chloral hydrate (Noctec®), if necessary, can be moistened with water and inserted rectally in the same way as a suppository; generally, however, if a soft capsule cannot be swallowed whole or dissolved in a small amount of water, an alternative dosage form should be prescribed.

Gelcaps®, gelatin-coated tablets, are smaller than most capsules and are advertised as being easier to swallow. An example of this more recently developed capsule formulation is the temazepam (Restoril®) gel-filled capsule. This formulation was developed in an effort to dissuade the illicit intravenous use of the liquid-filled capsule by people who have histories of problematic

---

[5] Scored formulations may be cut or broken along the score mark, if necessary, and will retain their sustained-release properties.

[6] Several brand name suffixes are commonly used to identify these drugs, including CR (controlled release or continuous release), Dur (duration), EC (enteric coated), en-tab or entabs (enteric tablets), LA (long acting), SA (sustained action), slo (slow), SR (sustained release or slow release), TD (time delay), TR (time release), XL (extended release), and XR (extended release). Attention should be given to these suffixes when psychotropic pharmacotherapy is prescribed, and patients should be taught the meanings of these suffixes to help them better understand the drug administration requirements associated with their required pharmacotherapy. They should be encouraged to seek clarification from their pharmacist at the time that the prescription is dispensed and, if necessary, to consult their prescribing psychologist.

patterns of benzodiazepine or other abusable psychotropic use. It is bioequivalent to the liquid-filled capsule that it replaced.

Administering solid dosage forms

Several factors that affect the transit of solid oral dosage forms through the esophagus have been identified, including size, shape, type of coating, and other physical properties of the tablet or capsule; volume of the liquid "chaser"; body position while swallowing; and esophageal function (e.g., presence of a motility disorder, mechanical obstruction). Capsules or tablets that become lodged in the esophagus can dissolve and release their contents in a concentrated form causing localized inflammation, stricture, or perforation and hemorrhage. Thus, if the consequences of delayed esophageal transit or irritation are to be avoided, patients should be advised to swallow all solid oral dosage forms, regardless of shape, size, or other factors, with a sufficient amount of liquid chaser (i.e., 120 ml to 240 ml) while standing. Solid oral dosage forms should *not* be ingested when lying down or immediately before retiring for bed. In addition, to further reduce "pill sticking," tablets and capsules can be ingested with food or meals, if not contraindicated, or "chased" with a few bites of a well-chewed banana or other soft food (e.g., bread).[7]

Before solid oral dosage forms of psychotropic drugs are prescribed to patients, their abilities to swallow the oral dosage form should be assessed. When solid oral dosage forms cannot be swallowed, various flavored syrups and other vehicles, such as jam or pureed fruit, can be used to increase the palatability of the drug when crushed or otherwise prepared to promote ingestion. Attention must be given to dietary restrictions (e.g., sugar or salt restrictions). When mixing crushed tablets and emptied capsules with liquid and foods, drug incompatibilities and individual preferences also must be considered. For example, tricyclic antidepressants should not be ingested with carbonated beverages or grape juice because of physical incompatibilities. Coffee and tea should not be used as liquid chasers for haloperidol, lithium, or monoamine oxidase inhibitors (MAOIs), and cola drinks should likewise be avoided with MAOIs. Applesauce or other pureed foods are commonly used as vehicles for mixing drugs, because they offer a consistency that allows mixing and ingestion without spills or loss of drug. Patients such as those who are elderly or have Alzheimer's or Parkinson's disease, who have difficulty swallowing, may find it easier to swallow their drugs when the drugs are mixed with textured foods (e.g., custards, rice pudding, toast, yogurt) rather than applesauce.[8]

Patients who require psychotropic drugs may not follow their prescribed pharmacotherapy for a variety of reasons. Exploring alterative dosage forms or methods of administration, focusing on the importance of pharmacotherapy as an adjunct to psychotherapy, and appropriately involving patients in all aspects of their therapy are helpful. Unpleasant-tasting drugs should not be mixed in large amounts of liquids or foods. They should be diluted in the smallest volume possible to ensure that the entire dose is swallowed. Some patients prefer to swallow an unpleasant-tasting drug "straight" and to "chase" it down with a compatible beverage. When patients require hospitalization, successful home routines should be followed as much as possible.

---

[7] An often missed symptom of esophagitis related to tablet sticking is prolonged hiccups. If patients complain of feeling that a tablet is stuck or lodged in the throat, or if they present with prolonged hiccups, "pill-induced" esophageal injury should be suspected, and patients should be appropriately referred for further evaluation.

[8] Several methods can assist dysphagic patients to swallow tablets and capsules that cannot be crushed (e.g., enteric-coated tablets) in order to prevent changing to less convenient dosage forms (liquid formations). Tablets can be placed on the "built-in shelf" of the Drink-a-Pill® cup. The cup should be filled halfway with water or a compatible liquid. As the person drinks, the liquid picks up the tablet or capsule and chases it down without triggering the gag reflex.

Familiar dosage forms and methods of administration should be used whenever possible, including similar drug brands, dosage forms, and procedures for administration (Table 4-4).[9]

When assisting nonambulatory or bedridden patients with the administration of prepared solid and liquid dosage forms, position them as for feeding to prevent aspiration and loss of drug. The head should be tilted forward, with the chin toward the chest (i.e., slightly flexed), rather than tilted backward (i.e., hyperextended) to prevent aspiration and to enhance swallowing. An oral drug syringe, drug cup, or spill-proof spoon can be used for liquid dosage forms. If an oral syringe is used, small amounts of the drug should be injected into the patient's cheek at the gums toward the back of the mouth. The patient should be allowed to swallow between each injection of the drug and should not be positioned in a lying (i.e., supine) or side-lying position until the drug has been completely swallowed. If necessary, the throat can be gently stroked in a downward motion to facilitate swallowing.

Sublingual and other transmucosal dosage forms

The oral cavity is well perfused by the circulatory system and, thus, provides an important site for drug absorption. It also offers considerable advantages for drugs that are extensively metabolized by the liver or those that are unstable (i.e., degraded) in the gastrointestinal tract. Drugs that are administered into the oral cavity, but are not swallowed, include: buccal tablets, which are placed in the cheek of the mouth; sublingual tablets, which are placed under the tongue; and medicated chewing gums and oral sprays. Both buccal and sublingual tablets are retained at their sites of placement for rapid dissolution and absorption into the systemic circulation. The therapeutic action of drugs administered by these dosage forms generally occurs within minutes. Although buccal formulations are not generally available for the psychotropic drugs, some psychotropic drugs have been formulated in sublingual dosages (e.g., lorazepam [Ativan®]) and as medicated chewing gums (e.g., nicotine [Nicorette®]).

Although the oral cavity offers some drug administration benefits, it offers a relatively small surface area for absorption. The buccal mucosa (i.e., inner lips and cheeks) appears to be thicker than the floor of the mouth but shows considerable variation in thickness (100 to 900 micromillimeters). However, it is more permeable than outer skin surfaces because it is not keratinized. Absorption depends on the physicochemical properties of the drug, with small lipophilic molecules displaying an absorption advantage. Decreased saliva production (i.e., xerostomia), particularly among elderly patients or those who are concurrently receiving pharmacotherapy with drugs that produce a dry mouth as an associated adverse drug reaction (e.g., anticholinergics, tricyclic antidepressants), can affect the absorption of drugs administered buccally or sublingually.[10] Therefore, patients should be assessed for xerostomia before buccal or

---

[9] Some patients who require psychotropic pharmacotherapy for the management of their mental disorders must take several drugs in tablet or capsule form each day, often at the same time. To prevent possible aspiration, they generally should be instructed to ingest their drugs one at a time. Most patients can ingest liquid oral dosage forms without difficulty. When ingesting solid oral dosage forms, they should be in a sitting or standing position to enhance swallowing and to prevent aspiration. For patients who have difficulty ingesting solid oral dosage forms, a sip of water and the placement of the tablet or capsule on the back of the tongue and the swallowing of the drug with another drink of water is often helpful. Drugs should be ingested with sufficient water, or other compatible liquid, to ensure drug transit to the stomach. Solid oral dosage forms should be taken with a minimum of 120 ml of water or compatible liquid. However, if patients require fluid restriction, have difficulty ingesting this recommended amount of liquid with their drugs, or are bedridden, an alternate dosage form (i.e., oral liquid formulation) should be selected. Oral drugs that are required at bedtime should generally be ingested 30 minutes before retiring.

[10] Dry mouth also is an ADR commonly associated with phenothiazines, tricyclic antidepressants, and other drugs that have anticholinergic actions. See Chapter 5, "Adverse Drug Reactions," for additional discussion and examples.

Table 4-4. Administering oral dosage forms.

Dosage form		General comments
Liquid dosage forms	Elixirs	Dilute in small amount of compatible food or fluid, monitor for gastric irritation. Contains alcohol. Contraindicated with disulfiram (Antabuse®) pharmacotherapy and for alcoholic patients.
	Solutions	Dilute in small amount of compatible food or fluid.
	Suspensions	Shake well, ingest immediately, obtain product of favorable flavor. Follow with adequate liquid chaser, particularly if required to promote drug action or minimize adverse reactions.
	Syrups	Contain significant amounts of sugar. When used for soothing effects (e.g., cough syrups containing opiates such as codeine or hydrocodone [Hycodan®]), do not chase with water or other beverages.
Solid dosage forms	CAPSULES	
	Gelatin capsules, hard	Administer with 100 to 120 ml of water or a compatible beverage. Patients should be in a standing position; *or* separate capsule, gently mix powder or timed beads in a compatible puree (e.g., applesauce), and administer from a spoon. Advise patients not to chew or crush timed beads.
	Gelatin capsules, soft	Administer with 100 to 120 ml of water or a compatible beverage. Patients should be in a standing position; *or* dissolve capsule, in a small amount of water and administer from a spoon.
	TABLETS	
	Chewable tablets	Instruct patients to chew completely and swallow, follow with 50 to 100 ml of water or a compatible beverage. If unable to chew, crush and administer as a suspension or select an alternate dosage form.
	Enteric-coated tablets	Administer with 100 to 120 ml of water or a compatible beverage. Patients should be in a standing position. If unable to swallow, do *not* crush or chew; select alternate dosage form. Do *not* administer with milk or antacids.
	Effervescent tablets	Must be completely dissolved in 100 to 240 ml of water or compatible beverage immediately before ingestion.
	Sugar-coated tablets	Administer with 100 to 120 ml of water or a compatible beverage. Patients should be in a standing position. If unable to swallow, crush, mix in a small amount of compatible puree (e.g., applesauce), and administer from a spoon.
	Sustained-release tablets	Administer with 100 to 120 ml of water or a compatible beverage. Patients should be in a standing position. If unable to swallow, do not crush or chew; select alternate dosage form.

Table 4-4. Administering oral dosage forms—Continued.

Dosage form	General comments
MISCELLANEOUS	
Granules	Sprinkle granules on compatible foods or gently mix in a small amount of water, or a compatible beverage, immediately before ingestion. For example, Depakote® Sprinkle (divalproex) may be swallowed whole as a capsule formulation or administered by carefully opening the capsule and sprinkling the entire contents on a small amount (teaspoonful) of soft food, such as applesauce or pudding. The drug/food mixture should be swallowed immediately (advise patients to avoid chewing) and not stored for future use.
Lozenges	Dissolve slowly in the mouth for optimal effect. Do not ingest foods or beverages for 30 minutes to 1 hour to promote optimum effect.
Powders	Mix completely in a small amount of compatible puree or semisolid food and administer from a spoon.

Note. Because gastric transit can effect drug absorption, see also Table 4-3.

sublingual pharmacotherapy is prescribed. If necessary, an alternate dosage form should be selected for those patients for whom xerostomia is problematic.

Sublingual administration

Sublingual tablets are small, soft tablets formulated to dissolve over several minutes in order to rapidly provide therapeutic drug levels. For example, peak blood levels of sublingual lorazepam (Ativan®) are obtained within 2 to 3 minutes as compared with 30 minutes for the oral tablet formulation. Patients must understand that sublingual tablets should not be swallowed. After placement, they should be allowed to dissolve under the tongue. Patients should be cautioned against swallowing their saliva for at least 2 to 3 minutes in order to allow sufficient time for sublingual absorption. Patients also should be advised to safely store their sublingual tablets in the original, or a suitable supplemental, container in order to prevent loss of drug potency.

Medicated chewing gums

Nicotine has been formulated as a chewable gum (e.g., Nicorette®) for adjunctive pharmacotherapy for the symptomatic management of smoking cessation. The formulation is well absorbed from the oral mucosa. Generally, patients should be instructed to slowly chew one piece of nicotine gum over 30 minutes when the desire to smoke occurs. Patients should be instructed to chew each piece of Nicorette® slowly and to stop chewing when they perceive a peppery taste or a slight tingling sensation in the mouth. They should then place the gum between the cheek and gums ("park" the gum) and resume chewing when the taste or tingling begins to disappear (approximately 1 minute). This procedure should be repeated over a period of 30 minutes. Patients should be encouraged to avoid swallowing while chewing the gum and to hold their saliva in their mouths for as long as possible before swallowing for maximum absorption of nicotine. Vigorous chewing can increase the occurrence of adverse drug reactions (e.g., canker sores, excessive salivation, hiccups, jaw pain, throat irritation) (see also nasal nicotine spray).

Oral sprays and other products

Oral spray products (e.g., oral nicotine spray) are increasingly being developed, as are such other alternative dosage forms as "fentanyl lollipops." Fentanyl lollipops (i.e., oral transmucosal fentanyl citrate) have been developed as a painless and effective preoperative drug formulation for both young children and adults. They also have been used for the treatment of cancer pain, providing a convenient, self-administered, easily titrated, and effective method of pain management. The further use of the oral transmucosal method of drug administration for fentanyl and other drugs requires continued research and evaluation.

Rectal dosage forms

Some psychotropic drugs (e.g., hydromorphone [Dilaudid®], chlorpromazine [Thorazine®], morphine [MS Contin®], pentobarbital [Nova Rectal®]) can be administered rectally in the form of rectal suppositories when oral administration is contraindicated (e.g., when patients are unconscious, vomiting, or, for any other reason, unable to ingest oral dosage forms). The use of rectal suppositories is contraindicated for patients who have inflammation or irritation of the anus or rectum, diarrhea, rectal bleeding, or other conditions (e.g., cancer pharmacotherapy) that would make them prone to rectal abscess or injury.

The rectum comprises the distal 15 cm to 20 cm of the large intestine. It produces approximately 2 ml to 3 ml of mucous fluid secretions, which have a pH of 7 to 8. The surface area of the rectum is relatively limited in regard to absorption (i.e., 200 to 400 cm^2) and usefulness as a route for drug administration because of the absence of villi and microvilli. The luminal pressure, degree of rectal motility, and presence of feces also affect the extent of drug dispersion after rectal insertion. These factors are altered by age, trauma, or disease processes (e.g., hemorrhoids, rectal cancer).

Although the rectal route has several limitations, it also has some advantages in regard to the administration of selected drugs. For example, it is independent of gastric emptying and intestinal transit time. The major source of blood supply to the rectum is provided by the superior rectal artery. The inferior and middle hemorrhoidal veins drain directly into the systemic circulation by way of the iliac vein and vena cava. The superior hemorrhoid vein drains directly into the portal vein, which then enters the liver. Thus, first-pass metabolism can be avoided depending on where in the rectum a drug is placed for systemic absorption. The extent of first-pass hepatic drug metabolism increases as the depth of drug insertion into the rectum increases. In addition, the rectum is well supplied with lymphatic vessels. First-pass hepatic metabolism also can be avoided when the drug is absorbed by the lymphatic system.

Rectal suppositories are formulated to melt or dissolve in rectal fluids after insertion. They are often poorly accepted by patients who find insertion difficult, distasteful, or embarrassing. Patients should be instructed in regard to the correct procedure for inserting suppositories, and it should not be assumed that they have had previous experience with the rectal administration of drugs. Suppositories formulated with synthetic oil bases should be warmed in the hands to facilitate insertion. Polyethylene glycol base suppositories should be moistened with warm tap water prior to insertion. Suppositories should be retained in the rectum for at least 20 to 30 minutes to ensure melting or dissolution of the base and release and absorption of the drug. A slight laxative effect may occur after the use of synthetic oil base suppositories.

Patients should be instructed to evacuate their bowels prior to insertion and to squat or bend forward to facilitate insertion. They should be encouraged to hold onto a hand rail or stable piece of furniture to assist them in maintaining their balance. They should know the reason for using the suppository, how it will be inserted, and what they can do to ensure correct insertion. They must understand that they should reinsert a suppository that is inadvertently expelled.

Patients who require assistance from family members or caregivers should be positioned on the left side with the upper leg bent at the knee (i.e., flexed). The anal area should be assessed for any changes in skin integrity (e.g., hemorrhoids, inflammation, or bleeding) and should be well exposed to prevent injury during insertion. However, adequate draping is required to ensure privacy and minimize embarrassment. The external anal sphincter should be gently dilated with a gloved index finger. To facilitate insertion, the suppository should be lubricated with water or a water-soluble jelly. Patients should be told to take a deep breath or to "bear down" as the suppository is inserted (rounded end first). This procedure distracts the patient and helps to relax the external sphincter muscle so that the suppository can be gently inserted. To ensure correct placement, the suppository should be inserted past the internal sphincter, the length of the finger, at an angle toward the navel (i.e., umbilicus). This technique is adapted according to patient size and health status (i.e., the fifth digit is used for children and frail or debilitated patients). The buttocks should be gently held together until the desire to expel the suppository passes.

Lower dosages of psychotropic pharmacotherapy may be required for patients who are elderly, frail, or debilitated or who have low body weight. However, suppositories should *not* be cut to provide lower dosages (e.g., halved or quartered). Cutting a suppository does not guarantee an accurate dose of drug because of the possible uneven drug migration in the suppository base. Instead, a lower dose suppository (e.g., children's formulation) should be prescribed, or another dosage form and route of administration should be considered.

Intranasal dosage forms

The nasal cavity is highly vascularized and consists of a central system, turbinates, and epithelial cilia and mucus, which assist in the removal of airborne particles and nasal debris. The intranasal route offers an effective option for the delivery of psychotropic drugs, as demonstrated by the illicit use of cocaine. It also offers a route of administration for drugs that are unstable in the gastrointestinal tract or that have a high first-pass hepatic metabolism. The deposition of a drug in the nasal cavity is affected by the dosage form and the droplet size delivered (i.e., intranasal drops versus intranasal sprays). Intranasal drops readily spread across nasal surfaces throughout the nasal cavity. Intranasal sprays, which deliver droplets larger than 10 μl, tend to deposit a drug over a small area toward the front of the nose. The initial loss of intranasal drops and sprays is rapid. Approximately 30% to 50% of the drug is lost within 10 minutes. Subsequent loss appears to be much slower, particularly for sprays, probably because the drug is deposited in nonciliated regions (intranasal drops spread quickly across ciliated areas). Thus, intranasal spray formulations may be preferred to drops. Although the intranasal route offers promise for psychotropic drug delivery, the rapid loss of drugs due to the mucociliary system limits its use. However, a few psychotropic drugs have been formulated as nasal sprays, including butorphanol

(Stadol NS®), an opiate analgesic, and nicotine (Nicotrol NS®), which is indicated for the symptomatic management of smoking cessation.

When intranasal sprays are prescribed, patients require instruction regarding their general use and safe storage. Instruct patients to sit or stand with their head straight or tilted slightly backward. The intranasal spray bottle tip should be introduced into a nostril after the opposite nostril has been occluded by pressing with the index and second fingers of the nondominant hand. The spray should be sniffed into the nostril as the spray container is squeezed. If indicated, the procedure should be repeated for the other nostril with the recommended number of sprays. To avoid contamination after use, the tip of the plastic intranasal spray bottle should be rinsed under warm running water and dried with a clean paper towel or tissue before recapping.

Butorphanol nasal spray

Stadol NS® is indicated for the symptomatic management of acute pain. It is formulated as a metered nasal spray product that is supplied in a child-resistant prescription vial containing a metered-dose spray pump with protective tip and dust cover, a bottle of nasal spray solution, and patient instructions for use. On average, one 2.5-ml bottle will deliver 14 to 15 doses. The patient's pharmacist will assemble the Stadol NS® prior to dispensing to the patient. The nasal spray is administered as a metered spray to the nasal mucosa, usually one spray in one nostril. If adequate pain relief is not achieved within 60 to 90 minutes, an additional nasal spray may be required. This two-spray sequence may be repeated in 3 to 4 hours, as needed.

The pump reservoir must be fully primed prior to initial use and reprimed if not used within 48 hours. Family members or others involved with the patient's pharmacotherapy should be advised that, during the priming process, a certain amount of butorphanol may be aerosolized. Therefore, the pump sprayer should be aimed away from the face and away from the patient, other people, or pets in the immediate environment.

Nicotine nasal spray

Nicotrol NS® is a nicotine nasal spray designed to deliver a nicotine dose for the relief of the signs and symptoms of the nicotine withdrawal syndrome associated with tobacco smoking cessation. The product delivers a 0.5-mg nicotine dose per 50-μl spray. Generally, a dose consists of two sprays, one in each nostril. Nicotine administered intranasally is rapidly absorbed. Peak levels are achieved within 10 minutes. This rapid nicotine absorption results in nicotine levels comparable to those produced by smoking a tobacco cigarette. The nasal spray is used whenever the patient has the urge to smoke (up to 40 doses per day). The most common ADRs associated with the use of the nicotine nasal spray are cough, throat and nasal irritation, runny nose, sneezing, and watering eyes. Other ADRs include headache, increased heart rate, and lightheadedness. Unfortunately, addiction appears to be *more* common with Nicotrol NS® than with the other nicotine replacement products. Thus, patients require monitoring to ensure that they are not using excessive quantities or using the spray product longer than recommended (i.e., 6 months). The incidence of addiction appears to increase when the product is used for longer than 6 months. The quantity of nicotine present in the nasal spray bottle can be toxic to a child or pet. Instruct patients to safely store the nasal spray out of the reach of children and pets.

Transdermal dosage forms

Transdermal drug delivery was first achieved with ointments, creams, and plasters. However, drug absorption was found to be unpredictable and highly variable. Subsequently, attention has been given to the design of transdermal drug delivery systems (TDDSs) that provide a more accurate rate of drug delivery and a prolonged duration of drug absorption. Transdermal drug delivery systems are thin, multilayered drug delivery patches that have a backing of drug-impermeable metallic plastic film. To ensure that drug bioavailability is independent of variations in skin permeability, the rate of drug delivery from the device to the skin surface is the rate-limiting step in transdermal absorption. Four-layer, three-layer, matrix diffusion, and microreservoir systems have been developed to control the rate and duration of transdermal drug delivery (see Figure 4-1). The rate of drug release is usually set below the mean steady-state flux of drug across the skin in order to help to ensure a controlled rate of drug delivery into the systemic circulation and avoid drug "dumping" among patients who have increased skin permeability.

The principal rate-limiting barrier for transdermal drug absorption through intact skin is the dense, keratinized stratum corneum outer layer of the epidermis, which is avascular. Thus, systemic drug absorption cannot occur until the drug reaches the dermis layer of the skin. The principal transport mechanism across the epidermis skin layer is passive diffusion. Several factors, including drug factors (e.g., pH, lipid solubility), dosage formulation variables (e.g., vehicle), and variation in skin condition (e.g., aging, disease, skin excretions), determine the rate and extent of transdermal absorption. Regional variations in skin drug permeability are due primarily to differences in the structure and thickness of this layer. Drugs that penetrate the stratum corneum undergo systemic absorption because underlying tissues offer little resistance to the passive diffusion of drug molecules. Drug absorption through intact skin also can occur by the transfollicular route. Drugs, particularly those composed of large molecules (e.g., antibiotics, corticosteroids), penetrate by diffusion down hair follicles in the secretions of the eccrine and sebaceous glands.

To be of clinical value, drugs administered by TDDSs must first permeate the skin in sufficient quantity to exert systemic effects and, second, be nonirritating and nonsensitizing to the skin. Several TDDSs have been marketed for the administration of nicotine (e.g., Nicoderm®, Nicotrol®) as an adjunct to tobacco smoking cessation. Transdermal clonidine (Catapres-TTS®) is under investigation for indications other than the management of hypertension (e.g., adjunctive symptomatic management of heroin withdrawal and tobacco smoking cessation), and transdermal

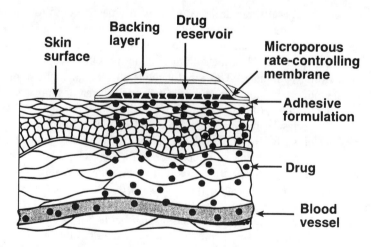

Figure 4-1. Example of a typical transdermal drug delivery system (TDDS) and its application to the external skin surface.

fentanyl (Duragesic®) appears to offer a viable alternative to the more conventional injectable routes of opiate analgesic administration (see later discussion).

Transdermal drug delivery systems allow continuous drug delivery over relatively long periods of time, reduce fluctuations in blood drug concentrations, are convenient to use because they provide longer dosing intervals that require less frequent administration, and are generally highly accepted by patients because of their ease of application and care. These benefits have resulted in an increased interest in the formulation of additional transdermal products, including those for the adjunctive symptomatic management of several psychological disorders.

The requirements for a drug to be incorporated into a TDDS are mainly related to the barrier properties and physicochemical characteristics of the skin. Generally, drugs that have a low molecular weight (i.e., less than 1,000 Daltons) and adequate solubility in both oil and water should easily penetrate the skin. The drug also must be of sufficient concentration so that only a small surface area is required for adequate absorption. Drugs for which the daily injectable dose is below 5 mg and the therapeutic blood levels are within the microgram per liter range are likely candidates for incorporation into a TDDS. In some cases, biotransformation of transdermally applied drugs can be facilitated by microorganisms present on the skin surface or by enzymes located within the epidermis. Drugs that are associated with topical irritation or allergic responses should be avoided. The most important requirement for incorporation into a TDDS is a drug's demonstrated need for controlled delivery (e.g., short half-life of elimination, adverse drug reactions associated with other methods of administration) or complex oral or intravenous dosing schedules. Although offering many advantages, TDDSs also have some disadvantages (see Table 4-5).

Transdermal administration

Although the administration of various psychotropic drugs formulated as TDDSs is relatively similar, certain differences among various products and different doses of the same product

Table 4-5. Advantages and disadvantages of transdermal drug delivery.

Advantages
- Accuracy of dose
- Elimination of variable drug bioavailability associated with the oral route; circumvents factors influencing gastrointestinal absorption, including variation of acidity, motility, and food content in the gastrointestinal tract
- Avoids first-pass intestinal and hepatic metabolism
- Controlled drug release generally leads to a steady pharmacologic response and convenient dosing intervals for drugs that have short biologic half-lives
- Possible increase in compliance because the frequency of dosing is reduced with prolonged administration periods (e.g., 24 hours, 72 hours, 1 week of effective drug release)
- Avoids peaks and troughs of conventional pharmacotherapy and related adverse drug reactions (i.e., therapeutic failure, overdosage) are minimized
- If necessary, can be rapidly terminated by removal from skin site, thus preventing further absorption and minimizing associated toxicity
- Avoids need for physical penetration of the protective barrier of the skin and the risks and inconveniences associated with injectable (e.g., IM, IV) pharmacotherapy (e.g., infection, tissue damage)

Disadvantages
- Sensitivity reactions related to the drug or adhesive used for the TDDS
- Prolonged, although milder, adverse drug reactions, as opposed to more severe short-term adverse drug reactions (e.g., low grade constant nitroglycerin headache with transdermal systems versus periodic splitting headache with buccal therapy)
- Individual variation in skin permeability and biological variability from patient to patient and site to site (i.e., 10-fold variation in individual skin permeability)

require attention. The most commonly used TDDSs are those formulated for the symptomatic management of tobacco cessation: the nicotine transdermal systems.

Nicotine TDDSs (e.g., Nicoderm®, Nicotrol®, Prostep®) have become useful adjuncts to smoking cessation programs, particularly when used in combination with appropriate psychotherapy. These systems offer several advantages over the chewing gum formulations because they do not require patients to learn proper chewing techniques and are not generally associated with such ADRs as hiccuping or nausea and vomiting. The dose is regulated, and slow absorption and relatively constant nicotine levels prevent the occurrence of signs and symptoms of nicotine withdrawal. The main adverse drug reaction associated with the nicotine TDDSs is local skin irritation, such as erythema and pruritus. This ADR is reportedly associated with the pharmacologic action of nicotine on local blood flow and generally resolves when the application site is changed or when pharmacotherapy with the TDDS is discontinued.

Transdermal drug delivery systems generally can be applied to any clean, dry, hairless skin area on the body. If a TDDS must be applied to a hairy skin site, hair should be clipped, not shaved, because shaving can irritate the skin and increase drug absorption. Sites on the extremities below the knee or elbow are generally not recommended, and injured skin sites (e.g., abrasions, cuts) should be avoided. Effective adhesion of the TDDS to the skin surface is critical for maintaining the diffusion gradient. Adhesive cover patches may be used over the delivery system, so that effective contact can be ensured during daily activities (e.g., showering, swimming) and for prolonged periods. Sites of application should be rotated when fresh systems are applied.

The rate of drug release remains constant as long as the diffusion gradient between the system and the skin site is maintained. Drug diffusion begins immediately after the saturation of binding sites in the skin, and the drug is released constantly to establish therapeutic blood concentrations. After removal, blood concentrations decrease at a rate determined by the half-life of the drug (see Chapter 3, "Pharmacokinetics and Pharmacodynamics"). The quantity of drug in the reservoir determines the duration of the action, because the size of the system determines the amount of drug absorbed per unit time. Thus, TDDSs deliver the drug at a controlled rate per unit area. Most systems are available in more than one size so that drug dosage can be individualized. Thus, attention to specific dosages among products is essential. Transdermal dosage should be carefully checked because dosing errors have occurred, particularly when one brand of a TDDS is replaced with another, perhaps for economic reasons.

Elderly, frail, or debilitated patients may require lower dosages. However, TDDSs should *not* be cut in order to obtain the desired dose. Cutting the TDDS destroys the drug reservoir and, thus, directly affects the amount of drug delivered and systemically absorbed. In some instances, cutting the TDDS may result in the release of the entire amount of drug stored in the reservoir and result in serious toxicity. Whenever possible, products with the most appropriate dosage for a particular patient should be selected. If such a product is not available, an alternative drug or method of administration is required.

Patients should be instructed regarding the correct application of TDDSs and their general care once applied. They also require instruction regarding the safe storage and disposal of their TDDSs. Advise patients to store TDDSs in their individual unopened packages and to dispose of used systems so that they are not accessible by children (and pets).[11] Patients also should be

---

[11] Discarded TDDSs may have sufficient amounts of drug remaining in the reservoir to pose significant risk of toxicity, and cases of poisoning have been reported among both small children and pets.

advised that aluminum-containing backing on some TDDSs may cause arcing during emergency defibrillation and, thus, require removal in these situations.

Injectable dosage forms

Many psychotropic drugs (e.g., antidepressants, such as amitriptyline [Elavil®]; antipsychotics, such as chlorpromazine [Largactil®, Thorazine®] and haloperidol [Haldol®]; opiate analgesics, such as anileridine [Leritine®], buprenorphine [Buprenex®], and morphine; and sedative-hypnotics, such as lorazepam [Ativan®]) have been formulated for subcutaneous, intramuscular, or intravenous pharmacotherapy as sterile pyrogen-free solutions, suspensions, emulsions, or powders for injectable use. Some psychotropic drugs (e.g., fluphenazine [Prolixin®]), depending on the clinical indication for use (e.g., immediate control of acute psychotic symptomatology, simplified long-term adjunctive pharmacotherapy for the management of schizophrenia or other psychotic disorders), have been specially formulated as various injectable salts (e.g., hydrochloride salt, decanoate salt, enanthate salt). The hydrochloride salt usually provides rapid action and may require additional dosing within a few hours. The decanoate and enanthate salts are generally used to provide prolonged action and can be dosed once a week or once monthly, depending on the specific formulation.

Although some formulations can be used for subcutaneous, intramuscular, or intravenous pharmacotherapy (e.g., meperidine hydrochloride [Demerol®]), others should not because of their unique physical and chemical properties (e.g., lipid solubility, tissue-irritating qualities). For example, suspensions should not be injected intravenously because of the risk of capillary blockage by insoluble particles that are part of the suspension formulation. Other injectables, such as chlorpromazine (Largactil®, Thorazine®), which are formulated with benzyl alcohol and sulfites for intramuscular use, should not be injected subcutaneously because they are extremely irritating to these tissues. Decisions regarding the type of injectable therapy to prescribe are influenced by the indication for injectable psychotropic pharmacotherapy and individual patient factors (e.g., age, weight, body system function, and condition of intramuscular, intravenous, and subcutaneous injection sites).

Solutions are the most common formulations for injectable pharmacotherapy. Most solutions are aqueous, but nonaqueous solutions also are available (e.g., polyethylene glycol–based solutions). Some aqueous solutions may contain varying proportions of water-miscible liquids (e.g., propylene glycol or glycerol) to increase drug solubility or stability. Water-immiscible oils (e.g., corn, peanut, sesame) are commonly used as alternatives to enhance drug solubility or stability or to prolong the rate of drug release when sustained action is desired. Ideal injectable formulations should provide a means for drug delivery that is nonirritating, nontoxic, nonsensitizing, and physiologically inert.[12] Psychotropic drugs that are unstable in solution are formulated as dry powders for reconstitution as solutions or suspensions with an appropriate diluent (e.g., bacteriostatic water for injection, normal saline) prior to their use. Some injectable formulations, such as chlordiazepoxide (Librium®), are marketed with their own special diluent for intramuscular use only. It is important to note that highly concentrated solutions of some drugs (e.g., Morphine HP®) have been formulated for injectable use. These highly concentrated solutions

---

[12] Note that propylene glycol, peanut oil, sesame oil, and other formulation ingredients (e.g., bisulfites) are capable of causing severe allergic reactions (see Chapter 5 "Adverse Drug Reactions") among susceptible patients. A careful history, including a detailed list of all known allergies and chronic medical conditions (e.g., asthma), is necessary to avoid prescribing such formulations to susceptible patients.

should not be confused with the standard injectable formulations that have lower dosage strengths. Overdosage and death may result.[13]

Injectable formulations of psychotropic drugs usually produce a more rapid onset of action than oral dosage forms and have a higher rate of absorption. The major disadvantage associated with their use, as compared with other dosage forms, is the need to penetrate the protective skin layer. Penetration of the skin layer can introduce pathogens into the body and cause injury to underlying blood vessels, bones, muscles, nerves, and subcutaneous tissues. Injectable pharmacotherapy requires a strict aseptic technique during all aspects of drug preparation and administration (e.g., reconstitution of powdered dosage forms, handling of needles, syringes, and intravenous tubing and solutions) and a knowledge of recommended injection sites and correct injection techniques. An understanding of the principles of universal precautions (i.e., the use of gloves and other precautions) also is needed because of the increased risk for contact with blood or other body fluids that may be infected with the human immunodeficiency virus (HIV).

When injectable psychotropic pharmacotherapy is required, it is imperative that patients be advised of the benefits and associated risks. Nonhospitalized patients who require injectable pharmacotherapy in the home setting also require individualized instruction in relation to the appropriate use and disposal of injection supplies and equipment, aseptic technique for drug preparation and administration, dose measurement, injection site selection and preparation for injection, monitoring of therapeutic effects, and the prevention of adverse drug reactions and other complications associated with their particular injectable pharmacotherapy.

Dosage forms and related equipment

Injectable psychotropic drugs are generally supplied in sterile glass ampules, multiple dose vials, or prefilled syringes or syringe cartridges (e.g., Carpuject®, Tel-E-Ject®, Tubex®).[14] Recommended guidelines for the preparation, storage, and disposal of injectable drugs, including reconstituted drugs, must be closely followed in order to help to ensure therapeutic benefit and prevent drug deterioration and contamination. In addition, all injectable drug products should be inspected for particulate matter and discoloration prior to use.[15] Prescribing psychologists also should be alert for evidence of drug product tampering, particularly in regard to drug products that are listed on the Food and Drug Administration (FDA) narcotics schedule (e.g., amphetamines, barbiturates, benzodiazepines, opiate analgesics).

[13] Highly concentrated solutions of morphine for injection (e.g., Morphine HP®) may be used with or without dilution. These formulations are indicated for the relief of severe pain among patients who are opiate tolerant (e.g., patients who have terminal cancer and require long-term opiate analgesic pharmacotherapy) and require intramuscular or subcutaneous opiate analgesia in dosages higher than those usually required by patients who are not opiate tolerant. These concentrated formulations allow smaller injection volumes and, thus, less of the discomfort usually associated with the injection of larger volumes of drug. These formulations also may generally be diluted in large-volume intravenous solutions (e.g., Dextrose 5% in water®, Sodium Chloride Injection®) and injected by slow continuous intravenous infusion.

[14] The Carpuject® unit dose system is available for codeine, diazepam, fentanyl, hydromorphone, lorazepam, meperidine, morphine, naloxone, pentazocine (Talwin®), phenytoin, and prochlorperazine. The psychotropic drugs that are available in Tubex® closed injection systems include codeine, hydromorphone, lorazepam, meperidine, morphine, pentobarbital, phenobarbital, prochlorperazine, and secobarbital. The Tubex® closed injection system delivers machine-measured doses of these drugs from sterile, clearly labeled, single-dose cartridge-needle units. These systems and similar cartridge systems help to reduce cross contamination of injectable products and dosage errors.

[15] Drug products that contain particulate matter, or are outdated or discolored, should *not* be used because they may be contaminated or their potency affected. These products should be returned to the dispensing pharmacy or directly to the manufacturer for proper and safe disposal. They should not be simply discarded into the trash, because several cases of death have been associated with their use by children and drug addicts who have found and used these discarded injectable drug products.

Ampules

Ampules, either glass or plastic (e.g., Polyamps®), are designed to hold a single dose of liquid drug. Most glass ampules are prescored around their stems so that they snap off easily to allow access to the drug contents. Plastic ampules are designed to come apart at the neck when the finger grip tab is twisted with the index finger and thumb. Before opening the ampule, ensure that all of the drug is in the base of the ampule. Any drug in the stem of the ampule can be brought down into the base by gently "flicking" the stem with the fingertips. This will help to prevent inadvertent drug loss when the stem of the ampule is snapped (or the neck twisted) off and ensure that sufficient volume of drug is available for preparing an accurate dose when the drug is withdrawn.[16]

To withdraw the desired volume of drug from an ampule, a sterile needle is inserted toward the bottom of the ampule with the bevel of the needle facing up. The required volume of drug is then withdrawn into the syringe.[17] Filter needles (e.g., Monoject Filter Needle®, Monoject Filter Aspirator®) are recommended when using glass ampules in order to avoid withdrawing glass particles that may otherwise be tracked through or deposited in the tissues during the injection. The drug also can be withdrawn with the ampule inverted. This technique is used in relation to personal preference or when shorter needles are used to withdraw the drug from the ampule. The needle must be kept in the solution to maintain capillary pressure and to prevent the drug from dribbling out of the ampule. Plastic ampules must be handled carefully because any squeezing pressure from the fingertips may also result in the loss of drug solution. With either method, the drug should be withdrawn quickly to prevent airborne contamination. The needle should be replaced with a dry, sterile needle before the drug is injected. Replacing the needle prevents the drug from being tracked through sensitive skin layers.

Vials

Some injectable psychotropic drugs are supplied in single or multiple dose vials (i.e., small sterilized glass bottles that are sealed with rubber stoppers). Drug vials are available in various sizes and usually hold from 0.5 ml to 50 ml of solution or powdered drug ready for reconstitution. To protect the rubber stopper, vials are usually packaged with a plastic cap that can be snapped off with the thumb or a soft metal lid that can be lifted off with a small metal file. The rubber stopper should be cleansed with an antiseptic before the drug is withdrawn. The drug is removed from the vial, which is a closed system, by injecting an amount of air equal to the volume of drug to be withdrawn.[18] To help ensure the accuracy of the dose, the drug should be withdrawn at eye level. The needle bevel should be kept below the surface of the solution.

Sterile bacteriostatic water for injection and sterile normal saline are diluents that are commonly used to reconstitute powdered drugs supplied in vials. The manufacturer's directions on the label or package insert regarding the type and the amount of diluent to use must be followed *exactly*. To facilitate dissolution of powders after a diluent is added, vials should be warmed in the hand and gently shaken. If shaking is contraindicated because of the possibility of frothing, the vial can be gently rolled in the hands for a few minutes. Vials should be

---

[16] Glass ampules are opened by snapping the stem off. The base of the ampule is grasped with the fingers of the nondominant hand, and the stem is grasped with the thumb and index finger of the dominant hand. The tips of the thumbs should be facing each other. If desired, a foil-packaged. sterile alcohol sponge can be placed on the stem under the thumbs for protection. The ampule should be held away from the face in order to prevent glass particles or solution droplets from inadvertently flying into the eyes, and the stem should be snapped off.

[17] The needle bevel must be under solution when the drug is withdrawn. Unlike multidose vials, injecting air into the ampule to displace the volume of drug withdrawn is not required because it is an open system. To prevent contamination, the needle should not be allowed to touch the open edge of the ampule during the procedure.

[18] To decrease the possibility of introducing rubber cores from the stopper into the drug solution, it is recommended that the needle be inserted into the stopper with slight lateral pressure. The bevel of the needle should be facing up.

examined carefully for any undissolved drug before the dose is withdrawn. After reconstitution, multiple dose vials should be stored according to the manufacturer's directions. In hospital and residential care settings, they must be labeled with the date and time of reconstitution, type and amount of diluent used for reconstitution, and the name or initials of the person who performed the reconstitution. However, because of a large number of reported incidents of improper care and handling of multiple dose vials (e.g., reentering a vial with a contaminated needle, withdrawing excessive dosages), which have resulted in drug contamination, an incorrect dose, or a lethal overdosage, it is recommended that all multidose vials be appropriately *discarded* after a single use. To avoid unnecessary waste and cost, single dose vials should be used whenever possible.[19]

Needles

The needles generally used for injectable pharmacotherapy are hyperchrome, stainless steel needles that are sterile, disposable, and individually packaged for convenience and to maintain sterility. Needles are designed to minimize the pain associated with insertion, penetrate skin and muscle without bending or breaking, and minimize tissue damage and the seepage of blood, lymph, and serum after the needle is withdrawn by making an incision that allows the close realignment of tissue edges. Needles are lubricated with a special medical-grade silicone that reduces the force needed to penetrate the skin and prevents the adherence of tissues when the needle is withdrawn.

Needles consist of several parts, including the cannula lumen (channel), hub, primary and secondary bevels (i.e., the point tip and the heel of the bevel), and sheath. The cannula is the shaft through which the drug is withdrawn or injected. The length of the cannula determines the depth of drug delivery. The hub is the part of the needle that attaches to the syringe. The bevel of the needle is designed to provide both a sharp-cutting and nontearing, stretching action on the skin. The slant of the needle bevel varies depending on its intended use and is an important consideration in proper needle selection. The longer the bevel, the sharper the needle. Regular bevels are used for subcutaneous and intramuscular injections. Short bevels are used for intravenous injections and to minimize the possibility of piercing the opposite vein wall when the venipuncture or injection is made. The sheath protects the needle point.

Needles should be selected carefully in relation to: the type, volume, and viscosity of the drug to be injected; the type of injection to be given (e.g., subcutaneous, intramuscular, intravenous); and the condition of the tissue to be injected (e.g., amount of subcutaneous fat, muscle size, health of veins). Needle gauge reflects the diameter of the needle. The lower the gauge number (e.g., 19 gauge), the larger the diameter. Conversely, the higher the gauge number (e.g., 25 gauge), the smaller the diameter. Generally, shorter needles with higher gauge numbers are used for subcutaneous injections (e.g., 0.5-inch, 27.5 gauge needles). Longer needles with lower gauge numbers are used for intramuscular injections (e.g., 1.5-inch, 21 gauge needles).[20]

Syringes

Sterile, disposable, plastic syringes are generally used for the preparation and administration of injectable drugs. These syringes are individually packaged for convenience and sterility. The

---

[19] In addition to ampules and vials, injectable drugs also are supplied in prefilled cartridges, such as the Tubex® or Carpuject® systems. These systems fit into reusable syringe holders that are designed to release their cartridges so that contact with needles after injections is minimized.

[20] The gauge refers to the outer diameter of the needle. Needles are available in various gauges ranging from 18 to 27.5. The highest gauge *number* (i.e., the smallest diameter needle) possible, considering drug and injection site factors, should be selected in order to minimize the tissue damage and pain associated with injectable pharmacotherapy. Viscous drugs usually require needles with lower gauge *numbers* (i.e., larger diameters, such as a 19 gauge needle), while aqueous drugs can be administered with needles that have higher gauge *numbers* (i.e., smaller diameters, such as a 25 gauge needle).

syringe consists of a barrel or reservoir for holding the drug, a syringe tip for the attachment of the needle to the syringe, a plunger tip or piston-like device for changing the volume in the barrel and preventing leakage of drug, calibrated markings for measuring the dose of a drug, a retainer ridge that prevents the plunger from being inadvertently withdrawn from the barrel, finger flanges for secure gripping during preparation and injection of the drug, and a thumb rest, which positions the thumb securely during the injection. Syringes are designed to meet needs for safety and accuracy of dose measurement. Several companies provide syringes with positive stops to prevent the plunger from being accidentally withdrawn from the barrel during aspiration and easier-to-read markings to help ensure accuracy of dose measurement. As with needle selection, syringe selection depends on the type and volume of drug solution to be injected and whether the injection is to be subcutaneous, intramuscular, or intravenous.

All injectable equipment should be disposed of immediately after use in appropriate and accessible puncture-resistant receptacles (e.g., Sharps Collector®, Monoject High Volume Sharps Container®) according to current Centers for Disease Control (CDC) recommendations. The safe and ecologically appropriate disposal of injectable equipment from the home setting and the clinic or hospital is a concern for the community at large (e.g., garbage collectors and neighborhood children), as well as psychologists and their patients.

Site preparation[21]

To prevent infection, injection sites should be cleansed with an appropriate antiseptic prior to injection. The two most common types of antiseptics are 70% isopropyl alcohol and iodorphors, such as povidone-iodine (Betadine®). Sensitivity to iodine (e.g., a previous hypersensitivity reaction to a specific iodine product or to shellfish) should be ascertained before iodophors are used. If a patient has an allergy to iodine, the site should be cleansed with 70% isopropyl alcohol.[22] If the skin site is dirty or covered with wound drainage or excrement, it first should be gently washed with warm soap and water, rinsed thoroughly, and allowed to dry.[23]

Subcutaneous injections

Small volumes (less than 2 ml) of aqueous solutions or suspensions are commonly administered by subcutaneous injection. Drug formulations for subcutaneous injection should be isotonic to prevent irritation and pain at the injection site. Concentrated or irritating drugs (e.g., chlorpromazine [Largactil®, Thorazine®]) should not be injected subcutaneously because they can cause

---

[21] Prescribing psychologists may not always be directly involved with the actual administration of injectable psychotropic pharmacotherapy. Depending on the clinical situation, the administration of injectable pharmacotherapy may be delegated, as appropriate, to registered nurses or other health care providers, patients, or family members. However, psychologists require an understanding of the principles of injectable pharmacotherapy and recommended techniques of administration so that they can prescribe dosage forms and methods of administration that will provide optimal therapeutic benefit for their patients who require injectable pharmacotherapy with a minimum of associated adverse drug reactions. In addition, they can: (1) apprise patients of the potential benefits and possible risks associated with their injectable pharmacotherapy; (2) appropriately instruct patients, or their family members, regarding correct administration procedures; and (3) recognize improper injection techniques that may compromise the achievement of optimal pharmacotherapy or patient health and safety.

[22] BD® disposable butterfly swabs are 70% isopropyl alcohol swabs commonly used for preparing injection sites for injectable therapy. These swabs form a handle when opened so that the fingertips do *not* touch the swabbed skin.

[23] The site should be cleansed with the antiseptic in a circular fashion, moving from the center of the injection site outward approximately 2 inches (5 cm). The area should be allowed to dry before the injection is made so that the antiseptic is not tracked through the tissues, which can cause irritation and pain.

such ADRs as sterile abscesses, pain, necrosis, and tissue sloughing at the injection site. The injection of certain psychotropic drugs (e.g., opiate analgesics) by subcutaneous infusion (i.e., hypodermoclysis) has received renewed interest in regard to the symptomatic management of chronic severe pain (e.g., cancer pain).

Drug absorption from subcutaneous tissues is generally slow and complete. However, any factor that affects blood flow to the subcutaneous tissues (e.g., edema, exercise, shock) also can affect the absorption rate of drugs injected by this route. To ensure that the drug is deposited in the subcutaneous tissue, a 25 to 27.5 gauge, $^1/_2$- to $^5/_8$-inch (1.27- to 1.59-cm) needle should be used, depending on the amount of subcutaneous tissue at the injection site. Obese patients may require a 1-inch or longer needle to ensure that the drug is deposited subcutaneously. Depending on the patient's size and the condition of the tissue, a *maximum* volume of 0.5 to 1.5 ml should be injected at any one subcutaneous injection site. Injection of larger volumes may result in pain and irritation at the injection site.

Subcutaneous injections deliver drug beneath the epidermal layer of the skin into the subcutaneous fat layer (Figure 4-2). The preferred subcutaneous injection sites (Figure 4-3) are the upper arms, lower abdomen (from the belt line to the symphysis pubis and 2 inches [5 cm] from the umbilicus), anterior thighs, and buttocks. Fatty sites on the upper back above the scapulae also can be used. The site selected must be free from excoriations, hematomas, lesions, and moles. If injections are frequently required, sites should be rotated to prevent ADRs such as unabsorbed drug deposits, subcutaneous nodules, and sterile abscesses.

Performing the injection
After the cooperation of the patient has been obtained and the site prepared, the needle should be inserted at a 90-degree angle to the skin surface (Figure 4-2). Depending on the characteristics of the skin, the skin can be held taut for the insertion of the needle with the fingertips of the nondominant hand, or, if preferred, the subcutaneous tissue can be gently lifted away from the

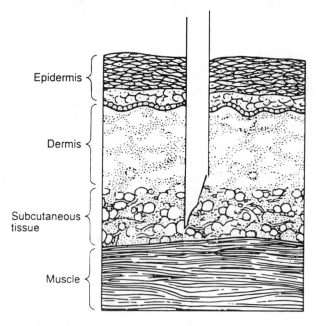

Figure 4-2. Subcutaneous injection.

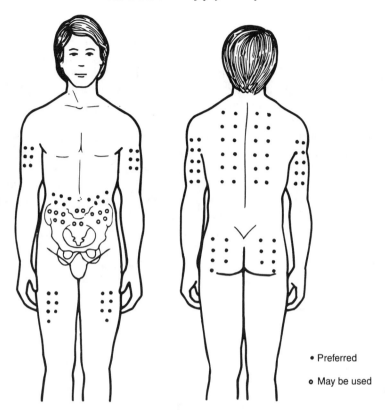

● Preferred

○ May be used

Figure 4-3. Subcutaneous injection sites.

muscle with the fingertips and the needle inserted into the "pocket" that is formed.[24] In order to prevent undue pain and discomfort, the needle should be inserted quickly, bevel-side up, with a darting motion. It should then be advanced smoothly into the tissue. Skin held taut should be released after inserting the needle and before injecting the drug to allow the drug to distribute readily into the tissues. Releasing the skin also helps to minimize painful stimulation of subcutaneous nerve endings.

The syringe plunger should be gently pulled back before injecting the drug to ensure that the needle has not penetrated a blood vessel. If no blood is aspirated into the syringe, the drug should be slowly injected. If blood is aspirated into the syringe, the needle should be removed and gentle pressure applied to the site with a dry, sterile gauze. The needle and syringe should be disposed of appropriately and a fresh dose prepared and injected at a different subcutaneous site.

After the drug is injected, the needle should be quickly withdrawn at the same angle by which it was inserted. A dry, sterile gauze should be held at the site as the needle is withdrawn to prevent the needle from clinging to and pulling on the tissues. After the needle is withdrawn, gentle pressure should be applied with the sterile gauze at the site to prevent bleeding. The site can then be gently massaged to increase drug absorption (unless it is contraindicated, such as when heparin [an anticoagulant] is injected). Tissue damage has been associated with frequent, repeated subcutaneous injections. These ADRs can be avoided or minimized by careful site rotation. It is generally recommended that no area 1 inch (2.5 cm) in diameter be used for subcutaneous injection more than once every 3 to 4 weeks.

---

[24] When the tissue "pocket" technique is used, the "pocket" should be maintained throughout the injection procedure.

Subcutaneous intermittent drug administration

Subcutaneous intermittent drug administration offers an alternative to intramuscular or intravenous analgesia for the management of severe chronic pain (e.g., cancer pain) in both hospital and home settings. Subcutaneous intermittent drug administration avoids repeated injections, facilitates adequate pain control, promotes maintenance of activities of daily living (e.g., ambulation), and prevents unnecessary infusion of excess fluids, as is needed with intermittent or continuous intravenous infusions.

A subcutaneous injection site is selected (e.g., abdomen, lateral upper chest, lateral or anterior thigh) and gently pinched to form a bulge. Care must be taken that the needle is not inserted into breast tissue when chest sites are used. An intermittent infusion set (e.g., EZ® set) with a 25 to 27 gauge, $^3/_4$-inch (1.75-cm) needle is used for the infusion. The site is prepared according to protocol. The needle is inserted at a 30- to 45-degree angle, secured with tape or a transparent dressing, and appropriately labeled (i.e., "for subcutaneous use only"). The injection port is cleansed with an antiseptic, and a maximum of 2 ml (i.e., the maximum volume of fluid that can be absorbed per hour from a subcutaneous site) of drug is slowly injected. Rapid injection can cause burning or stinging at the injection site and should be avoided. The site, usually maintained for 7 days, should be carefully monitored daily for signs of irritation or infection.

Subcutaneous opiate analgesic infusion

Subcutaneous opiate infusion offers patients with advanced cancer sustained pain relief without significant systemic ADRs. Unfortunately, a complication of therapy is the development of serious and painful subdermal plaques at the needle-insertion sites. Plaque formation seems unrelated to needle size, site or angle of insertion, duration of use, opiate dose or volume, or cancer diagnosis. Unfortunately, there are no dermatologic warning signs of plaque formation, although induration is sometimes noted at the site before plague formation occurs.

Although causes of plaque formation remain inconclusive, they appear to be related to hydraulic irritation, in which subdermal destruction may occur simply as a reaction to the infusion of a foreign substance into subcutaneous tissue. Administered drug appears to be distributed just as effectively from subcutaneous pockets with plaques as from those without. However, plaques do limit needle placement in the abdomen, a disadvantage when patients are elderly, frail, or debilitated and have little subcutaneous tissue. In addition, the lesions are painful and disfiguring.

Continuous subcutaneous infusion. Terminally ill patients are increasingly choosing to die in their own homes with the assistance of family caregivers and the help of palliative care professionals. The use of continuous subcutaneous infusion (CSCI) of opiate analgesics has been important for promoting patient comfort in relation to pain and symptom management. Patients and their families require accurate and complete information regarding how to manage CSCI and other related aspects of palliative home care.

Continuous subcutaneous infusion is of benefit to patients who have pain that is poorly controlled by orally ingested analgesics or who may be experiencing dysphagia or gastrointestinal obstruction. Continuous subcutaneous infusion also is indicated when prolonged use of other injectable routes for opiate analgesic pharmacotherapy (i.e., intravenous pharmacotherapy) is not feasible because of the need for close monitoring or activity limitations.

Continuous subcutaneous infusion involves the use of a portable, small, light, battery-operated, refillable pump (e.g., Cormed®, Graesby MS26®, CADD-PCA®) that administers drug subcutaneously through a butterfly needle inserted into one of several subcutaneous injection sites, including the subclavian and anterior chest regions, outer aspects of upper arms, abdomen, and thighs. Mobility is generally unaffected because the pump can be held in a shoulder bag or pyjama pocket. This method provides continuous drug administration and replaces the need for repeated injections.

An interdisciplinary approach, such as palliative care services, is required, and proper support and teaching is essential. In addition to a basic knowledge about the required opiate analgesics and how to obtain, store, and dispose of them safely and appropriately, patient instruction should include an overview of the basic parts and function of the infusion pump, general care of the pump during daily activities (e.g., ambulation, bathing, sleeping, traveling), specific ways to identify whether the pump is working properly, procedures for battery and drug cartridge changes, stopping and starting the pump, care of the tubing, and monitoring of alarm systems, including the meaning of various alarms and when and how to take appropriate action.

Monitoring and changing of CSCI sites also are important. Sites are usually changed every 3 to 7 days. Sites should be monitored for blockage, edema, seepage of blood or other body fluid, pain, poor absorption, redness, and other signs and symptoms that indicate the site should be changed.

Intramuscular injections

Essentially all of the injectable psychotropic drugs can be injected intramuscularly. Generally, drugs are absorbed rapidly and completely after intramuscular injection because of the high vascularity of healthy muscle. However, the rate of absorption may vary widely because of the physicochemical properties of a particular drug formulation. For example, drugs formulated as aqueous solutions are rapidly and completely absorbed after intramuscular injection. However, drugs such as fluphenazine [Modecon® Concentrate] and haloperidol [Haldol® Decanoate 50 or 100] are formulated in such a way that their absorption is slowed and their action sustained so that they can be injected once a month. Absorption also is affected by various physiologic factors, including blood flow to the muscle site, which can be influenced by a patient's age and general health state. These drug and patient factors also affect the volume of drug that can be injected into a muscle site. The maximum recommended volume for intramuscular injections for children and elderly, frail, or debilitated patients is 1 ml to 2 ml. Usually 1 ml to 5 ml is considered the recommended range for adults.

Thus, as with other injectable pharmacotherapy, the intramuscular injection of psychotropic drugs requires the consideration of several factors, including the indication for intramuscular psychotropic pharmacotherapy, the type of drug formulation to be injected (e.g., aqueous solution, suspension, or decanoate salt), volume of drug to be injected, equipment (i.e., size of needle and syringe), health of skin and underlying muscle, and the number of injections required.

Performing the injection

Intramuscular injections require careful selection of needles and syringes so that the drug is delivered deeply into healthy muscle sites where it can absorbed and therapeutic benefit obtained with a minimum of associated adverse effects. Site accessibility and individual preference also must be considered. Injections should be made into relaxed muscle to decrease associated pain and to increase dispersion of the drug into the muscle tissue. A patient's response to intramuscular injections depends on his or her previous experiences with injectable pharmacotherapy. Psychological support is often required, and various strategies can be used to help patients with their injectable pharmacotherapy. Mentally challenged or confused patients may require gentle manual restraint to prevent them from moving during the injection and inadvertently sustaining injury. Patients who are psychotic may be concerned that "their insides might leak out" and require the simple application of a plastic adhesive bandage to allay their fears.

Intramuscular injections are generally contraindicated for patients who are receiving anticoagulant (i.e., heparin [Hepalean®] or warfarin [Coumadin®, Warfilone®]) pharmacotherapy or those who have thrombocytopenia. Injections made deeply into the muscle can result in bleeding and severe tissue sloughing among these patients. Serum creatine phosphokinase (CPK) concentrations may rise after intramuscular injections, as a result of injury to muscle tissue, and may affect the interpretation of this laboratory test result.

Equipment selection

Intramuscular injections should be made with needles ranging in length from 1 to 3 inches (2.5 to 7.5 cm). The length of the needle is determined by the amount of subcutaneous fat over the injection site (Figure 4-4). For children or thin, elderly, frail, or debilitated patients, a 1-inch (2.5 cm) or smaller needle ($^5/_8$ inch) may be required. For most adults, a 1.5 inch needle is used. The needle gauge is determined by the viscosity of the drug formulation to be injected. A 19 gauge needle is used for viscous drug formulations, whereas 21 to 23 gauge needles are used for more aqueous formulations. As a general rule to avoid unnecessary tissue damage, the shortest length and highest gauge number needle possible for a particular drug and patient should be selected.[25]

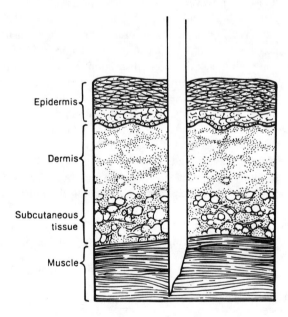

Figure 4-4. Intramuscular injection.

---

[25] A two-needle technique (replacing the wet needle used to prepare the injection with a sterile dry needle) can be used to avoid tracking an irritating drug through the epidermis, dermis, and subcutaneous tissues when the injection is made. An airlock technique (withdrawing 0.2 ml to 0.5 ml of air into the syringe after replacing the needle) alone or in combination with the Z-track injection technique (see later discussion) can be used to prevent the drug from seeping out of the injection site along the needle track after the injection has been made.

Intramuscular injection sites

The selection of a suitable intramuscular injection site is an important aspect of intramuscular psychotropic pharmacotherapy. Intramuscular injection sites must be carefully selected to avoid injuring blood vessels, bones, and nerves. Recommended intramuscular injection sites include the deltoid muscles of the upper arms, the gluteal muscles of the buttocks, and the rectus femoris and vastus lateralis muscles of the anterior and lateral thighs. The selection of a particular site depends on such factors as accessibility (e.g., a cast or dressing may prevent access to a site), size and health of muscle (i.e., only healthy muscle that is well vascularized should be selected), characteristics of the drug, number of injections required, and the patient's and clinician's personal preferences. Sites that are at risk for infection should be avoided (e.g., frequent diarrhea or urinary incontinence may increase the risk for infection of sites on the buttocks and thighs), as should sites that are sensitive,[26] are painful to touch, or have hardened masses (e.g., sterile abscesses) upon palpation.

Deltoid site.   The deltoid muscle is generally *not* recommended for intramuscular injections of psychotropic drugs because of its small size and close proximity to the radial nerve and major blood vessels. However, it is a recommended site for the injection of fluphenazine (Modecate®, Moditen®, Prolixin®). Although patients can generally receive 0.5 ml to 2 ml of drug at this site when the muscle is healthy and well developed, it is generally recommended that the site be used only when necessary and for small volumes (0.5 ml or less) of aqueous, nonirritating drugs (e.g., vitamin B_{12} [cyanocobalamin] injections). However, many nonambulatory patients who use nonmotorized wheelchairs have deltoid muscles that are better developed than other muscle sites. For these patients, the deltoid site offers an important site for intramuscular injections.

To locate the densest area of the deltoid muscle and avoid the radial nerve and major blood vessels, a point on the lateral aspect of the upper arm, about 1 to 2 inches (2.5 to 5 cm) inferior to the lower edge of the acromion process in line with the axilla, should be identified (Figure 4-5). The patient should be encouraged to relax the muscle by supporting the lower arm, and the needle should be inserted at a right angle to the skin or pointed slightly toward the acromion process.

Dorsogluteal site.   The gluteal muscles are the most commonly used muscles for intramuscular injection. Generally, patients should be instructed to position themselves comfortably, lying facedown. To relax the gluteal muscles, patients should be asked to point their toes in ("toe-in"). The needle should be inserted at a right angle to the surface that the patient is lying on. Although this position offers greater stability by restricting movement during the injection, the dorsogluteal site also can be injected when patients are lying on their sides or standing. To relax the gluteal muscles when patients are lying on their side, they should be instructed to position themselves with the knee and hip of the upper leg flexed forward and the lower leg straight. To relax the gluteal muscles when patients are standing, patients should be instructed to stand with the toes pointed in.

Accurate identification of landmarks is essential to avoid injuring the sciatic nerve and superior gluteal artery. To locate the dorsogluteal site, an imaginary line from the posterior superior iliac spine to the greater trochanter of the femur should be visualized. This imaginary line between the iliac spine and the greater trochanter is parallel and superior to the sciatic nerve. Thus, a site selected laterally and superiorly to this line avoids the sciatic nerve and the major blood vessels (Figure 4-6). The dorsogluteal site is recommended for the injection of

---

[26] When a site has been selected, the muscle should be rolled between the fingertips and assessed for twitching. Highly sensitive areas twitch when the muscle is rolled between the fingertips. The intramuscular injection of a drug into a sensitive area can result in referred or sharp pain that feels as if a nerve has been "hit."

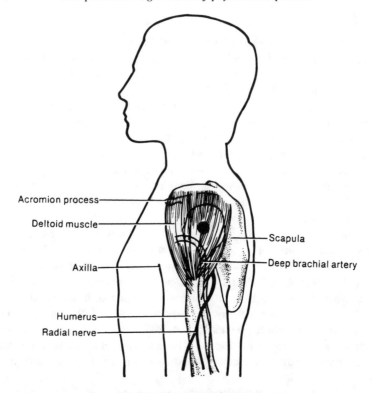

Figure 4-5. Deltoid intramuscular injection site.

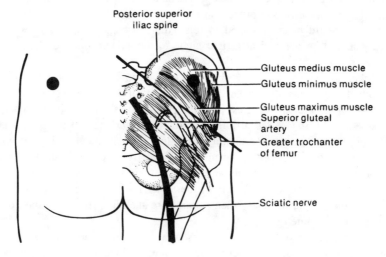

Figure 4-6. Dorsogluteal intramuscular injection site.

viscous or irritating psychotropic drugs and drugs that can stain the skin (see "Z-track technique" and Figure 4-10). The gluteal muscles are likely to be degenerated in patients who are nonambulatory, frail, or emaciated. The use of the dorsogluteal site is contraindicated for these patients. When healthy muscles are used, a maximum volume of up to 4 ml can be comfortably injected. *Ventrogluteal site.*   The ventrogluteal site, comprising the gluteus medius and gluteus minimus muscles, has a larger muscle mass and less subcutaneous tissue than the dorsogluteal site. This site is accessible when patients are lying down (faceup or facedown), lying on their sides, or standing. The ventrogluteal site is generally free of major nerves and blood vessels, which makes it a relatively safe site for intramuscular injection. However, care must be taken to avoid making the injection into a bone or joint. The ventrogluteal site is generally recommended for both ambulatory and nonambulatory patients. It offers an alternative intramuscular injection site for nonambulatory or frail patients whose muscle mass is likely to be degenerated at the dorsogluteal and vastus lateralis sites. Depending on the size and health of the muscle, patients can tolerate up to 5 ml.

The site can be located while patients are standing, lying on their abdomen or back, or lying on their side. The heel of the hand is placed over the greater trochanter of the femur, and the iliac crest is palpated with the fingertips pointed toward the patient's head. The right hand is used for identifying the site on the left hip, and the left hand is used for identifying the site on the right hip. The index and middle fingers are spread to form a "V" with the tip of the index finger at the anterior superior iliac spine and the tip of the middle finger just below the iliac crest. Injections should be made at the center of the triangle formed between the index finger, middle finger, and iliac crest (Figure 4-7), with the needle perpendicular to the skin or directed slightly toward the iliac crest. The ventrogluteal muscle can be relaxed by "toeing-in" when patients are standing or lying on their abdomens or backs. Patients can relax the ventrogluteal muscle by flexing the upper knee in front of the lower leg while in the side lying position.
Vastus lateralis site.   The vastus lateralis site has only a thin covering of subcutaneous tissue, tolerates up to 4 ml of drug volume, and can be used for deep intramuscular and Z-track injections for patients who have a healthy muscle site. This muscle is likely to be degenerated among nonambulatory, frail, or debilitated patients and, thus, should *not* be used for these patients.

The vastus lateralis is located on the anterolateral aspect of the thigh from a hand's breadth below the greater trochanter to a hand's breadth above the knee (Figure 4-8). Patients can be positioned in either a lying or sitting position for the injection. The needle should be inserted at a right angle to the muscle or directed slightly toward the knee. The injection should be made into the belly of the muscle by gently lifting the muscle away from the bone.
Rectus femoris site.   Although the rectus femoris is smaller in size than the vastus lateralis, it also is recommended as an intramuscular injection site for ambulatory patients who have healthy muscle sites. There are no major nerves or blood vessels in close proximity to this site, and it is readily accessible. The rectus femoris muscle is located on the anterior aspect of the thigh (Figure 4-9). Injections can be made into the mid-section of this muscle while patients are

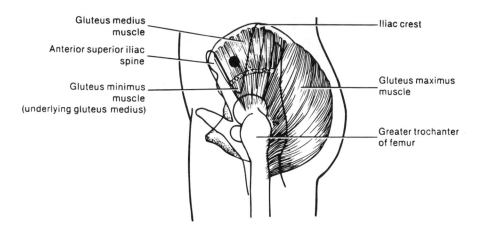

Figure 4-7. Ventrogluteal intramuscular injection site.

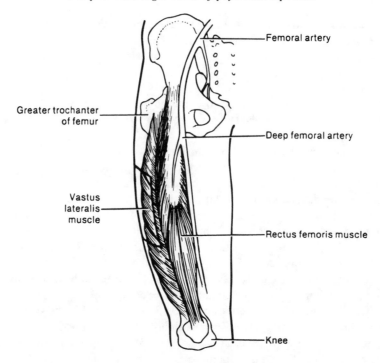

Figure 4-8. *Vastus lateralis intramuscular injection site.*

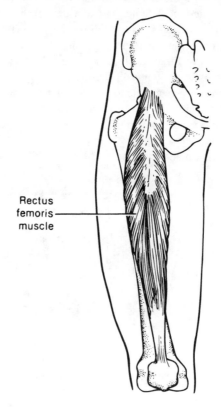

Figure 4-9. *Rectus femoris intramuscular injection site.*

sitting or lying down. Depending on the size and health of the muscle, up to 3 ml can be injected into this site. The site is identified in the same way as the vastus lateralis site, but the anterior aspect of the thigh is used.

The intramuscular injection

Before the drug is injected, the site must be prepared with an antiseptic by cleansing it in a circular fashion from the center out for approximately 2 inches (5 cm). With the syringe at a 90-degree angle to the skin surface, unless otherwise specified, the needle should be quickly inserted with a darting motion, which minimizes pain and facilitates penetration of the skin and underlying tissue. The tissue should be gently released and the plunger pulled back to determine whether the needle is in a blood vessel. If blood appears in the syringe during aspiration, the needle should be withdrawn, gentle pressure applied to the site with a dry sterile gauze, and another dose prepared. If no blood is aspirated into the syringe, the dose should be slowly injected to allow dispersion into the muscle tissue. The needle should then be withdrawn quickly and smoothly in the same direction that it was inserted. A sterile gauze should be held at the site to prevent any bleeding from the site after the injection has been made.

It is not uncommon for patients to experience pain and discomfort as a result of muscle damage associated with intramuscular injections. The diluent can be irritating to muscle tissues. For example, dextrose and saline solutions cause minimal damage, but alcohol and propylene glycol may cause moderate damage. Severe injury to muscle has resulted from the injection of diazepam (Valium®) and phenytoin (Dilantin®). When several intramuscular injections are required, rotation of injection sites is essential to prevent muscle injury and to ensure adequate drug absorption from intramuscular injection sites.

Generally, pain is minimized if the injection is made into a relaxed muscle and the site is gently massaged, unless contraindicated, after the injection is made.[27] Massaging the site also distributes the drug, increases absorption, and reduces pain associated with the stretching of the tissue resulting from the volume of drug injected. Exercise of the muscle also will increase drug absorption and reduce pain. Injection sites must be monitored for early signs of complications related to injectable pharmacotherapy, which can generally be avoided by site rotation. Elderly, frail, or debilitated patients may be at particular risk for injury and infection associated with injectable pharmacotherapy.

Z-track injection

The Z-track method of intramuscular injection (see Figure 4-10) is used to prevent irritation and discoloration of the skin and subcutaneous tissues when viscous, irritating, or staining drugs (e.g., iron dextran [INFeD®]) are injected. A 19 to 20 gauge, 1- to 3-inch (2.5- to 7.5-cm) needle is used to withdraw the drug from the ampule or vial. The needle should be replaced with a dry, sterile needle to avoid tracking the drug through the skin and subcutaneous tissue, and 0.2 ml to 0.5 ml of air should be withdrawn into the syringe as an airlock before administering the dose.

Although the Z-track method can be used at other intramuscular injection sites, it is most commonly used at the dorsogluteal site. A 4-inch (10-cm) skin area is prepared with an antiseptic and allowed to dry. With the ulnar side (heel) of the nondominant hand, the skin and subcutaneous tissue at the injection site are retracted inferiorly (down) and medially (toward the median plane

---

[27] A more recently developed technique for minimizing pain associated with injectable pharmacotherapy involves the use of a specially formulated topical anesthetic cream, EMLA®. EMLA® is a eutectic mixture of local anesthetics, equal parts lidocaine and prilocaine. It has been found to significantly reduce the pain associated with injectable pharmacotherapy.

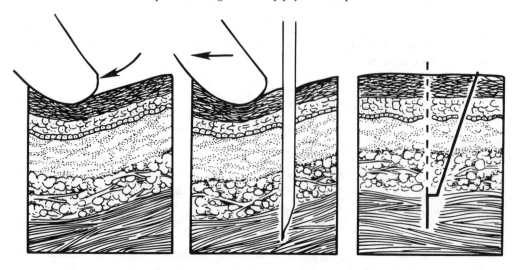

Figure 4-10. Z-track injection.

of the body) at least 1 inch (2.5 cm) before the needle is inserted at a 90-degree angle. Although the skin and subcutaneous layers are retracted, the muscle remains in the original landmarked position. The needle should be inserted quickly and smoothly in a darting manner and the syringe plunger gently pulled back. If no blood is aspirated into the syringe, the drug should be slowly injected. The skin should be held in the retracted position for 10 seconds to allow dispersion of the drug into the muscle tissue. The needle then should be quickly and smoothly withdrawn while the skin and subcutaneous tissue are allowed to return to their normal position. Pressure can be gently applied at the site; however, rubbing and massaging are contraindicated because of the possibility of tissue damage. No more than 2 ml of irritating or staining drug should be injected into any one site.[28] Patients should be cautioned not to rub the site, exercise, or wear tight clothing immediately after the injection. Following these recommendations minimizes the chance of the drug seeping into the subcutaneous tissues and causing irritation or staining.

Intravenous injections and infusions

Intravenous injections and infusions are often used to administer drugs with short elimination half-lives (i.e., that require frequent dosing), avoid the pain and injury associated with multiple subcutaneous or intramuscular injections when drug volumes greater than 5 ml must be administered frequently, facilitate the concurrent administration of several different injectable drugs, and administer psychotropic drugs (e.g., anticonvulsants, antipsychotics, opiate analgesics) when immediate drug action is required, such as in emergency situations. Intravenous injections and infusions also are used when subcutaneous and intramuscular injections are contraindicated because of the chemical characteristics or actions of a particular drug. For example, some drugs (e.g., diazepam [Valium®], phenytoin [Dilantin®]) are formulated in propylene glycol or alcohol solvents. These solvents encourage rapid dilution by interstitial fluid and precipitation at subcutaneous and intramuscular injection sites, which can result in slow and erratic absorption and

---

[28] For pharmacotherapy that requires more than one or two injections, intravenous pharmacotherapy with an appropriate injectable formulation should be considered.

irritation to subcutaneous tissues and muscle. Therefore, the intravenous route is preferred for these drugs when an injectable route is required.

Drug effects following intravenous injection or infusion are immediate and predictable, depending on the dose administered, protein binding, distribution, and rate of metabolism and excretion. The intravenous route is the route of choice for patients who have compromised peripheral circulation (e.g., congestive heart failure, shock) because absorption is immediate and, unlike subcutaneous and intramuscular injections, is independent of blood flow to different tissues.[29] With increased focus on home care, including palliative home care, intravenous drug therapy is becoming more commonplace in private and residential homes and extended care facilities. This trend is expected to continue with impetus from potential health care cost savings.

Patients and their family members, or others who may be involved with their care, can effectively manage home intravenous pharmacotherapy with appropriate instruction and assistance from the psychologist and community health resources (e.g., public health nurse; home health care assistants). They can learn to prepare intravenous admixtures, maintain peripheral and central venous access sites and devices (including Broviac/Hickman catheters and implantable devices), and operate electronic infusion pumps and controllers. Technological advances in the development of intravenous infusion devices offer economy, flexibility, and convenience to patients who require in-home intravenous pharmacotherapy.

Intravenous equipment

Solutions and containers

A variety of equipment is available for intravenous drug delivery for both hospitalized and nonhospitalized patients. The type of equipment selected for intravenous pharmacotherapy depends on several factors. Generally, intravenous pharmacotherapy can be individualized according to the specific needs of the patient by taking into consideration the patient's age, general health state, accessibility and number of venipuncture sites, required pharmacotherapy (e.g., type of drug to be injected, frequency and duration of pharmacotherapy), manufacturer guidelines for use of equipment (e.g., venous access devices and infusion control devices, including electronic pumps and controllers), equipment cost, and amount of waste (e.g., drug, intravenous tubing).

Intravenous solutions

A wide selection of intravenous solutions (e.g., sodium chloride 0.9% [normal saline], dextrose 5% in water [D_5W]) are supplied in sterile vacuum-sealed glass bottles or, more commonly, polyvinylchloride (PVC) bags. These products are provided in various volumes (e.g., 50, 100, 250, 500, and 1,000 ml) for convenience. The larger volumes (i.e., 500 and 1,000 ml) are used for fluid replacement and continuous intravenous infusions. The smaller volumes (i.e., 50, 100, and 250 ml) are used for intravenous drug dilution and intermittent drug delivery.

PVC bags have generally replaced glass bottles for the provision of intravenous pharmacotherapy and offer several advantages (e.g., easier storage, less weight, less breakage). However, some disadvantages have been noted, including the greater propensity of many drugs in solution to adsorb to the inner plastic surface of PVC bags. For example, approximately 50% of diazepam (Valium®) has been reportedly adsorbed after 5 hours of contact within a PVC bag. To avoid the potential significant adsorption of diazepam and other psychotropic drugs (e.g., chlorpromazine

---

[29] Recall from Chapter 3, "Pharmacokinetics and Pharmacodynamics" that, by definition, F = 1.0 for all intravenously administered drugs.

[Largactil®, Thorazine®]), it is recommended that these drugs be prepared in polyethylene bags (e.g., Stedim 6®) and administered with polyethylene infusion sets (see later discussion of "tubing and drip chambers").

Solution bottles are fitted with rubber stoppers and sealed with metal caps or collars. They should be inspected carefully before use to ensure that seals are intact and the glass is not cracked. Solution bags should be inspected for puncture marks and leaks, particularly at the additive ports. All intravenous solution containers should be held up to the light and inspected for cloudiness and particulate matter. The expiration dates on solution containers should be checked carefully to ensure that products are not outdated, and labels should be read three times to avoid using the wrong solution.

Intravenous solution bottles have a vacuum and require that an equal volume of air be introduced through an integral airway (vent) to replace the volume of solution removed from the bottle during the infusion. Some intravenous solution bottles do not have integral airways and require vented tubing to permit filtered air to enter the bottle as the solution is infused. Nonvented tubing can be used with solution bags because they compress as they empty.

Tubing and drip chambers

Specially designed intravenous tubing is supplied in sterile packages by various manufacturers for use with specific drug delivery systems and intravenous products. Tubing is available with drip chambers that make it easy to see and count drops of fluid so that required amounts of drugs and solutions can be administered accurately. The drip chamber is calibrated so that a specified number of drops deliver a milliliter of solution. Tubing also is available with in-chamber and in-line filter systems that can help to decrease the amount of contaminants and particulate matter delivered into the bloodstream.

There are several types of tubing that can be used for intravenous drug delivery. PVC tubing is commonly used and is adequate for most drugs and solutions. However, it is not appropriate for all drugs. For example, the vasodilator nitroglycerin is adsorbed by PVC intravenous tubing, and if used for infusion, underdosing can occur during the first 2 hours of the infusion until the tubing becomes saturated with nitroglycerin. If the infusion rate is increased during this initial period, to compensate for drug loss, toxicity can develop as the tubing becomes saturated. Polyethylene (PEL) tubing can avoid this adsorption problem, but use of PEL tubing has been limited because of its opacity and inflexibility. In an effort to avoid these problems, a PEL/PVC intravenous set has been developed, which has been associated with significantly less loss of drug than the standard set, regardless of drug concentration or infusion rate.

Newer delivery systems

Although small-volume intermittent infusions are commonly used for intravenous drug delivery, they have several limitations. These limitations include: unpredictable infusion rates, resulting in inconsistent and incomplete drug delivery; relatively high expense; and excessive waste of tubing and other equipment (e.g., needles and syringes). An increasing number of newer intravenous drug delivery systems (e.g., AddVantage®, Viaflex Plus®) are designed to facilitate intravenous pharmacotherapy, save time in preparing and administering doses, and prevent dosing errors that can occur when reconstitution of drugs is required. These drug delivery systems provide ready-to-use drugs and diluents or premixed drug solutions in containers that are easy to handle. Some drugs, primarily antibiotics (e.g., Fortaz®), are available frozen. The manufacturer's instructions for the use of these products should be followed.

Concerns about escalating health care costs and disposal of used injection equipment have focused attention on intravenous drug administration products that are cost effective and minimize waste. For example, several controlled-release membrane infusion devices have been studied in an effort to eliminate the need for small-volume bags and bottles, secondary infusion sets, and mechanical infusion devices.

Venous access devices

Veins can be accessed with peripheral venous access devices, central venous access devices, and implantable vascular access devices. The selection and use of these devices are based on the individual requirements of patients for intravenous psychotropic pharmacotherapy (e.g., volume of drug, frequency of dosing, duration of therapy), the patient's general health status, and the size and condition of the patient's veins.

Peripheral venous access devices.   Peripheral venous access devices include individually pack-aged, sterile, winged-tipped needles (e.g., Butterfly®) and over-the-needle catheters, which are available in a variety of gauges and lengths.[30] Needles and catheters should be carefully inspected for defects before use. Generally, needles and catheters are coated with silicone to decrease clotting at the bevel and tip and to facilitate insertion. The winged-tipped (e.g., Butterfly®) needle is 0.5 to 1.25 inches (1.3 to 3.1 cm) long with tubing 3 to 12 inches (7.5 to 30 cm) in length. It is commonly used for one-time (i.e., slow or rapid intravenous injection) or short-term, intermittent pharmacotherapy (i.e., 1 to 3 days). Over-the-needle catheters (e.g., Angiocath®) are radiopaque combination catheter and needle devices available in lengths ranging from 1.25 to 2 inches (3.1 to 5 cm). An over-the-needle catheter has an inner needle and an outer catheter. After the combination is inserted into a vein, the needle is removed, leaving the catheter in the vein. Generally, over-the-needle catheters are used when an irritating drug or long-term intrave-nous pharmacotherapy (more than 3 days) is required.

Several peripheral venous access devices have been developed to protect against accidental needle stick injury and infection with HIV, hepatitis B, or other infectious microorganisms. For example, the PROTECTIV® IV catheter safety system offers needle stick protection during and after venipuncture with an over-the-needle catheter. As the contaminated needle is removed from within the catheter, a protective guard glides over it. A reassuring click indicates when the needle is locked safely inside the guard.

Peripheral venous access devices (either needles or catheters after they have been inserted) are often capped with intermittent infusion control (IIC) caps (e.g., intermittent heparin lock) to promote freedom and mobility and to prevent the necessity of repeated venipunctures. The IIC cap provides ready access for intravenous injections (i.e., "push" or "bolus" injections) and intermittent intravenous drug infusions. Some drugs can be injected over 5 minutes or less (i.e., "IV push") directly into the IIC cap; alternatively, intravenous

---

[30] The selection of a peripheral access device often depends on personal preference (i.e., some health care providers prefer butterfly needles, but others prefer catheters). Winged-tip needles may be preferred because they are easily inserted. However, winged-tip needles are not as stable as catheters after insertion because they are rigid and can more easily damage or pierce the opposite vein wall, resulting in extravasation. Although winged-tip needles can be used for long-term pharmacotherapy, catheters may be preferred because they are more flexible and offer patients fewer activity restrictions. However, the catheter insertion site must be carefully assessed for infection and phlebitis because these problems tend to occur more often with catheters than with wing-tipped needles, particularly when irritating drugs are infused. Generally, the smallest possible diameter (i.e., the highest gauge number) needle or catheter should be used to maximize blood flow at the needle or catheter tip, which helps to rapidly dilute irritating drug solutions as they enter the bloodstream.

tubing can be attached to the IIC cap for slow, intermittent infusion with a volume-control device or a small-volume infusion set.[31]

The IIC cap is wiped with an alcohol swab, the site is checked for patency, and the drug is injected with a $^1/_2$ to 1 inch (1.25 to 2.5 cm) needle. Traditionally, 1 ml of sterile normal saline (0.9% sodium chloride solution for injection) has been injected into the IIC cap to flush the drug through the peripheral venous access device. The saline flush has been followed by a heparin flush (1 ml of heparin [100 units/ml]) to maintain the patency of the venous access device. Heparin flushes generally have been recommended every 8 hours and after drug administration. Irritation at the venipuncture site, phlebitis, and leakage of heparin have called into question the need for heparin flushes for the maintenance of peripheral venous access devices. Overall, the results of studies examining this question are conflicting. Normal saline has been found to avoid phlebitis and to be as effective as heparin for maintaining patency of IIC caps. However, cost-effectiveness research found that saline-flushed venous access devices had to be replaced twice as often as heparin-flushed devices and that increased discomfort and risk of phlebitis were associated with saline flushes. Therefore, the use of a heparin flush without a saline flush has been recommended after administering drugs that are compatible with heparin (for drugs that are incompatible with heparin, flush the venous access device with 1 ml normal saline, administer the drug, and flush the device with 1 ml normal saline and then with 1 ml heparin solution). The use of other intravenous solutions (e.g., dextrous 5% and water) also has been explored with encouraging results. Further research is required.

An example of a potentially safer method of intravenous drug delivery is the "needle-less" InterLink® intravenous access system. This system uses a blunt plastic cannula in place of a needle for extracorporeal intravenous drug delivery applications such as access to both single- and multiple-dose vials and intravenous tubing ports (i.e., "Y-sites"), preventing accidental needle stick injuries and infections. Similar needle-less systems have been developed by other manufacturers.

If the peripheral venous access device is inadvertently dislodged, patients should be provided with a protocol for immediate management of the bleeding (i.e., apply pressure to the venipuncture site with a sterile gauze) and with procedures for accessing emergency services if required; also, they should be instructed to notify their psychologist immediately so that a new venous access device can be inserted. The site should be observed for hemorrhage, discoloration, and other signs of prolonged clotting time. IIC caps are generally changed when peripheral venous access devices (i.e., needles and catheters) are changed, at least every 72 hours or more frequently if needed (e.g., if leaking occurs). Peripheral venous access devices are generally adequate for providing intravenous psychotropic pharmacotherapy to most patients. However, in some situations, other devices may be required, including central venous access devices (e.g., Broviac/Hickman catheters, multi-lumen central venous pressure catheters) and implantable venous access devices. These devices are usually reserved for use by patients who require intravenous opiate analgesics for the symptomatic

---

[31] The IIC cap can be carefully taped to prevent it from being inadvertently displaced. Patients and their family members, or others involved with their pharmacotherapy, should be instructed regarding the care and management of the site. They also should be instructed regarding the appropriate procedure to follow if the IIC capped access device becomes dislodged (e.g., apply firm pressure to the site with a sterile gauze to stop any bleeding and notify the prescribing psychologist or other specified health care provider so that any additional care to the site can be provided and the device replaced if necessary). The site should be observed for hemorrhage, discoloration, or other signs that may indicate a prolonged clotting time. These devices are generally changed every 72 hours or as needed. More research is required regarding the influence of various factors (e.g., drug factors, various needles and catheter factors, length of time a site is used for intravenous pharmacotherapy, venipuncture site care procedures) on the occurrence of infiltration, inflammation, or infection rates.

relief of severe long-term pain associated with cancer or other serious medical conditions (e.g., AIDS).

Central venous access devices.   Broviac/Hickman catheters are central venous catheters made of silicone designed for long-term infusion therapy. The Broviac catheter was introduced by Broviac in 1973 as a permanent indwelling right atrial catheter for delivering home nutritional support. It was modified by Hickman and colleagues in 1979 to allow blood withdrawal and the delivery of intravenous drugs and solutions and blood products. These catheters can have one to three lumens and are flushed every 24 hours (12 hours if not in use) and after each use with 2.5 ml heparin (100 units/ml) or according to protocol. Before inserting a needle into the access port of the catheter, all tubing and needle connections should be vigorously scrubbed with povidone-iodine and allowed to dry. Alternatively, each connection can be vigorously scrubbed with isopropyl alcohol for 2 minutes. Catheter insertion and removal is a minor surgical procedure completed medically under local or general anesthesia. In addition to infection, central venous access devices are subject to a variety of complications, including dislodgement and occlusion. If catheters are dislodged or occluded, they must be replaced or an alternative device selected.

The multi-lumen central venous pressure (ML-CVP®) catheter is an alternative to the Broviac/Hickman catheter. It uses a single insertion site and provides three separate polyurethane lumens. It is suitable for patients who require intermediate-length courses of intravenous therapy and avoids the more traumatic insertion required with Broviac/Hickman catheters. The ML-CVP® catheter can be used for other continuous and intermittent drug delivery and or for administering incompatible drugs simultaneously. The locations of the exit points are staggered, and lumens can be rotated for drug administration to avoid mixing incompatible drugs. The device can be inserted percutaneously or by surgical cutdown into the internal or external jugular or subclavian veins.

Peripherally inserted central venous catheters.   The peripherally inserted central venous catheter (PICC) is an intermediate-term silastic long-line catheter. It is inserted peripherally at the anticubital region, preferably of the nondominant arm, and centrally placed with the tip of the catheter in the superior vena cava. It is often recommended that the venipuncture site be at least two finger-breadths above or below the bend of the arm in order to allow maximum mobility of the extremity. Radiographic confirmation of the placement of the catheter tip is required in order to minimize complications associated with incorrect placement (e.g., occlusion, thrombus).

The PICC is a relatively new device that has gained wide acceptance as a comparatively low-risk and cost-effective alternative to ongoing venous access, particularly for patients who require intravenous therapy in the home setting. The insertion of most PICCs is performed by registered nurses with very good outcomes provided that the patient has adequate venous access and that the nurses have had appropriate training. Fluoroscopically assisted insertion may facilitate the correct placement of the PICC, particularly in patients with poor peripheral veins.

Common complications associated with PICCs, particularly with long-term use, include catheter and venous thrombosis, infection, occlusion, and phlebitis. In addition, because of the potential for severe tissue damage and resultant loss of limb associated with accidental extravasation, the continuous infusion of vesicant drugs (e.g., cancer chemotherapy) by PICCs is not recommended.

An alternative to the PICCs is the midline catheter. These catheters are inserted with aseptic technique, as per the PICCs, but are shorter and are advanced only into the veins of the upper arm below the axillary lateral line. Thus, the midline catheter does not require radiographic verification of catheter tip placement. Complications associated with use of midline catheters are essentially the same as those encountered with the use of PICCs.

The Landmark® midline catheters use a thromboresistent Aquavene® cannula that is relatively stiff during insertion but softens after hydration within the vein. The cannula lengthens approximately 0.5 inches (1.25 cm) and increases two gauge sizes after full hydration (approximately 2 hours after insertion). A catheter two gauge sizes smaller than normally required is selected for insertion, and the arm is measured from the proposed insertion site to the desired placement of the catheter tip (usually approximately 5 to 6 inches [13 to 15 cm] in most patients). After insertion, a sterile, occlusive dressing should be applied to the site and the catheter connected to IV luer-lock tubing or a heparin lock for intermittent use. The arm must be kept at rest in the extended position for 30 minutes after insertion in order to allow adequate hydration of the catheter. Aquavene® catheters should *not* be used for high-pressure injection (i.e., above 45 pounds per square inch, because the catheter may rupture) and hypertonic solutions (i.e., above 13% final glucose concentration, because the tonicity of these solutions is too high for peripheral veins and requires a central venous catheter).

Implantable venous access devices.   Implantable venous access devices include Infuse-a-Port®, Port-a-Cath®, and Mediport®, which provide central venous access for intravenous drugs and solutions, systemic and intra-abdominal cancer chemotherapy (the catheter is inserted into the abdominal cavity rather than a central vein), nutrition support (including lipid emulsions), and administration of blood products. They can also be used for blood sample withdrawal.

Implantable vascular access devices eliminate the need for daily flushing and dressing changes. However, they should be flushed with 5 ml of heparin (100 units/ml) every 5 days and after each use. If not accessed regularly, the devices should be flushed at least once a month with 10 ml of normal saline followed by 3 to 5 ml of heparin (100 units/ml). Implantable devices require a Huber® needle, which should be supported with 2 × 2-inch sterile gauze and SteriStrips® or a foam-padded Port-Gard® dressing during intravenous drug or solution infusion. The site should not be covered with a dressing when not in use. Insertion and removal require minor surgery.

Strict aseptic technique and universal precautions are required. Although implantable vascular devices offer advantages, their use is associated with several complications, including the need for the skin to be punctured to access the implanted access device, septicemia, thromboembolism, internal extravasation injury, and catheter migration. The most common and serious adverse effects occur at the site of infusion therapy and include pain, inflammation, and infection. The development of these adverse effects, particularly inflammation, may necessitate removal of the device. However, the use of implantable vascular access devices is expected to increase because of their overall benefits. The selection of a particular manufacturer's device (Infuse-A-Port®, Mediport®, or Port-a-Cath®) depends largely on the type of drug, other pharmacotherapy required, and familiarity with or preference of the surgeon or oncologist.

Electronic infusion control devices

When drugs with a narrow therapeutic index are administered by continuous intravenous infusion, it is essential that infusion rates be controlled accurately with an electronic infusion-control device (EICD) or system. Although there are many EICDs to choose from, there are only two main types: (1) the gravity controller; and (2) the infusion pump. Both types of EICDs are available in volumetric or nonvolumetric models. Volumetric EICDs are used when a specific volume of solution is required over a long period but the infusion rate is not critical. Nonvolumetric EICDs deliver solution at a constant drop rate and are used when the infusion rate must be measured with short-term accuracy. Cardiovascular drugs such as dopamine [Intropin®]

nitroglycerin, and sodium nitroprusside [Nipride®] are best infused with nonvolumetric EICDs, and nutrition support can be infused with volumetric EICDs.[32]

Gravity controllers
Gravity provides the driving force for intravenous solution delivery with controllers, although flow rate may be regulated by the electronic counting of droplets.

Infusion pumps
Infusion pumps can be classified by mechanism of operation, including peristaltic, syringe, cassette, and reservoir pump. They may also be classified according to the timing of drug delivery (i.e., rapid or slow intravenous injection, intermittent infusion, or continuous infusion), single- or multiple-solution delivery, or therapeutic application (e.g., patient-controlled analgesia).

Patient-controlled analgesia (PCA) is an increasingly common method of pain control whereby patients self-administer doses of an intravenous opiate analgesic when they need it, using a specially designed infusion pump programmed to prevent overdosage (e.g., Bard Harvard PCA®, Life Care PCA®). This method of pain control is generally well received by patients and is both safe and effective. In comparison with conventional intramuscular opiate analgesic pharmacotherapy, PCA is associated with fewer adverse drug reactions, better pulmonary recovery after abdominal surgery, less nursing time for drug administration tasks, and improved individualization of drug dosing in adults.

In the past, infusion pumps were designed for use in the acute hospital setting. However, portable infusion pumps (e.g., Bard Ambulatory PCA®) have been developed and are used increasingly. Generally, portable infusion pumps consist of a refillable drug reservoir with a large capacity that requires infrequent or no reservoir changes (so the risk of contamination and infection is low), a rate-controlling pump, an energy source, and a safety mechanism. As these infusion pumps become more cost-effective, their use is expected to increase because the inconvenience of using a device that requires care and attention can be offset by the benefits of freedom of movement and the opportunity to receive pharmacotherapy at home.

Advances in infusion therapy and computer technology have led to the development of infusion pumps with increasingly sophisticated drug-delivery capabilities such as multiple-rate and multiple-solution programming. Research in infusion pump technology has led to the development of devices such as implantable pumps, pumps with chronobiological applications, osmotic-pressure devices, and open- and closed-loop systems.

Performing the venipuncture and intravenous injection

Psychotropic drugs that are formulated for intravenous use can be administered by three general methods depending on their intended use and pharmacologic action: (1) intravenous push, which can be rapid (i.e., less than 30 seconds) or slow (i.e., 3 to 5 minutes); (2) intermittent infusion (i.e., over a period of 10 minutes to several hours); and (3) continuous infusion (i.e., over a period of 24 hours or longer). For example, diazepam (Valium®) and meperidine (Demerol®)

---

[32] EICDs are not failsafe in relation to such problems as empty solution chambers, air in the tubing, occluded tubing, and inaccurate infusion rates. Thus, EICDs require careful monitoring and calibration for safety. Although various models are equipped with alarm systems to indicate problems, they continue to deliver solution even when needles or catheters are displaced in the interstitial space. In these situations, severe tissue damage can occur, particularly when irritating or vesicant drugs are infused. Particular attention is required when patients cannot communicate pain at the infusion site.

are available as injectable solutions for use by slow intravenous push over 3 to 5 minutes. Flumazenil (Anexate®, Romazicon®) and naloxone (Narcan®) may be injected by rapid intravenous push over 30 seconds. Other injectable forms of psychotropic drugs (e.g., chlorpromazine [Largactil®, Thorazine®]) may be diluted in small volumes of compatible intravenous solutions (i.e., less than 100 ml) with small-volume bags, bottles, and volume-control devices (volumetric chambers such as Buretrol®, Metriset®, Soluset®, and Vol-U-Trol®) and administered by intermittent intravenous infusion over a short period (e.g., 30 to 60 minutes). Other psychotropic drugs (e.g., morphine) can be diluted in large volumes of intravenous solutions (e.g., 500 ml to 1,000 ml) and slowly administered as continuous infusions over long periods (e.g., 24 hours or longer).

Factors such as recommended diluent and concentration, pH, incompatibilities with other drugs and solutions, stability, and infusion rate, as well as patient factors (e.g., kidney function) and the pharmacologic effect of the drug (i.e., desired action and ADRs), must be considered when planning intravenous psychotropic pharmacotherapy.

Venipuncture

In many areas of practice, venipuncture and the establishment of the intravenous site (Figure 4-11) for administration of intravenous drugs is a shared responsibility among nurses and physicians. As clinical psychologists move increasingly into areas of drug prescription, it can be expected that they too may be responsible for venipuncture.[33]

Before intravenous therapy is initiated, patients must be carefully instructed regarding the reasons for their required intravenous pharmacotherapy, and they must know how and when it will be administered and how it will affect their mobility and other activities. Patients also should be instructed regarding the care and monitoring of their venipuncture sites. As with other forms of injectable pharmacotherapy, patients must be carefully prepared for the venipuncture procedure.

The venipuncture site is selected in relation to the physicochemical properties of the

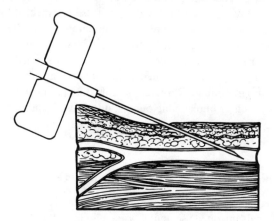

Figure 4-11. Intravenous injection.

[33] Psychologists are guided by state or provincial regulations; professional practice standards; and institutional policies in regard to their roles in the provision of intravenous psychotropic pharmacotherapy. There is significantly less margin for error with the intravenous injection of psychotropic drugs than with other methods of administration. Psychotropic drugs injected intravenously act immediately, and their effects are generally more difficult to reverse when an error is made. Hypersensitivity reactions and exaggerated or unusual pharmacologic effects can occur more readily. As a safeguard, intravenous drugs generally should be diluted in small volumes of appropriate intravenous solution and slowly infused over 30 to 60 minutes or longer, depending on the drug. The intravenous injection of psychotropic drugs by rapid or slow intravenous push should be avoided whenever possible. Thus, if an undesired reaction occurs, the infusion can be discontinued before the entire dose is delivered.

psychotropic drug, health of the veins and surrounding tissue, frequency and duration of drug administration, and individual patient preference (i.e., dominant or nondominant hand). Prominent veins with adequate blood flow and elasticity should be selected whenever possible. Generally, the smallest possible diameter (highest gauge number) needle and the largest possible vein should be used to optimize blood flow at the tip of the needle and dilution of the drug as it enters the vein, thus reducing vein irritation and avoiding the development of phlebitis. It is essential that venipunctures be made carefully so that veins are not damaged and sites are maintained to avoid the need for frequent venipunctures, particularly when patients have limited sites and require long-term pharmacotherapy. It is particularly essential that sites be maintained carefully, because of the limited number of sites available for many patients (e.g., elderly and debilitated patients).

In general, the basilic and cephalic veins on the back of the hand are the most commonly used veins for venipuncture (Figure 4-12).[34] Sites closer to the fingers should be selected first, and then sites toward the wrist can be used as needed. The needle or catheter should be inserted away from a movable joint to prevent inadvertent dislodgement and extravasation. The antecubital fossa sites are commonly used for rapid or slow intravenous injections or for blood withdrawal. They are *not* recommended for intermittent or continuous intravenous infusions because the elbow must be splinted to prevent dislodgement of the venous access device, resulting in stiffness and pain at the joint as a result of immobility.

Some patients may require gentle manual restraint of the extremity during the venipuncture to stabilize the site. They should be positioned comfortably and the site prepared. It is often

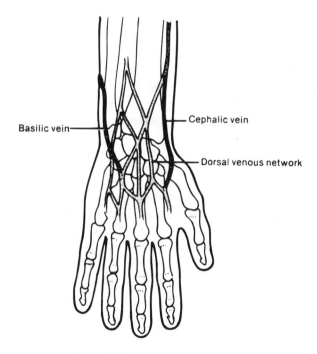

Figure 4-12. Intravenous injection sites.

[34] If the veins on the back of the hand are not readily visible, a warm compress can be applied to the site, or it can be lowered below the rest of the body to enlarge the veins. Gentle tapping at the site with the fingertips and asking the patient to "make a fist" also are helpful. If these measures are ineffective, a rubber tourniquet can be applied above the venipuncture site between the elbow and wrist. Before the tourniquet is secured, a piece of gauze can be placed between it and the skin to prevent pinching.

helpful to stabilize the extremity on a padded arm board before the venipuncture is made. Any equipment required for intravenous pharmacotherapy (e.g., intravenous solution, controller or infusion pump) should be prepared prior to the venipuncture so that it is ready for use once the venipuncture is completed.

After the site has been cleansed with an appropriate antiseptic and a tourniquet has been applied (if required), the skin should be pulled taut with the thumb of the nondominant hand below the venipuncture site, which helps to anchor the vein and prevent it from rolling to the side when the venipuncture is made. The needle should be inserted in the direction of blood flow to ensure that the injection or infusion is aimed in the same direction as the venous blood returning to the heart. It is particularly important to avoid arteries.[35] The needle should be inserted at a 20- to 30-degree angle to the skin with the bevel facing up. The skin should be entered just distal to the proposed site of vein entry (approximately $^1/_4$ to $^1/_2$ inch or 0.6 to 1.25 cm). After the skin has been penetrated, the angle should be decreased to 15 degrees and the needle gently and slowly advanced into the vein. Blood should appear in the tubing. The needle of an over-the-needle catheter should be advanced a little further and then removed, leaving the catheter in the vein.

Once the venipuncture is made, the tourniquet (if used) should be released, and the needle or catheter should be carefully secured with tape or a transparent adhesive dressing so that the site can be easily observed. The needle or catheter should be flushed with normal saline solution before any drugs are administered to ensure patency of the site. If intravenous tubing is used, it should be secured with tape so that it is free from kinks and does not pull on the needle or catheter. A padded arm board may be required to fully stabilize the site. When arm boards are used, the extremity should be kept in a natural anatomical position, and the fingers should be readily observable for monitoring circulation, voluntary movement, and sensation. All venous access devices should be labeled clearly with the dates and times they were inserted and the initials of the person who inserted the device. Needles and catheters that will remain in place can be flushed according to protocol and covered with a transparent dressing so that the site can be easily observed and monitored.[36]

Topical anesthesia

The fear and pain associated with venipunctures can be minimized with the application of a local topical anesthetic cream (i.e., EMLA®). The cream is applied 1 to 2 hours before the venipuncture is performed. Although the use of EMLA® is not feasible in all clinical situations (e.g., emergencies) because of the time required to achieve effective anesthesia, it offers, for selected patients, an effective means of reducing the pain perception and psychological trauma associated with venipunctures. The major disadvantage associated with the use of EMLA® is the required waiting period. However, the waiting time has been found to be generally acceptable among patients who require EMLA®.[37] EMLA® should be applied only to intact skin (i.e., avoid

---

[35] The brachial artery is close to the skin surface and adjacent to the cephalic vein. It can be inadvertently penetrated when sites above the wrist are used, including the antecubital fossa. If an artery is inadvertently punctured, the blood, which will be bright red in color, will pulsate from the site. In contrast, blood from a vein is darker red in color and will not pulsate. Firm pressure should be applied to the site for 10 minutes after the needle is withdrawn from an artery to stop bleeding from the site and to prevent bruising.

[36] Some patients may require an arm-board splint to immobilize the site or soft restraints to prevent the needle from being removed. A plastic drug cup that has been cut in half lengthwise may be gently taped over the site to protect the needle from becoming dislodged. If necessary, roll gauze (Kling®) can be gently wrapped over the site, or stretchable netting (i.e., Tuberoll®) can be used for protection. However, the roll gauze must be unwrapped frequently to monitor for dislodgement and extravasation.

[37] Patients can be taught to apply EMLA® in the home setting so that the site will be anesthetized upon arrival at the clinic or office, where the venipuncture can be performed readily without waiting.

abraded or denuded areas). Its use is contraindicated for patients who are hypersensitive to the amide-type local anesthetics (e.g., lidocaine [Xylocaine®]).

The use of EMLA® involves the following steps: (1) Apply a thick layer of the cream (approximately 1.5 to 2.5 g) to 1.5 inches squared (8 cm²) of skin surface at the injection site (the skin should be clean and dry to ensure an effective seal); (2) remove the perforated center area from the occlusive dressing provided (i.e., Tegaderm®) and peel away the protective backing; (3) holding the dressing edges, fold the nonadhesive sides toward each other to form a "U" and place the center of the "U" over the cream; (4) tap down the occlusive dressing over the skin around the mound of cream and smooth down the dressing edges to ensure that the cream will not leak out; (5) remove the paper frame and record the time of application directly on the exterior surface of the occlusive dressing; (6) after at least 1 hour (maximum of 5 hours), remove the occlusive dressing and any remaining cream; and (7) clean the site with alcohol and prepare the patient for the venipuncture. The venipuncture site will remain anesthetized for at least 1 hour after removal of the occlusive dressing. However, the venipuncture should be made as soon as possible after its removal.

The removal of Tegaderm® occlusive dressings, which are supplied with EMLA® cream, can be painful unless the correct method is used. The adhesive action of Tegaderm® dressings is eliminated by stretching. A corner edge of the dressing can be lifted simply and painlessly by gently dabbing it with the adhesive side of a piece of surgical tape. The lifted edge of the dressing is grasped with the dominant hand and stretched parallel to the skin in a downward motion while the other side of the dressing is anchored with the nondominant hand. The stretching is repeated in a circular pattern around the dressing until the last portion of the edge of the dressing is removed by peeling it back while massaging the cream into the place where the skin and the final edge of the dressing meet.

A newer formulation (i.e., EMLA Patch®) consists of a single-dose, prepackaged dressing containing EMLA® 5% emulsion (2.5% lidocaine and 2.5% prilocaine). This formulation is available to patients at pharmacies without a prescription. The patient simply removes the aluminum backing and attaches the patch, as directed, to a clean, dry area of skin to be used for the venipuncture site. The patch should remain in place (for a minimum of 1 hour) until the procedure. It is then removed, the area is cleaned, and the patient is prepared for the venipuncture. Although the EMLA® cream and patch formulations reportedly produce equivalent efficacy, the ease of patch administration appears to be a distinct advantage.

Slow and rapid intravenous injection (IV push)

Some psychotropic drugs are available commercially in ready-to-use formulations that require no further dilution and are injected directly into the vein through a needle, catheter, IIC cap, or injection port in the tubing of a primary (fluid maintenance or replacement) intravenous infusion. For example, diazoxide (Hyperstat®), an antihypertensive, is injected over 10 to 30 seconds because it is highly plasma protein bound, and rapid administration overcomes the effect of protein binding so that sufficient serum concentration and, thus, desired effects are achieved. Other drugs, such as atropine, may be delivered over a minute to achieve an immediate effect. For psychotropic drugs, the recommended rate of intravenous injection varies, but they generally should not be injected over less than 1 minute. The manufacturer's recommendations for administration rate should be closely followed. A red blood cell travels through the entire circulatory system in approximately 1 minute. If drugs are injected too rapidly, "speed shock" can occur, resulting in headache, tightness in the chest, shock, and cardiac arrest. Slow intravenous injection allows drugs to mix more thoroughly with the blood before delivery to the heart and brain, which can occur within 15 seconds.

Drugs can be injected into an injection port (sometimes called a "Y-site") in the tubing of a compatible primary (maintenance or replacement) continuous intravenous infusion. After the patency of the intravenous infusion site is verified by visual inspection of blood return, the tubing above the injection port should be occluded with a roller clamp or hemostat. The injection port should be wiped with an antiseptic and allowed to dry, and the needle should be inserted into the center of the port. The drug should be injected at the recommended rate. After the drug is injected, the roller clamp or hemostat is released, and the flow rate is readjusted. Patients should be observed closely for ADRs during the time the drug is administered and immediately after. The technique is adapted accordingly when EICDs are being used.

Intermittent infusion

Intravenous additive sets, small-volume bags or bottles, and volume-control devices (i.e., intermittent infusion control devices such as Burette®, Buretrol®, and Metriset®) are used for intermittent infusion of intravenous drugs that require dilution and infusion over 10 minutes to several hours. Intermittent infusion pharmacotherapy is used with IIC caps when patients require an IV drug several times a day but do not want the additional fluid or activity restrictions imposed by a continuous infusion. The use of additive sets, small-volume bags or bottles, and volume-control devices for intravenous drug delivery also avoids incompatibilities between drugs and between drugs and primary (maintenance or replacement) intravenous solutions.

When patients require continuous maintenance or replacement intravenous therapy, intermittent pharmacotherapy can be infused into an injection port in the tubing of the primary infusion. The use of various additive sets, small-volume bags and bottles, and small-volume control devices for the intermittent infusion of intravenous pharmacotherapy differs among facilities, so psychologists should be familiar with the equipment and procedures used in their clinical practice settings. Generally, psychotropic drugs can be infused simultaneously with compatible primary intravenous solutions. If the drug and primary intravenous solution are incompatible, they should be infused separately by occluding the tubing above the injection port with a roller clamp or hemostat or hanging the drug infusion container above the primary solution (gravity causes the solution in the higher position to infuse first). When psychotropic drugs are administered through the same tubing as an incompatible primary intravenous solution, the tubing must be flushed with a compatible intravenous solution before the drug is infused. After drug infusion, the tubing must be flushed again before infusion of the incompatible primary intravenous solution is resumed.[38]

Continuous infusion

Various psychotropic drugs can be added to large-volume primary (maintenance or replacement) intravenous solutions for slow continuous infusion. Incompatibility with the solution and bioavailability are important considerations with this type of intravenous pharmacotherapy. When drugs are added to primary solutions, an unexpected color change or cloudiness usually indicates an incompatibility. The most concentrated drug should be added first and mixed thoroughly before other drugs are added. Colored additives should be added last because they can mask precipitation and cloudiness. These same principles apply when preparing drugs for intermittent infusions. Some drugs can be added directly to the primary solution according to aseptic technique, while other drugs can be added only after they have been reconstituted according to the manufacturer's recommendations.[39]

---

[38] For further discussion and examples of both compatible and incompatible intravenous drugs and solutions, readers are referred to "Administering Intravenous Drugs to Infants and Children" (Stowe, Ivey, Kuhn, & Piecoro, 1995).

[39] A label specifying the drug added and its amount or concentration, time, date, and initials of the person who added the drug is attached to the container. A record of the infusion and any other pertinent observations are documented appropriately. Pharmacy departments at most hospitals are increasingly assuming primary responsibility for preparing intravenous admixtures because of the complexity of preparing such admixtures and the risks for contamination and error.

Complications of intravenous drug administration

Although the intravenous administration of various psychotropic drugs offers many advantages, there are disadvantages, including complications such as infection, hypersensitivity reactions, extravasation, phlebitis, and air emboli or thrombus formation. Additional complications associated with pharmacotherapy that involves continuous intravenous infusion include fluid overload and drug toxicity associated with "free-flow" (uncontrolled infusion) accidents. These complications can be particularly problematic for patients who have compromised body system function (e.g., heart, kidney, or liver dysfunction), including the very young and very old. Activity restriction associated with the maintenance of intravenous injection sites is also a concern, particularly when patients are confused or have psychoses. Furthermore, there is no room for error, particularly when psychotropic drugs are injected by rapid or slow intravenous injection, because the drug is injected directly into the bloodstream and effects are virtually immediate. Emergency drugs and support equipment and personnel should be readily available whenever intravenous drugs are administered. It is essential that patients who require intravenous pharmacotherapy be monitored for common complications and that these complications be prevented whenever possible.

Infection
The intravenous administration of psychotropic drugs poses a risk of infection because microbial organisms can be introduced directly into the systemic circulation by means of the vein. Psychologists should be alert to signs of local (e.g., redness and swelling at the injection site) and systemic (e.g., fever) infection. Infection can result from contaminated equipment or solutions, improper techniques, or poor injection or infusion site care. Several approaches to minimizing infection have been suggested, including stringent protocols for performing venipunctures and changing site dressings and infusion tubing. Collaboration with medical or nursing colleagues is indicated.

Infection can be prevented by the use of strict aseptic technique during venipuncture and the preparation and administration of intravenous drugs. Appropriate care of venipuncture sites also is important in preventing infection. Institutional venipuncture dressing procedures should be followed. In an increasing number of clinical facilities, pharmacists are preparing intravenous admixtures with the use of vertical laminar airflow hoods to maintain sterility. Likewise, pharmaceutical manufacturers are increasingly supplying psychotropic drugs in delivery systems ready for immediate intravenous use.

Hypersensitivity
Psychologists must be alert for signs of hypersensitivity when psychotropic drugs are injected or infused intravenously. Monitoring is particularly important when drugs are injected by rapid or slow intravenous injection. When drugs are administered intravenously, clinical psychologists must be alert to signs of drug sensitivity. Patients should be asked to report any unusual effects, including burning, chills, itching, local pain, or nausea. If these effects occur, the injection or infusion should be stopped immediately and appropriate intervention implemented. Emergency equipment and drugs (e.g., epinephrine) should be readily available in case of hypersensitivity reactions, particularly when the drug is used for the first time.

Extravasation
The most common local complication of intravenous pharmacotherapy is extravasation. Extravasation occurs when the needle or catheter is improperly positioned outside of the vein and

the drug or solution is mistakenly infused into the subcutaneous tissue. Swelling around the venipuncture site may be observed, and the patient may complain of pain. In assessing swelling, the involved extremity should be compared with the opposite extremity. An early sign of extravasation is a slowed rate of infusion, but this sign will be absent and intravenous solutions will continue to be infused if an EICD is being used.[40]

Phlebitis

Another important and common complication associated with intravenous psychotropic pharmacotherapy is phlebitis, which results from trauma to the vein caused by the needle, catheter, or drug. Some drugs, such as chlorpromazine (Largactil®, Thorazine®), are particularly irritating to the veins, and the venipuncture site and skin over the vein should be observed for redness and increased skin temperature.[41] A patient's complaints of burning and pain along the vein should be heeded. If these symptoms occur, the injection or infusion should be stopped immediately and restarted at another site. To prevent further damage to the vein, re-use of the affected site should be avoided. It is important that venipuncture sites not be covered so that they can be observed closely during intravenous pharmacotherapy. The use of collodion dressings is recommended, but they should be applied so that dressing changes will not result in the displacement of the needle or catheter.

Research regarding the development of phlebitis from intravenous pharmacotherapy has provided evidence to support changing tubing at least every 24 hours and changing intermittent infusion control devices (e.g., Buretrols®) at least every 72 hours. Using the smallest diameter needle or catheter possible in the largest possible vein reduces the risk for mechanical phlebitis and optimizes blood circulation and drug dilution to decrease the chances of chemical phlebitis.

Embolism

Air embolism is a concern for patients, although the amount of air required for fatal embolism has not been precisely determined. When injecting or infusing drugs, the inadvertent injection of air should be avoided. The amount of air contained in intravenous tubing is approximately 10 to 15 ml, but blood usually backs up into the tubing, occluding the needle or catheter before this air enters the vein. Thrombus formation may occur at the needle or catheter tip. Under *no* circumstances should the occluded needle or catheter be irrigated with normal saline or heparin solution because of the risk of thrombus detachment and severe complications (e.g., pulmonary embolus).

Fluid overload and drug toxicity

Pharmacotherapy that requires continuous intravenous infusion must be closely monitored, particularly because of the potential for fluid overload and drug toxicity. Careful regulation of

---

[40] To reduce the possibility of extravasation, insertion of the needle near a movable joint should be avoided. An IIC cap should be used if the patient requires frequent intravenous psychotropic pharmacotherapy but does not require continuous infusion. Some psychotropic drugs can be extremely irritating to tissues. For example, extreme care is required when pentobarbital (Nembutal®) or secobarbital (Seconal®) are injected because they are highly alkaline. Extravasation of these drugs into the surrounding tissues can result in pain and tissue necrosis. In addition, inadvertent intra-arterial injection has been associated with adverse effects ranging from transient pain along the course of the artery to gangrene of the limb, requiring amputation. It is imperative that the patency of the needle or catheter be ensured before psychotropic drugs are injected or infused to prevent extravasation. Psychologists are encouraged to develop treatment protocols for use in the event of extravasation associated with intravenous psychotropic pharmacotherapy. Psychologists also should be familiar with these protocols so that they can be readily implemented in the event of extravasation.

[41] To monitor for the development of phlebitis, the flash chamber or flash ball can be gently compressed and the patient observed for complaints of pain. This procedure dilates the vein at the entry site, which causes pain if the vein is inflamed. Patients requiring long-term intravenous pharmacotherapy may require frequent site changes to avoid phlebitis and other complications (e.g., infection). Sites should be alternated to allow healing between use.

infusion rate is essential because changes in a patient's body position can significantly increase or decrease the infusion rate of a gravity controller. Although nonelectric and electronic infusion-control devices often are used to limit the amount of intravenous solution delivered, these devices are not failsafe.

Fluid overload and free-flow accidents continue to pose a serious problem with regard to intravenous pharmacotherapy. Uncontrolled free-flow accidents involving meperidine (Demerol®) and other psychotropic drugs have resulted in serious injury and death. The use of devices that allow "free flow" should be avoided whenever psychotropic pharmacotherapy is required. To promote patient safety, only trained personnel should be authorized to set up, adjust, and remove administration sets. All psychologists and others who are involved with intravenous pharmacotherapy should receive periodic training and retraining to maintain competency and avoid complications such as fluid overload and drug toxicity.

The confused, mentally retarded, or psychotic patient

Patients who are confused, mentally retarded, or psychotic can present a special challenge to clinical psychologists in relation to the administration of psychotropic pharmacotherapy. Oral drugs are usually ingested in liquid forms or in prepared solid forms (e.g., crushed tablets, dissolved or emptied capsules) in a small amount of compatible food or liquid, because many of these patients have difficulty swallowing. Other patients may fear that the psychologist is poisoning them. Whole tablets and even the pieces of crushed tablets may be spit out by some of these patients. These patients, as well as those who have tardive dyskinesia, may be able to ingest small amounts of liquid dosage forms (e.g., Intensols®) much better than other oral dosage forms. The smallest amount of liquid or food possible to ensure that the entire amount of drug is ingested should be used.[42]

In all cases, the administration of psychotropic drugs should be individualized to the needs and abilities of each patient. Patients should be approached as if expected to take the drug, but they should never be threatened. Clinical psychologists should be honest and explain, as appropriate for their patients' cognitive and mental abilities (and reexplain, as necessary), any changes in drug regimens in order to allay any undue anxiety and to maintain trust.

The injection of psychotropic drugs to the psychotic or confused patient can be difficult. Getting a patient with paranoia, one who is belligerent, or one who is violent or uncooperative to comply with prescribed pharmacotherapy can be trying and may take much time and patience. Clinical psychologists may have to resort to creative approaches to drug administration. The confused, mentally retarded, or psychotic patient may react negatively to certain methods of drug administration, such as: the instillation of eye, ear, and nose drops; the insertion of suppositories; the administration of injections; and intravenous pharmacotherapy. These procedures can be painful and frightening for these patients and may be misinterpreted as an "attack." In addition, confused, mentally retarded, or psychotic patients may have a hyper-responsiveness to pain; thus, their reactions to intrusive procedures involved in pharmacotherapy may not always seem appropriate. They may have a magnified response to even simple procedures.

---

[42] In institutional inpatient settings, drugs should never be placed in foods provided as meals (e.g., bowl of pudding, sandwich) and left with patients to eat. It is not uncommon for patients to share or trade foods in these settings. In addition, it cannot be ensured that the total amount of food will be ingested. Foods used to mix drugs should be selected carefully, because aversions to these foods can occur among some patients. Required drugs are usually ingested if individualized routines are established and if the patient is hungry. If drugs are refused, the clinical psychologist should ascertain the reason for refusal and, if necessary, explore the use of other oral dosage forms that may be more acceptable to the patient.

Advanced preparation and appropriate timing for procedures may enhance their ability to cope and cooperate with their pharmacotherapy. Preparation for injections, intravenous therapy, and other intrusive procedures should be planned individually in relation to the patient's cognitive and mental abilities, coping style, physical abilities, and previous experiences with pharmacotherapy and psychotherapy. The maintenance of patient dignity, including personal rights and freedoms, and the prevention of injury are major concerns.

The confused, mentally retarded, or psychotic patient should be approached calmly and with confidence, and the drug should be administered promptly. Undue physical restraint should be avoided because it can increase combativeness, fear, and protest. Clinical psychologists should acknowledge the patient's fear or confusion. Depending on mental age and state, a warm touch or hug after completion of the procedure, if appropriate, can be effective. A caring and understanding approach is essential. Patients should be allowed to object, and their anger should be accepted. However, they must be protected from harming themselves or others. Aggression should be redirected and not punished or "treated" with undue use of physical or chemical restraints.

With the confused, mentally retarded, or psychotic patient, explanations regarding drug therapy should be kept simple and concrete. Teaching sessions should be completed in areas where there are few distractions and noise is minimal. Body diagrams, simple models, and the actual equipment required for pharmacotherapy should be used along with demonstrations to enhance verbal explanations. These patients may need continued reminders and re-explanations each time the drug is administered.

The confused, mentally retarded, or psychotic patient will usually take the required drug after a simple explanation and with a little encouragement. A positive approach is important. To maintain independence, patients should be allowed and encouraged to make decisions regarding aspects of their pharmacotherapy as appropriate for their cognitive and mental abilities. For example, a confused, mentally retarded, or psychotic person may not have a legal say regarding required pharmacotherapy. However, he or she may be able to choose how the drug will be ingested (e.g., in a particular beverage or soft food, in tablet or liquid form) and where it will be ingested (e.g., at the dispensary, in the television room, sitting in a favorite chair in the residence).

In order to promote appropriate participation in their pharmacotherapy, confused, mentally retarded, and psychotic patients should be acknowledged for demonstrating an understanding of any aspect of their therapy and for cooperating in various ways with their pharmacotherapy. For example, they could be told "The medicine helps you not to shake and to walk better"; "Yes, the medicine helps your hands to feel better and your fingers to move easier"; or "Yes, your Thorazine® at this higher dosage helps you get along better with the other men on your unit." Psychotic or confused patients should be treated not in a condescending manner but in a warm, respectful, and understanding way. They should not be told that they are "good" for taking their drugs; rather, they should be thanked for making an effort to participate in their pharmacotherapy.

Summary

Professional responsibilities of psychologists are expanding in relation to the increased complexity of clinical psychological services, including the provision of psychotropic pharmacotherapy as an adjunct to psychotherapy. In order to provide optimal psychological services to their patients, clinical psychologists must have and apply knowledge of the use and effects of psychotropic drugs. Recommended guidelines for the administration of psychotropic drugs have been provided in this chapter. Although prescribing psychologists generally will not be involved with the direct administration of psychotropics to their patients, they require a thorough knowledge and understanding of the various dosage forms available for psychotropic drugs and correct methods of administration so that they can better provide appropriate and individualized pharmacotherapy for their patients. With the information presented in this chapter and the other chapters of this text, psychologists will be better prepared to prescribe and manage optimal psychotropic pharmacotherapy with a minimum of ADRs for their patients who require psychotropic drugs as an adjunct to their psychotherapy.

5

Adverse Drug Reactions

Introduction

An adverse drug reaction (ADR) is any undesired consequence of pharmacotherapy, including expected and unexpected toxic effects and therapeutic failure in instances in which therapeutic success could reasonably be expected.[1] This definition does not include accidental drug poisoning or intentional drug overdosage. All psychotropic drugs are capable of producing ADRs. Thus, psychologists must be ever vigilant for their occurrence and plan to prevent or minimize them whenever possible. This goal requires that psychologists be familiar with the nature and extent of ADRs involving the psychotropics and apply this knowledge when prescribing and managing pharmacotherapy for their patients who require these drugs as an adjunct to their psychotherapy.[2]

As noted almost a decade ago by Bapna (1989), who addressed physician prescribing practices:

> Irrational drug prescribing is considered a common
> occurrence. Several reasons identified for this include: inadequate
> physician education and training in clinical pharmacology, which is
> the basis for rational drug use; promotional activities of
> pharmaceutical companies to popularize their products; physician
> efforts to reduce the number of patient revisits by dispensing an initial
> heavy drug load; uncertainty of diagnosis; reliance on favorable but
> limited experience with just a few drugs; and demand from the patient
> for a drug to treat each of his or her symptoms. (p. 217)

The human and economic costs of these actions has been significant (see Table 5-1). As described in a subsequent editorial (1994) in the same journal:

> Physicians want to prescribe the safest and most cost-effective
> drugs for their patients. However, after the second year of medical
> school, physicians have little if any opportunity for balanced

---

[1] A closely related, but not synonymous, term is adverse drug event (ADE). An ADE is an indirect consequence of drug usage that occurs as a result of an ADR. For example, ADRs associated with the use of alcohol would include impaired psychomotor skills and decreased cognitive functioning, while an associated ADE would be a motor vehicle crash that occurred while the driver was intoxicated. Another common example involves the use of sedative-hypnotics among elderly patients. When they are used to induce sleep, associated ADRs of the sedative-hypnotics may include confusion, drowsiness, and postural (orthostatic) hypotension upon awakening and arising. If, as a result of these ADRs, the elderly patient falls and breaks a hip upon getting out of bed, then the broken hip would be considered to be an ADE of sedative-hypnotic use.

[2] The anticonvulsants, although not generally expected to be prescribed by psychologists, have been formally included in this chapter because they are frequently used concurrently by patients who are being treated for various psychological disorders. Thus, the ADRs associated with the anticonvulsants have the potential to adversely affect the therapy provided by psychologists, particularly if they are unaware of and unfamiliar with these ADRs.

education on the basic principles of therapeutics and the comparative
effectiveness and safety of the drugs they prescribe. The
informational systems and drug research conducted in the United
States are far less than adequate to enable physicians to prescribe
medications in the safest and most cost-effective manner. It is no
surprise that prescribing errors are frequently seen and are the second
most common basis for malpractice claims in the United
States.

Table 5-1. General summary of findings from published ADR studies.

- ~30% of general medical patients experience at least one ADR during their hospitalizations
- ~3% of *all* hospital admissions are the result of an ADR
- ~14% of *all* hospital occupancy days are due to ADRs
- ~9 additional days, on average, are added to the stay of hospitalized patients who experience an ADR
- 0.3% of hospitalized general medical patients *die* as a result of ADRs
- ~300 people *die* daily in North America as a result of ADRs

---

However, this need not be the case, because an entire body of scientific knowledge concerning ADRs has been developed. This body of knowledge is readily available to prescribing physicians, as well as prescribing psychologists. The purpose of this chapter is to acquaint psychologists with this body of knowledge so that they can optimally prescribe the psychotropics to their patients who may require appropriate pharmacotherapy as an adjunct to their psychotherapy. A knowledge and understanding of these data are *not* an option but, rather, a required part of the professional responsibility of psychologists. As noted in the American Psychological Association (APA) Code of Conduct, Section 1.14, "Avoiding Harm":

> Psychologists take reasonable steps to avoid harming their
> patients or clients, research participants, students, and others with
> whom they work, and to minimize harm where it is foreseeable and
> unavoidable.

For the most part, ADRs are both "foreseeable" and "avoidable" if logical, rational principles of pharmacotherapy are applied. For example, ADRs are commonly associated with the following:

1. Failure to adjust dosages for age, body weight, gender, or body system (e.g., heart, kidney, and liver) function.
2. Failure to recognize possible individual variation in drug response (e.g., deficient parahydroxylation of phenytoin [Dilantin®], a rare genetic biotransformation defect necessitating a reduced dosage of phenytoin).[3]
3. Failure to monitor carefully psychotropic drugs that have a narrow therapeutic index (e.g., lithium [Eskalith®, Lithane®]) (Tables 5-2 and 5-3).

Table 5-2. Psychotropic drugs associated with a high risk for serious ADRs.

Anticonvulsants (e.g., phenytoin [Dilantin®])
Antipsychotics (e.g., chlorpromazine [Largactil®, Thorazine®])

Note. See Table 5-6 and Appendix 3 for additional details.

---

[3] Fortunately, genetic variation in drug response (i.e., pharmacogenetics) occurs only rarely in relation to the psychotropics. See Chapter 3, "Pharmacokinetics and Pharmacodynamics," for additional discussion.

Table 5-3. Psychotropic drugs with narrow therapeutic indexes that may predispose patients to ADRs.

Anticonvulsants (e.g., phenytoin [Dilantin®])
Antimanics (e.g., lithium [Eskalith®, Lithane®])
General anesthetics (e.g., halothane [Fluothane®])

Note. See Table 5-6 and Appendix 3 for additional details.

4. Failure to gradually discontinue long-term pharmacotherapy (e.g., anticonvulsants, benzodiazepines) (Table 5-4).
5. Failure to appropriately consider risk of addiction and habituation when prescribing the abusable psychotropics (e.g., opiate analgesics, sedative-hypnotics) (see Table 5-4).
6. Failure to anticipate adverse drug *interactions* whenever pharmacotherapy involves more than one drug (e.g., oversedation from concurrent opiate analgesic and tricyclic antidepressant pharmacotherapy [see Chapter 6, "Drug Interactions"]).
7. Failure to identify patient membership in certain groups (e.g., the elderly, women) that have been identified for various reasons as being at particular risk for significant ADRs (see Table 5-5).
8. Failure to stay in control of pharmacotherapy (e.g., giving in to pressures from patients or third-party payers for a quick and ostensibly easy solution [i.e., prescribing psychotropics]

Table 5-4. Categories of psychotropics for which abrupt discontinuation of pharmacotherapy (or personal use) may result in ADRs.

Nonabusable psychotropics
    Anticonvulsants [see also Abusable psychotropics; Sedative-hypnotics]
    (e.g., carbamazepine [Tegretol®]; phenytoin [Dilantin®])
Abusable psychotropics[a]
  CNS depressants
    Opiate analgesics
    (e.g., heroin, meperidine [Demerol®], morphine [M.O.S.®])
    Sedative-hypnotics
    (e.g., alcohol, barbiturates, and benzodiazepines)
  CNS stimulants
    (e.g., amphetamines, cocaine, caffeine, nicotine)

Note. The frequency and severity of ADRs are generally related to the dosage and duration of pharmacotherapy or personal use prior to sudden discontinuation. See Table 5-6 and Appendix 3 for additional details.
[a] CNS depressants and CNS stimulants have the potential for withdrawal syndromes associated with abrupt discontinuation of long-term pharmacotherapy or regular personal use. The intensity of these syndromes will be directly related to the dosage and duration of pharmacotherapy prior to its abrupt discontinuation.

Table 5-5. Patients at high risk for ADRs.

• Patients who require pharmacotherapy with multiple drugs
• Patients who require pharmacotherapy with drugs that have narrow therapeutic indexes
• Patients who are seriously ill
• Elderly, frail, or debilitated patients and those who have decreased functional reserve capacity[a]
  (e.g., chronically ill patients)

Note. As a group, the elderly are generally highly ranked on each of these individual risk parameters and are, therefore, at significantly higher risk for ADRs than are patients in other age groups.
[a] Body organ systems reach peak performance at variable rates (e.g., 1 to 25 years) (i.e., skin versus brain). Following peak performance, organ function begins to decline. This decline is not initially noticed because of the "reserve capacity," particularly of the vital organs (i.e., heart, lungs, liver, and kidneys). After the age of 25 years, the decline, on average, is equal to approximately 1% per year in the absence of disease pathology and is related primarily to decreased cardiac output (see Chapter 3, "Pharmacokinetics and Pharmacodynamics").

when equally effective, but perhaps more costly or time-consuming, treatments [i.e., psychotherapy] could be used without the risk of ADRs).

The incidence of ADRs can be minimized by rational prescription and monitoring of pharmacotherapy. Psychologists must consider the factors that predispose patients to ADRs (Figure 5-1), and they must take action to minimize the severity of ADRs when pharmacotherapy cannot be altered and expected ADRs cannot be avoided (i.e., they must ensure that the therapeutic benefits outweigh the risks). In addition to these professional responsibilities, psychologists are

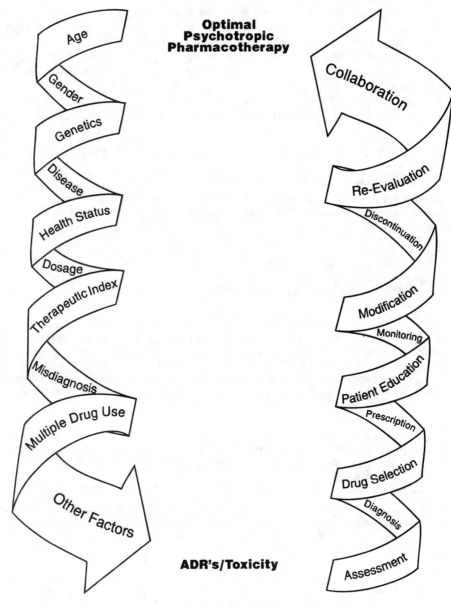

Figure 5-1. ADRs and related factors.

asked to report any ADRs that they observe in their clinical practices (Figures 5-2 and 5-3). Formally reporting ADRs will contribute to the development of a more accurate and comprehensive database[4] so that optimal psychotropic pharmacotherapy can be provided with a minimum of ADRs.

Allergic, idiosyncratic, and pharmacologic ADRs

Adverse drug reactions can be categorized according to three major types: pharmacologic, allergic, and idiosyncratic. Each of these is briefly discussed.

Pharmacologic ADRs

Pharmacologic ADRs are dose-related ADRs associated with a particular drug. Thus, they can occur in any patient provided that a sufficient quantity of the drug is ingested, inhaled, inserted, or injected. Most pharmacologic ADRs conform to a sigmoid, or "S"-type, response curve (see Chapter 1, "Introduction to the Basic Principles of Pharmacotherapy"). Accordingly, they may be observed among a small number of patients who are exposed to a low dose of a drug. As the dose is increased, the number of patients reacting also increases. An example of this type of ADR is the troublesome drowsiness observed following the use of the antihistamine diphenhydramine (Benadryl®). However, this ADR (i.e., drowsiness) is frequently used clinically as a "beneficial" drug reaction (i.e., as a nonprescription sleep aid; see Chapter 2, "The Psychotropics," for further discussion of this example). Some pharmacologic ADRs, such as the sedation associated with amitriptyline (Elavil®) pharmacotherapy, subside with continued use as the body becomes accustomed or sensitized to the effects of the drug.[5]

Allergic ADRs

Allergic ADRs are caused by an immune (antigen-antibody) response. Therefore, these ADRs do not occur when a patient is first exposed to a particular drug; rather, they occur in conjunction with a subsequent exposure. Allergic ADRs involve the body's response to foreign or exogenous proteins (antigens). Generally, drugs do not, by themselves, act as antigens because they are not usually composed of protein. However, following their metabolism, drugs may combine with endogenous proteins to form reactive compounds against which antibodies may be formed. Following the initial sensitizing contact to the drug, subsequent exposure may produce an allergic hypersensitivity reaction. Allergic ADRs are not dose–related and involve only a small portion of the total number of patients who receive a particular psychotropic.

Allergic reactions are difficult to predict and, thus, prevent. A careful and complete drug history will enable psychologists to avoid prescribing psychotropics to patients who report *prior* allergic reactions to particular psychotropic drugs.[6] In addition, whenever patients are prescribed

---

[4] This is particularly important for newer psychotropics (i.e., those that have been in widespread clinical use for less than 5 years) because the pattern and incidence of unusual or rare ADRs may not yet have been clearly established.

[5] In these cases, careful patient education and monitoring, instead of dosage reduction or changing drugs, would be the preferred approach for handling these ADRs.

[6] Cross hypersensitivity has been documented among members of the same chemical drug group (class). If a patient has displayed hypersensitivity to one member of a drug group, as a matter of caution, *all* other drugs in this group should be generally avoided.

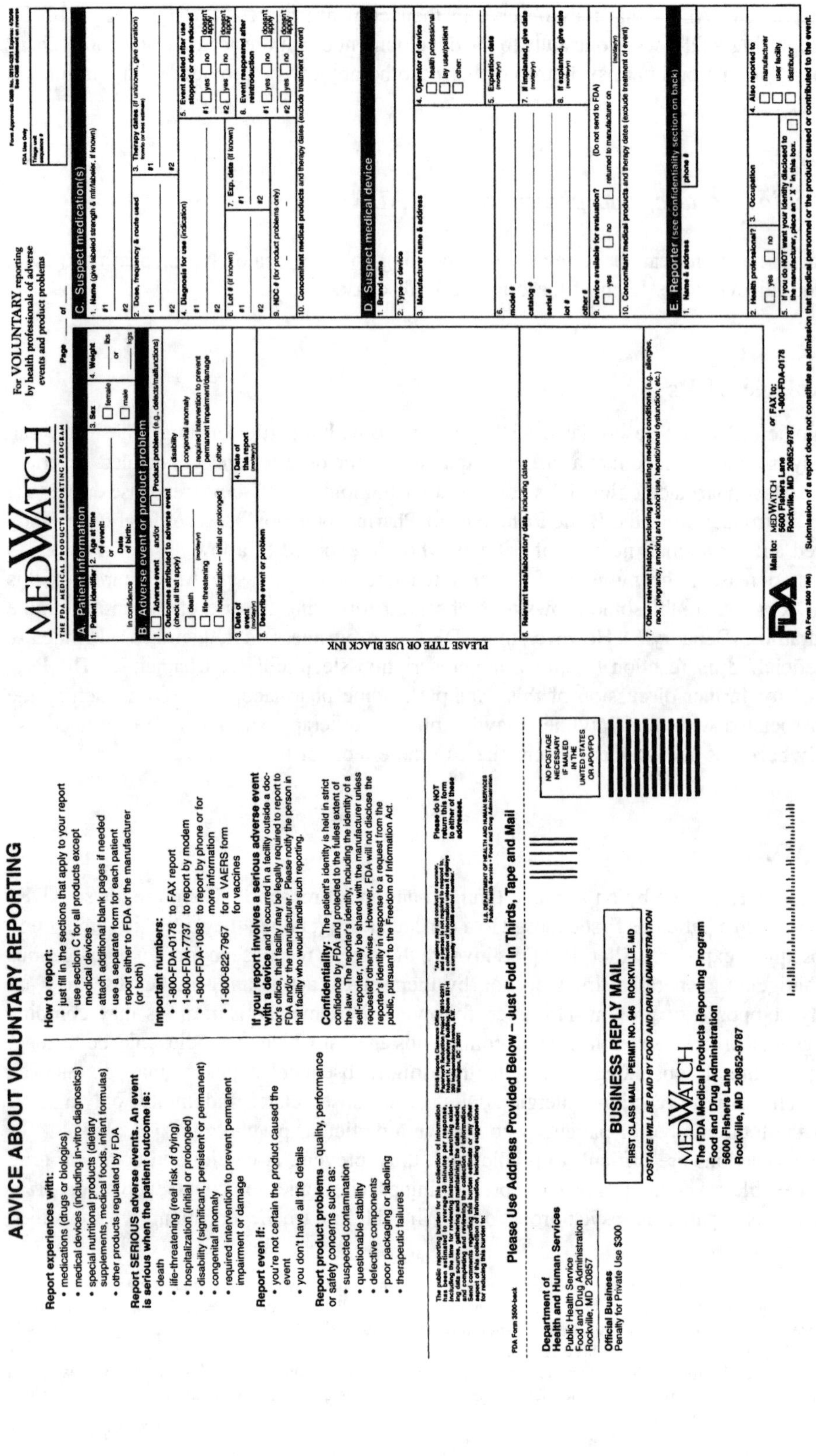

Figure 5-2. *Food and Drug Administration (FDA) ADR reporting form.*

	Health Canada	Santé Canada	PROTECTED PROTÉGÉ

Report of adverse reaction suspected due to drugs, cosmetics and biological products (Vaccines excluded)
- See reverse for return address

Notification concernant un effet indésirable présumé dû à des médicaments, cosmétiques et produits biologiques (Vaccins exclus)
- Voir à l'endos l'adresse de retour

FOR H.P.B. USE ONLY
RÉSERVÉ à LA D.G.P.S.

Patient Data - Données relatives au patient

Initials - Initiales	Chart number - Numéro de dossier	Age - Âge	Sex - Sexe	Weight -Poids	Height - Taille	Ethnic origin - Origine éthnique
			☐ Male Homme ☐ Female Femme			

Allergies or previous adverse reactions
Allergies ou effets indésirables précédents ☐ No Non ☐ Yes (Specify) Oui (Préciser)

Relevant medical history - Historie médicale pertinente

Adverse Reaction - Effet indésirable

Onset - Début
☐ Gradual / Graduel ☐ Sudden(specify in min. and hrs.) Soudain (préciser en min. et hres) ☐ Other(Specify) Autre (Préciser)   Date

Description of adverse reaction - Description de l'effet indésirable   Laboratory results - Résultats de laboratoire

Intensity of reaction
Intensité de l'effet ☐ Minor Légère ☐ Moderate Modérée ☐ Major Grave   Hospitalized because of reaction Hospitalisé à cause de l'effet ☐ No Non ☐ Yes Oui

Treatment of reaction - Traitement de l'effet
Suspected drug - Produit suspect   Treatment drugs or therapy Médicaments de traitement ou thérapie
☐ Discontinued Discontinué ☐ Dose reduced Dose réduite ☐ Unchanged Non changé ☐ Other (Specify) Autre (Préciser)   ☐ No Non ☐ Yes (Specify) Oui (Préciser)

Outcome of reaction - Suites de l'effet
☐ Recovered Rétabli ☐ Recovered with residual effects Rétabli avec séquelles ☐ Not yet recovered Pas encore rétabli ☐ Unknown Inconnues ☐ Fatal Décès → Date   Cause

Product Data - Données relatives au produit

Suspected drugs or products - Trade name / Chemicals / Lot number Médicaments ou produits suspects - Nom déposé / Produit chimique / No. de lot	Started (D-M-Y) Début (J-M-A)	Ended (D-M-Y) Fin (J-M-A)	Daily dose Dose quotidienne	Route Voie d'administration	Reason for use Raison de l'usage

Drugs taken concomitantly
Produits associés ☐ No Non ☐ Yes (Specify) Oui (Préciser)   Other comments Autres commentaires

Reporter's name - Nom du déclarant	City - Ville	Province

Name of institution - Nom de l'établissement		Telephone number - Numéro de téléphone

HC/SC 4016 (02-95)

Canadä

Figure 5-3. Health Protection Branch (HPB) ADR reporting form.

drugs they have not used previously, they should be monitored appropriately and advised as to what to do (e.g., discontinue the use of the offending drug, contact the prescriber, or seek emergency symptomatic medical treatment if signs and symptoms are severe) should they have an allergic reaction to a particular psychotropic drug.

Allergic ADRs manifest themselves in a variety of ways because they can affect several different body systems. For example, an allergic ADR affecting the blood may produce agranulocytosis (e.g., chlorpromazine [Largactil®, Thorazine®]), thrombocytopenia (e.g., carbamazepine [Tegretol®]), or neutropenia (e.g., phenytoin [Dilantin®]). On the basis of their immunologic mechanisms, allergic ADRs may be further classified into four types: Type I, anaphylactic reactions; Type II, cytotoxic reactions; Type III reactions; and Type IV reactions.

Type I

Type I (anaphylactic) reactions are acute, life-threatening reactions that occur within 30 minutes of drug exposure. Although anaphylactic reactions can occur in a susceptible person regardless of the method of administration, they are observed most frequently following intravenous injections. The reaction results from an antigen reacting with an antibody that is fixed to the surface of mast cells or basophils. Signs and symptoms of anaphylaxis include bronchospasm, hypotension, increased gastrointestinal (GI) contractility, laryngeal edema, and urticaria. Anaphylactic reactions require immediate emergency symptomatic medical support of body systems. Anaphylactic reactions are associated, for the most part, with nonpsychotropics, such as aspirin, local anesthetics, penicillins, and sulfonamides. However, they also can occur as a result of a nonmedicinal ingredient in a particular drug formulation (e.g., tartrazine coloring of tablets or other formulations of some drugs, including the following psychotropics: Butisol® 30 mg tablets, Chlorpromanyl®-20, -40 liquid, Depakene® capsules, Dexedrine Spansule® capsules, Dexedrine® tablets, Morphitec® syrup, Nembutal Sodium® capsules, Orap® 4 mg tablets, Oxycodan® tablets, PMS-Hydromorphone® tablets, and Sanorex® 2 mg tablets).

Type II

Type II (cytotoxic) reactions occur when the antigen (drug–protein combination) attaches to a cell surface. Circulating antibodies may then react with the antigen and destroy the cells. These ADRs frequently result in damage to specific body organs, such as the liver, kidneys, and skin. The thrombocytopenia associated with meprobamate (Equanil®, Miltown®) pharmacotherapy and the Stevens–Johnson syndrome, associated with carbamazepine (Tegretol®) pharmacotherapy, are examples of cytotoxic reactions.

Type III

Type III reactions involve circulating antigen-antibody complexes that destroy various tissues. The best-known example of this type of allergic reaction is the "serum sickness" associated with phenytoin (Dilantin®) and other pharmacotherapy. Signs of Type III reactions include arthritis, fever, lymphadenopathy, nephritis, and rash.

Type IV

Type IV reactions occur when the antigenic material produces tissue inflammation after interacting with antibodies that are attached to lymphocytes. The tuberculin skin reactions that occur after Mantoux testing are an example of Type IV reactions.

Idiosyncratic ADRs

Idiosyncratic ADRs are usually considered to be a catchall category for ADRs that are inadequately understood. As more clinical information becomes available, many psychotropic drugs associated with idiosyncratic ADRs may be reclassified according to the observed mechanisms of their ADRs. Idiosyncratic ADRs are not generally dose–related, affect only a small portion of the total patient population, and are usually associated with a genetic predisposition. The latter is frequently caused by genetically linked deficiencies in specific enzymes, which results in some patients responding adversely to certain drugs. For example, patients vary in regard to the rates at which they metabolize procainamide (Pronestyl®), an antidysrhythmic. Patients who have decreased amounts of N-acetyltransferase, the liver enzyme responsible for inactivating procainamide, metabolize this drug more slowly. If slow metabolizers and rapid metabolizers receive the same dose of procainamide, toxic levels may accumulate more quickly in the slow metabolizer group. Indeed, patients who are slow acetylators of procainamide develop systemic lupus erythematosus more frequently than do patients who are rapid acetylators. This process appears to be mediated by the 2D6 subfamily of the cytochrome P_{450} hepatic microsomal enzymes. Psychotropic drugs affected by this mechanism include codeine, desipramine (Pertofrane®), and nortriptyline (Pamelor®) (see Chapter 3, "Pharmacokinetics and Pharmacodynamics," for additional discussion).

Toxic ADRs

Toxic ADRs are generally associated with drug overdosages but can occur by other means. For example, clinicians who are unfamiliar with the special dosage requirements of children and the elderly (see Chapter 1, "Introduction to the Basic Principles of Pharmacotherapy," and Chapter 3, "Pharmacokinetics and Pharmacodynamics") may inadvertently overdose these patients if simply treating them as "little" or "smaller" adults. More commonly, drug overdosage occurs as the result of accidental childhood poisoning, the deliberate ingestion of a large amount of a particular drug in a suicide attempt, or the inadvertent ingestion, inhalation, or injection of an unknown quantity of an illicit drug, such as occurs in circumstances of substance abuse. In other situations, overdosage may occur as a result of kidney or liver dysfunction, which affects the normal metabolism or excretion of a particular drug and, thus, allows toxic amounts to accumulate in the body. The signs and symptoms of overdosage are generally manifested as an exacerbation of the desired pharmacologic action of a particular drug (e.g., the severe central nervous system [CNS] depression associated with opiate analgesic and sedative-hypnotic overdosages).

There are relatively few specific antidotes for treating drug overdosage.[7] Emergency symptomatic medical support of body systems, along with preventing further absorption of the drug (e.g., inducing vomiting, administering activated charcoal) and increasing elimination, is the most important aspect of treatment. The prevention of toxic ADRs is essential and includes providing patients with appropriate instruction, according to their cognitive and mental abilities, regarding their required pharmacotherapy and the safe storage of drugs out of the reach of children. Attention to suicide precautionary measures among suicidal patients and the promotion

---

[7] Among the psychotropics, two specific antidotes are available to treat drug overdosage: (1) the benzodiazepine antagonist flumazenil (Anexate®, Romazicon®) and (2) the opiate antagonist naloxone (Narcan®). See Chapter 2, "The Psychotropics," for additional details and discussion.

of substance abuse awareness and treatment programs can be helpful general strategies. Ascertaining kidney and liver function before initiating pharmacotherapy, prescribing the lowest effective dosage, monitoring when appropriate drug blood levels (see discussion of *therapeutic drug monitoring* in Chapter 3, "Pharmacokinetics and Pharmacodynamics"), and properly adjusting the dosage according to the individual needs of each patient can generally circumvent most potential toxic ADRs, even among susceptible patients. Other areas of professional responsibility include instructing patients as to what to do should an overdosage occur (e.g., immediately discontinue the use of the drug, notify the prescribing psychologist, or access emergency medical treatment).

ADRs associated with various drug interactions

Whenever pharmacotherapy involves more than one psychotropic drug, concurrent pharmacotherapy is prescribed by another prescriber (e.g., a patient's dentist may have prescribed penicillin to treat an abscessed tooth, or a patient's physician may have prescribed digoxin for the treatment of congestive heart failure), or a patient self-prescribes with nonprescription drugs (e.g., treats a headache with aspirin), the possibility of a drug–drug interaction exists. Drug interactions occur by several mechanisms. The most common interactions involve either cumulative or antagonistic effects. For example, excessive sedation may be observed among patients who have been prescribed several CNS depressants (e.g., flurazepam [Dalmane®] for sleep, codeine for pain, and diazepam [Valium®] to relieve anxiety) by their various health care prescribers (e.g., advanced practice nurse, dentist, family physician). Drugs also may interact pharmacokinetically to influence the input, distribution, and output of one another. The mechanisms involved in these interactions are often complex and incompletely understood (see Chapter 6, "Drug Interactions," for a comprehensive discussion of this topic).

ADRs involving specific body organ systems

ADRs can mimic virtually any naturally occurring medical disorder (see Tables 5-6 through 5-9). Therefore, distinguishing between a drug-induced clinical condition and one caused by natural disease factors may be extremely difficult and generally requires collaboration with medical and nursing colleagues (e.g., advanced practice nurse, physician) in order to perform required laboratory tests and physical assessments to appropriately rule out natural disease processes. However, an awareness of ADRs associated with a particular psychotropic drug, careful patient assessment (i.e., a comprehensive patient history), and close monitoring of patient response to prescribed pharmacotherapy will help to ensure a rapid detection of ADRs.

In order to properly establish an ADR, psychologists can begin by:

(1) *Ruling out* other possible causes (e.g., other drugs, disease states, laboratory test errors, and environmental factors).
(2) *Establishing* temporal eligibility (i.e., Did the suspected ADR occur after drug therapy had begun?).
(3) *Identifying linkages* between the alleged causative drug and the observed reaction. For example, did the reaction subside when the drug was discontinued? Did the patient experience a similar reaction when rechallenged with the drug? Has the suspected ADR been reported previously in the published literature?

Table 5-6. Medical and psychological disorders caused, mimicked, or exacerbated by commonly used psychotropics.

Medical or psychological disorder	Possible causative psychotropic
Acne	Barbiturates and lithium
Aggressive behavior	Alcohol, amphetamines, anticonvulsants (large doses), benzodiazepines, cocaine, and triazolam
Akathisia (*see also* "extrapyramidal reactions")	Antidepressants (e.g., paroxetine) and antipsychotics (e.g., chlorpromazine, olanzapine, and haloperidol)
Akinesia (*see also* "extrapyramidal reactions")	Antipsychotics (e.g., chlorpromazine and haloperidol)
Amnesia	(see "memory impairment")
Anorexia	CNS stimulants (e.g., amphetamines) and opiate analgesics (e.g., codeine) that irritate the gastrointestinal system
Anorgasmia	Antidepressants, particularly selective serotonin reuptake inhibitors
Asterixis	Carbamazepine, haloperidol, phenothiazines, and phenytoin
Asthenia	Dexfenfluramine, lamotrigine, and nefazodone
Ataxia	Benzodiazepines, carbamazepine, chloral hydrate, clonazepam, gabapentin, lamotrigine, phenobarbital, phenytoin, and primidone
Athetosis	Carbamazepine, levodopa, and phenytoin
Behavioral disturbance	Alcohol, cocaine, and most psychotropic drugs (with large doses or upon abrupt discontinuation after long-term use)
Blood dyscrasias	
Agranulocytosis	Carbamazepine, clozapine, mirtazapine, phenothiazines, phenytoin, and tricyclic antidepressants
Aplastic anemia	Carbamazepine, felbamate, mephenytoin, and phenytoin
Eosinophilia	Carbamazepine and phenothiazines
Leukocytosis	Haloperidol, lithium, and phenothiazines
Leukopenia	Carbamazepine, haloperidol, phenytoin, and primidone
Megaloblastic anemia	Phenobarbital, phenytoin, and primidone
Neutropenia	Phenytoin
Thrombocytopenia	Alcohol, carbamazepine, phenytoin, primidone, and valproic acid
Bradycardia	Lithium
Cardiac dysrhythmias (*see also* "bradycardia," "tachycardia," and "torsade de pointes")	Haloperidol, lithium, trazodone, and tricyclic antidepressants
Chorea	Amphetamines, anticonvulsants, antipsychotics, cocaine, levodopa, lithium, and tricyclic antidepressants
Cognitive dysfunction	(see "confusion," "learning impairment," and "memory impairment")
Coma	Barbiturates, benzodiazepines, tricyclic antidepressants, and valproic acid
Confusion	(see Table 5-7)
Constipation	Nefazodone, olanzapine, opiate analgesics, phenothiazines, and tricyclic antidepressants

continued. . .

Table 5-6. Medical and psychological disorders caused, mimicked, or exacerbated by commonly used psychotropics—Continued.

Medical or psychological disorder	Possible causative psychotropic
Convulsions	Amoxapine (overdosage), clozapine, CNS stimulants, haloperidol, lithium, meperidine, phenothiazines, and risperidone
Decreased libido	Alprazolam, chlorpromazine, fluphenazine, lithium, maprotiline, and tricyclic antidepressants
Delirium	Anticonvulsants, benzodiazepines, chlorpromazine, clozapine, disulfiram, lithium, opiate analgesics, sedative-hypnotics, thioridazine, and tricyclic antidepressants
Dementia	Alcohol, anticonvulsants, antipsychotics, lithium, and sedative-hypnotics
Depression	(see Table 5-8)
Diarrhea	Dexfenfluramine, lithium, and valproic acid
Dizziness	(see "vertigo")
Drowsiness	Anticonvulsants, dexfenfluramine, gabapentin, lamotrigine, mirtazapine, nefazodone, opiate analgesics, phenothiazines, sedative-hypnotics, trazodone, tricyclic antidepressants, venlafaxine, and vigabatrin
Dystonia	Antipsychotics, carbamazepine, fluoxetine, levodopa, and phenytoin
Encephalopathy	Alcohol, carbamazepine, lithium, phenytoin, valproic acid, and vigabatrin
Exfoliative dermatitis	Carbamazepine, phenobarbital, and phenytoin
Extrapyramidal reactions (*see also* individual reactions [e.g., akathisia])	Haloperidol, phenothiazines, and risperidone
Fever	Clozapine and phenytoin
Gingival hyperplasia	Phenytoin
Goiter	(see "hypothyroidism")
Gynecomastia (including galactorrhea in females)	Amoxapine, antipsychotics, fluoxetine, maprotiline, and tricyclic antidepressants
Hallucinations (*see also* "psychosis")	Alcohol, amphetamines, benzodiazepines, cocaine, haloperidol, methylphenidate, phenytoin, psychedelics (e.g., LSD, cannabis), and tricyclic antidepressants
Headaches	Dexfenfluramine, ethosuximide, fluoxetine, lamotrigine, moclobemide, nicotine, pimozide, sertraline, trazodone, and venlafaxine
Hepatic dysfunction (including hepatitis and liver failure)	Alcohol, barbiturates, chlorpromazine, diazepam, haloperidol, pemoline, phenothiazines, phenytoin, and valproic acid
Hirsutism	Phenytoin
Hyperprolactinemia	Chlordiazepoxide, clozapine, cocaine, fenfluramine, haloperidol, monoamine oxidase inhibitors, opiate analgesics, and tricyclic antidepressants
Hypersensitivity reaction (*see also* "anaphylaxis")	Virtually all drugs, including the psychotropics, can produce hypersensitivity reactions among susceptible patients. However, some drugs may have a greater propensity for producing hypersensitivity reactions than others. In addition, some drug formulations contain "inactive" ingredients (e.g., sulfites, tartrazine) that may produce hypersensitivity reactions

Table 5-6. Medical and psychological disorders caused, mimicked, or exacerbated by commonly used psychotropics—Continued.

Medical or psychological disorder	Possible causative psychotropic
Hypertension	Amphetamines, cocaine, and methylphenidate
Hyponatremia (see also "syndrome of inappropriate secretion of antidiuretic hormone")	Antidepressants
Hypotension	Alcohol, clozapine, lithium, monoamine oxidase inhibitors, olanzapine, phenothiazines, trazodone, and tricyclic antidepressants
Hypothermia	Alcohol, barbiturates (large doses or acute overdosage), lithium, and opiate analgesics
Hypothyroidism	Lithium
Impotence	Amoxepine, butyrophenones, lithium, monoamine oxidase inhibitors, phenothiazines, trazodone, and tricyclic antidepressants
Insomnia	Amphetamines, buspirone, caffeine, cocaine, dexfenfluramine, methylphenidate, monoamine oxidase inhibitors, nicotine (transdermal patch), risperidone, and selective serotonin reuptake inhibitors
Learning (cognitive function) impairment (*see also* "memory impairment")	Alcohol (acute intoxication and fetal alcohol syndrome), anticonvulsants, antipsychotics, cannabis, cocaine, lithium, opiate analgesics, sedative-hypnotics, and tricyclic antidepressants
Liver failure	(see "hepatic dysfunction")
Lymphadenopathy	Primidone
Mania	Amphetamines, antidepressants, and cocaine
Memory impairment (*see also* "confusion")	Alcohol, benzodiazepines, cannabis, levodopa, lithium, sedative-hypnotics, and tricyclic antidepressants
Mental confusion	(see Table 5-7)
Myoclonus	Antipsychotics, carbamazepine, phenytoin, and tricyclic antidepressants
Nausea	Virtually *all* orally ingested drugs
Neuroleptic malignant syndrome	Antipsychotics
Nightmares	Alcohol, benzodiazepines, chloral hydrate, fenfluramine, and nicotine (transdermal patch)
Nystagmus (*see also* "visual dysfunction/ impairment")	Amitriptyline, barbiturates, benzodiazepines, carbamazepine, chloral hydrate, disulfiram, fenfluramine, gabapentin, glutethimide, lithium, meperidine, phenelzine, phenobarbital, phenytoin, and valproic acid
Oculogyric crisis	Antipsychotics, carbamazepine, lithium, and pentazocine
Orthostatic hypotension	(see "hypotension")
Pancreatitis	Valproic acid (rare)
Parkinsonism, drug-induced	Antipsychotics, disulfiram, fluoxetine, lithium, meperidine, and valproic acid
Peripheral neuropathy	Amitriptyline, anticonvulsants, glutethimide, imipramine, lithium, phenelzine, and zimeldine

continued. . .

Table 5-6. Medical and psychological disorders caused, mimicked, or exacerbated by commonly used psychotropics—Continued.

Medical or psychological disorder	Possible causative psychotropic
Polyuria	Lithium
Postural hypotension	(see "hypotension")
Priapism	Amitriptyline, desipramine, lithium, phenothiazines, and trazodone
Psychosis	(see Table 5-9)
Pulmonary hypertension	CNS stimulants
Respiratory depression	Alcohol, opiate analgesics, and sedative-hypnotics
Restless legs syndrome	Benzodiazepines, carbamazepine, and levodopa
Schizophrenia	(see "psychosis")
Seizures	(see "convulsions")
Sexual dysfunction	(see "anorgasmia," "decreased libido," "gynecomastia," "impotence," and "priapism")
Sleepwalking	Benzodiazepines, chloral hydrate, lithium, and zolpidem
Serotonin syndrome (*see also* Chapter 6, "Drug Interactions")	Clomipramine, fluoxetine, fluvoxamine, moclobemide, paroxetine, phenelzine, sertraline, and tranylcypromine (note: almost all cases of serotonin syndrome associated with single drug pharmacotherapy (i.e., monotherapy) have been associated with overdosages)
Syndrome of inappropriate secretion of antidiuretic hormone (SIADH)	Antipsychotics, benzodiazepines, carbamazepine, and tricyclic antidepressants
Tachycardia (*see also* "cardiac dysrhythmias")	Clozapine, CNS stimulants, risperidone, and tricyclic antidepressants
Tardive dyskinesia	Antipsychotics (e.g., chlorpromazine, haloperidol) and fluoxetine (relatively rare)
Torsade de pointes	Haloperidol
Tourette's syndrome (tics)	Amphetamines, carbamazepine, cocaine, dextroamphetamine, methylphenidate, and pemoline
Toxic epidermal necrolysis (*see also* "exfoliative dermatitis")	Carbamazepine, phenobarbital, and phenytoin
Tremor	Amphetamines, caffeine, fenfluramine, gabapentin, levodopa, lithium, methylphenidate, pemoline, tricyclic antidepressants, and valproic acid
Urinary retention	Monoamine oxidase inhibitors, phenothiazines, trazodone, and tricyclic antidepressants
Vertigo/vestibular dysfunction	Gabapentin, haloperidol, lamotrigine, mirtazapine, nefazodone, olanzapine, phenytoin, primidone, and venlafaxine
Visual dysfunction/impairment (*see also* "nystagmus")	Alcohol, cannabis, ethosuximide, felbamate, lamotrigine, lithium, nefazodone, phenothiazines, thioridazine, and tricyclic antidepressants
Vomiting	Virtually *all* orally ingested psychotropics
Weight gain	Cannabis, clozapine, mirtazapine, olanzapine, tricyclic antidepressants, and vigabatrin

Table 5-6. Medical and psychological disorders caused, mimicked, or exacerbated by commonly used psychotropics—Continued.

Medical or psychological disorder	Possible causative psychotropic
Weight loss (*see also* "anorexia")	Molindone
Xerostomia	Antidepressants (e.g., tricyclic), antipsychotics (e.g., chlorpromazine and haloperidol), and mirtazapine

Note. Drugs other than those listed in this table may cause these medical and psychological disorders, as well as other ADRs. However, this list is an attempt to identify some of the more common examples that have been observed and reported in the clinical literature. Psychologists can quickly refer to this table to determine whether or not psychotropic pharmacotherapy needs to be ruled out as a possible cause of various disorders with which the patient presents. In addition, the data in this table can be of assistance in the selection of psychotropic pharmacotherapy that will not exacerbate or complicate a clinical condition(s) being treated by another prescriber. Alcohol, cannabis, and cocaine, although not prescribed, are widely used by patients who have mental disorders. Thus, these abusable psychotropics have been included in this table in order to both (1) assist psychologists in the recognition of related signs and symptoms of their use and (2) remind psychologists to appropriately rule out their use among patients presenting with the noted clinical disorders.

Table 5-7. Drugs that can aggravate or cause confusion.

• Acyclovir	• Corticosteroids
• **Alcohol**	• Digoxin
• **Anticonvulsants**	• Ephedrine
• **Antidepressants**	• Indomethacin
• Antidiabetics	• **Lithium**
• Antihistamines	• Methyldopa
• Antihypertensives	• **Nefazodone**
• **Anti-parkinsonian drugs**	• **Opiate analgesics**
• **Antipsychotics**	• **Phenytoin**
• Atropine-like drugs	• Quinidine
• Calcium channel blockers	• Ranitidine
• Cimetidine	• Reserpine
• Clonidine	• **Sedative-hypnotics**

Note. Psychotropics are listed in boldface.

Table 5-8. Drugs that can aggravate or cause depression.

• **Alcohol**	• Indomethacin
• Amantadine	• **Levodopa**
• Anabolic steroids	• Methyldopa
• **Anticonvulsants**	• Metoclopramide
• **Antipsychotics**	• Naptroxen
• Baclofen	• **Opiate analgesics**
• Cimetidine	• Oral contraceptives
• Corticosteroids	• Propranolol
• Digoxin	• Reserpine
• Guanethidine	• **Sedative-hypnotics**

Note. Psychotropics are listed in boldface.

Careful monitoring and the identification of certain factors aid in making an association between prescribed pharmacotherapy and an ADR. When considering a potential ADR, psychologists must identify whether there is a reasonable temporal association between the use of the drug and the occurrence of the observed or reported reaction (i.e., Did pharmacotherapy precede the onset of the reaction?). In addition, other factors that could contribute to a patient's ADR

Table 5-9. Drugs that can aggravate or cause psychosis.

• Amantadine	• **Lithium**
• **Amphetamines**	• **LSD**
• Anabolic steroids	• Mefloquine
• **Anticonvulsants**	• **Methylphenidate**
• **Antipsychotics**	• Nalidixic acid
• Baclofen	• Nifurtimox
• Bromocriptine	• Nitroprusside
• **Bupropion**	• Phenacemide
• **Carbamazepine**	• Prazosin
• **Cocaine**	• Procainamide
• Corticosteroids	• Propafenone
• Cyclopentolate	• Quinacrine
• Digoxin	• Quinidine
• Disopyramide	• Scopolamine
• Disulfiram	• Sulfonamides
• Isoniazid	• Vidarabine
• **Levodopa**	• Vigabatrin

Note. Psychotropics are listed in boldface.

(e.g., clinical status) also should be explored. For some ADRs, the results of a "dechallenge" should be observed (i.e., If the drug is discontinued, does the patient's condition improve?).

An awareness of potential ADRs can prevent misdiagnosis and encourage appropriate modification of pharmacotherapy. In this section, ADRs involving specific body organ systems are discussed. Special attention is given to the specific psychotropic drugs that have been implicated in causing body organ toxicity that may mimic selected medical and psychological disorders or other clinical conditions (see also Table 5-6 and Appendix 3).

The following body organ systems are considered:[8,9] (1) cardiovascular, (2) CNS, (3) cutaneous or skin, (4) fever,[10] (5) hematologic, (6) hepatic, (7) ocular (8) otic, (9) pulmonary/respiratory, (10) renal, and (11) reproductive/genitourinary.

Emphasis here is on the various physical ADRs. These ADRs are briefly described and discussed in order to enable psychologists to reasonably anticipate and identify them in their clinical practices. When such ADRs are encountered, appropriate actions are required that may include modification of dosage, changes in dosage forms, or selection of an alternative psychotropic drug from a similar or different class. When there is concern that the observed physical ADR(s) may pose a significant hazard for a patient, collaboration with or *referral* to another health care professional (e.g., advanced practice nurse, dentist, physician) may be required for confirmation of the ADR and other appropriate intervention.

Cardiovascular system (CVS)

ADRs associated with the cardiovascular system (CVS) can be grouped into three major categories: (1) effects on blood pressure, (2) effects on cardiac conduction, and (3) effects on cardiac rhythym (which can be considered as a specialized subset of cardiac conduction disorders).

---

[8] Note that ADRs associated with gastrointestinal toxicities have not been included because nearly all drugs, particularly when orally ingested, can cause abdominal distress, constipation, diarrhea, nausea, or vomiting.

[9] For comprehensive information regarding specific types of ADRs occurring with a particular drug, the reader is referred to Jain (1996), Kane and Lieberman (1995), or Pagliaro and Pagliaro (1986, 1995) or to the companion volume to this text, *Psychologists' Psychotropic Desk Reference* (Pagliaro & Pagliaro, 1998).

[10] Fever, obviously, is not an organ system. However, because this phenomenon involves several organ systems, it has been listed and discussed separately.

Effects on blood pressure

Blood pressure can change in only one of two ways (i.e., it can increase or decrease). Increased blood pressure (i.e., hypertension), which can cause intracranial hemorrhage and strokes in susceptible patients, is associated with the use of CNS stimulants (e.g., amphetamines, methylphenidate [Ritalin®]). Decreased blood pressure (i.e., hypotension), which can cause syncope, particularly among elderly frail, and debilitated patients, and those who have serious heart disease, is associated with the use of various psychotropics, including the monoamine oxidase inhibitors, the phenothiazines, and the tricyclic antidepressants (see Table 5-10 for the relative risk associated with various individual antidepressants).[11]

Effects on cardiac conduction[12]

Disturbances in cardiac conduction result in various degrees of dissociation between normal sinus pacemaker function and contraction of the ventricles. These effects are reflected in changes to the electrocardiogram (ECG) (see Footnote 12 for a brief review and discussion of the ECG). Prolonged P-R intervals, indicative of first-degree AV block, are related to the use of the tricyclic antidepressants. This ADR is generally not clinically significant but may be so in patients who have preexisting cardiac disease, particularly bundle branch block. In addition, this effect would tend to be synergistic with similar therapeutic actions of the antidysrhythmics and may prove problematic when both drugs are used concurrently. Lithium pharmacotherapy is often accompanied by a flattening or, rarely, inversion of the T wave. This effect, which has its onset shortly after the start of lithium pharmacotherapy and appears to be benign, reverts to normal within a few days of the discontinuation of lithium pharmacotherapy.

Effects on cardiac rhythm

ADRs can result in various cardiac dysrhythmias, including bradycardia (decreased heart rate to less than 60 beats per minute in an adult at rest) and tachycardia (increased heart rate of more than 100 beats per minute in an adult at rest). Lithium use may result in sinus bradycardia, which is usually asymptomatic but may cause symptoms of ataxia, dizziness, or syncope. Tachycardia is commonly associated with tricyclic antidepressant pharmacotherapy and is related to the anticholinergic actions of the tricyclic antidepressants. Torsade de pointes, a potentially malignant form of ventricular tachycardia that is generally associated with the use of Type I antidysrhythmics, has also been associated with haloperidol (Haldol®) pharmacotherapy.

Central nervous system (CNS)

The ADRs affecting the CNS most frequently involve either: (1) overstimulation (CNS excitation), resulting in associated signs and symptoms such as insomnia, mania, or seizures; or (2)

---

[11] Orthostatic hypotension, particularly when combined with the ADRs of drowsiness or confusion (see Tables 5-6 and 5-7), can result in syncope and the associated ADE of hip fracture, particularly among elderly patients. Risk of hip fracture among elderly patients has been estimated to be several-fold greater for those who are receiving pharmacotherapy with psychotropics that are capable of causing orthostatic hypotension and confusion or drowsiness.

[12] The sinoatrial (SA) node acts as the heart's pacemaker, generating an electrical impulse that is transmitted to the atrioventricular (AV) node and then further by means of the ventricular specialized conducting system (VSCS), composed of the bundle of His, bundle branches, and peripheral Purkinje fibers. This electrical impulse triggers synchronized contractions of the heart muscle. The electrocardiogram (ECG) is used to measure the related electrical activity within the heart. Specific elated measures include the P wave, which is the first event seen in a normal ECG and corresponds to depolarization of the atrial muscle; the Q, R, and S waves (i.e., QRS complex), which corresponds to depolarization of the ventricles; the P-R interval, which is the time interval between depolarization of the atrial muscle and depolarization of the ventricles; the T wave, which corresponds to repolarization of the ventricles; the ST segment, which represents the completion of depolarization and the beginning of repolarization of the ventricles and corresponds to the actual time during which the ventricles contract; and the Q-T interval, which is the time interval from the beginning of depolarization to full repolarization of the ventricles.

Table 5-10. Comparative ADR profiles for the antidepressants.

	ADR (key: 0 = absent or rare; 4+ = relatively common)						
	Central nervous system			Cardiovascular system		GI system	Other
Antidepressant	Anticholinergic effects[a]	Drowsiness	Insomnia/ agitation	Orthostatic hypotension	Cardiac dysrhythmias	Nausea/ vomiting	Weight gain (>6 kg)
Monoamine oxidase inhibitors (MAOIs)							
(e.g., tranylcypromine)	1+	1+	2+	2+	0	1+	2+
Selective serotonin reuptake inhibitors (SSRIs)							
(e.g., fluoxetine, paroxetine, sertraline)	0	0	2+	0	0	3+	0
Tricyclic antidepressants (TCAs)							
Amitriptyline	4+	4+	0	4+	3+	0	4+
Desipramine	1+	1+	1+	2+	2+	0	1+
Doxepin	3+	4+	0	2+	2+	0	3+
Imipramine	3+	3+	1+	4+	3+	1+	3+
Nortriptyline	1+	1+	0	2+	2+	0	1+
Protriptyline	2+	1+	1+	2+	2+	0	0
Trimipramine	1+	4+	0	2+	2+	0	3+
Miscellaneous							
Amoxapine	2+	2+	2+	2+	3+	0	1+
Bupropion	0	0	2+	0	0	1+	0
Maprotiline	2+	4+	0	0	1+	0	2+
Mirtazapine	3+	4+	0	0	0	0	4+
Nefazodone	1+	1+	0	0	0	2+	1+
Trazodone	0	4+	0	1+	1+	1+	1+
Venlafaxine[b]	1+	1+	1+	0	0	3+	0

[a] Anticholinergic effects include blurred vision, confusion, constipation, drowsiness, dry mouth, increased heart rate (tachycardia), and urinary retention.
[b] Venlafaxine can be categorized as an SSRI (see Chapter 2, "The Psychotropics"). However, because its ADR profile differs slightly, it has been included, for the purposes of this table, under the "miscellaneous" category.

oversedation (CNS depression), resulting in associated signs and symptoms such as confusion, drowsiness, or respiratory depression. In addition, several specific syndromes mediated by the CNS and generally associated with the psychotropics have been identified. Two of the most common and clinically significant of these syndromes are the "neuroleptic (antipsychotic) malignant syndrome" and the "serotonin syndrome." These and a constellation of reactions commonly associated with the use of the antipsychotics (i.e., extrapyramidal reactions) are briefly discussed.

Neuroleptic (antipsychotic) malignant syndrome
The neuroleptic malignant syndrome (NMS) is a rare, poorly understood but potentially fatal reaction to therapeutic dosages of the antipsychotics.[13] NMS appears to be produced by extensive, abrupt dopamine receptor blockade within the nigrostriatal and hypothalamic pathways of the CNS and appears to require a pre–existing defect in skeletal muscle metabolism that is exacerbated by antipsychotic use. The incidence of this syndrome has been estimated at approximately 1% of patients treated with antipsychotics. Although NMS has generally been characterized as an idiosyncratic reaction, its risk factors appear to include age (mean age ~40 years), dosage and method of administration of the antipsychotic (i.e., high dosages, rapid dosage escalation, and use of the injectable formulations of an antipsychotic), gender (i.e., NMS is twice as common among males as among females), and use of antipsychotics among patients who have affective disorders (e.g., clinical depression, bipolar manic-depressive disorder), for whom antipsychotics are generally not indicated.

The classic diagnostic signs and symptoms of NMS include: (1) altered consciousness (i.e., coma, confusion, disorientation, mutism, or stupor; (2) autonomic nervous system (ANS) dysfunction (i.e., incontinence, increased pulse and respiratory rates, profuse sweating [diaphoresis], unstable [fluctuating] blood pressure); (3) hyperthermia (i.e., body temperature of 39°C [104°F] or higher); and (4) muscular rigidity. NMS is sometimes confused with the serotonin syndrome (see following discussion) because of some overlapping (common) signs and symptoms (i.e., diaphoresis, hyperthermia).

Medical complications of NMS include cardiac dysrhythmias, kidney failure, and respiratory distress that result in death in up to 20% of patients who develop NMS. Therefore, if NMS is suspected, patients should be referred for medical evaluation and, if needed, symptomatic emergency care. The treatment of NMS generally includes: (1) discontinuation of all antipsychotic pharmacotherapy; (2) intensive supportive care of vital body systems (i.e., heart, lungs, and liver); and (3) administration, as indicated, of bromocriptine (Parlodel®), a dopamine agonist, and dantrolene (Dantrium®), a skeletal muscle relaxant.[14] NMS may persist and require treatment for up to 2 weeks following discontinuation of antipsychotic pharmacotherapy. Following recovery from NMS, antipsychotic pharmacotherapy may be successfully resumed for most patients who have schizophrenia (~90%). Lower dosages of a less potent antipsychotic should be prescribed.[15]

Serotonin syndrome
The serotonin syndrome, as the name implies, is due to an oversupply of serotonin (5-hydroxytryptamine) in the CNS. It is most commonly the result of drug interactions involving monoamine

---

[13] It has been postulated that NMS is not a true distinct clinical entity but, rather, simply a special case of antipsychotic-induced extrapyramidal reactions accompanied by fever.
[14] The efficacy of these drugs for the treatment of NMS has been questioned because of the inconsistency of the clinical results associated with their use.
[15] Some patients may tolerate the same antipsychotic that caused the NMS, but, whenever possible, it is preferable to restart the patient on a different antipsychotic.

oxidase inhibitors and serotonergics (e.g., selective serotonin reuptake inhibitors, tryptophan) (see Chapter 6, "Drug Interactions"). The serotonin syndrome can also result from an overdosage of serotonergics (see Table 5-6).

The signs and symptoms of the serotonin syndrome include agitation, diaphoresis, hyper-reflexia, hyperthermia, incoordination, and myoclonus. The severity of the syndrome can range from benign transient cases to those that have resulted in death. Treatment generally involves discontinuation of the offending drug, symptomatic medical support of body systems, and, where indicated, the administration of serotonin antagonists such as cyproheptadine (Periactin®) and methysergide (Sansert®).

Extrapyramidal reactions

Disorders of the basal ganglia[16] in the forebrain result in various forms of involuntary movements characterized by either hyperkinesia or hypokinesia and specific postural changes. The antipsy-chotics, presumably as a result of their propensity to block dopamine receptors, can cause drug-related syndromes that mimic all of the organic basal ganglia disorders.[17] Following is a brief list and associated definitions of the specific "extrapyramidal reactions" that have been associated with antipsychotic pharmacotherapy, including acute dystonia, akathisia, Parkinson's syndrome, and tardive dyskinesia.

Acute dystonia.   Acute dystonia involves intermittent or sustained muscle contractions that result in abnormal, bizarre postures and repetitive twisting movements. It is somewhat similar in nature and appearance to athetosis. Acute dystonias usually first occur within the first few days of antipsychotic pharmacotherapy. The reactions can last from a few seconds to several hours. Acute dystonias generally remit upon discontinuation of antipsychotic pharmacotherapy and/or initiation of anticholinergic treatment (e.g., benzotropine [Cogentin®], trihexyphenidyl [Artane®]).

Akathisia.   Akathisia is the inability to sit still. The patient has a feeling of restlessness and a conscious, urgent need for movement. Signs include lateral knee movements, pacing, repeated leg crossings, rocking movements from foot to foot while standing, swinging of one leg when sitting, and walking on the spot. Akathisia, both acute and chronic, is the most frequently reported extrapyramidal reaction associated with antipsychotic pharmacotherapy, reportedly occurring in approximately 30% of treated patients. It also has been reported in association with the use of all of the various types of antidepressants, particularly the selective serotonin reuptake inhibitors (SSRIs), but at a significantly lower incidence than that reported for the antipsychotics.

Risk factors for the development of akathisia associated with antipsychotic pharmacotherapy are poorly understood. However, the occurrence of akathisia appears to be higher among patients who have the following conditions or characteristics: affective disorders, cognitive dysfunction, drug-induced Parkinsonism, female gender, high dosage of antipsychotics, iron deficiency,[18] mental retardation, and negative symptoms of schizophrenia.

Parkinson's syndrome.   Parkinson's syndrome[19] is a hypokinetic movement disorder with four

---

[16] The basal ganglia, composed of the caudate nucleus, putamen, globus pallidus, and substantia nigra, is a group of interrelated structures that lie deep within the forebrain. CNS transmission via the basal ganglia is directed rostrally through the thalamus to the cerebral cortex (rather than passing caudally directly through the pyramidal tract); hence, this system is also known as the *extrapyramidal system*.

[17] Other psychotropics, in addition to the antipsychotics, can also cause extrapyramidal reactions (see Table 5-6).

[18] Iron appears to interact with the dopamine (D2) receptor, but the clinical significance of this interaction is not yet fully understood.

[19] Also referred to as drug-induced Parkinsonism or secondary Parkinson's syndrome (disease) in order to etiologi-cally differentiate this syndrome from idiopathic Parkinson's disease.

characteristic features: (1) bradykinesia (i.e., slowness and poverty of movement); (2) muscular rigidity of the limbs (often described as being either "lead pipe" or "cogwheel" in nature); (3) postural instability, including a tendency to fall forward or backward when the center of gravity is displaced and a related gait that varies from shuffling to festination (i.e., increase in speed of walking to slow running to keep from falling forward); and (4) resting tremor (i.e., characteristically a 4 to 8 Hz "pill-rolling" tremor of the hand while at rest, although the tremor can spread to other limbs). Treatment of drug-induced Parkinsonism can include dosage reduction, discontinuation of antipsychotic pharmacotherapy, substitution of an antipsychotic with a lower propensity for causing drug-induced Parkinsonism (e.g., clozapine [Clozaril®]), and/or addition of anticholinergic drugs (e.g., benzotropine [Cogentin®], trihexyphenidyl [Artane®]) to the antipsychotic pharmacotherapy (see related discussion in Chapter 2, "The Psychotropics").

Tardive dyskinesia.   Tardive dyskinesia[20] is a defect in voluntary movement associated with long-term, generally high-dosage, antipsychotic pharmacotherapy. Characteristics of tardive dyskinesia include choreiform movements of the buccal-lingual fascial muscles commonly resembling "lip smacking" and "tongue darting." Tardive dyskinesia is generally irreversible, even upon discontinuation of antipsychotic pharmacotherapy, and is resistant to standard treatments for related movement disorders. Thus, prevention is the "treatment of choice" (see Chapter 2, "The Psychotropics," for additional discussion).

Cutaneous or skin

The ADRs affecting the cutaneous or skin system may be produced by almost any drug, including the psychotropics. In many instances, a single drug may produce a variety of ADRs, including rashes, lesions, and eruptions. The diagnosis of an ADR affecting the skin is often made difficult because ADRs can mimic common dermatologic diseases. Immediate identification of the offending drug and modification of pharmacotherapy are of prime importance. Collaboration with other health care providers (e.g., advanced practice nurses, dermatologists, family physicians) may often be required in these situations to either confirm or rule out suspected dermatological reactions or conditions.

The drug-induced cutaneous ADRs reviewed in this section include acneform eruptions, alopecia, erythema multiforme (minor), fixed drug eruptions, photosensitivity reactions, and toxic epidermal necrolysis.

Acneform eruptions

Drug-induced acneform eruptions resemble true acne but are characterized by a sudden onset, absence of comedones, and involvement of unusual sites. A classic example of drug-induced acneform eruption is the severe acne that was once commonly considered to be a "telltale" sign of barbiturate abuse.[21]

---

[20] Tardive dyskinesia is often not included as part of the extrapyramidal reactions but is instead considered to be a separate ADR because of its late occurrence in antipsychotic pharmacotherapy and its general resistance to treatment. Either categorization of tardive dyskinesia is acceptable.

[21] Barbiturate abuse has significantly abated over the last 30 years, commensurate with decreased clinical use, production, and availability. See Chapter 2, "The Psychotropics," for related discussion. See also *Substance Use Among Children and Adolescents: Its Nature, Extent, and Effects from Conception to Adulthood* (Pagliaro & Pagliaro, 1996) for detailed discussion of barbiturate abuse.

Alopecia
Hair loss induced by drugs may affect any portion of the body. However, scalp hair is most notably affected, because 90% of scalp hairs are in the active phase of growth (anagen). While potentially emotionally and cosmetically troublesome to most patients, drug-induced alopecia is not life threatening and usually resolves with discontinuation of the offending drug.

Erythema multiforme (minor)
As implied by its name, erythema multiforme can involve variable skin lesions, including urticarial, macular, papular, vesicular, and purpuric eruptions. These lesions involve generally the skin and mucous membranes and are most commonly observed among children and young adults. The duration of erythema multiforme reactions is 2 to 6 weeks. A more serious variant is the Stevens–Johnson syndrome, which can be fatal, with death estimated to occur in 5% to 18% of patients (see section on toxic epidermal necrolysis).

Fixed drug eruptions
Fixed drug eruptions represent a hypersensitivity reaction in which repeated exposure to the offending drug produces lesions at the same, or almost identical, sites as previously affected. Fixed eruptions often are characterized by bullous, erythematous, pruritic, or urticarial plaques. These lesions resolve when the drug is discontinued. However, hyperpigmented areas may remain.

Photosensitivity reactions
Drug-induced photosensitivity reactions occur when patients who are receiving pharmacotherapy with certain offending drugs (e.g., chlorpromazine [Largactil®, Thorazine®]) are exposed to the ultraviolet rays of direct sunlight. When considering drug-induced photosensitivity reactions, it is important to differentiate between photoallergic and phototoxic reactions.

Photoallergic reactions. Photoallergic reactions: (1) are preceded by an initial sensitizing exposure; (2) are unrelated to the use of a particular drug; (3) exhibit cross sensitivity between chemically related drugs; (4) usually involve a light spectrum of longer wavelengths than phototoxic reactions; (5) may occur at distant dermatologic sites from those previously exposed to the offending drug; (6) take a wide variety of morphologic forms, including bullous eruptions, erythematous papules or nodules, sunburn-like reactions, and urticarial lesions; and (7) occur within 2 days of exposure to the offending drug.

Phototoxic reactions. In contrast to photoallergic reactions, phototoxic reactions: (1) may occur with the first exposure to the drug, usually within 6 hours; (2) occur at wavelengths close to the absorption peak of the drug; (3) are dose related; (4) do not exhibit cross reactivity; and (5) are sunburn-type reactions, occurring only on light-exposed areas of the skin.

   Patients who are prescribed known photosensitizing drugs should be cautioned to avoid direct exposure to sunlight, particularly during midday. They also should be advised to wear a hat and other protective clothing and to use a chemical sunscreening agent (e.g., PABA) when direct exposure to the sun cannot be avoided.

Toxic epidermal necrolysis
Toxic epidermal necrolysis (erythema multiforme major) is a life-threatening hypersensitivity reaction. During the early stages, toxic epidermal necrolysis is characterized by skin eruptions of an erythematous and tender nature. This early-stage reaction is followed by large flaccid

bullae that easily rupture and peel. These lesions involve predominantly the epidermis, and, thus, there is usually little or no dermal involvement. Healing occurs within 2 weeks without residual scarring unless complicated by infection. When death occurs, it is frequently a result of a secondary infection. In addition to psychotropics (e.g., carbamazepine [Tegretol®], phenobarbital [Luminal®], phenytoin [Dilantin®]) and other drugs, bacterial metabolites and foods have been implicated as etiologic factors in the development of toxic epidermal necrolysis. However, irrespective of cause, the pathogenesis appears to be the same.

Fever[22]

The precise mechanism by which drug-induced fever occurs is incompletely understood. However, five types of "drug fever" have been described. The most common type involves an immunologic response in which fever becomes manifest either alone or in combination with other signs and symptoms (e.g., eosinophilia, rash, and urticaria). On subsequent use of an offending drug, the fever will often ensue within hours. Idiosyncrasy is a second mechanism by which drugs have been implicated in fever. Such a reaction occurs when pharmacotherapy with depolarizing skeletal muscle relaxants is prescribed for certain patients who have abnormal muscle metabolism. Febrile reactions also may occur as a direct result of the pharmacologic action of a particular drug (e.g., bactericidal effect of antibiotics on sensitive microorganisms), such as the release of endotoxins (e.g., Jarisch–Herxheimer reaction).

A fourth mechanism is associated with drugs that elevate body temperature by a direct effect on the physiologic mechanisms involved with temperature regulation. The mechanisms by which drugs have been implicated include interference with the dissipation of heat (e.g., cocaine), increases in metabolism (e.g., amphetamines), and alterations in the thermoregulatory center in the CNS (e.g., phenothiazines).

A final mechanism for drug-induced febrile reactions results from impurities or pyrogens present in a drug formulation (e.g., injectable dosage form). Although this mechanism is not truly caused by the drug, it is an important source of unexplained fever among patients who are receiving injectable psychotropic pharmacotherapy.

Whenever drug fever is suspected, the best therapy is the discontinuation of the offending drug. In cases in which the use of the drug is essential, concurrent use of corticosteroids, unless contraindicated, often suppresses the fever and other accompanying symptomatology. Collaboration with an advanced practice nurse or physician is indicated to rule out infection and other medical disorders associated with fever.

Hematologic ADRs

Numerous drugs have been implicated in causing ADRs such as blood dyscrasias or untoward effects on the development and production of blood cells (i.e., hemopoietic system) (see Table 5-6). Diagnosis can be confirmed only by hematologic laboratory analysis. Therefore, collaboration with other health care providers (e.g., advanced practice nurse, family physician, hematologist) may be indicated.

The ADRs affecting the hematologic system usually involve the destruction of blood cells in the general circulation or the inhibition of their development in the bone marrow. Blood cells

---

[22] As noted in the introduction to this section of the chapter, fever actually involves several body organ systems, including the CNS, cutaneous, and cardiovascular systems.

disappear more rapidly in the former than in the latter instance. Five categories of drug-induced blood dyscrasias are presented here: (1) agranulocytosis, (2) aplastic anemia, (3) hemolytic anemia, (4) leukopenia, and (5) thrombocytopenia.

Agranulocytosis

Agranulocytosis, or neutropenia, is characterized by a severe decrease in the number of granulo-cytes, or neutrophils, in the blood. Patients with agranulocytosis are at increased risk for bacterial and fungal infections. Symptoms associated with agranulocytosis include chills; fever; necrosis of the mucous membranes of the mouth, throat, rectum, and vagina; and prostration. Red blood cells and platelets are usually unaffected. Frequently, recovery is complete, occurring within 2 weeks of the discontinuation of the offending drug. However, in cases in which the reaction is complicated by infection, death may result.

Aplastic anemia

Aplastic anemia is characterized by bone marrow that has few, if any, hemopoietic cells and a preponderance of fatty spaces. This drug-induced reaction is the most severe of the hematologic toxicities but occurs less frequently than do the other drug-induced blood dyscrasias. Death frequently occurs and is associated with infection and hemorrhage.

Hemolytic anemia

Drug-induced hemolytic anemia is associated with a rapid fall in the number of red blood cells (i.e., erythrocytes). This ADR is due to hemolysis of the erythrocytes and normoblastic hyperpla-sia of the bone marrow.

Leukopenia

Leukopenia is an abnormal decrease in white blood cell counts. It is also referred to as granulocy-topenia or leukocytopenia. Leukopenia subjects the patient to increased risk from infections.

Thrombocytopenia

A fall in platelets characterizes drug-induced thrombocytopenia. Thus, the major signs of this ADR are easy bruising and bleeding from the skin and mucous membranes. However, internal bleeding also may be present. Recovery is rapid once the causative drug is discontinued.

Hepatic

As with other ADRs, drug-induced liver dysfunction may occur as a result of drug toxicity, hypersensitivity, or idiosyncrasy. The severity of the associated signs and symptoms, including mortality, depends on the type of liver damage produced. In general, the ADRs affecting the liver take the form of cholestatic, cytotoxic, or mixed hepatitis. The latter involves a combination of the cholestatic and cytotoxic forms. Mortality is highest with cytotoxic hepatitis.

Cholestatic hepatitis may be canalicular (i.e., without portal inflammation) or hepatocanali-cular (i.e., with portal inflammation). Canalicular hepatitis is characterized clinically by a normal or slightly elevated serum alkaline phosphatase. In hepatocanalicular hepatitis, alkaline phosphatase levels are relatively high (i.e., more than three times normal), and cholesterol levels also may be markedly elevated. Both canalicular and hepatocanalicular hepatitis are associated with modest elevations in serum transaminase levels. Jaundice and pruritus predominate. Death rarely occurs. In comparison, cytotoxic hepatitis includes necrosis or steatosis. Both of these reactions involve overt parenchymal damage and show a moderate elevation in alkaline phosphatase. Necrotic lesions resemble viral hepatitis. Serum glutamic pyruvic transaminase (SGPT) and serum glutamic oxaloacetic transaminase (SGOT) are markedly elevated.[23]

Several drugs have been implicated as causative factors in hepatotoxicity. Acetaminophen (Tylenol®), for example, is hepatotoxic at high dosages. In the event of acute hepatic necrosis, the rates of metabolism for many drugs, including acetaminophen (Tylenol®), phenobarbital (Luminal®), and phenytoin (Dilantin®), are reduced significantly. Although many drugs in clinical use can produce liver toxicity, only a few, such as chloroform and carbon tetrachloride, are true hepatotoxins.[24] Most drugs that adversely affect the liver appear to act as liver sensitizers. The following drugs can produce major hepatotoxicity among susceptible people.

Major Hepatotoxic Drugs[25]
Acetaminophen (Tempra®, Tylenol®)
Alcohol
Allopurinol (Zyloprim®)
Aminosalicylic acid (PAS®)
Barbiturates
Bupropion (Wellbutrin®)
Chlorambucil (Leukeran®)
Chloramphenicol (Chloromycetin®)
Chlorpromazine (Largactil®, Thorazine®)
Chlorpropamide (Diabinese®)
Chlortetracycline (Aureomycin®)
Contraceptives, oral
Cortisone
Diazepam (Valium®)
Digoxin (Lanoxin®)
Ethosuximide (Zarontin®)
Furosemide (Lasix®)
Hydralazine (Apresoline®)
Indomethacin (Indocin®)
Isoniazid (in combination with aminosalicylic acid)
Mercaptopurine (Purinethol®)
Methyldopa (Aldomet®)
Methotrexate (Mexate®)
Nitrofuradantoin (Macrodantin®)
Nitroglycerin
Oxytetracycline (Terramycin®)
Pemoline (Cylert®)
Penicillin
Perphenazine (Trilafon®)
Phenelzine (Nardil®)

continued. . .

[23] SGPT is also known as alanine transaminase, and SGOT is also known as aspartate transaminase.

[24] The recognition of major associated hepatotoxic effects has led to the discontinuation of the common use of the general anesthetic chloroform and the cleaning solvent carbon tetrachloride.

[25] Psychotropics are listed in boldface.

Phenylbutazone (Novo-Butazone®)
Phenytoin (Dilantin®)
Prochlorperazine (Compazine®)
Promazine (Sparine®)
Sulfonamides
Tetracycline (Achromycin®)
Thioridazine (Mellaril®)
Tranylcypromine (Parnate®)
Trifluoperazine (Stelazine®)
Valproic Acid (Depakene®, Depakote®, Epival®)

Ocular

The ADRs affecting the ocular system may occur following the use of systemic or topically applied ophthalmic drugs. A wide variety of others may adversely affect almost any portion of the eye, producing a wide range of reactions from temporary blurred vision to permanent blindness. For example, thioridazine (Mellaril®) has been associated with pigmentary retinopathy. Other commonly encountered examples include exophthalmos and papilloedema associated with lithium (Eskalith®, Lithane®), cornea and lens changes associated with phenothiazines, and interference with visual accommodation associated with tricyclic antidepressants. In addition, the use of tricyclic antidepressants, such as amitriptyline (Elavil®), for patients who have narrow angle glaucoma can precipitate an acute attack. Initial and subsequent ophthalmic examinations are recommended for patients who are prescribed pharmacotherapy with any psychotropic drug known to be associated with producing ADRs affecting the eye or its related structures because their occurrence often cannot be predicted. It should be noted that the use of alcohol and cannabis also is associated with ocular ADRs such as blurred and double vision. Collaboration with an ophthalmologist is indicated for further evaluation of the patient and appropriate treatment when drug-induced visual impairment is suspected.

Otic

The ADRs affecting the ear and its structures may range from an annoying ringing in the ear (i.e., tinnitus), which is commonly associated with aspirin toxicity, to total and irreversible deafness, which is associated with aminoglycoside antibiotic toxicity. Reactions are usually associated with hearing loss (auditory toxicity) or dysfunction of the vestibular apparatus. Frequently, these ADRs may be traced to alterations in the neural structures of the inner ear and the eighth cranial nerve. The inner ear contains all of the receptors required for hearing (cochlea) and equilibrium (utricle for static equilibrium and semicircular canals for dynamic equilibrium).

Pulmonary/respiratory

The ADRs affecting the pulmonary/respiratory system are relatively uncommon. However, when patients are seen with a respiratory disorder of unknown etiology, drugs should be considered in the differential diagnosis. As with renal ADRs, the exact mechanisms by which drugs cause pulmonary/respiratory ADRs are poorly defined. As the mechanisms become better understood, recognition of these drugs may increase. The ADRs most often affecting the pulmonary/respiratory system include (1) asthma, (2) interstitial pulmonary fibrosis, (3) pulmonary eosinophilia (infiltrates), and (4) respiratory depression (associated, for example, with overdosages of the CNS depressants). A relatively rare, but potentially fatal, pulmonary ADR is primary pulmonary hypertension (see "CNS Stimulants" in Appendix 3 for further discussion).

Renal

The ADRs affecting the kidney may include signs and symptoms associated with (1) acute renal failure, (2) chronic renal failure, (3) acute nephrotic syndrome, (4) chronic nephrotic syndrome, (5) renal colic, (6) hematuria, (7) tubular defects, and (8) obstructive nephropathy. Therefore, patients who require pharmacotherapy with nephrotoxic psychotropics and who have a history of kidney dysfunction require referral to an advanced practice nurse, family physician, or nephrologist for a thorough assessment *before* pharmacotherapy is initiated. They also require careful, periodic monitoring of kidney function during the course of pharmacotherapy. When a drug is suspected of causing ADRs affecting the kidneys, it should be discontinued until appropriate investigations have ruled out this suspicion.

Renal ADRs associated with psychotropic pharmacotherapy are relatively uncommon but include polyuria associated with lithium (Eskalith®, Lithane®) use and acute renal failure associated with amoxapine (Asendin®) overdosage. Surprisingly, relatively few studies have been conducted on the nephrotoxicity of selected drugs. Those drugs that are recognized as being nephrotoxic among susceptible people are identified in the following list. Fortunately, the psychotropics have not been generally recognized as presenting a significant risk for nephrotoxicity.

Nephrotoxic Drugs[26]
Analgesics
Acetaminophen (Tempra®, Tylenol®)
Salicylates (e.g., aspirin)
Antibiotics
Amikacin (Amikin®)
Amphotericin B (Fungizone®)
Bacitracin (Bacitin®)
Gentamicin (Garamycin®)
Kanamycin (Kantrex®)
Neomycin (Mycifradin®)
Penicillins
Polymyxin B (Aerosporin®)
Streptomycin
Sulfonamides
Tetracyclines
Vancomycin (Vancocin®)

continued. . .

[26] Psychotropics are listed in boldface.

Other drugs
    Aminosalicylic acid (PAS®)
    Paramethadione (Paradione®)
    Phenylbutazone (Novo-Butazone®)
    Trimethadione (Tridione®)

Reproductive/genitourinary

Data describing ADRs affecting the reproductive/genitourinary system are relatively sparse. The ADRs associated with sexual function include anorgasmia, decreased libido, erectile problems (e.g., impotence, priapism), gynecomastia, and impaired ejaculation (see Table 5-6).[27] The psychotropic drugs that significantly interfere with sexual function are generally those that have secondary anticholinergic actions (e.g., antipsychotics, tricyclic antidepressants). The antihypertensives, and other drugs that cause hypotension as an ADR, also have been implicated. The mechanisms by which drugs adversely affect sexual function involve the autonomic and central nervous systems and hormonal imbalance. The SSRIs commonly cause anorgasmia or decreased libido because of their effects on serotonin.

Urinary ADRs associated with psychotropic pharmacotherapy predominantly involve urinary retention (including urinary hesitancy and difficulty urinating). Psychotropics with anticholinergic activity (e.g., phenothiazines, tricyclic antidepressants) are those that have been most often and commonly associated with causing urinary retention. However, monoamine oxidase inhibitors and the miscellaneous antidepressant, trazodone (Desyrel®), which do not have significant anticholinergic activity, also have been reported to cause urinary retention.

Clinical considerations

The subject of ADRs affecting specific body organ systems is complex and varied. An understanding of the different classes of ADRs and their underlying mechanisms makes it possible for clinical psychologists to anticipate potential ADRs and to conduct thorough drug histories and collaborate with their patients' other health care providers, including advanced practice nurses, dentists, and physicians, in relation to the prevention, detection, and treatment of ADRs.

In an effort to assist prescribing psychologists to provide optimal pharmacotherapy while preventing or minimizing ADRs, several major tables have been specifically developed for inclusion in this chapter as well as Appendix 3, "Psychotropics: Associated ADRs and Clinical Comments," which lists psychotropic drugs arranged according to their pharmacologic classification together with major reported ADRs and relevant clinical comments. For a comprehensive listing and discussion of the ADRs associated with each individual psychotropic, readers are referred to the second volume in this series, the *Psychologists' Psychotropic Desk Reference* (Pagliaro & Pagliaro, 1998).

---

[27] These ADRs are often ignored by clinicians unless specifically brought to their attention by the patient. It is important to proactively consider these possible drug-induced effects on sexual function because, if ignored, they not only adversely affect the quality of the patient's life but can also cause or aggravate other psychological disorders such as depression, low self-esteem, and partner relational problems. In addition, priapism (see Table 5-6) is considered to be a urological emergency, and patients must be properly and fully informed, in advance, of what to do if this condition occurs (i.e., to go directly to their urologist or to a hospital emergency room for appropriate evaluation and treatment).

Summary

The potential for ADRs is a major concern for psychologists who prescribe psychotropic pharmacotherapy as an adjunct to their psychotherapy. The occurrence of ADRs appears to be primarily related to: (1) age, probably because of age-related physiologic changes in major body organ systems (i.e., heart, kidneys, and lungs); (2) gender (i.e., women, probably because of increased prescription of the psychotropics and greater relative percentage of adipose tissue) (see Chapter 3, "Pharmacokinetics and Pharmacodynamics," and Chapter 6, "Drug Interactions"); (3) use of unnecessary drugs (e.g., overprescription); (4) use of high-risk drugs, such as those that have a narrow therapeutic index (e.g., lithium [Eskalith®, Lithane®]); (5) genetic predisposition; and (6) general health status.

The incidence and consequences of ADRs can be substantial, as reflected by current estimates of approximately 300 deaths daily in North America due to ADRs. Psychologists must intervene to reduce the risk for and negative impact associated with ADRs among their patients. Increased efforts to report ADRs will improve the accuracy of ADR incidence databases and their analysis in terms of promoting optimal pharmacotherapy for patients who require psychotropics as an adjunct to their psychotherapy. A knowledge and understanding of the information presented in this chapter should assist psychologists to prevent or minimize ADRs among their patients as they strive to promote optimal psychological health.

6

Drug Interactions

Introduction

Significant efforts have been made to identify and prevent drug interactions that adversely affect psychotropic pharmacotherapy. However, increased attention to this common problem in prescribing and managing psychotropic pharmacotherapy is still required. This chapter focuses primarily on common drug interactions that involve the various psychotropics. These interactions can result in increased or decreased therapeutic actions, increased adverse drug reactions and toxic effects, unexpected pharmacologic effects, or *no* clinically significant pharmacologic effects.[1] To assist clinical psychologists to prescribe and manage optimal pharmacotherapy, specific information regarding psychotropic drug interactions that have been confirmed as clinically significant is provided in Appendix 4, "Major Clinically Significant Drug Interactions Involving the Psychotropics."

Types of drug interactions

Drug interactions can involve drug–drug interactions, drug–nutrient or drug–food interactions, drug–disease state interactions, and drug–laboratory test interactions. Drug–drug interactions can be classified into one of two major types based on the mechanism and site of the interaction: (1) *pharmacodynamic* interactions; and (2) *pharmacokinetic* interactions.[2] These drug–drug interactions are illustrated in an excellent model developed by Hansten (1986) (see Figure 6-1). Examples of each of these major types of drug–drug interactions are briefly presented (see also Appendix 4).

Pharmacodynamic interactions

Pharmacodynamic interactions, which occur at the sites of drug action, are caused by the combined pharmacologic actions of each of the interacting drugs at these sites. An example of a pharmacodynamic interaction is the interaction between one central nervous system (CNS) depressant and another (e.g., alcohol and diazepam [Valium®]). This interaction results in additive or synergistic CNS depressant actions, which may be manifested by oversedation and respiratory depression in a particular patient. Another example of a pharmacodynamic interaction

---

[1] Fortunately, for patients and prescribers alike, most drug interactions fall into the last category, for reasons discussed within this chapter.

[2] See Chapter 3, "Pharmacokinetics and Pharmacodynamics," for additional discussion of these concepts.

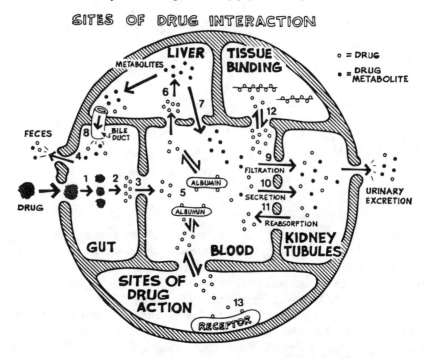

Figure 6-1. Sites of drug interactions. Gastrointestinal absorption of an ingested drug is influenced by the disintegration of the solid oral dosage form (1), dissolution of the solid oral dosage form (2), and absorption across the gut wall (3). Elimination of the drug and its metabolites in the feces (4) may be affected by concurrent pharmacotherapy. Some drugs bind to plasma proteins (primarily albumin) (5) and may be displaced from these binding sites by other drugs that are more highly plasma protein bound. Hepatic metabolism of certain drugs may be enhanced (6) or inhibited (7) by concurrent pharmacotherapy. Metabolites formed in the liver may undergo biliary excretion (8), which can be affected by other drugs. Renal drug elimination processes that can be affected by concurrent pharmacotherapy include: glomerular filtration (9); active tubular secretion (10); and passive tubular reabsorption (11). Tissue binding (12) of one drug may be affected by another. Drug interactions that involve these twelve sites are often referred to as pharmacokinetic *interactions because they affect the processes of absorption, distribution, metabolism, and excretion. Drugs may also have an additive or antagonistic pharmacologic effect at the receptor site (13). Drug interactions involving the receptor site are often referred to as* pharmacodynamic *interactions.*

is the concurrent use of a tricyclic antidepressant (e.g., amitriptyline [Elavil®]) and an anticholinergic (e.g., atropine). This interaction can result in the signs and symptoms of anticholinergic toxicity (e.g., blurred vision, constipation, dry mouth, urinary retention). Although most clinically significant pharmacodynamic drug interactions result in additive or synergistic effects with resultant toxicity (as noted in the previous two examples), some may have significant therapeutic benefits. For example, naloxone (Narcan®), an opiate antagonist, competitively displaces opiate analgesics (e.g., heroin, morphine) from their receptor sites and, thus, is useful for the treatment of opiate analgesic overdosage. Flumazenil (Anexate®, Romazicon®) similarly competitively displaces benzodiazepines (e.g., diazepam) from benzodiazepine receptors and, thus, is useful for the treatment of benzodiazepine overdosage.[3]

Pharmacokinetic interactions

Pharmacokinetic drug interactions involve the processes of drug input, distribution, and output.[4] Each of these types of pharmacokinetic interaction is briefly discussed.

[3] See Chapter 1, "Introduction to the Basic Principles of Pharmacotherapy," for a review of the mechanism of action for both naloxone and flumazenil.

[4] See also Chapter 3, "Pharmacokinetics and Pharmacodynamics."

Input

One of the most common examples of a pharmacokinetic drug interaction involving the process of input is that which occurs when tetracycline (Achromycin®, Sumycin®), an antibiotic, is ingested with a drug that has a divalent or trivalent cation.[5] In this situation, the cation binds (chelates) with the tetracycline and decreases or prevents its absorption. Consequently, the therapeutic benefit of both drugs is decreased.[6] Other common examples of drug interactions involving the process of input include interactions involving any drug that affects gastrointestinal (GI) transit time. For example, when metoclopramide (Reglan®), an upper GI tract motility modifier, is concurrently ingested with levodopa (Dopar®), an anti-parkinsonian, the absorption of levodopa is increased by prolonging gastric transit time (see also Appendix 4).

Distribution

An example of a clinically significant drug–drug interaction involving the process of distribution is the interaction of phenytoin (Dilantin®), an anticonvulsant, and warfarin (Coumadin®), an anticoagulant, when they are concurrently prescribed to a patient. Phenytoin displaces warfarin from its plasma protein-binding sites (see Table 6-1). This displacement results in a decreased volume of distribution and, consequently, an increased free drug concentration of warfarin with an increased risk for hemorrhage.[7]

Output

Drug–drug interactions involving the processes of output can be categorized into three types: (1) enzyme induction interactions, (2) enzyme inhibition interactions, and (3) renal excretion interactions. Each of these three types of interaction is briefly discussed.

Table 6-1. Drugs that can displace other drugs from plasma protein-binding sites.

Barbiturates (e.g., pentobarbital [Nembutal®], phenobarbital [Luminal®], secobarbital [Seconal®])
Clofibrate (Atromid-S®)
Diazoxide (Hyperstat®, Proglycem®)
Ethacrynic acid (Edecrin®)
Mefenamic acid (Ponstan®, Ponstel®)
Methotrexate (Mexate®, Rheumatrex®)
Nonsteroidal Anti-Inflammatory Drugs (NSAIDs) (e.g., ibuprofen [Motrin®], indomethacin [Indocin®], naproxen [Anaprox®, Synflex®], piroxicam [Feldene®])
Phenylbutazone (Novo-Butazone®)
Phenytoin (Dilantin®)
Salicylates (e.g., aspirin)
Sulfonamides
Sulfonylureas (e.g., chlorpropamide [Diabinese®], tolbutamide [Orinase®])
Warfarin (Coumadin®)

Note. These drugs can also be displaced by other drugs from plasma protein-binding sites. Whether a drug displaces, or is displaced by, another drug is determined by the relative affinity of each of the drugs for the plasma protein-binding sites and their relative concentrations at these sites (see Chapter 1, "Introduction to the Basic Principles of Pharmacotherapy"). Psychotropics are listed in boldface.

---

[5] A divalent or trivalent cation refers to an inorganic metal element with a plus charge (valence) of 2 or 3, such as calcium (Ca^{++}), iron (Fe^{++}, Fe^{+++}), or magnesium (Mg^{++}). Note that these cations also are found in nutrients such as milk and nutritional supplements.

[6] This also is the reason for the familiar precaution to avoid ingesting tetracyline with milk or other dairy products. Milk and dairy products contain the divalent cation, calcium.

[7] Recall from Chapter 1, "Introduction to the Basic Principles of Pharmacotherapy," that only the "free" drug is able to bind at receptor sites and elicit a pharmacologic effect.

Interactions involving enzyme induction.　　Several drugs can induce or inhibit the hepatic metabolizing enzyme systems and, thus, increase or decrease the hepatic metabolism of other drugs. Some of these drugs also can induce or inhibit their own hepatic metabolism.

Enzyme inducers include phenobarbital (Luminal®) and several other drugs (see Table 6-2). Enzyme induction generally requires 2 to 3 weeks of pharmacotherapy to reach maximal effect. Pharmacotherapy with enzyme inducers increases (1) liver weight and blood flow, (2) total liver protein (including microsomal protein) per unit weight of liver, (3) amount of smooth endoplasmic reticulum, and (4) the cytochrome P450 system, which is involved in metabolic oxidation reactions.[8]

There are virtually hundreds of drugs that reportedly induce metabolic oxidation reactions; of these drugs, however, only a few are involved in virtually all of the related clinically significant drug interactions (see Table 6-2). An often-cited example of a clinically significant enzyme induction interaction is that which occurs with concurrent phenobarbital (Luminal®) and warfarin (Coumadin®, Panwarfin®) pharmacotherapy. For anticoagulants like warfarin, dosage differences between ineffective blood levels and those that are likely to produce dangerous hemorrhage are small. Thus, drug-induced enzyme induction can pose a significant risk for a patient. For example, the desired mean prothrombin time associated with warfarin pharmacotherapy is about 20 seconds. This time is reduced if concurrent phenobarbital pharmacotherapy is initiated for 2 weeks. To maintain the desired prothrombin time, the prescriber of the warfarin may need to increase the dosage by 30% to 50%. It also is important to note that, for patients for whom concurrent phenobarbital and warfarin pharmacotherapy has been stabilized, a dangerous overdosage of warfarin could result if the concurrent phenobarbital pharmacotherapy was discontinued without a corresponding decrease in warfarin dosage.

In many instances, drugs that stimulate hepatic microsomal enzyme production also may

Table 6-2. Hepatic microsomal enzyme inducers.

Alcohol (*chronic use*)
Barbiturates (e.g., pentobarbital [Nembutal®], phenobarbital [Luminal®], secobarbital [Seconal®])
Carbamazepine (Tegretol®)
Glutethimide (Doriden®)
Griseofulvin (Fulvicin P/G®, Grisovin-FP®)
Marijuana smoke
Meprobamate (Equanil®, Miltown®)
Phenytoin (Dilantin®)
Primidone (Mysoline®)
Rifampin (Rifadin®, Rimactane®)
Sulfinpyrazone (Antazone®, Anturan®)
Tobacco smoke

Note. Psychotropics are listed in boldface.

[8] The cytochrome P450 system consists of multiple drug-metabolizing enzymes. These cytochrome P450 isoenzymes are denoted by an alphanumerical label and have been shown to have specific differential effects with various psychotropics. For example, CYP1A2, which is involved in the metabolism of caffeine, clozapine (Clozaril®), and imipramine (Tofranil®), is significantly inhibited by fluvoxamine (Luvox®); CYP3A4, which is involved in the metabolism of carbamazepine (Tegretol®) and various benzodiazepines (e.g., alprazolam [Xanax®], midazolam [Versed®], triazolam [Halcion®]), is significantly inhibited by fluoxetine (Prozac®), fluvoxamine (Luvox®), nefazodone (Serzone®), and sertraline (Zoloft®); CPY2C19, which is involved in the metabolism of diazepam (Valium®) and phenytoin (Dilantin®), is significantly inhibited by fluoxetine (Prozac®), flouvoxamine (Luvox®), and sertraline (Zoloft®); and CYP2D6, which is involved in the metabolism of desipramine (Norpramin®), phenothiazines, and risperidone (Risperdal®), is significantly inhibited by all of the SSRIs, particularly fluoxetine (Prozac®) and paroxetine (Paxil®). Knowledge of the various isoenzymes within the cytochrome P450 system can assist prescribing psychologists to anticipate and, thus, avoid related pharmacokinetic drug interactions.

stimulate their own metabolism. This phenomenon is known as "self-induction" or "auto-induction." This process partially explains the phenomenon of tolerance (i.e., why long-term pharmacotherapy with some drugs requires an increase in dosage in order to maintain desired effects).

Drugs That Induce Their Own Hepatic Metabolism[9]
Carbamazepine (Tegretol®)   **Diazepam** (Valium®)   **Glutethimide** (Doriden®)   **Meprobamate** (Miltown®)   Nitroglycerin   **Phenobarbital** (Luminal®)   Phenylbutazone (Novo-Butazone®)   **Phenytoin** (Dilantin®)   Tolbutamide (Orinase®)

Many environmental chemicals also stimulate drug metabolism. For example, exposure to insecticides (e.g., DDT, lindane) may decrease the half-lives of many drugs, whereas exposure to polycyclic hydrocarbons (e.g., cigarette smoke and industrial effluents) may induce the metabolism of many drugs. Cigarette smokers usually develop lower plasma levels of drugs than nonsmokers when both are given comparable doses of certain drugs (see Appendix 4).

Interactions involving enzyme inhibition. Concurrent fluoxetine (Prozac®) and other pharmacotherapy (see Table 6-3) may inhibit the metabolism of other drugs and, thus, prolong their pharmacologic actions. This interaction often is the result of substrate competition for metabolic enzymes. If concurrent pharmacotherapy is prescribed with drugs that are both metabolically oxidized by the cytochrome P450 enzyme system, one will act as a competitive inhibitor of the metabolism of the other. Typical examples of this competitive inhibition include the interactions between monoamine oxidase inhibitors and sympathomimetic amines (e.g., epinephrine), disulfiram (Antabuse®) and alcohol, and phenytoin (Dilantin®) and the antibiotic chloramphenicol (Chloromycetin®) (see Appendix 4). Enzyme inhibition can occur after only a few days of pharmacotherapy.

Interactions involving kidney excretion. Drugs that compete for active renal tubular secretion can affect the excretion of other drugs (see Table 6-4). A common example of this type of interaction involves the antimanic lithium (Eskalith®, Lithane®, Lithobid®) and thiazide diuretics (e.g., hydrochlorothiazide [Esidrix®, HydroDIURIL®]). Thiazide diuretics increase the renal excretion of sodium and correspondingly decrease the excretion of lithium. This interaction can result in elevated lithium serum levels and toxicity.

Drug–nutrient interactions (DNIs)

Psychotropic drugs can interact with various vitamins, minerals, and trace elements (see Table 6-5); selected foods and beverages (see Tables 6-6 and 6-7); and a patient's general nutritional state (see Table 6-8). Most drug–nutrient interactions are of the pharmacokinetic type and involve input (i.e., gastrointestinal absorption) or output (i.e., liver metabolism or kidney excretion processes). The rate and extent of drug absorption from the gastrointestinal tract can be

---

[9] Psychotropics are listed in boldface.

Table 6-3. Hepatic microsomal enzyme inhibitors.

Alcohol *(acute intoxication)*
Allopurinol (Zyloprim®)
Amiodarone (Cordarone®)
Chloramphenicol (Chloromycetin®)
Chlorpromazine (Thorazine®)
Chlorpropamide (Diabinese®)
Cimetidine (Tagamet®)
Ciprofloxacin (Cipro®)
Diltiazem (Cardizem®)
Disulfiram (Antabuse®)
Erythromycin (E-Mycin®)
Fluoxetine (Prozac®)
Fluvoxamine (Luvox®)
Imipramine (Tofranil®)
Isoniazid (INH®)
Ketoconazole (Nizoral®)
Methyldopa (Aldomet®)
Methylphenidate (Ritalin®)
Metoprolol (Lopressor®)
Metronidazole (Flagyl®)
Miconazole (Monistat®)
Nefazodone (Serzone®)
Nortriptyline (Aventyl®, Pamelor®)
Paroxetine (Paxil®)
Perphenazine (Trilafon®)
Phenylbutazone (Novo-Butazone®)
Primaquine
Propoxyphene (Darvon®)
Propranolol (Inderal®)
Quinidine (Cardioquin®, Quinate®)
Sertraline (Zoloft®)
Thioridazine (Mellaril®)
Trimethoprim (Proloprim®)
Valproic acid [divalproex sodium, sodium valproate] (Depakene®)
Verapamil (Isoptin®)

Note. Psychotropics are listed in boldface. Although not a drug, naringenin, a bioflavonoid found in grapefruit juice (but *not* orange juice), also is a hepatic microsomal enzyme inhibitor. The ingestion of grapefruit juice is potentially clinically significant for several nonpsychotropics (e.g., the immunosuppressant cyclosporine [Sandimmune®] and the cardiovascular drug nisoldipine [Sular®]). However, grapefruit juice does *not* appear to be related to any clinically significant drug interactions involving the psychotropics except for midazolam, which is not expected to be prescribed by psychologists.

Table 6-4. Drugs excreted by active renal tubular secretion.

Cephalosporins (e.g., cefaclor [Ceclor®], ceftazidime [Tazidime®], cephalothin [Keflin®])
Digoxin (Lanoxin®)
Methotrexate (Mexate®, Rheumatrex®)
Penicillins (e.g., ampicillin [Ampicin®], penicillin G [Pfizerpen®])
Phenylbutazone (Novo-Butazone®)
Probenecid (Benemid®)
Salicylates (e.g., aspirin)
Thiazide diuretics (e.g., chlorthalidone [Hygroton®], hydrochlorothiazide [HydroDIURIL®])

Table 6-5. Psychotropic and vitamin interactions.

Drug (drug classification) and vitamin effects	Mechanism	Possible clinical result
Anticonvulsants (e.g., phe-nobarbital,[a] phenytoin) *and*		
Folic acid, decreased	Decreased absorption Enzyme induction Competitive inhibition of vitamin coenzymes	Megaloblastic anemia
Vitamin D, decreased	Enzyme induction	Osteomalacia Rickets

[a] Phenobarbital can be alternatively classified as a barbiturate sedative-hypnotic (see Chapter 2, "The Psychotropics").

Table 6-6. Foods high in pyridoxine content.

Avocados	Pork
Bacon	Salmon
Beef kidney	Skim milk, dry
Beef liver	Soy beans
Bran	Split peas
Kidney beans	Sweet potatoes
Lentils	Tuna
Lima beans	Walnuts
Malted milk	Wheat germ
Molasses	Yams
Navy beans	Yeast
Oatmeal	

Note. Pyridoxine can significantly interact with levodopa.

affected by nutrients that: (1) affect the rate of gastric emptying; (2) change intestinal transit time; (3) increase the viscosity of the contents in the gastrointestinal tract; (4) form a complex with the psychotropic drug; (5) alter pH, particularly in the gastric region; (6) affect bile secretion; and (7) affect gastrointestinal membrane permeability and, thus, absorption. In addition, nutrients can induce or inhibit hepatic drug metabolizing enzymes. They also can affect the excretion of several different psychotropic drugs by changing urinary pH (see Tables 6-9 and 6-10).

Several psychotropic drugs also may contribute to diminished nutrition. For example, amphetamines can alter appetite and nutritional needs by their direct stimulant and anorexiant, or anorexigenic, actions on the CNS. Other drugs (e.g., opiate analgesics) can cause gastric upset, including nausea and vomiting, while others (e.g., chloral hydrate [Noctec®]) may cause anorexia because of their unpleasant taste or smell. Psychotropic drugs that affect bowel elimination also can influence nutritional status. For example, some psychotropics (e.g., amitriptyline [Elavil®], meperidine [Demerol®]) can slow gastrointestinal motility and cause constipation. Others (e.g., fluoxetine [Prozac®], sertraline [Zoloft®]) can increase gastrointestinal motility and cause diarrhea.

Clinical considerations

Four basic points should be kept in mind when considering drug interactions among patients who require psychotropic pharmacotherapy as an adjunct to their psychotherapy. First, not all

Table 6-7. Foods and beverages high in tyramine content.[a]

Food or beverage	Pressor amine content (μg/g or μg/ml)					Amount of food (g) or beverage (ml) containing 25 mg of tyramine[b]
	Dopamine	2-phenyl-ethylamine	Serotonin (5-hydroxy-tryptamine)	Tryptamine	Tyramine	
Foods						
Caviar, Russian	—	—	—	—	680	27
Cheese[c]						
American, processed	—	—	—	—	50	500
Blue (Gorgonzola type), Danish	—	—	—	—	31–256	98–806
Boursault, French	—	—	—	—	1,116	22
Brick, natural, Canadian	—	—	—	—	524	48
Brie	—	—	—	—	180	139
Brie type, Danish	—	—	—	—	0	—
Camembert	—	—	—	—	86	291
Camembert type, Danish	—	—	—	—	23	1,087
Camembert type, Mycella, Danish	—	—	—	—	1,340	19
Camembert type, South African	—	—	—	—	13	1,923
Cheddar, South African	—	—	—	—	175–775	32–143
Cheddar, Canadian	—	—	—	—	120–1,530	16–208
Cheddar, New York State	—	—	—	—	1,416	18
Cheddar, processed, pasteurized, Canadian	—	—	—	—	26	962
Cheshire, South African	—	—	—	—	297	84
Colby	—	—	—	—	100–560	45–250
Cottage	—	—	—	—	<0.2	>12,500
Cream	—	—	—	—	<0.2	>12,500
Cream (cottage), South African	—	—	—	—	5–7	3,571–5,000
Edam	—	—	—	—	300–320	78–83
Emmenthaler	—	—	—	—	225	111
Gouda type, Canadian	—	—	—	—	20	1,250
Gruyère	—	—	—	—	516	48
Gruyère, South African	—	—	—	—	30	833
Mozzarella, Canadian	—	—	—	—	410	61
Parmesan, Italian	—	—	—	—	65	385
Parmesan type, USA	—	—	—	—	4–290	86–6,250
Provolone, Italian	—	—	—	—	38	658
Romano, Italian	—	—	—	—	238	105

Cheese *Continued*						
Roquefort, French	—	—	—	—	27–520	48–926
Roquefort type, South African	—	—	—	—	656	38
Stilton	—	—	—	—	466–2,170	11.5–54
Swiss	—	—	—	—	0–1,800	≥14
Chocolate	—	—	≥107	—	—	—
Condiments						
Soya sauce	—	—	—	—	1.76	14,204
Fruits						
Avocado	4–5	10	—	0	23	1,087
Banana (skin or peel)	700	50–150	—	0	65	385
Banana (pulp)	8	28	—	0	7	3,571
Grape	0	0	—	0.1	0	—
Orange (pulp)	0	0	—	—	10	2,500
Plantain (pulp)	—	45	—	5	—	—
Plum, blue	0	0	—	2	—	—
Plum, blue-red	—	8	—	—	6	4,167
Plum, red	0	10	—	0–2	13–93	269–1,923
Raspberry	—	—	—	—	3,030	8
Herring, pickled	—	—	—	—	470	53
Herring, salted, dry	—	—	—	—	274	91
Liver, beef	—	—	—	—	100	250
Liver, chicken	—	—	—	—	2,300	11
Marmite (yeast extract)	—	—	—	—	1,090–1,640	15–23
Marmite (yeast extract), English	—	—	—	—	190	132
Marmite (yeast extract), salt-free, English	—	—	—	—	10–151	165–2,500
Sausage,[d] dry, fermented, Belgian	—	—	0–6	—	—	—
Vegetables						
Broad (fava) beans	—[e]	2	—	0.5–3	3	8,333
Eggplant	0	0	—	0	1	25,000
Potato	0	—	—	—	37	676
Sauerkraut	—	—	—	—	1	25,000
Spinach	0	12	—	4	4	6,250
Tomato	—	—	—	—	—	11–12
Yeast extracts, Brand A, English	—	—	—	—	2,057–2,256	≥298
Yeast extracts, Brand B, Canadian	—	—	—	—	0–84	—

Table 6-7. Foods and beverages high in tyramine content—Continued.

Food or beverage	Pressor amine content (µg/g or µg/ml)					Amount of food (g) or beverage (ml) containing 25 mg of tyramine[b]
	Dopamine	2-phenyl-ethylamine	Serotonin (5-hydroxy-tryptamine)	Tryptamine	Tyramine	
Yogurt	—	—	—	—	<0.2	>12,500
Beverages						
Ale and beer						
Unspecified brands	—	—	—	—	2–4	6,250–12,500
Unspecified brands, Canadian	—	—	—	—	6–11	2,273–4,167
Ale, Canadian	—	—	—	—	9	2,778
Milk, sweet, South African	—	—	—	—	22	1,136
Wines[f]						
Chianti	—	—	—	—	2–12; 25	1,000–12,500
Sherry	—	—	—	—	4	6,250

[a] From Block (1983).

[b] Note that 25 mg is the amount of tyramine that generally can provoke a hypertensive crisis in a patient prescribed pharmacotherapy with a MAOI (i.e., phenelzine [Nardil®], tranylcypromine [Parnate®]). In order to cause a similar response among patients receiving the *selective* MAOI moclobemide (Manerix®), patients, on average, would need to consume six times the amount of food listed (i.e., an amount of food sufficient to contain 150 mg of tyramine). Thus, although the interaction can still occur, it is unlikely, and moclobemide pharmacotherapy generally does not require special dietary restrictions. Patients should, however, be urged to report immediately any atypical or unusual signs and symptoms.

[c] Ripened or aged cheeses tend to have substantial concentrations of tyramine in comparison with unripened cheeses (e.g., cottage cheese, cream cheese).

[d] Other fermented sausages (e.g., bologna, pepperoni, salami) should be considered potential problems as well.

[e] Broad beans have been shown to have little or no pressor amine content but do have a considerable amount of dopa that can be converted to dopamine.

[f] Prolonged contact with grape skins during processing may result in the introduction of extraneous fermenting organisms and the subsequent production of appreciable amounts of tyramine. This is true of red and, to a lesser extent, rosé wines.

Table 6-8. Psychotropics that affect body weight.

Psychotropic	Effect on body weight	Mechanism[a]
Amphetamines	Decrease	Anorexigenic; increases physical activity and caloric requirements
Antidepressants (all)	Decrease/increase	Returns abnormal food intake toward "normal"
Benzodiazepines	Decrease/increase	Returns abnormal food intake toward "normal"
Cannabis preparations	Increase	Stimulation of appetite
Fluoxetine (Prozac®)	Decrease	Anorexigenic
Lithium (Eskalith®, Lithane®)	Decrease/increase	Returns abnormal food intake toward "normal"
Phenothiazines	Decrease/increase	Returns abnormal food intake toward "normal"

[a] "Normal" refers to what is "usual" for the patient in the absence of the corrected mental disorder.

Table 6-9. Foods that acidify the urine.

Bacon	Fish
Brazil nuts	Fowl
Breads	Lentils
Cakes	Macaroni
Cheeses	Meats
Cookies	Noodles
Corn	Peanuts
Crackers	Plums
Cranberries	Prunes
Eggs	Shellfish
Filbert nuts	Walnuts

Note. The "typical" North American diet produces an *acidic* urine.

Table 6-10. Foods that alkalinize the urine.

Almonds
Buttermilk
Chestnuts
Coconut
Cream
Fruit (*except* cranberries, plums, and prunes)
Milk
Vegetables (*except* corn, lentils)

drug interactions are detrimental. Consider, for example, the life-saving effect of naloxone (Narcan®) when used to counteract an opiate analgesic overdosage. Second, with appropriate recognition and management, it is rarely necessary to avoid interacting drug combinations, particularly when attention is given to the mechanisms of their interactions. For example, an interaction between two orally ingested drugs that interact in the stomach usually can be avoided by dosing these drugs 2 or more hours apart. If that is not feasible, the two drugs can be prescribed by alternate methods of administration (e.g., oral and intravenous). In many other cases, dosages of the interacting drugs can be adjusted to appropriately compensate for an expected drug interaction. Third, few interactions cause immediate reactions. For example, the use of hepatic enzyme inhibitors or inducers does not immediately produce observable effects on the blood level of a drug that is metabolized by the liver. Inhibitors require several days, and inducers several weeks, for maximum clinically significant effects to occur. Fourth, the significance of a particular drug interaction is usually affected by several drug and patient factors. Drug factors include: the dose and dosage form; method, sequence, and timing of administration; dosing schedule; and duration of pharmacotherapy. Patient factors include: age; general state of health; gender; heart, kidney, and liver function; plasma albumin concentration; urinary pH; diet and nutritional status; genetics; and various other factors. Large interpatient variability is commonly observed, and, thus, a significant drug interaction may occur in one patient but not in another patient under seemingly similar circumstances.

Prescribing psychologists can prevent or minimize drug interactions by: (1) obtaining current and detailed drug histories from their patients; (2) prescribing the least possible number of psychotropics as an adjunct to a patient's psychotherapy; (3) avoiding, whenever possible, changes in pharmacotherapy; (4) using special care when prescribing and managing psychotropic pharmacotherapy with drugs that have a narrow therapeutic index; (5) using special care when prescribing pharmacotherapy with drugs that affect the elimination (i.e., metabolism or excretion) of other drugs; (6) monitoring for drug interactions whenever pharmacotherapy is modified (i.e., when a psychotropic drug is added to, or removed from, a therapeutic plan) and whenever major dietary changes are made; (7) collaborating with other prescribers (e.g., dentists, advanced practice nurses, physicians); and (8) instructing patients about their pharmacotherapy, including the possible occurrence of drug interactions, how to avoid drug interactions, and required actions to take should an interaction occur.

Summary

Drug interactions may have several possible clinical outcomes, ranging from those that are of benefit to patients to those that can result in serious morbidity or mortality. Drug–drug and drug–nutrient interactions are of particular concern to prescribing psychologists. This chapter has reviewed the topic of drug interactions. With a knowledge of the clinically significant drug interactions and their mechanisms of action, prescribing psychologists can better anticipate avoidable interactions and be prepared to intervene appropriately when unavoidable interactions occur. Specific details of clinically significant drug interactions involving the psychotropics are presented in Appendix 4.

References[1,2]

Airaudo, C. B., Gayte-Sorbier, A., Bianchi, C., & Verdier, M. (1993). Interactions between six psychotherapeutic drugs and plastic containers. *International Journal of Clinical Pharmacology, Therapy and Toxicology, 31*, 261–266.

Alcohol-medication interactions. (1995, January). *National Institute on Alcohol Abuse and Alcoholism, Alcohol Alert*, No. 27, PH355, pp. 1–4.

Andrews, J. M., & Nemeroff, C. B. (1994). Contemporary management of depression. *American Journal of Medicine, 97*, 24S–32S.

Ascher, J. A., Cole, C. O., Colin, J. N., Feighner, J. P., Ferris, R. M., Ribiger, H. C., Goldern, R. N., Martin, P., Potter, W. Z., & Richelson, E. (1995). Bupropion: A review of its mechanism of antidepressant activity. *Journal of Clinical Psychiatry, 56*, 395–401.

Ashton, H. (1994). Guidelines for the rational use of benzodiazepines. When and what to use. *Drugs, 48*, 25–40.

Ashton, H. (1994). The treatment of benzodiazepine dependence. *Addiction, 89*, 1535–1541.

Azorin, J. M. (1995). Long-term treatment of mood disorders in schizophrenia. *Acta Psychiatrica Scandinavica, 388*, 20–23.

Bailey, R. T., Jr., Bonavina, L., Nwakama, P. E., DeMeester, T. R., & Cheng, S. C. (1990). Influence of dissolution rate and pH of oral medications on drug-induced esophageal injury. *Annals of Pharmacotherapy, 24*, 571–573.

Baldassano, C. F., Truman, C. J., Nierenberg, A., Ghaemi, S. N., & Sachs, G. S. (1996). Akathisia: A review and case report following paroxetine treatment. *Comprehensive Psychiatry, 37*, 122–124.

Bapna, J. S. (1989). Education on the concept of essential drugs and rationalized drug use. *Clinical Pharmacology & Therapeutics, 45*, 217–219.

Barden, N., Reul, J. M., & Holsboer, F. (1995). Do antidepressants stabilize mood through actions on the hypothalamic-pituitary-adrenocortical system? *Trends in Neurosciences, 18*, 6–11.

Beasley, C. M., Jr., Masica, D. N., Heiligenstein, J. H., Wheadon, D. E., & Zerbe, R. L. (1993). Possible monoamine oxidase inhibitor-serotonin uptake inhibitor interaction: Fluoxetine clinical data and preclinical findings. *Journal of Clinical Psychopharmacology, 13*, 312–320.

Benet, L. Z., & Pagliaro, L. A. (1986). Pharmacokinetic considerations in drug response. In A. M. Pagliaro & L. A. Pagliaro (Eds.), *Pharmacologic aspects of nursing* (pp. 118–129). St. Louis, MO: C. V. Mosby.

---

[1] The references cited here were used in the writing of this text. They were integrated with more than 30 years of clinical experience and academic knowledge of each of the coauthors. As noted in the Preface, this text and the others in this series were based on the "Hierarchial Series of Graduate and Postgraduate Courses in Pharmacopsychology." This series was developed by the coauthors in 1989 and continues to be taught by the coauthors. Thus, the references are not meant to provide an exhaustive review of the related literature but may be better interpreted as a starting point. Additional comprehensive referencing, particularly to earlier classical and initial foundational works in the field, can be found in previous textbooks by the coauthors.

[2] The references are meant to provide readers with examples that document the data (e.g., ADRs and drug interactions) cited in the body of this text. They are not meant to provide an exhaustive review of the related literature but may be better interpreted as a starting point. For this reason, secondary reviews have been cited where possible. Readers are encouraged to perform CD-ROM searches of relevant computerized databases (e.g., Medline, PsychLIT) to obtain additional references. Although the Internet provides databases reporting ADRs and drug interactions, these reports generally have *not* been externally reviewed and should be interpreted with caution.

Bhatara, V. S., & Bandettini, F. C. (1993). Possible interaction between sertraline and tranylcypromine. *Clinical Pharmacy, 12*, 222–225.

Bhatara, V. S., & Bandettini, F. (1993). Serotonin syndrome and drug interactions [Letter]. *Clinical Pharmacology & Therapeutics, 53*, 230.

Biegon, A., & Volkow, N. D. (Eds.). (1995). *Sites of drug action in the human brain.* Boca Raton, FL: CRC Press.

Blaisdell, G. D. (1994). Akathisia: A comprehensive review and treatment summary. *Pharmacopsychiatry, 27*, 139–146.

Block, L. H. (1983). Drug interactions in the geriatric client. In L. A. Pagliaro & A. M. Pagliaro (Eds.), *Pharmacologic aspects of aging* (pp. 140–191). St. Louis, MO: C. V. Mosby.

Bloomfield, S. S., Cissell, G. B., Mitchell, J., Barden, T. P., Kaiko, R. F., Fitzmartin, R. D., Grandy, R. P., Komorowski, J., & Goldenheim, P. D. (1993). Analgesic efficacy and potency of two oral controlled-release morphine preparations. *Clinical Pharmacology and Therapeutics, 53*, 469–478.

Borison, R. L. (1995). Clinical efficacy of serotonin-dopamine antagonists relative to classic neuroleptics. *Journal of Clinical Psychopharmacology, 15*(Suppl. 1), 24S–29S.

Bostrom-Ezrati, J., Dibble, S., & Rizzuto, C. (1990). Intravenous therapy management: Who will develop insertion site symptoms? *Applied Nursing Research, 3*, 146–152.

Bowden, C. L. (1996). Role of newer medications for bipolar disorder. *Journal of Clinical Psychopharmacology, 16*(Suppl. 1), 48S–55S.

Boyer, W. F., & Blumhardt, C. L. (1992). The safety profile of paroxetine. *Journal of Clinical Psychiatry, 53*, 61–66.

Bristow, M. R. (1993). Changes in myocardial and vascular receptors in heart failure. *Journal of the American College of Cardiology, 22*(Suppl. A), 61A–71A.

Brodde, O. E. (1993). Beta-adrenoceptors in cardiac disease. *Pharmacology & Therapeutics, 60*, 405–430.

Brosen, K. (1995). Drug interactions and the cytochrome P450 system. The role of cytochrome P450 1A2. *Clinical Pharmacokinetics, 29*(Suppl. 1), 20–25.

Brosen, K. (1996). Are pharmacokinetic drug interactions with the SSRIs an issue? *International Clinical Psychopharmacology, 11*(Suppl. 1), 23–27.

Bruera, E., Legris, M. A., & Kuehn, N. (1990). Hypodermoclysis for the administration of fluids and narcotic analgesics in patients with advanced cancer. *Journal of Pain and Symptom Management, 5*, 218–220.

Buchanan, R. W. (1995). Clozapine: Efficacy and safety. *Schizophrenia Bulletin, 21*, 579–591.

Buck, M. L., & Blumer, J. L. (1991). Phenothiazine associated apnea in two siblings. *Annals of Pharmacotherapy, 25*, 244–247.

Butler, S. H. (1986). Analgesics and narcotic antagonists. In A. M. Pagliaro & L. A. Pagliaro (Eds.), *Pharmacologic aspects of nursing* (pp. 299–324). St. Louis, MO: C. V. Mosby.

Caccia, S., & Garattini, S. (1990). Formation of active metabolites of psychotropic drugs: An updated review of their significance. *Clinical Pharmacokinetics, 18*, 434–459.

Cardella, J. F., Fox, P. S., & Lawler, J. B. (1993). Interventional radiologic placement of peripherally inserted central catheters. *Journal of Vascular & Interventional Radiology, 4*, 653–660.

Cohen, M. R., & Davis, N. M. (1992). Free flow associated with electronic infusion devices: An underestimated danger. *Hospital Pharmacy, 27*, 384–390.

Connolly, M. J. (1993). Ageing, late-onset asthma and the beta-adrenoceptor. *Pharmacology & Therapeutics, 60*, 389–404.

Cooper, J. R., Bloom, F. E., & Roth, R. H. (1996). *The biochemical basis of neuropharmacology* (7th ed.). New York: Oxford University Press.

Corso, D. M., Pucino, F., DeLeo, J. M., Calis, K. A., & Gallelli, J. F. (1992). Development of a questionnaire for detecting potential adverse drug reactions. *Annals of Pharmacotherapy, 26*, 890–892.

Costa, E., & Guidotti, A. (1996). Benzodiazepines on trial: A research strategy for their rehabilitation. *Trends in Pharmacological Sciences, 17,* 192–200.

Davis, J. M., Matalon, L., Watanabe, M. D., Blake, L., & Metalon, L. (1994). Depot antipsychotic drugs. Place in therapy. *Drugs, 47,* 741–773.

Denny, D. F. (1993). Placement and management of long-term central venous access catheter ports. *American Journal of Roentgenology, 161,* 385–393.

DeVane, C. L. (1994). Pharmacokinetics of the newer antidepressants: Clinical relevance. *American Journal of Medicine, 97,* 13S–23S.

DeVane, C. L. (1995). Brief comparison of the pharmacokinetics and pharmacodynamics of the traditional and newer antipsychotic drugs. *American Journal of Health-System Pharmacy, 52*(Suppl. 1), S15–S18.

Devinsky, O., & Pacia, S. V. (1994). Seizures during clozapine therapy. *Journal of Clinical Psychiatry, 55*(Suppl. B), 153–156.

Dewhurst, W. G. (1986). Drugs used to treat affective disorders. In A. M. Pagliaro & L. A. Pagliaro (Eds.), *Pharmacologic aspects of nursing* (pp. 352–381). St. Louis, MO: C. V. Mosby.

Diagnostic and statistical manual of mental disorders (4th ed.). (1994). Washington, DC: American Psychiatric Association.

DiPadova, C., Roine, R., Frezza, M., Gentry, R. T., Baraona, E., & Lieber, C. S. (1992). Effects of ranitidine on blood alcohol levels after ethanol ingestion. *Journal of the American Medical Association, 267,* 83–86.

DiSalvo, T. G., & O'Gara, P. T. (1995). Torsade de pointes caused by high-dose intravenous haloperidol in cardiac patients. *Clinical Cardiology, 18,* 285–290.

Dockens, R. C., Greene, D. S., & Barbhaiya, R. H. (1996). Assessment of pharmacokinetic and pharmacodynamic drug interactions between nefazodone and digoxin in healthy male volunteers. *Journal of Clinical Pharmacology, 36,* 160–167.

Drug/drug interaction: Fluoxetine/phenytoin. (1994). *Drug Evaluations Monitor, 2,* 7.

Drugs that cause psychiatric symptoms. (1993). *Medical Letter on Drugs and Therapeutics, 35,* 65–70.

Dubovsky, S. L., & Thomas, M. (1996). Tardive dyskinesia associated with fluoxetine. *Psychiatric Services, 47,* 991–993.

Ellingrod, V. L., & Perry, P. J. (1994). Venlafaxine: A heterocyclic antidepressant. *American Journal of Hospital Pharmacy, 51,* 3033–3046.

Ellingrod, V. L., & Perry, P. J. (1995). Nefazodone: A new antidepressant. *American Journal of Health-System Pharmacy, 52,* 2799–2812.

Ereshefsky, L., Riesenman, C., & Lan, Y. W. (1995). Antidepressant drug interactions and the cytochrome P450 system. The role of cytochrome P450 2D6. *Clinical Pharmacokinetics, 29*(Suppl. 1), 10–18.

Estes, J. W. (1995). The road to tranquillity: The search for selective anti-anxiety agents. *Synapse, 21(1),* 10–20.

Evans, R. J., Miranda, R. N., Jordan, J., & Krolikowski, F. J. (1995). Fatal acute pancreatitis caused by valproic acid. *American Journal of Forensic Medicine & Pathology, 16,* 62–65.

Feighner, J. P. (1994). The role of venlafaxine in rational antidepressant therapy. *Journal of Clinical Psychiatry, 55*(Suppl. A), 62–68.

Fernstrom, M. H. (1995). Drugs that cause weight gain. *Obesity Research, 3*(Suppl. 4), 435S–439S.

Fleischhacker, W. W. (1995). New drugs for the treatment of schizophrenic patients. *Acta Psychiatrica Scandinavica, 388*(Suppl.), 24–30.

Friesen, A. J. D. (1983). Adverse drug reactions in the geriatric client. In L. A. Pagliaro & A. M. Pagliaro (Eds.), *Pharmacologic aspects of aging* (pp. 257–293). St Louis, MO: C. V. Mosby.

Garcia, B., Zaborras, E., Areas, V., Obeso, G., Jimenez, I., de Juana, P., & Bermejo, T. (1992).

Interaction between isoniazid and carbamazepine potentiated by cimetidine [Letter]. *Annals of Pharmacotherapy, 26,* 841.

Geller, J. L., Gaulin, B. D., & Barreira, P. J. (1992). A practitioner's guide to use of psychotropic medication in liquid form. *Hospital and Community Psychiatry, 43,* 969–971.

Generali, J. A. (1996). Drug-nutrient interactions: New drug update. *Drug Newsletter, 15*(6), 42–44.

Generali, J. A. (1996). Serotonin syndrome. *Drug Newsletter, 15*(10), 76–77.

Gerlach, J. (1994). Oral versus depot administration in relapse prevention. *Acta Psychiatrica Scandinavica, 382*(Suppl.), 28–32.

Gerlach, J. (1995). Depot neuroleptics in relapse prevention: Advantages and disadvantages. *International Clinical Psychopharmacology, 9*(Suppl. 5), 17–20.

Gibaldi, M. (1992). Drug interactions: Part I. *Annals of Pharmacotherapy, 26,* 709–713.

Gibaldi, M. (1992). Drug interactions: Part II. *Annals of Pharmacotherapy, 26,* 829–834.

Gitlin, M. J. (1994). Psychotropic medications and their effects on sexual function: Diagnosis, biology, and treatment approaches. *Journal of Clinical Psychiatry, 55,* 406–413.

Gitlin, M. J. (1995). Effects of depression and antidepressants on sexual functioning. *Bulletin of the Menninger Clinic, 59,* 232–248.

Givens, B., Oberle, S., & Lander, J. (1993). Taking the jab out of needles. *The Canadian Nurse, 89*(10), 37–40.

Goff, D. C., Henderson, D. C., & Amico, E. (1992). Cigarette smoking in schizophrenia: Relationship to psychopathology and medication side effects. *American Journal of Psychiatry, 149,* 1189–1194.

Gold, P. W., Licinio, J., Wong, M. L., & Chrousos, G. P. (1995). Corticotropin releasing hormone in the pathophysiology of melancholic and atypical depression and in the mechanism of action of the antidepressant drugs. *Annals of the New York Academy of Sciences, 771,* 716–729.

Goodnick, P. J. (1994). Pharmacokinetic optimisation of therapy with newer antidepressants. *Clinical Pharmacokinetics, 27,* 307–330.

Graber, M. A., Hoehns, T. B., & Perry, P. J. (1994). Sertraline-phenelzine drug interaction: A serotonin syndrome reaction. *Annals of Pharmacotherapy, 28,* 732–735.

Graham, D. R., Keldermans, M. M., Klemm, L. W., Semenza, N. J., & Shafer, M. L. (1991). Infectious complications among patients receiving home intravenous therapy with peripheral, central, or peripherally placed central venous catheters. *American Journal of Medicine, 91*(3B), 95S–100S.

Haggett, R. R., & Gionet, P. J. (1992). Peripherally inserted central catheters—Review and case reports. *Alaska Medicine, 34,* 140–141.

Hansten, P. D. (1986). Drug interactions. In A. M. Pagliaro & L. A. Pagliaro (Eds.), *Pharmacologic aspects of nursing* (pp. 170–179). St. Louis, MO: C. V. Mosby.

Hansten, P. D. (1995). Pediatric drug interactions. In L. A. Pagliaro & A. M. Pagliaro (Eds.), *Problems in pediatric drug therapy* (3rd ed., pp. 463–504). Hamilton, IL: Drug Intelligence.

Haria, M., Fitton, A., & McTavish, D. (1994). Trazodone: A review of its pharmacology, therapeutic use in depression and therapeutic potential in other disorders. *Drugs & Aging, 4,* 331–355.

Harth, Y., & Rapoport, M. (1996). Photosensitivity associated with antipsychotics, antidepressants and anxiolytics. *Drug Safety, 14,* 252–259.

Hedges, C., & Karas, B. S. (1993). Peripherally-inserted central catheters: Challenges for hospital management. *Medical Surgical Nursing, 2,* 443–450.

Hensley, J. R. (1991). Continuous SC morphine for cancer pain. *American Journal of Nursing,* 98–101.

Hirschfeld, R. M. (1994). Guidelines for the long-term treatment of depression. *Journal of Clinical Psychiatry, 55*(Suppl.), 61–69.

Hoener, B. (1986). Drug availability and distribution. In A. M. Pagliaro & L. A. Pagliaro (Eds.), *Pharmacologic aspects of nursing* (pp. 78–94). St. Louis, MO: C. V. Mosby.

Holsboer, F., Grasser, A., Friess, E., & Wiedemann, K. (1994). Steroid effects on central neurons and implications for psychiatric and neurological disorders. *Annals of the New York Academy of Sciences, 746,* 345–359.

Human, S. E., & Nestler, E. J. (1996). Initiation and adaptation: A paradigm for understanding psychotropic drug action. *American Journal of Psychiatry, 153,* 151–162.

Hunt, N., & Stern, T. A. (1995). The association between intravenous haloperidol and torsade de pointes. Three cases and a literature review. *Psychosomatics, 36,* 541–549.

International classification of diseases (10th ed.). (1993). Geneva: World Health Organization.

James, L., Bledsoe, L., & Hadaway, L. C. (1993). A retrospective look at tip location and complications of peripherally inserted central catheter lines. *Journal of Intravenous Nursing, 16,* 104–109.

Janai, H. (1990). Adverse drug reactions: United States experience. Part I. *Pediatric Infectious Disease Journal, 9,* S115–S116.

Janicak, P. G. (1993). The relevance of clinical pharmacokinetics and therapeutic drug monitoring. Anticonvulsant mood stabilizers and antipsychotics. *Journal of Clinical Psychiatry, 54*(Suppl.), 35–41.

Johnson, M. S., Pesko, L. J., Wood, C. F., & Reinders, T. P. (1990). Cost and acceptability of three syringe-pump infusion systems. *American Journal of Hospital Pharmacy, 47,* 1794–1798.

Joyce, T. H. (1993). Topical anesthesia and pain management before venipuncture. *Journal of Pediatrics, 22*(5, Part 2), S24–S29.

Kalow, W. (1993). Pharmacogenetics: Its biologic roots and the medical challenge. *Clinical Pharmacology & Therapeutics, 54,* 235–241.

Kane, J. M., Jeste, D. V., & Barnes, T. R. E. (1992). *Tardive dyskinesia: A task force report of the American Psychiatric Association.* Washington, DC: American Psychiatric Association.

Kane, J. M., & Lieberman, J. A. (Eds.). (1992). *Adverse effects of psychotropic drugs.* New York: Guilford Press.

Keck, P. E., Caroff, S. N., & McElroy, S. L. (1995). Neuroleptic malignant syndrome and malignant hyperthermia: End of a controversy? *Journal of Neuropsychiatry & Clinical Neurosciences, 7,* 135–144.

Ketter, T. A., Flockhart, D. A., Post, R. M., Denicoff, K., Pazzaglia, P. J., Marangell, L. B., George, M. S., & Callahan, A. M. (1995). The emerging role of cytochrome P450 3A in psychopharmacology. *Journal of Clinical Psychopharmacology, 15,* 387–398.

Kittel, J. F. (1986). Sedative-hypnotics. In A. M. Pagliaro & L. A. Pagliaro (Eds.), *Pharmacologic aspects of nursing* (pp. 252–283). St. Louis, MO: C. V. Mosby.

Koch, K. E. (1990). Use of standardized screening procedures to identify adverse drug reactions. *American Journal of Hospital Pharmacy, 47,* 1314–1320.

Kopala, L. C. (1996). Risperidone for child and adolescent schizophrenia. *Child & Adolescent Psychopharmacology News, 1*(2), 1–4.

Kostowski, W. (1995). Recent advances in the GABA-A-benzodiazepine receptor pharmacology. *Polish Journal of Pharmacology, 47,* 237–246.

Kunovac, J. L., & Stahl, S. M. (1995). Future directions in anxiolytic pharmacotherapy. *Psychiatric Clinics of North America, 18,* 895–909.

Latimer, P. R. (1995). Tardive dyskinesia: A review. *Canadian Journal of Psychiatry, 40*(Suppl. 2), S49–S54.

Levinson, M. L., Lipsy, R. J., & Fuller, D. K. (1991). Adverse effects and drug interactions associated with fluoxetine therapy. *Drug Intelligence and Clinical Pharmacy, 25,* 657–661.

Lindenmayer, J. P. (1995). New pharmacotherapeutic modalities for negative symptoms in psychosis. *Acta Psychiatrica Scandinavica, 388*(Suppl.), 15–19.

Logan, M., & Fothergill-Bourbonnais, F. (1990). Continuous subcutaneous infusion of narcotics (CSCI)—Preparing family caregivers for managing chronic pain in the home. *Canadian Nurse, 85*(4), 31–32.

Marder, S. R. (1994). The role of dosage and plasma levels in neuroleptic relapse prevention. *Acta Psychiatrica Scandinavica, 382*(Suppl.), 25–27.

Marti-Masso, J. F., Lopez de Munain, A., & Lopez de Dicastillo, G. (1992). Ataxia following gastric bleeding due to omeprazole-benzodiazepine interaction. *Annals of Pharmacotherapy, 26,* 429–430.

McLean, D. R. (1986). Antiparkinsonian medications and stimulants. In A. M. Pagliaro & L. A. Pagliaro (Eds.), *Pharmacologic aspects of nursing* (pp. 382–404). St. Louis, MO: C. V. Mosby.

McLean, D. R. (1986). Drugs used to treat epilepsy. In A. M. Pagliaro & L. A. Pagliaro (Eds.), *Pharmacologic aspects of nursing* (pp. 405–432). St. Louis, MO: C. V. Mosby.

Medication errors. (1996). *Prescriber's Letter, 3*(12), 72.

Megens, A. A., Awouters, F. H., Schotte, A., Meert, T. F., Dugovic, C., Niemegeers, C. J., & Leysen, J. E. (1994). Survey on the pharmacodynamics of the new antipsychotic risperidone. *Psychopharmacology, 114,* 9–23.

Merrell, S. W., Peatross, B. G., Grossman, M. D., Sullivan, J. J., & Harker, W. G. (1994). Peripherally inserted central venous catheters: Low-risk alternatives for ongoing venous access. *Western Journal of Medicine, 160*(1), 25–30.

Meyer, F. P., Tröger, U., & Röhl, F.-W. (1996). Pharmacoepidemiology and drug utilization. *Clinical Pharmacology & Therapeutics, 60,* 347–352.

Mitchell, J. F., & Pawlicki, K. S. (1994). Oral dosage forms that should not be crushed: 1994 revision. *Hospital Pharmacy, 29,* 666–668, 670–675.

Morton, W. A., Sonne, S. C., & Verga, M. A. (1995). Venlafaxine: A structurally unique and novel antidepressant. *Annals of Pharmacotherapy, 29,* 387–395.

Moulin, D. E., Kreeft, J. H., Murray-Parsons, N., & Bouquillon, A. I. (1991). Comparison of continuous subcutaneous and intravenous hydromorphone infusions for management of cancer pain. *Lancet, 337,* 465–468.

Mulligan, S. C., Masterson, J. G., Devane, J. G., & Kelly, J. G. (1990). Clinical and pharmacokinetic properties of a transdermal nicotine patch. *Clinical Pharmacology & Therapeutics, 47,* 331–337.

Murray, M. (1992). P450 enzymes: Inhibition mechanisms, genetic regulation and effects of liver disease. *Clinical Pharmacokinetics, 23,* 132–146.

Naganuma, H., & Fujii, I. (1994). Incidence and risk factors in neuroleptic malignant syndrome. *Acta Psychiatrica Scandinavica, 90,* 424–426.

Naranjo, C. A., Shear, N. H., & Lanctot, K. L. (1992). Advances in the diagnosis of adverse drug reactions. *Journal of Clinical Pharmacology, 32,* 897–904.

Nemeroff, C. B. (1994). Evolutionary trends in the pharmacotherapeutic management of depression. *Journal of Clinical Psychiatry, 55*(Suppl.), 3–15.

Nemeroff, C. B., DeVane, C. L., & Pollock, B. G. (1996). Newer antidepressants and the cytochrome P450 system. *American Journal of Psychiatry, 153,* 311–320.

Nestler, E. J. (1992). Molecular mechanisms of drug addiction. *Journal of Neuroscience, 12,* 2439–2450.

Neuvonen, P. J., Pohjola-Sintonen, S., Tacke, U., & Vuori, E. (1993). Five fatal cases of serotonin syndrome after moclobemide-citalopram or moclobemide-clomipramine overdoses [Letter]. *Lancet, 342,* 1419.

Neuvonen, P. J., Varhe, A., & Olkkola, K. T. (1996). The effect of ingestion time interval on the interaction between itraconazole and triazolam. *Clinical Pharmacology & Therapeutics, 60,* 326–331.

New Wyeth gel filled temazepam capsules. (1990). *Pharmaceutical Journal, 244,* 593.

Nilsson, A., Boman, I., Wallin, B., & Rotstein, A. (1994). The EMLA patch—A new type of local anaesthetic application for dermal analgesia in children. *Anaesthesia, 49,* 70–72.

Nimmo, W. S. (1990). The promise of transdermal drug delivery. *British Journal of Anaesthesia, 64,* 7–10.

Nordin, C., & Bertilsson, L. (1995). Active hydroxymetabolites of antidepressants. Emphasis on E-10-hydroxy-nortriptyline. *Clinical Pharmacokinetics, 28*, 26–40.

Obesity. (1996). *Prescriber's Letter, 3*(12), 68.

Olkkola, K. T., Backman, J. T., & Neuvonen, P. J. (1994). Midazolam should be avoided in patients receiving the systemic antimycotics ketoconazole or itraconazole. *Clinical Pharmacology & Therapeutics, 55*, 481–485.

O'Mara, N. B., & Nahata, M. C. (1995). Drugs excreted in human breast milk. In L. A. Pagliaro & A. M. Pagliaro (Eds.), *Problems in pediatric drug therapy* (3rd ed., pp. 245–335). Hamilton, IL: Drug Intelligence.

Oshika, T. (1995). Ocular adverse effects of neuropsychiatric agents. *Drug Safety, 12*, 256–263.

Owens, D. G. (1996). Adverse effects of antipsychotic agents. Do newer agents offer advantages? *Drugs, 51*, 895–930.

Pagliaro, A. M. (1985, October). *Diet, vitamins, and nutrient interactions with drugs in the elderly.* Paper presented at the International Holistic Gerontology Symposium, Ponoka, Alberta, Canada.

Pagliaro, A. M. (1995). Administering drugs to infants, children, and adolescents. In A. M. Pagliaro & L. A. Pagliaro (Eds.), *Problems in pediatric drug therapy* (pp. 1–101). Hamilton, IL: Drug Intelligence.

Pagliaro, A. M., & Pagliaro, L. A. (Eds.). (1986). *Pharmacologic aspects of nursing.* St. Louis, MO: C. V. Mosby.

Pagliaro, A. M., & Pagliaro, L. A. (1996). *Substance use among children and adolescents: Its nature, extent, and effects from conception to adulthood.* New York: John Wiley & Sons.

Pagliaro, L. A. (1985, October). *Drug interactions in the elderly: Overview and basic principles.* Paper presented at the International Holistic Gerontology Symposium, Ponoka, Alberta, Canada.

Pagliaro, L. A. (1986). Mechanisms of drug action. In A. M. Pagliaro & L. A. Pagliaro (Eds.), *Pharmacologic aspects of nursing* (pp. 71–77). St. Louis, MO: C. V. Mosby.

Pagliaro, L. A. (1994). Pharmacopsychology updates: Attention-deficit/hyperactivity disorder. *Psymposium, 4*(3), 14–15.

Pagliaro, L. A. (1995). Pharmacopsychology updates: Drugs and sexual (dys)function. *Psymposium, 4*(6), 20–21.

Pagliaro, L. A. (1995). Pharmacopsychology updates: Psychotropic teratogens. *Psymposium, 5*(1), 18–19.

Pagliaro, L. A. (1995). The straight dope: A consideration of substance-induced disorders. *Psynopsis, 17*, 14.

Pagliaro, L. A. (1996). Pharmacopsychology updates: Drug prescription privileges for psychologists. *Psymposium, 5*(4), 11–12.

Pagliaro, L. A. (1996). Should Canadian psychologists follow the APA trend and seek prescription privileges?: Of course they should!—An invited critical commentary of Dozois and Dobson. *Canadian Psychology, 36*, 305–312.

Pagliaro, L. A., & Benet, L. Z. (1975). Critical compilation of terminal half-lives, percent excreted unchanged, and changes of half-life in renal and hepatic dysfunction for studies in humans with references. *Journal of Pharmacokinetics and Biopharmaceutics, 3*, 333–383.

Pagliaro, L. A., & Locock, R. A. (1992). Nutritional products. In *Self-medication: Reference for health professionals* (4th ed.). Ottawa: Canadian Pharmaceutical Association.

Pagliaro, L. A., & Pagliaro, A. M. (Eds.). (1983). *Pharmacologic aspects of aging.* St. Louis, MO: C. V. Mosby.

Pagliaro, L. A., & Pagliaro, A. M. (1986). Adverse drug reaction index. In A. M. Pagliaro & L. A. Pagliaro (Eds.), *Pharmacologic aspects of nursing* (pp. 1727–1745). St. Louis, MO: C. V. Mosby.

Pagliaro, L. A., & Pagliaro, A. M. (1986). Age-dependent drug selection and response. In A. M. Pagliaro & L. A. Pagliaro (Eds.), *Pharmacologic aspects of nursing* (pp. 130–139). St. Louis, MO: C. V. Mosby.

Pagliaro, L. A., & Pagliaro, A. M. (1986). Drugs used to treat psychotic disorders. In A. M. Pagliaro & L. A. Pagliaro (Eds.), *Pharmacologic aspects of nursing* (pp. 325–351). St. Louis, MO: C. V. Mosby.

Pagliaro, L. A., & Pagliaro, A. M. (1992). Alcohol metabolism in a native patient [Letter]. *Canadian Medical Association Journal, 146,* 2141.

Pagliaro, L. A., & Pagliaro, A. M. (1992). Drug induced aggression. *The Medical Psychotherapist, 8*(2–3), 9.

Pagliaro, L. A., & Pagliaro, A. M. (1992). Pharmacopsychology as distinct from psychopharmacology: The initial results of a historical and philosophical inquiry [Abstract]. *Canadian Psychology, 33,* 437.

Pagliaro, L. A., & Pagliaro, A. M. (1993). Carbamazepine-induced Stevens-Johnson syndrome. *Hospital and Community Psychiatry, 44,* 999–1000.

Pagliaro, L. A., & Pagliaro, A. M. (1995). Abuse potential of the antidepressants: Does it exist? *CNS Drugs, 4*(4), 1–6.

Pagliaro, L. A., & Pagliaro, A. M. (1995). Alcoholic cognitive impairment and reliability of eyewitness testimony: A forensic case report. *The Medical Psychotherapist, 11*(1), 9–10.

Pagliaro, L. A., & Pagliaro, A. M. (1995). Drug prescription privileges for Canadian psychologists: Attainable and necessary. *Canadian Clinical Psychologist, 5*(3), 2–5.

Pagliaro, L. A., & Pagliaro, A. M. (Eds.). (1995). *Problems in pediatric drug therapy* (3rd ed.). Hamilton, IL: Drug Intelligence.

Pagliaro, L. A., & Pagliaro, A. M. (1998). *Psychologists' psychotropic desk reference.* Washington, DC: Taylor & Francis.

Pagliaro, L. A., & Pagliaro, A. M. (in press). *Clinical psychopharmacotherapeutics for psychologists.* Washington, DC: Taylor & Francis.

Perry, P. J. (1995). Clinical use of the newer antipsychotic drugs. *American Journal of Health-System Pharmacy, 52*(Suppl. 1), S9–S14.

Perry, P. J., Zeilmann, C., & Arndt, S. (1994). Tricyclic antidepressant concentrations in plasma: An estimate of their sensitivity and specificity as a predictor of response. *Journal of Clinical Psychopharmacology, 14,* 230–240.

Perucca, E., Gatti, G., & Spina, E. (1994). Clinical pharmacokinetics of fluvoxamine. *Clinical Pharmacokinetics, 27,* 175–190.

Petursson, H. (1994). The benzodiazepine withdrawal syndrome. *Addiction, 89,* 1455–1459.

Popli, A. P., Kando, J. C., Pillay, S. S., Tohen, M., & Cole, J. O. (1995). Occurrence of seizures related to psychotropic medication among psychiatric inpatients. *Psychiatric Services, 46,* 486.

Prosser, T. R., & Kamysz, P. L. (1990). Multidisciplinary adverse drug reaction surveillance program. *American Journal of Hospital Pharmacy, 47,* 1334–1339.

Reiss, R. A., Haas, C. E., Karki, S. D., Gumbiner, B., Welle, S. L., & Carson, S. W. (1994). Lithium pharmacokinetics in the obese. *Clinical Pharmacological Therapeutics, 55,* 392–398.

Reynolds, G. P. (1994). Antipsychotic drug mechanisms and neurotransmitter systems in schizophrenia. *Acta Psychiatrica Scandinavica, 380,* 36–40.

Ritschel, W. A. (1983). Pharmacokinetics in the aged. In L. A. Pagliaro & A. M. Pagliaro (Eds.), *Pharmacologic aspects of aging.* St. Louis, MO: C. V. Mosby.

Robinson, D. S., Roberts, D. L., Smith, J. M., Stringfellow, J. C., Kaplita, S. B., Seminara, J. A., & Marcus, R. N. (1996). The safety profile of nefazodone. *Journal of Clinical Psychiatry, 57*(Suppl. 2), 31–38.

Robinson, T. E., & Berridge, K. C. (1993). The neural basis of drug craving: An incentive-sensitization theory of addiction. *Brain Research and Brain Research Reviews, 18,* 247–291.

Roose, S. P., & Glassman, A. H. (1994). Antidepressant choice in the patient with cardiac disease: Lessons from the Cardiac Arrhythmia Suppression Trial (CAST) studies. *Journal of Clinical Psychiatry, 55*(Suppl. A), 83–87.

Rose, J. E., Levin, E. D., Behm, F. M., Adivi, C., & Schur, C. (1990). Transdermal nicotine facilitates smoking cessation. *Clinical Pharmacology & Therapeutics, 47*, 323–330.

Ryder, M. A. (1993). Peripherally inserted central venous catheters. *Nursing Clinics of North America, 28*, 937–971.

Sachdev, P. (1995). The epidemiology of drug-induced akathisia: Part I. Acute akathisia. *Schizophrenia Bulletin, 21*, 431–449.

Sachdev, P. (1995). The epidemiology of drug-induced akathisia: Part II. Chronic, tardive, and withdrawal akathisias. *Schizophrenia Bulletin, 21*, 451–461.

Schmidt, C. J., Sorensen, S. M., Kehne, J. H., Carr, A. A., & Palfreyman, M. G. (1995). The role of 5-HT2A receptors in antipsychotic activity. *Life Sciences, 56*, 2209–2222.

Schneider, J. K., Mion, L. C., & Frengley, J. D. (1992). Adverse drug reactions in an elderly outpatient population. *American Journal of Hospital Pharmacy, 49*, 90–96.

Schneider, P. J., Gift, M. G., Lee, Y. P., Rothermich, E. A., & Sill, B. E. (1995). Cost of medication-related problems at a university hospital. *American Journal of Health-System Pharmacology, 52*, 2415–2418.

Schumock, G. T., & Thornton, J. P. (1992). Focusing on the preventability of adverse drug reactions. *Hospital Pharmacy, 27*, 538.

Segraves, R. T. (1995). Antidepressant-induced orgasm disorder. *Journal of Sex & Marital Therapy, 21*, 192–201.

Sharma, H., & Pompei, P. (1996). Antidepressant-induced hyponatraemia in the aged. Avoidance and management strategies. *Drugs & Aging, 8*, 430–435.

Sheiner, L. B., Benet, L. Z., & Pagliaro, L. A. (1981). A standard approach to compiling clinical pharmacokinetic data. *Journal of Pharmacokinetics and Biopharmaceutics, 9*, 59–127.

Slattery, J. R., Nelson, S. D., & Thummel, K. E. (1996). The complex interaction between ethanol and acetaminophen. *Clinical Pharmacology & Therapeutics, 60*, 241–246.

Smiley, R. M., & Finster, M. (1996). Do receptors get pregnant too? Adrenergic receptor alterations in human pregnancy. *Journal of Maternal-Fetal Medicine, 5*, 106–114.

Smith, M., & Buckwalter, K. C. (1992). Medication management, antidepressant drugs, and the elderly: An overview. *Journal of Psychosocial Nursing and Mental Health Services, 30*(10), 30–36.

Stahl, S. M. (1992). Serotonin neuroscience discoveries usher in a new era of novel drug therapies for psychiatry. *Psychopharmacology Bulletin, 28*, 3–9.

Stahl, S. (1994). 5HT1A receptors and pharmacotherapy. Is serotonin receptor down-regulation linked to mechanism of action of antidepressant drugs? *Psychopharmacology Bulletin, 30*, 39–43.

Stanton, J. M. (1995). Weight gain associated with neuroleptic medication: A review. *Schizophrenia Bulletin, 21*, 463–472.

Steward, D. J. (1993). Eutectic mixture of local anesthetics (EMLA): What is it? What does it do? *Journal of Pediatrics, 22*(5, Part 2), S21–S23.

Stolley, P. D. (1990). How to interpret studies of adverse drug reactions. *Clinical Pharmacology & Therapeutics, 48*, 337–339.

Stowe, C. D., Ivey, M. M., Kuhn, R. J., & Piecoro, J. J. (1995). Administering intravenous drugs to infants and children. In L. A. Pagliaro & A. M. Pagliaro (Eds.), *Problems in pediatric drug therapy* (3rd ed., pp. 541–675). Hamilton, IL: Drug Intelligence.

Taddio, A., Nulman, I., & Reid, E. (1992). Effect of lidocaine-prilocaine cream (EMLA®) on pain of intramuscular Fluzone® injection. *Canadian Journal of Hospital Pharmacy, 45*, 227–230.

Taddio, A., Robieux, I., & Koren, G. (1992). Effect of lidocaine-prilocaine cream on pain from subcutaneous injection. *Clinical Pharmacy, 11*, 347–349.

Tatro, D. S. (1991). Food-drug interactions—Part I. *Facts and Comparisons Drug Newsletter, 10*(6), 41–42.

Tatro, D. S., Ow-Wing, S. D., & Huie, D. L. (1986). Drug toxicity. In A. M. Pagliaro & L. A.

Pagliaro (Eds.), *Pharmacologic aspects of nursing* (pp. 180–187). St Louis, MO: C. V. Mosby.

Taylor, D. P., Carter, R. B., Eison, A. S., Mullins, U. L., Smith, H. L., Torrente, J. R., Wright, R. N., & Yocca, F. D. (1995). Pharmacology and neurochemistry of nefazodone, a novel antidepressant. *Journal of Clinical Psychiatry, 56*(Suppl. 6), 3–11.

Taylor, D., & Lader, M. (1996). Cytochromes and psychotropic drug interactions. *British Journal of Psychiatry, 168,* 529–532.

Thomas, N. R. (1986). Review of the anatomy, physiology, and assessment of the central nervous system. In A. M. Pagliaro & L. A. Pagliaro (Eds.), *Pharmacologic aspects of nursing* (pp. 207–222). St. Louis, MO: C. V. Mosby.

Thomson, P. D., Rowland, M., & Melmon, K. L. (1971). The influence of heart failure, liver disease, and renal failure on the disposition of lidocaine in man. *American Heart Journal, 82,* 417–421.

Toth, P., & Frankenburg, F. R. (1994). Clozapine and seizures: A review. *Canadian Journal of Psychiatry, 39,* 236–238.

Ueda, C. T., & Hoie, E. B. (1995). Pediatric pharmacokinetics. In A. M. Pagliaro & L. A. Pagliaro (Eds.), *Problems in pediatric drug therapy* (3rd ed., pp. 713–735). Hamilton, IL: Drug Intelligence.

Varhe, A., Olkkola, K. T., & Neuvonen, P. J. (1994). Pharmacokinetics and drug disposition: Oral triazolam is potentially hazardous to patients receiving systemic antimycotics ketoconazole or itraconazole. *Clinical Pharmacology & Therapeutics, 56,* 601–607.

Volpicelli, J. R., Alterman, A. I., & Hayashida, M. (1992). Naltrexone in the treatment of alcohol dependence. *Archives of General Psychiatry, 49,* 876–880.

Watsky, E. J., & Salzman, C. (1991). Psychotropic drug interactions. *Hospital and Community Psychiatry, 42,* 247–256.

Weiner, M., & Weiner, G. J. (1996). The kinetics and dynamics of responses to placebo. *Clinical Pharmacology & Therapeutics, 60,* 247–254.

Williams, L., Davis, J. A., & Lowenthal, D. T. (1993). The influence of food on the absorption and metabolism of drugs. *Medical Clinics of North America, 77,* 815–829.

Yee, G. C., Stanley, D. L., Pessa, L. J., Dalla Costa, T., & Beltz, S. E. (1995). Effect of grapefruit juice on blood cyclosporin concentration. *Lancet, 345,* 955–956.

Yee, L. Y., & Lopez, J. R. (1992). Transdermal fentanyl. *Annals of Pharmacotherapy, 26,* 1393–1399.

Zaleon, C. R., & Guthrie, S. K. (1994). Antipsychotic drug use in older adults. *American Journal of Hospital Pharmacy, 51,* 2917–2943.

Zimmer, R., Gieschke, R., Fischbach, R., & Gasic, S. (1990). Interaction studies with moclobemide. *Acta Psychiatrica Scandinavica, 360,* 84–86.

Appendix 1: Abbreviations

ADE	adverse drug event
ADHD	attention-deficit/hyperactivity disorder
ADR	adverse drug reaction
AIDS	acquired immune deficiency syndrome
ANS	autonomic nervous system
ATP	adenosine triphosphate
AUC	area under the curve
Ca^{++}	calcium ion(s)
cAMP	cyclic adenosine monophosphate
CDC	Centers for Disease Control
CL_R	renal clearance
CL_T	total clearance
cm	centimeter(s)
CNS	central nervous system
COPD	chronic obstructive pulmonary disease
C_p	plasma concentration
$C_{p\ ave}$	average plasma concentration
CPK	creatine phosphokinase
CR	controlled release; continuous release
CSCI	continuous subcutaneous infusion
CTZ	chemoreceptor trigger zone
CVS	cardiovascular system
D_2	dopamine-2 (receptor)
DEA	Drug Enforcement Agency
DNA	deoxyribonucleic acid
DNI	drug–nutrient interaction
DSM-IV	*Diagnostic and Statistical Manual of Mental Disorders* (4th ed.)
D_5W	dextrose 5% in water
EAC	Editorial Advisory Committee
ECT	electroconvulsive therapy
ED_{50}	average dose that is effective for 50% of the population
EICD	electronic infusion control device
F	fraction of the administered drug dose that is available to the systemic circulation
FDA	Food and Drug Administration
Fe^{++}	ferrous iron ion(s)
GABA	gamma-aminobutyric acid
GABA-T	gamma-aminobutyric acid transaminase
GI	gastrointestinal
HCl	hydrochloride; hydrochloric acid
HIV	human immunodeficiency virus

HPB	Health Protection Branch
hr	hour(s)
IAA	indole acetic acid
ICD	*International Classification of Diseases*
IHL	intermittent heparin lock
IIC	intermittent infusion control
IM	intramuscular
INR	international normalized ratio
IQ	intelligence quotient
IV	intravenous
Ka	rate constant of absorption
kg	kilogram(s)
L	liter(s)
LA	long acting
LD_{50}	average dose that is lethal for 50% of the population
MAOI	monoamine oxidase inhibitor
mEq	milliequivalent(s)
mg	milligram(s)
Mg^{++}	magnesium ion(s)
min	minute(s)
ml	milliliter(s)
mmol	millimole(s)
NAD	nicotinamide adenine dinucleotide
NAPQI	N-acetyl-para-benzoquinone
ng	nanogram(s)
nmole	nanomole(s)
NMS	neuroleptic malignant syndrome
N-REM	non–rapid eye movement
NS	normal saline
NSAIDS	nonsteroidal anti-inflammatory drugs
PABA	para-aminobenzoic acid
Pb^{++}	lead ion(s)
PCA	patient-controlled analgesia
PEL	polyethylene
pH	hydrogen ion potential
PICC	peripherally inserted central (venous) catheter
pKa	ion dissociation constant
PNS	peripheral nervous system
PO	by mouth; orally
PT	prothrombin time
PVC	polyvinylchloride
RBF	renal blood flow
REM	rapid eye movement
SAR	structure–activity relationship
SC	subcutaneous
SCOI	subcutaneous opiate infusion
SD	standard deviation
SDAs	serotonin–dopamine antagonists
SIDS	sudden infant death syndrome

SGOT	serum glutamic oxaloacetic transaminase; aspartate transaminase
SGPT	serum glutamic pyruvic transaminase; alanine transaminase
SR	slow release; sustained action
SSRI	selective-serotonin reuptake inhibitor
$T_{1/2}$	half-life of elimination
TBC	total body clearance
TCA	tricyclic antidepressant
TD	time delay
TDDS	transdermal drug delivery system
TDM	therapeutic drug monitoring
TENS	transcutaneous electrical nerve stimulation
THC	delta-9-tetrahydrocannabinol
TI	therapeutic index
TR	time release
Vd	volume of distribution
V_{max}	maximum possible rate of drug metabolism
®	registered trademark symbol
°C	degree(s) Centigrade
°F	degree(s) Fahrenheit
>	greater than
<	less than
~	approximately
τ	tau (dosing interval)
μg	microgram(s)
μmol	micromole(s)
5-HIAA	5-hydroxyindoleacetic acid
5-HT	5-hydroxytryptamine; serotonin
$5\text{-}HT_2$	serotonin-2 (receptor)
5-HTP	5-hydroxytryptophan

Appendix 2: Glossary[1]

abulia: absence of ability to exercise independent willpower (e.g., demonstrate initiative, make decisions). Abulia is associated most commonly with cerebral vascular accidents (i.e., strokes) and is characterized by signs and symptoms including brief spoken responses, lack of spontaneity, and slow reaction to stimuli.

acid-base regulator: drug (e.g., sodium bicarbonate) that is involved in adjusting the acidity and alkalinity of body fluids, particularly blood and urine.

active transport: movement of molecules of endogenous compounds (e.g., various amino acids, ions, and sugars) or drugs (see discussion of renal excretion in Chapter 3, "Pharmacokinetics and Pharmacodynamics," for examples) across a biological membrane against a concentration (or electrochemical) gradient. This process requires the expenditure of energy (i.e., metabolic work) by the cells involved. See "passive diffusion."

acute dystonia: muscle contractions primarily affecting the back, face, neck, and tongue. These contractions cause twisting and repetitive movements or abnormal posture. See also "extrapyramidal reactions."

addiction: phenomenon accompanying prolonged used of a drug that involves the processes of acquired tolerance to the pharmacologic effects of the drug and a distinct physiological withdrawal syndrome upon abrupt discontinuation of drug use. All of the abusable psychotropics, except for the psychedelics, are capable of causing addiction. Use of the nonabusable psychotropics (e.g., antidepressants, antipsychotics) is not associated with the development of addiction. See also "habituation."

adrenolytic: pertaining to the inhibition of the activity of nerves and receptors that are stimulated by epinephrine (adrenaline).

adverse drug event: indirect consequence of pharmacotherapy that occurs as a result of an adverse drug reaction (e.g., a motor vehicle crash and resultant injuries that occur as a result of the adverse drug reaction, such as impaired psychomotor skills, associated with alcohol use). See "adverse drug reaction."

adverse drug reaction: any undesired consequence of pharmacotherapy, including expected and unexpected toxic effects and therapeutic failure where therapeutic success could reasonably be expected. This definition does *not* include accidental drug poisoning or intentional drug overdosage. See also "adverse drug event."

affinity: measure or degree of a drug's (or endogenous compound's) attraction to and ability to bind to a specific receptor. When two different drugs, each capable of binding to a specific receptor, are simultaneously present at a receptor in equal concentrations, the drug with the higher affinity will preferentially bind to the receptor. If the receptor is already occupied by the drug with lower affinity, then the drug with the higher affinity is capable of displacing it from the receptor site. See "receptor." See also Chapter 6, "Drug Interactions."

agonist: drug that binds to a receptor and stimulates the receptor's function. See also "antagonist."

agranulocytosis: physical disorder characterized by a significant deficit or absolute lack of granulocytic

---

[1] The terms in this glossary have been identified for inclusion by the members of the Editorial Advisory Committee as those that might be unfamiliar to some psychologists and psychology students using this text. With the recognition of the introductory nature of this text and in an attempt to make the glossary as helpful as possible, these terms generally have been defined in a expanded manner from that found in the body of the text, with examples and/or brief additional discussion included where appropriate.

This glossary is not intended to be comprehensive. Psychological disorders and terminology generally have not been included because it is expected that psychologists and psychology students already will, for the most part, be familiar with these disorders and terms. For the same reasons, terms related to the anatomy and physiology of the central nervous system also generally have not been included in this glossary. For definitions of additional terms not found in this glossary, readers are referred, as noted in the Preface, to standard medical, pharmaceutical, or psychological dictionaries.

white blood cells (i.e., basophils, eosinophils, and neutrophils). Also referred to as "granulocytopenia." See also "neutropenia."

akathisia: motor disorder characterized by restlessness and an inability to sit still. Signs include lateral knee movements, pacing, repeated knee crossings, rocking movements from foot to foot while standing, swinging of one leg when sitting, and walking on the spot. Akathisia is the most frequently reported extrapyramidal reaction associated with antipsychotic pharmacotherapy. See "extrapyramidal reactions."

albumin: type of simple protein found in both plant and animal tissues (e.g., ovalbumin that is found in the white of eggs). In pharmacotherapy, the most important albumin is plasma (or serum) albumin. It is the principal protein to which drugs bind in the blood and, as such, acts as both a carrier and reservoir system for many drugs in the systemic circulation. See "protein" and "protein binding." See also Chapter 6, "Drug Interactions," for a discussion of protein-binding interactions involving drugs that are highly bound to plasma albumin.

amide: organic compound containing the -$CONH_2$ group. Typically, these compounds are formed when the hydroxyl portion (i.e., -OH) of a carboxyl group (i.e., -COOH) is replaced by an amino group (i.e., -NH_2).

amine: nitrogen (N) containing organic compound. Typically, these compounds are formed when one or more of the hydrogen atoms (H) attached to the nitrogen in ammonia (NH_3) is replaced by a hydrocarbon group (e.g., -CH_3, -C_2H_5, etc.).

amino acid: one of approximately 80 organic compounds possessing both an amino group (i.e., NH_2) and a carboxyl group (i.e., COOH). Amino acids are the "building blocks" from which proteins are constructed and are the end product of protein catabolism. Twenty amino acids are necessary for human growth and metabolism. Of these, 11 are classified as essential because they cannot be produced in the body and must be obtained from food sources. See also "protein."

aminoglycoside: family of older, potent, broad-spectrum antibiotics, including amikacin (Amikin®), gentamicin (Garamycin®), kanamycin (Kantrex®), streptomycin, and others, noted for adverse drug reactions that affect the otic and renal systems. See "otic" and "renal."

analgesic: drug that provides relief from pain. The analgesics are generally divided into opiate and nonopiate groups, with the nonopiates being further divided into acetaminophen (Tylenol®) and nonsteroidal anti-inflammatory drugs (NSAIDs) such as aspirin (Bufferin®, Excedrin®) and ibuprofen (Motrin®).

anaphylactic reaction: acute, life-threatening allergic reaction that occurs within 30 minutes of drug exposure. Signs and symptoms include brochospasm, hypotension, increased gastrointestinal contractility, laryngeal edema, and urticaria. See "hypotension," "laryngeal edema," and "urticaria."

anemia: a reduction from the normal number of red blood cells (RBC). Anemia may result from excessive blood loss, decreased RBC production, or excessive RBC destruction. Over 20 different types of anemia have been identified. See also "aplastic anemia."

angina pectoris: physical disorder characterized by severe pain and a sensation of constriction or pressure in the region of the heart. It occurs when cardiac work and oxygen demand exceed the ability of the coronary circulation to supply sufficient amounts of oxygenated blood and is, thus, typically precipitated by physical exertion.

angioneurotic edema: physical disorder characterized by urticaria and edematous areas of mucous membranes and skin. Also referred to as "angioedema." See "urticaria."

anion: negatively charged ion (e.g., chloride ion, Cl^-).

anorectic: having no appetite. Also a drug that suppresses appetite.

antagonist: drug that binds to a receptor and inhibits the receptor's function by preventing agonists from binding to that receptor. See "agonist" and "receptor."

antecubital region: area on the front surface of the arm at the bend of the elbow. Also referred to as the "antecubital fossa." This is the area from which blood samples are most frequently drawn in adults.

anticholinergic effects: effects that impede the normal actions of the cholinergic, particularly parasympathetic, nervous system. These effects result in a constellation of signs and symptoms, including blurred vision, confusion, constipation, dry mouth, orthostatic hypotension, tachycardia, and urinary retention. Several groups of drugs are associated with causing anticholinergic effects, including the anticholinergic drugs (e.g., atropine) and drugs with anticholinergic actions (e.g., phenothiazines, tricyclic antidepressants). Also referred to as "parasympatholytic effects." See Chapter 5, "Adverse Drug Reactions," for additional details and discussion.

anticoagulant: drug that prevents blood coagulation. Heparin is the primary example of an injectable anticoagulant, and warfarin (Coumadin®) is an example of an oral anticoagulant.

antidote: substance that neutralizes poisons or their effects.

antiemetic: drug that prevents vomiting.

antitoxin: antibody that is produced in response to a specific biologic toxin and is capable of neutralizing that toxin.

antitussive: drug (e.g., codeine, dextromethorphan) that prevents coughing.

anxiolytic: drug (e.g., benzodiazepines) that can alleviate anxiety.

aplastic anemia: anemia due to insufficient production of red blood cells within the bone marrow. See "anemia."

apnea: temporary cessation of breathing.

ataraxia: state of complete calm or tranquility achieved without significant depression of consciousness or loss of cognitive facilities.

ataxia: defective voluntary muscular coordination and movement.

athetosis: condition of involuntary movement in which the upper extremities, particularly the hands and fingers, move in an irregular, slow, twisting fashion.

axon: part of a neuron that conducts electrochemical impulses away from the cell body. When the axon is surrounded by a myelin sheath or neurilemma (i.e., sheath of Schwann), it is referred to as a nerve fiber. See also "dendrite" and "neuron."

basophils: type of granulocytic white blood cell. See also "agranulocytosis."

binding: forces of chemical attraction that "hold together" chemical compounds and also hold drugs in place with respective receptor sites. See "receptor."

bioavailability: amount of administered drug that is available to the systemic circulation and, thereby, capable of eliciting systemic pharmacotherapeutic effects. Bioavailability can range from 0% to 100% and is denoted by F, the fraction of the administered dose (i.e., 0 to 1.0) available to the systemic circulation. By definition and convention, $F = 1.0$ for drugs that are administered intravenously. See also "bioequivalence."

bioequivalence: comparative bioavailability of two drug formulations. In order to be considered bioequivalent, the two formulations are compared in relation to (1) peak concentration, (2) time to peak concentration, and (3) area under the blood concentration–time curve. See "bioavailability." See Chapter 3, "Pharmacokinetics and Pharmacodynamics," for additional discussion and application.

buccal: pertaining to the cheek or mouth.

bullae: large skin vesicles (e.g., blisters) filled with fluid.

cachectia: state of severe malnutrition and wasting. May be associated with terminal phases of AIDS and many types of cancer.

cardiac glycosides: family of cardiac drugs (e.g., digoxin [Lanoxin®]) that exert a positive ionotropic effect on heart muscle and are used primarily in the treatment of heart failure. See "positive ionotropic effect."

catabolic: pertaining to catabolism (i.e., the metabolic conversion of complex substances into simple ones).

catalyst: compound that increases the rate of a chemical reaction. The catalyst accomplishes this function without being permanently altered in the reaction and can, thus, be used again in subsequent reactions.

cation: positively charged ion (e.g., calcium ion, Ca^{++}). See also "anion."

chelation: binding of metal ions (e.g., iron [Fe^{++}, Fe^{+++}], lead [Pb^{++}]) within a heterocyclic chemical ring structure(s) so that the ion is tightly held by bonds from each of the rings in a "claw-like" or "pincher" fashion. See "binding."

chemoreceptor trigger zone (CTZ): area within the CNS that can stimulate the vomiting center in the medulla. The butyrophenone and phenothiazine antipsychotics appear to elicit their antiemetic effects by selectively depressing the CTZ.

chorea: movement disorder characterized by involuntary muscle twitching of the limbs or facial muscles.

cirrhosis: disease of the liver characterized by an inability of the liver to perform its functions because of widespread fibrosis of the liver tissue. It is one of the top five causes of death among adults in North America and is primarily the direct result of the sequelae of chronic alcohol abuse.

coenzyme: specific chemical compound that acts in conjunction with certain enzymes to cause an enzymatic reaction. In the absence of a required coenzyme, the enzymatic reaction either would not occur or would be significantly reduced. See "enzyme."

congener: chemical that is similar in function, origin, or structure to another chemical.

congenital: present at birth.

corticosteroid: group of natural (e.g., cortisol) and synthetic (e.g., prednisone) hormonal steroid chemicals derived from the cortex of the adrenal gland. The corticosteroids are commonly classified, according to their biologic activity, into three groups: glucocorticosteroids, which affect carbohydrate and protein metabolism; mineralocorticosteroids, which affect fluid and electrolyte status, primarily by effects on ion transport and the renal tubules; and androgens, which stimulate the development of primary and secondary male characteristics. Also referred to as "adrenocorticosteroids." See "glucocorticosteroid."

Cushing's syndrome: physical disorder consisting of a constellation of signs and symptoms (e.g., "buffalo hump," mental abnormalities, "moon" facies, muscle weakness, osteoporosis, slender fingers, thin skin, truncal obesity) due to chronic exposure to excess amounts of corticosteroids. The etiology can be either endogenous (e.g., excessive production of cortisol as the result of an adrenocortical carcinoma) or exogenous (e.g., excessive dosage of corticosteroids such as dexamethasone [Decadron®] or prednisone). See "corticosteroids."

cutaneous: pertaining to the skin. Also referred to as "dermatologic."

cyanosis: slightly bluish or grayish discoloration of the skin due to the presence of excessive amounts of reduced hemoglobin in the blood.

cytochrome C reductase: enzyme that accelerates the process of reduction of cytochrome C (a pigment that is important in cellular respiration). See "enzyme."

cytotoxic reaction: allergic reaction mediated by the interaction between circulating antibodies and drug–protein complex (e.g., the Stevens–Johnson syndrome associated with carbamazepine [Tegretol®] pharmacotherapy). See "Stevens–Johnson syndrome."

decarboxylation: chemical metabolic reaction in which the carboxyl group (i.e., -COOH) is removed from an organic compound.

dendrite: branched process of a neuron that conducts electrochemical impulses to the cell body. See "neuron." See also "axon."

deoxyribonucleic acid (DNA): complex high molecular weight nucleic acid containing deoxyribose, phosphoric acid, and four bases (i.e., adenine, guanine, cytosine, and thymine) arranged in a spiraling double helix structure. It has been called the "building block of life." DNA is present in the chromosomes of cell nuclei and is the chemical basis of heredity.

dermatologic: pertaining to the skin. Also referred to as "cutaneous."

detoxify: to make an organic compound less toxic. Also to treat patients for drug toxicity or overdosage.

diplopia: double vision.

dosage: specified amount of drug that a patient is to receive over a specified time period (i.e., frequency of dose) and including the method of administration (e.g., 10 mg orally three times daily, 50 mg orally at bedtime, 150 mg intramuscularly once monthly). See "dose."

dosage form: physical vehicle for a drug (e.g., capsule, solution, tablet). See also Chapter 4, "Administration of Psychotropics," for discussion of dosage forms.

dose: specified amount of drug that a patient is to receive at one time including the method of administration (e.g., 10 mg orally, 50 mg intravenously). See also "dosage."

dose–response relationship: direct relationship between dose, or plasma concentration, and observed pharmacologic effect. This relationship does *not* apply to drugs that elicit their effects by the mechanisms of "physical effect" or "placebo effect." Nor does it apply to drugs with an indirect mechanism of action. See "dose" and "placebo effect." See Chapter 1, "Introduction to the Basic Principles of Pharmacotherapy," for additional discussion.

down regulation: process by which the normal response of an organ or system is inhibited or suppressed. For example, the immune system is down regulated or immunocompromised in patients with AIDS. Drug receptors can also be down regulated so that usual doses of drugs do not cause the expected usual pharmacologic response. See "receptor."

duodenal: pertaining to the duodenum. The duodenum is the first part of the small intestine that connects the pylorus of the stomach (i.e., the lower orifice of the stomach) to the second part of the small intestine (i.e., the jejunum).

dysarthria: difficult and defective speech due to neuronal functional impairment of the tongue and other muscles required for speech. Mental function is intact, and, if literate, the patient can read and write.

dyskinesia: defect in voluntary movement. See also "tardive dyskinesia."

dysphagia: inability to swallow or difficulty in swallowing.

dysrhythmia: abnormal, disordered, or disturbed (cardiac) rhythm, including abnormally slow rhythms (i.e., bradycardia) and abnormally fast rhythms (i.e., tachycardia and fibrillation). Also referred to as "arrhythmia."

efficacy: measure of the ability of a drug to achieve a specified therapeutic effect. Drugs can be equally efficacious and differ significantly in relation to adverse drug reactions and potency. See "adverse drug reactions" and "potency."

emphysema: form of chronic obstructive pulmonary disease (COPD). Associated pathology includes enlargement of the air spaces distal to the terminal nonrespiratory bronchioles and destructive changes affecting the alveolar walls.

endogenous: produced or arising from within the cell or organism. See also "exogenous."

enteric coated: drug formulation in which a capsule or tablet has a special coating that is designed to resist dissolving in the acidic pH of the stomach and dissolve instead in the alkaline pH of the small intestine. This formulation is used to protect drugs that may be degraded in the acidic environment of the stomach and to protect the stomach from the effects of irritating drugs (e.g., aspirin). See Chapter 4, "Administration of Psychotropics," for additional discussion and examples.

enzyme: complex proteins that are produced by living cells and are capable of catalyzing organic reactions without being changed themselves. See also "coenzyme."

enzyme induction: increase in the amount of drug metabolizing enzymes secondary to stimulation of the hepatic microsomal enzyme system by specific drugs. See also "enzyme inhibition." See Chapter 6, "Drug Interactions," for additional discussion and examples.

enzyme inhibition: decrease in the amount of drug metabolizing enzymes secondary to inhibition of the hepatic microsomal enzyme system by specific drugs. See also "enzyme induction." See Chapter 6, "Drug Interactions," for additional discussion and examples.

epiphyseal: pertaining to the epiphysis. See "epiphysis."

epiphysis: center of ossification at each extremity of long bones.

erythematous: diffuse redness of the skin caused by capillary congestion.

eutectic: easily melted. A eutectic mixture of two or more chemical substances has a lower melting point than any of its individual chemical constituents.

excipient: substance added to drug formulations to enhance or facilitate the manufacturing process. These substances (e.g., binders, coloring agents, fillers, agents to improve palatability), although generally considered to be inert, may cause untoward adverse drug reactions among patients who are allergic or sensitive to them.

exogenous: produced or arising from outside of the cell or organism. See also "endogenous."

extracellular: outside the cell. See also "intracellular."

extrapyramidal reactions: constellation of signs and symptoms related to the extrapyramidal system. The extrapyramidal reactions include akathisia, dystonia, neuroleptic malignant syndrome, Parkinsonism, perioral tremor, and tardive dyskinesia. Also referred to as "extrapyramidal effects." See Chapter 2, "The Psychotropics," and Chapter 5, "Adverse Drug Reactions," for additional details and discussion. See also "akathisia," "dystonia," "extrapyramidal system," "neuroleptic malignant syndrome," "Parkinsonism," "perioral tremor," and "tardive dyskinesia."

extrapyramidal system: functional system of the CNS involved in maintaining equilibrium and muscle tone. It includes all of the descending fibers arising in the cortical and subcortical motor centers that reach the medulla and spinal cord by pathways other than the pyramidal tracts. See also "extrapyramidal reactions."

fibrillation: cardiac dysrhythmia characterized by extremely rapid, incomplete, uncoordinated contractions of the atria or ventricles. Ventricular fibrillation commonly accompanies sudden cardiac arrest. During ventricular fibrillation, the ability of the heart to pump blood is significantly reduced, and, if the condition is not rapidly corrected, brain damage will ensue as a direct result of lack of blood flow to the brain. Treatment includes both electrical defibrillation and antidysrhythmic pharmacotherapy. Uncorrected ventricular fibrillation ultimately results in death. See also "dysrhythmia" and "tachycardia."

first pass metabolism: metabolism that occurs upon the first pass through the liver when a drug is absorbed from a site (e.g., gastrointestinal tract) from which the majority of the blood supply first passes through the liver before going to the general or systemic circulation. The amount of drug metabolized in this fashion never has a chance to elicit a systemic action outside of the liver and is therefore said to be "lost" to the systemic circulation. See Chapter 3, "Pharmacokinetics and Pharmacodynamics," for additional details, discussion, and examples.

functional reserve capacity: extra capacity that an organism has available to assist with situations of increased need (e.g., the extra brain cells or an "extra" kidney that individuals could generally function normally even without). However, the extra capacity generally proves useful in cases of accident, disease, and aging.

galactorrhea: abnormal lactation in men and in women. Can be an ADR associated with the use of several drugs, including the opiate analgesics and the phenothiazine antipsychotics.

gastrointestinal: pertaining to the stomach and the intestines, including the mouth, esophagus, and rectum.

glucocorticosteroid: natural (e.g., cortisol) or synthetic (e.g., prednisone) adrenal cortical hormones that are primarily active in providing physiologic responses to deal with stress by affecting carbohydrate and protein metabolism. Also referred to as "glucocorticoids" or "glucocorticosteroids," these compounds are a subfamily of the adrenocorticosteroids (corticosteroids) that includes both the glucocorticosteroids and the mineralocorticosteroids. See "corticosteroid."

glycol: family of dihydric alcohols related to ethylene glycol.

habituation: psychological dependence. It is the psychological process of becoming accustomed to and mentally dependent on a drug. It is generally associated with frequent drug use and characterized by craving for the drug and loss of control over its use. See also "addiction."

half-life of elimination: amount of time that it takes the existing concentration of a drug to decrease to one-half concentration. It takes the time equivalent of approximately five half-lives for a drug to achieve steady state concentrations at a constant dosage. It also takes the time equivalent of approximately five half-lives for a drug to be totally eliminated from the body after discontinuation of use.

hepatic: pertaining to the liver. See also "cirrhosis."

hepatitis: inflammation of the liver characterized by hepatocellular necrosis. A variety of forms of hepatitis occur. The major causes are infections and the use of various drugs, including, notably, alcohol.

homeopathy: school of medicine that uses what are generally considered to be subtherapeutic or subthreshold doses of drugs to elicit a therapeutic effect. The school is based generally on the theory that if large doses of certain drugs cause symptoms of disease in healthy patients, then very small doses of these drugs should "cure" these same symptoms in sick patients. See also "threshold dose."

hydrolysis: chemical reaction in which a compound is split into simpler component compounds by the addition or removal of water (i.e., H_2O). These reactions occur very commonly in the human body (e.g., conversion of fat to glycerol and fatty acids, conversion of protein to amino acids). Most of these reactions are reversible. The reversed reaction is often referred to as a neutralization or condensation reaction.

hydroxylation: chemical reaction in which the hydroxyl group (i.e., $-OH$) is added to an organic compound.

hyperreflexia: excessive or hypersensitive reaction of the reflexes.

hyperplasia: overdevelopment (i.e., excessive proliferation) of a body tissue. See also "hypoplasia."

hypertension: increased blood pressure above normal. See also "hypotension."

hypnotic: drug that can induce sleep. Generally these drugs (i.e., sedative-hypnotics) cause sedation at lower dosages and hypnosis at higher dosages. See also Chapter 2, "The Psychotropics."

hypodermoclysis: injection of large amounts of fluids into the subcutaneous tissues. See Chapter 4, "Administration of Psychotropics," for further details and discussion.

hypoplasia: underdevelopment of a body tissue. See also "hyperplasia."

hypotension: decreased blood pressure below normal. See also "hypertension."

induration: area of hardened tissue.

international normalized ratio: standardized blood clotting time laboratory test. It is used to help monitor the effects of the oral anticoagulants (e.g., warfarin [Coumadin®]).

intracellular: inside the cell. See also "extracellular."

iodophor: combination of iodine and a solubilizing carrier that liberates free iodine in solution. Some of these compounds are used as antiseptics (e.g., povidone-iodine [Betadine®]).

ion channel: a channel in a cellular membrane through which various ions (e.g., calcium ion [Ca^{++}], chloride ion [Cl^-], hydrogen ion [H^+], potassium ion [K^+], and sodium ion [Na^+]) pass. The passage of these charged ions from extracellular to intracellular locations (or vice versa) causes a change in the electrical status (i.e., polarity) of the membrane and results in physiologic, (pharmacologic, if drug induced) effects.

isotonic solution: solution that has an equivalent osmotic pressure with another solution with which it is being compared.

keratin: hard protein substance found in hair, nails, and skin. Keratin is insoluble in water and unaffected by most proteolytic enzymes.

laryngeal edema: localized condition in which the larynx becomes swollen with excessive tissue fluid. Laryngeal edema is usually the result of an allergic reaction. It is considered to be a medical emergency because it can result in airway obstruction and death. Treatment often requires the performance of an emergency tracheostomy. See also "larynx."

larynx: upper, wider end of the trachea below the root of the tongue. The larynx is the organ of voice and is often commonly referred to as the "voice box." See also "laryngeal edema."

law of conservation of dose: law that states that, within the usual therapeutic range (i.e., above the minimum effective dose and below any "ceiling" effect), the observed pharmacologic effect of a drug is directly proportional to the dose administered. Thus, doubling the dosage would be expected, for most drugs, to result in a doubling of effect. See Chapter 3, "Pharmacokinetics and Pharmacodynamics," for a discussion of the concepts of bioavailability and dose-dependent kinetics that might result in exceptions to this law.

ligand: endogenous chemical that binds to a receptor site. See "endogenous" and "receptor."

lipid soluble: fat soluble. A measure of the degree to which a compound dissolves in fat solvents such as alcohol as opposed to water. See also "lipophilic."

lipophilic: compound with an affinity for fat (e.g., a drug that preferentially distributes into fatty tissue). See also "lipid soluble" and "volume of distribution."

loading dose: a larger than regular dose that is administered, generally at the beginning of pharmacotherapy, to rapidly achieve steady state plasma concentrations (i.e., without having to wait for the time equivalent of five half-lives of elimination). See "half-life of elimination."

luminal pressure: pressure within a hollow organ (e.g., stomach) or tubular structure (e.g., blood vessel).

lymphadenopathy: disease involving the lymph glands.

macromolecule: large molecule such as a protein molecule. See "protein." See also "receptor."

mast cell: cells that synthesize, store, and release histamine and mediators of the inflammatory process (e.g., leukotrienes). Mast cells are found in the cutaneous connective tissue.

medial: toward the median plane of the body. See "median plane."

median plane: imaginary plane that divides the body vertically into right and left halves. Also referred to as the "midsagittal plane." See also "medial."

microsomal enzyme system: a system of metabolic enzymes found in the endoplasmic reticulum of liver cells. This is the system that is primarily responsible for drug metabolism. See "enzyme." See also related discussion in Chapter 6, "Drug Interactions."

mitochondria: organelle within cells that provides energy and is involved in protein synthesis and lipid metabolism. See "protein."

molecular weight: weight of a molecule obtained by totaling the atomic weights of its constituent atoms.

monovalent: ion or chemical group with a single positive charge (i.e., having the combining power of a single hydrogen atom [H^+]). Also referred to as "univalent." See also "cation."

nephritis: inflammation of the kidney.

nephron: kidney cell. See also "renal."

neurasthenia: unexplained chronic fatigue and lassitude.

neuroleptic malignant syndrome (NMS): antipsychotic-induced medical disorder characterized by catatonia, fever, myoglobinemia, stupor, and unstable blood pressure. NMS is a potentially life-threatening condition with a mortality rate of up to 20%. See Chapter 5, "Adverse Drug Reactions," for additional discussion. See also "extrapyramidal reactions."

neuromodulating compound: compound that diminishes or enhances the effects of neurotransmitters. See "neurotransmitter."

neuron: nerve cell. Neurons are the basic structural and functional unit of the nervous system. Each neuron consists of a cell body (perikaryon), an axon, and one or more dendrites. See "axon" and "dendrite."

neurotransmitter: chemical substance (e.g., acetylcholine, dopamine, norepinephrine [noradrenaline], and serotonin [5-hydroxytryptamine]) that is released into the synaptic cleft from the axon terminal of a presynaptic neuron when it is electrochemically excited. This substance then travels across the synaptic cleft to receptors on the postsynaptic neuron, where it binds, eliciting an excitatory or inhibitory effect. See "axon" and "synaptic cleft." See also Chapter 2, "The Psychotropics," for related discussion.

neutropenia: abnormally small number of neutrophils in the blood. Neutrophils are the most common type of granulocytic while blood cells. Acute, malignant neutropenia is referred to as agranulocytosis. See also "agranulocytosis."

nomogram: figure illustrating relationships among numerically quantified variables. For example, the body surface nomogram allows the estimation of body surface area from a knowledge of height and weight.

nystagmus: constant, rapid, involuntary, cyclic movement of the eyeball.

oleaginous: oily.

osmosis: passage of a solvent (e.g., water) through a semipermeable membrane that separates solutions of different concentrations. The rate of osmosis is dependent on differences in the osmotic pressure of the solutions on the two sides of the semipermeable membrane, the permeability of the membrane, the electrical potential across the membrane, and the electrical charge upon the walls of the pores of the membrane.

orthostatic hypotension: decrease in blood pressure upon standing. This is a normal physiologic response; if pronounced, however, it may result in syncope. Also referred to as "postural hypotension." See "hypotension" and "syncope."

otic: pertaining to the ears.

oxidation: chemical reaction in which electrons are lost and positive valence is increased. See also "reduction."

parahydroxylation: hydroxylation in the "para" (i.e., opposite) position of a chemical compound. See "hydroxylation."

Parkinsonism: idiopathic or drug-induced CNS disorder with four characteristic features: muscular rigidity, postural instability, resting tremor, and slowness and poverty of movement (e.g., bradykinesia, shuffling gait). Can be caused by virtually all of the antipsychotics, although incidence varies significantly from the phenothiazines to the atypical antipsychotics. Also referred to as "Parkinson's disease." See Chapter 2, "The Psychotropics," for additional discussion. See also "extrapyramidal reactions."

passive diffusion: movement of molecules of endogenous compounds (e.g., various amino acids, ions, and sugars) or drugs (for examples, see discussion of renal excretion in Chapter 3, "Pharmacokinetics and Pharmacodynamics") across a biological membrane from a region of higher concentration to a region of lower concentration. This process does not require the expenditure of energy (i.e., metabolic work) by the cells involved. Also referred to as "simple diffusion." See also "active transport."

patency: state of being freely and wide open. Term used to describe the status of blood vessels and intravenous needles, catheters, and tubing.

percutaneous: through the skin. Term used to describe processes (e.g., drug absorption) or procedures (e.g., removal of fluid by needle).

perioral tremor: involuntary quivering tremor involving the mouth. See "extrapyramidal reactions."

periostitis: inflammation of the periosteum (i.e., the fibrous membrane investing the surface of bone).

pharmacodynamics: study of the relationship between drug concentration (i.e., blood level) and pharmacologic effect. See Chapter 4, "Pharmacokinetics and Pharmacodynamics," for additional discussion. See also "pharmacokinetics."

pharmacokinetics: study of the processes of drug absorption, distribution, metabolism, and excretion. See Chapter 3, "Pharmacokinetics and Pharmacodynamics," for additional discussion. See also "pharmacodynamics."

pharmacotherapy: drug therapy (i.e., the use of drugs to treat medical and psychological disorders).

phlebitis: inflammation of a vein. Also referred to as "thrombophlebitis."

photosensitivity: abnormal sensitivity to light.

pigmentary retinopathy: degenerative disorder of the retina of the eye with widespread pigmentary changes.

pinocytosis: method of drug or nutrient transfer across a biological membrane. In this process, the drug or nutrient can be transferred without first undergoing dissolution. A hollowed-out portion of the biological membrane is formed and filled with the drug or nutrient. The area then closes to form a small sac or vacuole that subsequently opens on the "inside," making the drug or nutrient available on the other side of the biological membrane.

placebo: an inert substance that traditionally has been given to patients to satisfy pathologic demands for pharmacotherapy or to act as a control factor in experimental drug studies (e.g., double-blind, placebo-controlled studies). See also "placebo effect."

placebo effect: effect caused by a drug that possesses no inherent pharmacologic activity. The effect is mediated through psychological processes. See Chapter 1, "Introduction to the Basic Principles of Pharmacotherapy," for a discussion of the placebo effect as one of the basic mechanisms of drug action. See also "placebo."

platelet: blood cells that do not contain hemoglobin. The platelets are the principal blood component involved in blood coagulation, hemostasis, and thrombus formation. Also referred to as "thrombocytes." See "thrombus." See also "thrombocytopenia."

polydipsia: excessive thirst. See also "polyuria."

polypharmacy: prescription of several different drugs for one patient. Polypharmacy may be appropriate in situations in which the patient has multiple medical or psychological conditions, all of which are amenable to and appropriately treated by pharmacotherapy. However, it is more often the inappropriate result of a patient receiving prescriptions from several different prescribers without any coordination or checks and/or the over-reliance by prescribers on drugs as a quick solution to conditions that are amenable to other forms of therapy (e.g., diet, exercise, psychotherapy). Appropriate or not, polypharmacy is directly correlated with an increased incidence of both adverse drug reactions (see Chapter 5, "Adverse Drug Reactions") and drug interactions (see Chapter 6, "Drug Interactions").

polyuria: excessive urine production and elimination. See also "polydipsia."

positive inotropic effect: increase in the contractility of heart muscle in a dose-dependent manner. See also "cardiac glycosides."

potency: the "strength" of a drug. Potency is generally measured and considered in comparison with other drugs. For example, if Drug A required 5 mg to achieve a certain therapeutic effect and Drug B required 50 mg to achieve the same therapeutic effect, then Drug A would be considered to be 10 times more potent than Drug B. See also "efficacy."

prodrug: drug that is inert but is converted to a pharmacologically active form after absorption into the systemic circulation. For example, divalproex (Epival®) is a prodrug that dissociates into valproic acid prior to absorption from the gastrointestinal tract; levodopa (Dopar®) is a prodrug that is metabolically converted after absorption and crossing the blood–brain barrier to dopamine. Some prodrugs are administered in order to enhance bioavailability (i.e., they may be more readily absorbed or less susceptible to metabolic processes, such as first-pass metabolism). For example, dopamine does not cross the blood–brain barrier; however, levodopa does, and, once across the blood–brain barrier, it is converted to dopamine.[2] Others have been formulated to avoid patent violation of popular drugs. See also Chapter 3, "Pharmacokinetics and Pharmacodynamics," for related discussion.

protein: complex nitrogenous compound that occurs naturally in both plants and animals. Protein is made up of amino acids and serves as a source of amino acids for the growth and repair of tissues. Complete proteins are those that contain all of the essential amino acids. See also "amino acids."

protein binding: attachment of drugs or endogenous compounds to proteins. In the human, plasma albumin is the principal protein to which drugs bind. See "albumin," "binding," and "protein."

proteolytic enzyme: enzyme that enhances the hydrolysis of protein. See "enzyme" and "protein."

prothrombin time: standardized laboratory test to determine blood clotting time. It is used to help monitor the effects of the oral anticoagulants (e.g., warfarin [Coumadin®]).

pruritus: severe itching.

psychotropic: drug that works within the CNS and has effects on cognition, learning, memory, behavior, or mental disorders. The psychotropics can be divided into abusable and nonabusable psychotropics. See Chapter 1, "Introduction to the Basic Principles of Pharmacotherapy," for additional discussion, classification, and examples.

pulmonary: pertaining to the lungs.

pyridoxine: vitamin B_6.

pyrogen: substance that is capable of producing fever.

radiopaque: impenetrable by X-rays or other forms of radiation. Radiopaque items appear as a light area on the radiograph (i.e., X-ray film).

receptor: a macromolecular protein complex that is capable of binding with certain drugs, thereby eliciting a pharmacologic effect. See "binding" and "protein." See Chapter 1, "Introduction to the Basic Principles of Pharmacotherapy," for additional discussion and examples.

receptor down regulation: decrease in the number and/or sensitivity of functioning receptors (i.e., receptors that are capable of binding to a ligand and eliciting a characteristic response). It has been suggested that down regulation may occur as a result of various factors, including clinical conditions (e.g., pregnancy), disease states (e.g., chronic heart failure), and drug therapy (e.g., chronic antidepressant pharmacotherapy). See "receptor" and "ligand."

reduction: chemical reaction in which electrons are gained and positive valence is decreased. See also "oxidation."

renal: pertaining to the kidneys.

septicemia: presence of pathogenic bacteria in the blood.

silastic: type of silicone material. It can be used in tubing for drug delivery and plastic surgery to help form body structures.

---

[2] Levodopa is also converted (decarboxylated) to dopamine after absorption into the systemic circulation. This extracerebral or peripheral metabolism essentially nullifies the intended pharmacologic effect of levodopa because the dopamine produced cannot cross the blood–brain barrier. In order to facilitate the use of levodopa, peripheral decarboxylase inhibitors, such as carbidopa and benserazide, have been developed and are generally co-administered with levodopa (e.g., benserazide and levodopa [Prolopa®], carbidopa and levodopa [Sinemet®]) to prevent the peripheral decarboxylation of levodopa and allow a maximal amount to cross the blood–brain barrier. The peripheral decarboxylase inhibitors do not themselves cross the blood–brain barrier; thus, the levodopa, once across the blood–brain barrier, can be readily metabolized to dopamine.

simple diffusion: See "passive diffusion."

smooth endoplasmic reticulum: portion of the endoplasmic reticulum (i.e., an organelle of microtubules found in the nucleus and cytoplasm of cells) that is free of ribosomes (i.e., submicroscopic cell structure that synthesizes protein). See "protein."

status epilepticus: the occurrence of seizures in rapid succession without an intervening period of consciousness. Status epilepticus may result in death, often from cardiovascular collapse, and is considered to be a medical emergency.

Stevens–Johnson syndrome: severe form of erythema multiforme characterized by bullae on the anogenital region, conjunctiva of the eye, oral mucosa, and pharynx. See "bullae."

stricture: constriction or narrowing of the lumen of a duct (e.g., ureter, urethra), hollow organ (e.g., esophagus, intestine), or tube (e.g., intravenous tubing).

structure–activity relationship: relationship between the physical–chemical structure of a drug and its pharmacologic activity, particularly in terms of efficacy and potency. This relationship is predicated upon the necessity of a drug to be physically compatible with its biologic receptor. See "efficacy" and "potency." See also Chapter 1, "Introduction to the Basic Principles of Pharmacotherapy," for additional discussion.

stupor: physiological or psychological condition of diminished responsiveness to external stimuli.

subclavian: under or beneath the clavicle or collarbone. Also referred to as "subclavicular."

subcutaneous: under or beneath the skin. Also referred to as "hypodermic."

sublingual: under or beneath the tongue.

sympathomimetic: drug or chemical compound that mimics the action of sympathetic nervous system agonists. Examples of some of the major sympathomimetics include: albuterol (Ventolin®), amphetamine, benzphetamine (Didrex®), diethylpropion (Tenuate®), dopamine (Intropin®), epinephrine (adrenaline), isoproterenol (Isuprel®), mephentermine (Wyamine®), norepinephrine (noradrenaline), phenylpropanolamine, and tyramine. The sympathomimetics have varying affinity for the three major types of adrenergic receptors (i.e., α-1, α-2, and β) and, therefore, varying pharmacologic activity (e.g., anorexiant, bronchodilator, CNS stimulant, hypertensive, increased heart rate, nasal decongestant). Also referred to as "adrenergic."

symphysis pubis: bony eminence under the pubic hair.

synapse: junction point between two neurons in which the termination of the axon of one neuron comes into close proximity to the cell body or dendrites of another neuron. See "axon," "dendrites," and "neuron."

syncope: a transient loss of consciousness due to inadequate blood flow to the brain. Also referred to as "fainting."

tachycardia: increased heart rate. See also "fibrillation."

tardive dyskinesia: late occurring dyskinesia characterized by choreiform movements of the facial muscles. Tardive dyskinesia is associated with long-term antipsychotic pharmacotherapy. It is particularly troublesome because it generally persists following the discontinuation of antipsychotic pharmacotherapy and is resistant to treatment. See "chorea." See also "extrapyramidal reactions." See Chapter 5, "Adverse Drug Reactions," for additional discussion.

teratogenic: capable of causing birth defects.

therapeutic index (TI): ratio of the minimum effective to the minimum toxic dose of a drug. The TI is a measure of the "safety" inherent in the use of a particular drug (i.e., the higher the TI, the greater the degree of safety). See "efficacy" and "toxicity." See Chapter 1, "Introduction to the Basic Principles of Pharmacotherapy," for additional discussion and examples.

threshold dose: minimal dose required to elicit a pharmacologic effect. Dosages below this level would not be expected to elicit a pharmacologic effect and are referred to as homeopathic. See "homeopathic." See also "efficacy."

thrombocytopenia: abnormal decrease in the number of blood platelets. Platelets are involved in blood coagulation process; therefore, thrombocytopenia is associated with increased bleeding. See "platelet."

thromboembolism: blockage of a blood vessel by a thrombus that has become detached from its site of formation on the blood vessel wall. See "thrombus."

thrombophlebitis: inflammation of a vein as a result of the formation of a thrombus. See "thrombus."

thrombosis: existence of a thrombus within the vascular system. See "thrombus."

thrombus: blood clot that obstructs a blood vessel. See also "thromboembolism," "thrombophlebitis," and "thrombosis."

thyrotoxicosis: toxic condition due to hyperactivity of the thyroid gland. The most frequent signs and symptoms include hypersensitivity to heat, increased activity, increased appetite, fatigue, insomnia, nervousness, tachycardia, and weight loss. Also referred to as "hyperthyroidism."

tonicity: state of normal tension of muscle fibers while at rest. Also referred to as "tone."

torticollis: abnormal position of the head to one side with the chin pointing to the opposite side.

toxicity: degree of being poisonous. Drug toxicity generally refers to signs and symptoms associated with drug overdosage, not adverse drug reactions that occur at usual therapeutic dosages. See "adverse drug reaction." See Chapter 5, "Adverse Drug Reactions," for additional discussion.

transdermal drug delivery system (TDDS): drug dosage form designed to deliver fixed amounts of drug across intact skin surfaces. See Chapter 4, "Administration of Psychotropics," for further discussion and examples.

trigeminal neuralgia: pain disorder of the sensory nucleus of the trigeminal nerve. The pain produced is severe and (although brief in duration), if recurrent at regular intervals, can be incapacitating. The etiology of trigeminal neuralgia is generally unknown.

tryptophan pyrrolase: enzyme that catalyzes the catabolism of the essential amino acid tryptophan. See also "amino acid," "catabolism," and "enzyme."

ultrafiltration: filtration of colloidal substances from their liquid dispersion medium.

urticaria: vascular skin reaction characterized by the development of wheals and severe itching. Also referred to as "hives." See "wheal."

vesicant: drug or chemical that causes blistering of the skin.

volume of distribution: volume in which a drug is apparently distributed in the body in order to adequately account for the relationship between administered dose and resultant plasma concentration. See "dose." See Chapter 3, "Pharmacokinetics and Pharmacodynamics," for further discussion and examples.

wheal: round elevation of the skin characteristically white in the center with a pale red periphery. Wheals are most often the result of anaphylaxis, insect bites, or urticaria and are accompanied by itching. See "anaphylactic reaction" and "urticaria."

withdrawal syndrome: signs and symptoms associated with the abrupt discontinuation of an abusable psychotropic. The signs and symptoms of the withdrawal syndrome vary from drug to drug but generally consist of the opposite of the expected pharmacologic effect of the abusable psychotropic. For example, if the drug caused increased wakefulness, then its withdrawal syndrome would be expected to include increased drowsiness or sleep. As another example, if the drug decreased pain sensation, then its withdrawal syndrome would be expected to include increased sensitivity to painful stimuli. See "psychotropic."

xerostomia: dryness of the mouth associated with an abnormal reduction in the amount of salivary secretion. See also "anticholinergic effects."

Appendix 3: Commonly Prescribed Psychotropics— Associated ADRs and Clinical Comments

The ADRs associated with commonly prescribed psychotropics are discussed in this appendix. These drugs were chosen for inclusion here because of their association with clinically significant ADRs. Thus, this appendix is *not* meant to be an all-inclusive list. For additional information regarding the ADRs associated with a particular psychotropic drug, whether listed or not listed, readers are encouraged to also consult the tables in Chapter 5 and other authoritative reference sources (e.g., Friesen, 1983; Kane & Lieberman, 1992; Pagliaro & Pagliaro, 1986; Pagliaro & Pagliaro, 1995; Pagliaro & Pagliaro, 1996), along with the companion volume to this text, *Psychologists' Psychotropic Desk Reference* (Pagliaro & Pagliaro, 1998).

Some ADRs are ubiquitous with pharmacotherapy. For example, virtually *every drug* has the potential to cause hypersensitivity reactions among susceptible patients. In addition, virtually all *intravenously* injected psychotropics have the potential to cause phlebitis or thrombophlebitis. Likewise, virtually all *orally* ingested psychotropics have the potential to cause some degree of GI distress (e.g., dyspepsia, nausea, vomiting). These essentially "universal" ADRs generally are *not* specifically mentioned (repeated) in each monograph unless warranted by some special consideration (e.g., particularly high incidence).

As a means of facilitating the use of this appendix, the psychotropic drugs have been arranged by generic name in alphabetical order according to their pharmacologic or therapeutic classification. Drugs that fall into two pharmacologic or therapeutic categories (e.g., anticonvulsants and sedative-hypnotics [e.g., diazepam, Valium®]); anticonvulsants and antimanics [e.g., carbamazepine, Tegretol®] have been arbitrarily assigned to only one of the categories (i.e., carbamazepine is listed under Anticonvulsants, not under Antimanics). Readers may use this outline, or the comprehensive index at the end of this text, to locate a particular psychotropic for which they require information.

Analgesics

Opiate analgesics

  Opiate agonists (pure)
    Anileridine (Leritine®)
    Codeine (methylmorphine)
    Fentanyl (Duragesic®, Sublimaze®)
    Heroin (diacetylmorphine, diamorphine)
    Hydromorphone (Dilaudid®)
    Levorphanol (Levo-Dromoran®)
    Meperidine [pethidine] (Demerol®)
    Methadone (Dolophine®)
    Morphine (M.O.S.®)
    Oxycodone (OxyContin®, Supeudol®)
    Oxymorphone (Numorphan®)
    Propoxyphene (Darvon®)
Opiate agonists/antagonists (mixed)
    Butorphanol (Stadol®)
    Dezocine (Dalgan®)
    Nalbuphine (Nubain®)
    Pentazocine (Talwin®)

Anticonvulsants

(*see also* SEDATIVE-HYPNOTICS)

Barbiturates
    Phenobarbital (Luminal®)
    Primidone (Mysoline®)
Benzodiazepines
    Clobazam (Frisium®)
    Clonazepam (Klonopin®)
    Diazepam (Valium®)
    Lorazepam (Ativan®)
    Nitrazepam (Mogadon®)
Miscellaneous anticonvulsants
    Carbamazepine (Tegretol®)
    Divalproex (see *Valproic acid*)
    Ethosuximide (Zarontin®)
    Felbamate (Felbatol®)
    Gabapentin (Neurontin®)
    Lamotrigine (Lamictal®)
    Methsuximide [mesuximide] (Celontin®)
    Paraldehyde (Paral®)
    Phenytoin [*diphenylhydantoin*] (Dilantin®)
    Valproate sodium (see *Valproic acid*)
    Valproic acid [*divalproex sodium; valproate sodium*] (Depakene®, Depakote®, Epival®)
    Vigabatrin (Sabril®)

Antidepressants

Monoamine oxidase inhibitors
    Moclobemide (Manerix®)
    Phenelzine (Nardil®)
    Tranylcypromine (Parnate®)
Selective serotonin reuptake inhibitors
    Fluoxetine (Prozac®)
    Fluvoxamine (Luvox®)
    Paroxetine (Paxil®)
    Sertraline (Zoloft®)
Tricyclic antidepressants
    Amitriptyline (Elavil®)
    Clomipramine (Anafranil®)
    Desipramine (Norpramin®, Pertofrane®)
    Doxepin (Adapin®, Sinequan®)
    Imipramine (Tofranil®)
    Nortriptyline (Pamelor®)
    Protriptyline (Triptil®, Vivactil®)
    Trimipramine (Surmontil®)

Antimanics

Carbamazepine (Tegretol®)
Divalproex (see *Valproic acid*)
Lithium salts (Eskalith®, Lithane®, Lithobid®)
Valproate sodium (see *Valproic acid*)
Valproic acid [*divalproex; valproate sodium*] (Depakene®, Depakote®, Epival®)

Antipsychotics

Butyrophenones
  Droperidol (Inapsine®)
  Haloperidol (Haldol®)

Phenothiazines
  Chlorpromazine (Largactil®, Thorazine®)
  Fluphenazine (Moditen®, Permitil®, Prolixin®)
  Mesoridazine (Serentil®)
  Methotrimeprazine (Nozinan®)
  Perphenazine (Trilafon®)
  Prochlorperazine (Compazine®, Stemetil®)
  Promazine (Sparine®)
  Thioridazine (Mellaril®)
  Trifluoperazine (Stelazine®)
  Triflupromazine (Vesprin®)

Miscellaneous (atypical) antipsychotics
  Clozapine (Clozaril®)
  Olanzapine (Zyprexa®)
  Risperidone (Risperdal®)

CNS Stimulants

Amphetamines and amphetamine-like CNS stimulants
  Amphetamine salts, mixed combination (Adderall®)
  Benzphetamine (Didrex®)
  Dextroamphetamine (Dexedrine®)
  Methylphenidate (Ritalin®)
  Pemoline (Cylert®)

Miscellaneous (anorexiant) CNS stimulants
  Dexfenfluramine (Redux®)
  Diethylpropion (Tenuate®)
  Fenfluramine (Ponderal®, Pondimin®)
  Mazindol (Sanorex®)
  Phendimetrazine (Prelu-2®)
  Phenmetrazine (Preludin®)
  Phentermine (Ionamin®)

Sedative-Hypnotics/Anxiolytics

(*see also* ANTICONVULSANTS)

Barbiturates
  Amobarbital (Amytal®)
  Butabarbital (Butisol®)
  Mephobarbital (Mebaral®)
  Pentobarbital (Nembutal®)
  Phenobarbital (Luminal®)
  Secobarbital (Seconal®)

Benzodiazepines
  Alprazolam (Xanax®)
  Bromazepam (Lectopam®)
  Chlordiazepoxide (Librium®)
  Clorazepate (Tranxene®)
  Diazepam (Valium®)
  Estazolam (ProSom®)
  Flurazepam (Dalmane®)
  Ketazolam (Loftran®)

Lorazepam (Ativan®)
Midazolam (Versed®)[1]
Nitrazepam (Mogadon®)
Oxazepam (Serax®)
Quazepam (Doral®)
Temazepam (Restoril®)
Triazolam (Halcion®)

Miscellaneous sedative-hypnotics
Buspirone (BuSpar®)
Chloral hydrate (Noctec®)
Clormezanone (Trancopal®)
Ethchlorvynol (Placidyl®)
Meprobamate (Equanil®, Miltown®)
Methaqualone
Paraldehyde (Paral®)
Zolpidem (Ambien®)

Analgesics

Note: Long-term pharmacotherapy (i.e., several weeks) with opiate analgesics can result in addiction and habituation. Addiction is characterized by both tolerance and an opiate withdrawal syndrome that occurs upon abrupt discontinuation of the opiate analgesic after regular long-term pharmacotherapy or regular personal use. Habituation is characterized by an intense craving for the drug.

Opiate Analgesics

Opiate agonists (pure)
Anileridine (Leritine®)
Codeine [*methylmorphine*]
Fentanyl (Duragesic®, Sublimaze®)
Heroin [*diacetylmorphine; diamorphine*]
Hydromorphone (Dilaudid®)
Levorphanol (Levo-Dromoran®)
Meperidine [*pethidine*] (Demerol®)
Methadone (Dolophine®)
Morphine (M.O.S.®)
Oxycodone (OxyContin®, Supeudol®)
Oxymorphone (Numorphan®)
Propoxyphene (Darvon®)

Opiate agonists/antagonists (mixed)
Butorphanol (Stadol®)
Dezocine (Dalgan®)
Nalbuphine (Nubain®)
Pentazocine (Talwin®)

Opiate analgesics can cause constipation, dizziness, mental clouding, miosis, nausea, respiratory depression, sedation, and vomiting. Toxicity is usually dose–related. Overdose can be effectively treated with the opiate antagonist naloxone (Narcan®). Addiction, including the phenomena of acquired tolerance and an opiate withdrawal syndrome upon abrupt discontinuation of use, can develop after several weeks of pharmacotherapy or regular personal use.

Anticonvulsants

Note: Therapeutic drug monitoring should be performed during anticonvulsant pharmacotherapy to optimize therapeutic effect and minimize the incidence of ADRs (see Chapter 3, "Pharmacokinetics and Pharmacodynamics"). Abrupt discontinuation of anticonvulsant pharmacotherapy, particularly among patients who have received long-term, high-dosage pharmacotherapy, is not recommended because of the

---

[1] Midazolam is a short-acting benzodiazepine that is administered by injection to provide sedation for brief diagnostic procedures and for anesthesia.

possibility of increased seizure activity, including the occurrence of status epilepticus. Most anticonvulsants raise the seizure threshold, at least in part, by reducing the rate of CNS neurotransmission. This mechanism of action also is associated with impairment of cognition, learning, and memory. The degree of impairment will depend upon both drug factors (e.g., dosage) and patient factors (e.g., IQ).

Benzodiazepines

(*see also* SEDATIVE-HYPNOTICS)

> *Clobazam* (Frisium®)
> *Clonazepam* (Klonopin®)
> *Diazepam* (Valium®)
> *Lorazepam* (Ativan®)
> *Nitrazepam* (Mogadon®)

Ataxia, drowsiness, and sedation are common dose–related ADRs associated with benzodiazepine pharmacotherapy and occur in approximately 50% of patients. These ADRs usually subside with continued pharmacotherapy. Behavioral effects occur less frequently (approximately 25% of patients) but can be troublesome. These ADRs include aggression, hyperactivity, irritability, and difficulty concentrating. Abrupt discontinuation of benzodiazepine pharmacotherapy, particularly among patients who have received long-term, high-dosage pharmacotherapy, may precipitate status epilepticus. Addiction, including the phenomena of acquired tolerance and a benzodiazepine withdrawal syndrome upon abrupt discontinuation of use, can develop after several weeks of pharmacotherapy. Habituation also can develop during several weeks of pharmacotherapy.

Miscellaneous Anticonvulsants

Carbamazepine (Tegretol®)

The most frequent ADRs associated with carbamazepine pharmacotherapy include ataxia, blurred vision, diplopia, dizziness, drowsiness, nausea, and nystagmus. Tolerance to these effects may occur with continued pharmacotherapy. Hypersensitivity-related skin rash occurs in ~3% of patients; altered pigmentation, photosensitivity, exfoliative dermatitis, Stevens–Johnson syndrome, and aggravation of systemic lupus erythematosus can occasionally occur. A variety of blood dyscrasias, such as aplastic anemia, leukopenia, agranulocytosis, eosinophilia, and thrombocytopenia, have been associated with the use of carbamazepine. Carbamazepine and the tricyclic antidepressants share some of the same ADRs (e.g., anticholinergic effects) because they are chemically (structurally) related (see Chapter 1, "Introduction to the Basic Principles of Pharmacotherapy"). Contraindications to carbamazepine pharmacotherapy include a history of hypersensitivity to carbamazepine or the tricyclic antidepressants (to which carbamazepine is structurally related). Carbamazepine pharmacotherapy should be initiated with low dosages, and carbamazepine blood concentrations should be monitored monthly to minimize the incidence of ADRs. Complete blood counts, kidney and liver function, and vision should be periodically monitored to ensure early detection of carbamazepine toxicity. Optimum blood concentrations for controlling seizures are 6–12 mg/L (25–50 µmol/L). Moderate overdosages may paradoxically increase seizure frequency. When desired, carbamazepine pharmacotherapy should be gradually discontinued to minimize the risk of precipitating status epilepticus.

Divalproex

After oral ingestion, divalproex dissociates in the gastrointestinal tract into valproic acid. Thus, the pharmacologic activity, including ADRs and toxicity, associated with divalproex is one and the same with valproic acid. See *valproic acid.*

Ethosuximide (Zarontin®)

Common ADRs associated with ethosuximide pharmacotherapy include ataxia, dizziness, drowsiness, GI upset, headache, hiccoughs, and lethargy. Tolerance to these effects usually develops with continued pharmacotherapy. The ADRs involving the GI system can be minimized by instructing patients to ingest oral dosage forms with food or milk. Photophobia and blurred vision also may occur. Periodic complete blood counts are recommended because ethosuximide may cause a variety of blood dyscrasias. Skin rash, Stevens–Johnson syndrome, systemic lupus erythematosus, and urticaria also have been reported. Ethosuximide pharmacotherapy should be discontinued if blood dyscrasias or dyskinesias, Stevens–Johnson syndrome, systemic lupus erythematosus, or mental disorders occur. Ethosuximide is contraindicated for patients who have experienced a hypersensitivity reaction to ethosuximide or other succinimides. Ethosuximide is used primarily to manage absence seizures. It may increase the frequency of grand mal seizures if it is used alone for mixed seizure types. Ethosuximide pharmacotherapy should be discontinued gradually to avoid precipitation of absence seizures. Ethosuximide blood concentrations should be monitored to minimize the incidence of ADRs. The optimum blood concentration for seizure control is 40–110 mg/L (280–780 μmol/L).

Felbamate (Felbatol®)

Fatigue, headache, nausea, and somnolence are the most common ADRs associated with felbamate pharmacotherapy. Photosensitivity also may occur among some patients. Widespread use of felbamate has been limited by the rare occurrence of the potentially fatal hematologic toxicity aplastic anemia.

Gabapentin (Neurontin®)

The most commonly observed ADRs associated with the use of gabapentin include ataxia, dizziness, fatigue, nystagmus, somnolence, and tremor. The blood concentration range for optimal seizure control has not been established, and there appears to be no direct correlation between gabapentin blood levels and observed therapeutic effect. Overdosages do not appear generally to be life threatening and can be managed with appropriate emergency supportive medical care.

Lamotrigine (Lamictal®)

The most commonly observed ADRs associated with the use of lamotrigine are asthenia, ataxia, blurred vision, diplopia, dizziness, headache, nausea, rash, rhinitis, and somnolence. Most of these ADRs are mild and resolve within the first 2 weeks of pharmacotherapy. Although reportedly occurring infrequently, greater clinical concern may be with allergic or autoimmune-related toxicity that may occur generally within the first 6 weeks of treatment. These potentially fatal ADRs include angioedema, hypersensitivity syndrome with facial swelling and hematologic or hepatic involvement, and the Stevens–Johnson syndrome. Overdosage has resulted in coma.

Paraldehyde (Paral®)

Addiction and habituation may develop with regular long-term paraldehyde use. Paraldehyde has a strong, characteristic (unpleasant) odor that can be detected on the breath for up to 24 hours after use. Overdosage is associated with metabolic acidosis and may result in death.

Phenobarbital (Luminal®)

Drowsiness and sedation are the most common ADRs associated with phenobarbital pharmacotherapy. However, paradoxical excitement resembling the attention-deficit/hyperactivity disorder (ADHD) occurs in approximately 10% of young children prescribed phenobarbital pharmacotherapy for seizure disorders. Phenobarbital suppresses rapid-eye movement (REM) sleep. Mild skin reactions develop in 1% to 3% of patients; serious skin reactions (e.g., exfoliative dermatitis and Stevens–Johnson syndrome) occur only rarely. Ataxia, nystagmus, and respiratory depression occur with excessive doses. Phenobarbital pharmacotherapy is contraindicated for patients who have a history of hypersensitivity to barbiturates, impaired liver function, severe respiratory disease, or porphyria. Doses should be based on blood phenobarbital concentrations to reduce the incidence and severity of ADRs. The recommended blood concentration for optimum seizure control is 10–40 μg/ml (65–180 μmol/L). Phenobarbital pharmacotherapy should be discontinued gradually to minimize the risk of precipitating status epilepticus. Addiction and habituation can develop with regular long-term phenobarbital pharmacotherapy or regular personal use. In general, the use of phenobarbital and other barbiturates is not recommended because of their associated ADRs, the potential for addiction and habituation, and the availability of safer alternatives (e.g., benzodiazepines).

Methsuximide (Celontin®)

Methsuximide is a succinimide anticonvulsant that is very closely related to ethosuximide. Thus, the pharmacologic activity, including ADRs and toxicity, associated with methsuximide is very similar to that associated with ethosuximide. The optimal blood concentration for seizure control has not been determined. See "*Ethosuximide.*"

Phenytoin [diphenylhydantoin] (Dilantin®)

Gingival hyperplasia, GI disturbances, hirsutism, and skin rash are the most common ADRs associated with phenytoin pharmacotherapy. Meticulous oral hygiene, including thorough brushing of the teeth with a soft toothbrush after every meal, may lessen the severity of gingival hyperplasia. Hematologic disorders, including agranulocytosis, aplastic anemia, leukopenia, neutropenia, and thrombocytopenia, occur occasionally. Long-term high dosage phenytoin pharmacotherapy may cause peripheral neuropathy. Long-term phenytoin pharmacotherapy also may result in folate deficiency and megaloblastic anemia. Rare ADRs include Stevens–Johnson syndrome, systemic lupus erythematosus, and fatal hepatic necrosis. Doses should be individualized by monitoring phenytoin blood concentrations to reduce the incidence of ADRs and to optimize therapeutic response. The recommended blood concentration for optimum seizure control is 10–20 μg/ml (40–80 μmol/L). Moderate overdosage produces a variety of CNS effects, including ataxia, blurred vision, confusion, hallucinations, hyperactive tendon reflexes, hyperactivity, mydriasis, sedation, and vertigo. When desired, phenytoin pharmacotherapy should be gradually discontinued to minimize the risk for precipitating status epilepticus.

Primidone (Mysoline®)

Common ADRs associated with primidone pharmacotherapy include ataxia, diplopia, dizziness, nausea, nystagmus, sedation, vertigo, and vomiting. Acute psychotic reactions have been reported among patients who have temporal lobe epilepsy. The dosage should be individualized by monitoring blood concentrations. The recommended blood concentration for optimum seizure control is 6–12 μg/ml (27–55 μmol/L). Primidone is converted to two active metabolites, phenobarbital and phenylethylmalonamide. Thus, phenobarbital blood concentrations also may be monitored to reduce the risk for ADRs and to optimize therapeutic response.

Valproic acid [divalproex sodium, sodium valproate] (Depakene®, Depakote®, Epival®)

The ADRs associated with valproic acid pharmacotherapy primarily involve the GI system and include anorexia, diarrhea, indigestion, nausea, and vomiting. These effects occur frequently when pharmacotherapy is initiated but can be minimized by ingesting oral dosage forms with food. Temporary hair loss, asthenia, dizziness, fine tremor, headache, and insomnia also can occur. The incidence of ataxia, lethargy, and sedation associated with valproic acid pharmacotherapy is lower than for other anticonvulsants. Contraindications to valproic acid pharmacotherapy include a history of hypersensitivity to valproic acid and liver dysfunction. Valproic acid is a human teratogen, and its use should therefore be avoided among women who are or who may become pregnant. Although rare, hepatitis, liver failure resulting in death, and pancreatitis have been associated with valproic acid pharmacotherapy, particularly among young children during the first 6 months of pharmacotherapy. It is, therefore, advisable to periodically refer patients for monitoring for increased bleeding time, increased blood ammonia concentrations, and decreased platelet counts, which are early signs of liver toxicity. Dosages should be individualized by measuring valproic acid blood concentrations. The recommended blood concentration for optimum seizure control is 50–100 μg/ml (350–700 μmol/L).

Vigabatrin (Sabril®)

Vigabratrin is an inhibitor of gamma-aminobutyric acid transaminase (GABA-T), the enzyme responsible for the catabolism of GABA in the CNS. The anticonvulsant activity of vigabatrin and its ADRs are, therefore, presumably due to increased levels of GABA within the CNS. The most frequently reported ADRs associated with vigabatrin use are fatigue, somnolence, and weight gain. When used for children, the most frequently reported ADRs also include signs and symptoms resembling ADHD. Overdosages do not appear generally to be life threatening and can be managed with appropriate supportive medical care.

Antidepressants[2]

Note: All antidepressants increase the synaptic concentration of one or more stimulatory neurotransmitters (e.g., dopamine, norepinephrine, serotonin) and, thus, have the potential to cause signs and symptoms of excess CNS stimulation (e.g., agitation, anxiety, insomnia, and mania). In addition, they may affect variably cognition, learning, and memory among patients depending on several factors, including antidepressant dosage, patient IQ, and the variable effects that depression itself can have on cognition, learning, and

---

[2] See Chapter 5, "Adverse Drug Reactions," Table 5-10 for a comparison of the ADRs both within and among the various groups of antidepressants.

memory. Anorgasmia is commonly associated with antidepressant pharmacotherapy and appears to be mediated by antagonism of the adrenergic mechanisms that facilitate normal orgasm.

Monoamine Oxidase Inhibitors (MAOIs)

> *Moclobemide* (Manerix®)
> *Phenelzine* (Nardil®)
> *Tranylcypromine* (Parnate®)

The ADRs associated with MAOI pharmacotherapy are generally among the lowest, in terms of both incidence and severity, of all the various groups of antidepressants. CNS stimulation (e.g., agitation, insomnia, restlessness, tremor) and postural (orthostatic) hypotension may occur. Overdosage may result in variable signs and symptoms, depending on the amount of overdosage, and include agitation, convulsions, dizziness, drowsiness, hallucinations, hyperpyrexia, hyperreflexia, hypertension, hyporeflexia, hypotension, and insomnia. Edema and weight gain are particularly associated with phenelzine pharmacotherapy. See also Chapter 5, "Adverse Drug Reactions," Table 5-10.

Selective Serotonin Reuptake Inhibitors (SSRIs)

> *Fluoxetine* (Prozac®)
> *Fluvoxamine* (Luvox®)
> *Paroxetine* (Paxil®)
> *Sertraline* (Zoloft®)

The ADRs associated with the SSRIs are primarily related to their enhancement of the effects of serotonin in the CNS and include anorexia, anorgasmia, anxiety, diarrhea, headache, impotence, insomnia, nausea, and nervousness. Although the SSRIs are generally better tolerated than the TCAs, their associated ADRs contribute to their discontinuation in approximately 10% of patients prescribed SSRI pharmacotherapy. See also Chapter 5, "Adverse Drug Reactions," Table 5-10.

Tricyclic Antidepressants (TCAs) (partial list)

> *Amitriptyline* (Elavil®)
> *Clomipramine* (Anafranil®)
> *Desipramine* (Norpramin®, Pertofrane®)
> *Doxepin* (Adapin®, Sinequan®)
> *Imipramine* (Tofranil®)
> *Nortriptyline* (Pamelor®)
> *Protriptyline* (Triptil®, Vivactil®)
> *Trimipramine* (Surmontil®)

The most common and potentially troublesome ADRs associated with the TCAs are their anticholinergic actions. These ADRs occur as a result of the blockade of muscarinic receptors. The anticholinergic effects include blurred vision, constipation, dry mouth, drowsiness, sinus tachycardia, and urinary retention. The TCAs also, because of both their anticholinergic and sedative actions, impair learning, memory, and cognition. Sedation and weight gain frequently occur as well. The ADRs associated with the TCAs are generally more pronounced and problematic among elderly patients. The various ADRs contribute to the discontinuation of TCA pharmacotherapy in approximately 30% of patients. See also Chapter 5, "Adverse Drug Reactions," Table 5-10.

Antimanics

Carbamazepine (Tegretol®)

See discussion of carbamazepine ADRs earlier in this appendix under "miscellaneous anticonvulsants."

Divalproex

See discussion of divalproex ADRs earlier under *valproic acid* in the "miscellaneous anticonvulsants" section.

Lithium salts (Eskalith®, Lithane®, Lithobid®)

Lithium has a narrow therapeutic index. Thus, dosing must be carefully individualized in relation to lithium blood concentrations and patient response (see Chapter 3, "Pharmacokinetics and Pharmacodynamics"). Patients who require lithium pharmacotherapy must maintain a relatively consistent intake of liquids and sodium. Any drug that affects blood sodium concentrations will cause an opposite effect on blood lithium concentrations. This effect occurs because blood lithium concentrations are inversely proportional to blood sodium concentrations. Up to 50% of patients prescribed lithium pharmacotherapy develop one or more of the following ADRs: dry mouth, fatigue, hand tremor (generally benign), lethargy, leukocytosis (reversible), mental confusion, muscle weakness, nephrogenic diabetes insipidus (with attendant polyuria and polydipsia), and electrocardiogram T-wave depression (benign and reversible). Adverse GI reactions (e.g., abdominal pain, anorexia, bloating, diarrhea, nausea, vomiting) occur initially among approximately 25% of patients. These ADRs generally resolve with continued lithium pharmacotherapy. Lithium-induced acneiform eruptions and symptomatic hypothyroidism occur in approximately 1% of patients.

Valproic acid (Depakene®, Depakote®, Epival®)

See discussion of valproic acid ADRs earlier under "miscellaneous anticonvulsants."

Antipsychotics

Note: All of the antipsychotics have the potential to cause both minor and serious ADRs. Anticholinergic effects and extrapyramidal reactions, including movement disorders, Parkinsonian symptoms, and tardive dyskinesia, occur with varying severity depending on the specific antipsychotic, including the dosage of the antipsychotic prescribed and the duration of pharmacotherapy.

Butyrophenones

Droperidol (Inapsine®)
Haloperidol (Haldol®)

Anticholinergic effects, hypotension, and sedation are less frequently observed with haloperidol pharmacotherapy than with phenothiazine pharmacotherapy. However, haloperidol has a greater tendency to cause extrapyramidal reactions, including acute dystonic reactions, akathisia, aphasia, Parkinsonian tremor, and tardive dyskinesia. Agitation, anorexia, confusion, hallucinations, headache, insomnia, nausea, vertigo, and vomiting may occur. Although relatively rare, torsades de pointes, a potentially fatal cardiac dysrhythmia, has been associated with haloperidol use.

Phenothiazines[3]

Chlorpromazine (Largactil®, Thorazine®)
Fluphenazine (Moditen®, Permitil®, Prolixin®)
Mesoridazine (Serentil®)
Methotrimeprazine (Nozinan®)
Perphenazine (Compazine®, Stementil®)
Promazine (Sparine®)
Thioridazine (Mellaril®)
Trifluoperazine (Stelazine®)
Triflupromazine (Vesprin®)

The ADRs commonly associated with the phenothiazines include dizziness, drowsiness, extrapyramidal reactions, postural (orthostatic) hypotension, sedation, skin rash, and tachycardia. Anticholinergic effects (e.g., blurred vision, constipation, dry mouth, and urinary retention) also may occur. Extrapyramidal reactions include acute dystonic reactions, akathisia, neuroleptic malignant syndrome, parkinsonian symptoms, perioral tremor, and tardive dyskinesia. The incidence of extrapyramidal reactions is significantly increased among children who have acute viral infections (e.g., varicella-zoster [chickenpox] infection, measles). Severe extrapyramidal reactions can be treated with anti-parkinsonians or amantadine. However, levodopa should be avoided because it tends to aggravate psychoses. Phenothiazines may cause seizures among patients who have epilepsy. Phenothiazine pharmacotherapy for children younger than 2 years of age is generally not recommended because of its reported association with sleep apnea and sudden infant death syndrome (SIDS). Apnea monitoring should be provided for young children who require

---

[3] See also Chapter 2, "The Psychotropics," for discussion of aliphatic, piperazine, and piperidine subclasses.

phenothiazine pharmacotherapy (see also Chapter 2, "The Psychotropics," for a discussion of phenothiazine ADRs associated with the three individual chemical subgroups of the phenothiazines).

Atypical Antipsychotics (partial list)

Clozapine

Sedation, which may be profound and prolonged, is the most frequently encountered ADR associated with clozapine pharmacotherapy. Other ADRs commonly encountered include anticholinergic effects (e.g., blurred vision, constipation, dry mouth), dizziness, enuresis, fever,[4] hypotension, increased salivation, tachycardia, and weight gain. Seizures can occur in up to 10% of patients.[5] The most troublesome ADR associated with clozapine pharmacotherapy is the potentially fatal hematologic ADR agranulocytosis, which occurs in approximately 2% of patients who are prescribed clozapine pharmacotherapy. In order to minimize the incidence of agranulocytosis, it is recommended that blood counts be monitored at least weekly during the first 4 months of clozapine pharmacotherapy and monthly thereafter. "Rebound" psychosis has been reported with abrupt discontinuation of clozapine pharmacotherapy. (See Chapter 2, "The Psychotropics," for additional related discussion.)

Risperidone (Risperdal®)

The most common ADRs associated with risperidone pharmacotherapy include agitation, anxiety, extrapyramidal reactions, headache, and insomnia. Constipation, dizziness, fatigue, nausea, rhinitis, and somnolence also occur in a significant minority of patients (generally less than 5%). The most serious ADRs include rare cases of atrioventricular (A-V) block, seizures, and tachycardia.

CNS Stimulants

Amphetamines and Amphetamine-Like CNS Stimulants

> *Amphetamine salts, mixed combination* (Adderall®)
> *Benzphetamine* (Didrex®)
> *Dextroamphetamine* (Dexedrine®)
> *Methylphenidate* (Ritalin®)
> *Pemoline* (Cylert®)

Amphetamines and amphetamine-like CNS stimulant pharmacotherapy have been associated with such ADRs as anorexia, insomnia, growth suppression among children, tremor, and weight loss. Tachycardia and hypertension are more commonly associated with methylphenidate than pemoline pharmacotherapy. All of these CNS stimulants can aggravate seizure disorders and precipitate Tourette's syndrome, or tics, among susceptible patients, particularly children who have ADHD. Pemoline causes liver dysfunction among some patients.[6] Addiction and habituation may develop with long-term pharmacotherapy with any of these drugs. Contraindications to the use of these CNS stimulants include agitated states, known hypersensitivity, and known severe idiosyncratic reactions. Neither methylphenidate nor pemoline pharma-cotherapy is recommended for children younger than 6 years of age because safety and efficacy have not been established for this age group. The mixed amphetamine salts combination is approved for use in children 3 years of age and older. The incidence and severity of ADRs among older children who require

---

[4] A "benign" fever (37.7° to 39.4°C [100° to 103°F]) may occur, particularly during the first few months of clozapine pharmacotherapy. The etiology of the fever is unknown, but it can be managed with appropriate antipyretics (e.g., acetaminophen, aspirin). The fever will usually spontaneously remit with continued clozapine pharmacotherapy. It is imperative, however, to appropriately rule out both NMS and infection as possible causes of the fever. Use consultation and/or referral to an appropriate health care professional (e.g., advanced practice nurse, patient's family physician) as needed.

[5] The majority of clozapine-related seizures are of the tonic–clonic type, although myoclonic seizures also can occur. Risk factors for this ADR appear to include concurrent use of other epileptogenic drugs, history of neurological abnormalities, rapid upward titration of dosage, and use of clozapine in the higher dosage range. Clozapine-induced seizures generally respond favorably to dosage reduction and/or the addition of an anticonvulsant to the patient's drug regimen.

[6] This liver dysfunction can be severe enough to result in death or the need for a liver transplant. It is particularly problematic because it can occur suddenly or after years of continuous use. Patients (and/or their parents, depending on the age and mental ability of the patient) should be instructed to observe for signs and symptoms of liver dysfunction (e.g., dark urine, fatigue, jaundice, nausea) and to report these immediately. The pemoline should then be discontinued pending the results of liver function tests. Collaboration with the patient's family physician or pediatrician is indicated.

pharmacotherapy with these drugs can be minimized by ensuring that a correct diagnosis of attention-deficit/hyperactivity disorder is made and that the lowest effective dosage is used.

Miscellaneous (Anorexiant) CNS Stimulants

> *Dexfenfluramine* (Redux®)
> *Diethylpropion* (Tenuate®)
> *Fenfluramine* (Ponderal®, Pondimin®)
> *Mazindol* (Sanorex®)
> *Phendimetrazine* (Prelu-2®)
> *Phenmetrazine* (Preludin®)
> *Phentermine* (Ionamin®)

These drugs were extremely popular as anorectics during the 1960s and 1970s. However, a lack of sustained significant long-term weight reduction and widespread habituation, together with stricter DEA controls, resulted in the severe curtailment of their use during the 1980s. Interest and use have again increased in the 1990s, commensurate with the introduction of newer drugs (e.g., dexfenfluramine) with the promise of better therapeutic effects and fewer ADRs. However, long-term efficacy remains to be demonstrated. In addition, these stimulants still have the potential to commonly cause anxiety, depression, dry mouth, headache, insomnia, nervousness, and habituation. A potentially fatal ADR, although relatively rare (occurring in approximately 1 out of 50,000 patients), is primary pulmonary hypertension. This ADR appears to be most often associated with dexfenfluramine and fenfluramine pharmacotherapy, particularly when continued for longer than 3 months.

Sedative-Hypnotics

Note: All of the sedative-hypnotics cause central nervous system depression and respiratory depression. Regular long-term use may lead to addiction and habituation.

Barbiturates

> *Amobarbital* (Amytal®)
> *Butabarbital* (Butisol®)
> *Mephobarbital* (Mebaral®)
> *Pentobarbital* (Nembutal®)
> *Phenobarbital* (Luminal®)
> *Secobarbital* (Seconal®)

The use of barbiturates, which were once popular as hypnotic drugs for the promotion of sleep, has decreased considerably. However, they continue to be used for the management of some seizure disorders (see ANTICONVULSANTS).

Benzodiazepines

> *Alprazolam* (Xanax®)
> *Bromazepam* (Lectopam®)
> *Chlordiazepoxide* (Librium®)
> *Clorazepate* (Tranxene®)
> *Diazepam* (Valium®)
> *Estazolam* (ProSom®)
> *Flurazepam* (Dalmane®)
> *Ketazolam* (Loftran®)
> *Lorazepam* (Ativan®)
> *Midazolam* (Versed®)
> *Nitrazepam* (Mogadon®)
> *Oxazepam* (Serax®)
> *Quazepam* (Doral®)
> *Temazepam* (Restoril®)
> *Triazolam* (Halcion®)

Although the benzodiazepines, including diazepam, have a wide therapeutic index, benzodiazepine pharmacotherapy has been associated with several ADRs. Excessive sedation, which is dose–related, is one of the most common ADRs. Other ADRs include amnesia, ataxia, confusion, impaired memory, and impaired psychomotor performance. Addiction may occur with long-term, high-dosage pharmacotherapy or regular personal use. Habituation also may develop with long-term pharmacotherapy, even at recommended therapeutic dosages. Anxiety, hostility, and paradoxic excitement have been reported among some patients. Tolerance to sedative-hypnotic effects develops rapidly with regular use over a period of 4 to 6 weeks. Thus, benzodiazepines should be prescribed for no longer than 1 month and only "as needed" to promote sleep. Failure of insomnia to resolve after 1 month's time may indicate the presence of a primary mental disorder or other condition that requires patient reassessment and reevaluation of therapy. Abrupt discontinuation of benzodiazepine pharmacotherapy should be avoided among patients who have been using benzodiazepines regularly for more than a month. For these patients, the dosage should be gradually reduced over a period of a few weeks to avoid the benzodiazepine withdrawal syndrome. Severe overdosage can be medically treated with flumazenil (Anexate®, Romazicon®), a benzodiazepine antagonist that competitively blocks the benzodiazepine receptor.[7]

Miscellaneous sedative-hypnotics (partial list; see Chapter 2, "The Psychotropics," for additional discussion)

Chloral hydrate (Noctec®)

Ataxia, epigastric distress, light-headedness, malaise, nightmares, unpleasant taste, and aggravation of peptic ulcers are the most frequently reported ADRs associated with chloral hydrate pharmacotherapy. Epigastric distress can be reduced by either diluting the liquid formulation of chloral hydrate in a small amount of water or milk before ingestion or ingesting the capsule form with a glassful of milk or some food. Addiction and habituation can develop with regular long-term use. Additive CNS depressant effects can be expected with concurrent use of chloral hydrate and alcohol or other CNS depressants. Excessive doses of chloral hydrate may cause respiratory depression.

---

[7] This action may result in the acute benzodiazepine withdrawal syndrome among patients who are addicted to benzodiazepines.

Appendix 4: Major Clinically Significant Drug Interactions Involving the Psychotropics[1,2,3,4]

Acenocoumarol (Sintrom®)

—See "oral anticoagulants"

Acetylsalicylic acid

—See "aspirin"

Adrenocorticosteroids

—See "corticosteroids"

Alcohol	**Acetaminophen**
(ethanol)	**(paracetamol)**

The use of alcohol appears to exacerbate the well-recognized liver toxicity associated with acetaminophen (Tylenol®) overdosage. In addition, acetaminophen liver toxicity has been reported among people who have long-term alcoholism and who use normally high dosages of acetaminophen (i.e., without overdosage). Patients should be advised of these possible interactions.

The mechanism of this interaction is complex. Apparently alcohol has a modulating effect on the formation of the toxic metabolite of acetaminophen (i.e., N-acetyl-para-benzoquinone amine [NAPQI]). Under some circumstances of use (e.g., the ingestion of a single dose of alcohol by a person who does not have alcoholism), alcohol can actually decrease acetaminophen toxicity. However, the combined use

---

[1] This appendix is as comprehensive and up to date as possible as of the time of publication. However, generally a more conservative approach for inclusion has been taken than that found in many listings of drug interactions, and only those interactions that are thought to pose a *significant* potential risk to patients requiring psychotropics and that have been substantiated in the clinical literature have been included. Interactions lacking sufficient documentation of clinical significance (e.g., unsubstantiated case reports in the published literature, undocumented reports submitted to pharmaceutical manufacturers) have not been included in this listing. In addition, as new knowledge is discovered and reported in the clinical literature, some of the information presented may change.

[2] Therapeutically desired drug interactions that have been clearly established and recognized, such as in the case of antidotes (e.g., naloxone and heroin), are not generally discussed in this appendix, nor are most drug interactions that involve straightforward additive pharmacologic effects (e.g., barbiturates and benzodiazepines) or that involve solely nonpsychotropic drugs (e.g., antibiotics, oral contraceptives). Drug interactions involving antineoplastics or the general anesthetics likewise are generally not addressed in this appendix. In addition, the majority of vitamin, mineral, and nutrient interactions with drugs are discussed in the body of Chapter 6 and in Tables 6-5 to 6-9. Therefore, they are generally *not* repeated in this appendix.

[3] As a means of facilitating the use of this appendix, common drug trade names, designated with the registered trademark symbol (®), have been added (minimally, as a result of space considerations, at the first occurrence of each generic drug name). These additions should assist those prescribing psychologists who may be more familiar with the trade names than the generic names of the drugs discussed. These trade name listings, however, are not meant to be comprehensive, nor are they meant to imply that a particular brand of drug is preferentially involved in the listed drug interaction.

[4] Psychotropics interact with other psychotropics and with nonpsychotropics. Clinical psychologists must be aware of, and be familiar with, interactions involving nonpsychotropic drugs because of their potential to adversely affect psychotropic pharmacotherapy. They also must be able to discuss these possible interactions with prescribers of the nonpsychotropics, particularly when it is determined that a change in the nonpsychotropic pharmacotherapy is the best way in which to prevent or manage a drug interaction involving a psychotropic.

of alcohol and acetaminophen generally results in increased toxic metabolite formation coupled with decreased plasma glutathione (glutathione is involved chemically in detoxifying NAPQI) and, therefore, significantly increases the risk of toxicity. Thus, the use of acetaminophen should be generally avoided among patients who have long-term alcoholism.

Alcohol   Barbiturates

—See "alcohol + sedative hypnotics"

Alcohol   Benzodiazepines

—See "alcohol + sedative hypnotics"

Alcohol   Chlorpropamide

Excessive use of alcohol may intrinsically induce hypoglycemia and augment the action of hypoglycemic drugs such as chlorpropamide (Diabinese®). In addition, a disulfiram-like reaction (e.g., facial flushing, headache, nausea, tachycardia) has been associated with the consumption of moderate to excessive amounts of alcohol by people who are receiving chlorpropamide pharmacotherapy for the management of non-insulin-dependent diabetes (see also "alcohol + disulfiram").

Inform patients who are receiving chlorpropamide pharmacotherapy for the management of non-insulin-dependent diabetes of the possibility of this interaction. These patients should be advised to avoid or limit to small amounts their consumption of alcohol (e.g., an occasional single drink consumed with dinner).

Alcohol   Cimetidine

The first-pass metabolism of alcohol is significantly decreased by cimetidine (Tagamet®), a histamine-inhibiting antiulcer drug. This interaction can significantly increase the bioavailability of alcohol and its corresponding blood levels. Ranitidine (Zantac®) has a similar effect. However, famotidine (Pepsid®) does not appear to significantly affect the metabolism of alcohol.

Although the results of this interaction have been variable in terms of significance, patients who use alcohol and are receiving cimetidine or ranitidine pharmacotherapy should be warned of this interaction. They also should be advised of the possibility of impaired cognitive and psychomotor function after the consumption of amounts of alcohol that were previously not associated with impaired functioning prior to this pharmacotherapy. Collaboration with the prescriber of the cimetidine or ranitidine pharmacotherapy may be indicated (note that these drugs are also available, in reduced strength formulations, without a prescription).

Alcohol   Disulfiram

The consumption of alcohol by patients receiving disulfiram (Antabuse®) pharmacotherapy as part of a drinking cessation program will result in the "disulfiram" or "Antabuse®" reaction. The signs and symptoms of this reaction include blurred vision, dyspnea, flushing, headache, hyperventilation, hypotension, nausea, palpitations, sweating, tachycardia, vertigo, and vomiting. Severe reactions may result in cardiovascular collapse and death. Although the exact mechanism of this interaction has not yet been fully determined, it is due, at least in part, to the inhibition of acetaldehyde dehydrogenase metabolism by disulfiram. Alcohol is normally metabolized to acetaldehyde, which is metabolized by the enzyme acetaldehyde dehydrogenase to carbon dioxide, water, and fatty acids. Thus, when patients who are receiving disulfiram pharmacotherapy consume alcohol, their acetaldehyde serum levels increase, resulting in the "disulfiram reaction."

These patients should be carefully forewarned about the mechanism and effects of this interaction. In addition, all patients prescribed disulfiram pharmacotherapy to reinforce abstinence or punish alcohol use should be advised to avoid, during their pharmacotherapy, the use of alcohol and all alcohol-containing products (e.g., aftershave lotions, colognes, pharmaceutical elixirs, mouthwash), because some patients have experienced the disulfiram reaction after exposure to even small amounts of alcohol (i.e., ingestion of 15 ml [approximately 1 tablespoonful] of alcohol or topical contact with alcohol-containing solutions).

Alcohol   Insulin

The effects of alcohol on blood glucose levels may vary depending on the circumstances of use. The acute ingestion of alcohol in conjunction with a meal may enhance insulin response to the increased blood glucose and improve glucose tolerance. However, the acute ingestion of alcohol during the fasting state may inhibit hepatic gluconeogenesis, resulting in hypoglycemia. Drinking to the point of intoxication may cause irreversible hypoglycemia-mediated neurological damage among people who have insulin-dependent diabetes.

Diabetic patients should be advised to avoid drinking alcohol while fasting. If they choose to drink alcohol, they should be encouraged to drink in moderation and to drink in conjunction with a meal.

Alcohol	**Nilutamide**

Alcohol consumption by patients receiving nilutamide (Anandron®), an antineoplastic used in the pharmacotherapy of advanced prostate cancer, can result in a disulfiram-like reaction (see "alcohol + disulfiram").

Patients should be advised to avoid the consumption of alcoholic beverages while receiving nilutamide pharmacotherapy.

Alcohol   *Ranitidine*

—See "alcohol + cimetidine"

Alcohol	**Sedative-Hypnotics** **(e.g., barbiturates, benzodiazepines, chloral hydrate [Noctec®])**

The pharmacologic and toxicologic effects of alcohol and other sedative-hypnotics are increased primarily because of their combined CNS depressant effects. These combined effects can cause heavy sedation, diminished psychomotor abilities, and severe respiratory depression. Overdosages involving the combined use of these psychotropic drugs can be fatal.

Advise patients who are receiving sedative-hypnotic pharmacotherapy, particularly elderly patients who appear to be at increased risk for severe combined CNS depressant effects, to avoid consuming moderate to large amounts of alcohol. Prescribe cautiously sedative-hypnotics to patients who have current or past histories of problematic patterns of alcohol use, and monitor carefully their pharmacotherapy.

Amitriptyline

—See "tricyclic antidepressants"

Amphetamines	**Furazolidone** **(e.g., dextroamphetamine [Dexedrine®])**

Amphetamines are primarily metabolized by monoamine oxidase. Thus, furazolidone (Furoxone®), an antiprotozoal with significant monoamine oxidase inhibitor activity, can inhibit their metabolism. This inhibition of amphetamine metabolism can increase norepinephrine levels at the adrenergic nerve terminals and, consequently, increase blood pressure.

Concurrent amphetamine and furazolidone pharmacotherapy places patients at unnecessary risk for hypertension and related sequelae (e.g., stroke), and, therefore, should be avoided.

Amphetamines	**Monoamine Oxidase** **Inhibitors (MAOIs)** **(e.g., phenelzine [Nardil®], tranylcypromine [Parnate®])**

Amphetamines cause catecholamine (e.g., norepinephrine) release, and monoamine oxidase inhibitors impair the major route of metabolism of norepinephrine. Therefore, concurrent use of amphetamines and MAOIs may result in hypertensive crisis and hemorrhagic stroke as a result of the release and accumulation of large amounts of norepinephrine in the CNS.

Avoid prescribing amphetamines to patients who are receiving pharmacotherapy with MAOIs and for several weeks after MAOI pharmacotherapy has been discontinued. Note that the hypertensive reaction may occur even if amphetamines are prescribed up to 2 weeks after discontinuing the MAOI. Patients who have histories of amphetamine addiction and who require MAOI pharmacotherapy should be warned of this interaction and strongly cautioned to avoid resumed amphetamine use. If in doubt regarding the patient's use of amphetamines and an antidepressant is required, prescribe an antidepressant from a noninteracting class (e.g., tricyclic antidepressants).

Amphetamines

Urinary Alkalinizers
(e.g., drugs such as sodium bicarbonate and foods such as almonds [see Chapter 6, "Drug Interactions," Table 6-8])

An alkaline urine increases the proportion of nonionized amphetamine in the urine. This effect increases renal tubular absorption of the amphetamines and amphetamine blood levels, with resultant toxicity. Conversely, an acid urine increases the renal excretion of the amphetamines. Thus, urine acidification can be used in the treatment of amphetamine overdosage or toxicity.

Advise patients who are prescribed amphetamines to eat, in moderation, foods that can alkalinize the urine. Monitor for amphetamine toxicity when urinary alkalinizers are prescribed concurrently, and adjust amphetamine dosage accordingly. Collaboration with the prescriber of the urinary alkalinizer may be indicated.

Antidepressants

—See "monoamine oxidase inhibitors [MAOIs], selective serotonin reuptake inhibitors [SSRIs], tricyclic antidepressants [TCAs], and individual drugs"

Aspirin   Valproic Acid

—See "valproic acid + aspirin"

Barbiturates   Alcohol

—See "alcohol + sedative-hypnotics"

Barbiturates
(e.g., pentobarbital [Nembutal®], phenobarbital [Luminal®], secobarbital [Seconal®])

Corticosteroids
(e.g., cortisone, prednisone)

Concomitant use of barbiturates and corticosteroids may result in decreased blood levels and diminished pharmacologic effects of the corticosteroids. This interaction appears to be primarily related to the induction of hepatic microsomal enzymes by the barbiturates.

When prescribing barbiturates to patients who require corticosteroid pharmacotherapy, collaboration with the prescriber of the corticosteroid is indicated, because an increase in corticosteroid dosage may be necessary. Preferably, an alternative sedative-hypnotic (e.g., benzodiazepine) that does not significantly interact with the corticosteroids should be prescribed in place of the barbiturate.

Barbiturates

Opiate Analgesics
(e.g., meperidine [Demerol®], morphine)

Concurrent use of barbiturates and opiate analgesics may increase CNS and respiratory depression by means of additive effects. Barbiturates and opiate analgesics may be safely prescribed concurrently. However, patients should be monitored for desired therapeutic effects and excessive CNS or respiratory depression. If necessary, the dosage should be adjusted accordingly.

Barbiturates

Oral Anticoagulants
(e.g., warfarin [Coumadin®])

The barbiturates increase the metabolism of the oral anticoagulants by inducing the production of hepatic microsomal enzymes.

When barbiturate pharmacotherapy is initiated or discontinued, patients requiring oral anticoagulants should be carefully observed, prothrombin time closely monitored, and anticoagulant dosage adjusted accordingly. Thus, collaboration with the prescriber of the anticoagulant is indicated. Whenever possible, an alternative sedative-hypnotic (e.g., benzodiazepine) should be prescribed in place of the barbiturate in order to avoid this interaction.

Barbiturates

Oral Contraceptives

Barbiturates, particularly phenobarbital, can induce the hepatic microsomal enzyme metabolism of the estrogen present in oral contraceptives. This interaction results in oral contraceptive failure and appears to be particularly clinically significant with low-dose estrogen formulations.

Higher dose estrogen oral contraceptives (e.g., those containing 50 μg ethynyl estradiol in each daily dose) are more resistant to this interaction and may provide greater protection against pregnancy. However, in any event, if breakthrough bleeding occurs, a change in anticonvulsant or, more likely, an alternative method of contraception should be considered. Collaboration with the prescriber of the oral contraceptive is indicated.

Barbiturates	**Quinidine**

Barbiturates can reduce the serum levels and pharmacologic effects of quinidine (Duraquin®, Quinaglute®), a cardiac antidysrhythmic. The mechanism of this interaction appears to involve barbiturate induction of the hepatic microsomal enzymes responsible for quinidine metabolism.

Changes in serum levels can result in fatal dysrhythmias; thus, collaboration with the prescriber of the quinidine pharmacotherapy is indicated so that patient response and serum quinidine levels can be monitored and quinidine dosage adjusted accordingly. To avoid this interaction, an alternative sedative-hypnotic (i.e., a benzodiazepine) should be prescribed whenever possible.

Barbiturates	**Theophylline**

The barbiturates induce the hepatic microsomal enzymes responsible for the metabolism of the bronchodilator theophylline (Theolair®). As a result of this interaction, the blood concentration and pharmacologic effects of theophylline may be reduced.

When barbiturate pharmacotherapy is prescribed or discontinued for patients who require theophylline pharmacotherapy, collaboration with their prescribers is indicated so that serum theophylline concentrations can be monitored and dosage appropriately adjusted. In order to avoid this interaction, an alternative sedative-hypnotic (i.e., a benzodiazepine) should be prescribed whenever possible.

Barbiturates	**Valproic Acid** **(divalproex sodium, sodium valproate)**

The hepatic metabolism of barbiturates, particularly phenobarbital (Luminal®), is inhibited by valproic acid (Depakene®, Depakote®, Epival®). Thus, this interaction can result in increased barbiturate blood concentrations and corresponding pharmacologic effects.

Monitor for changes in barbiturate blood concentrations and patient response when valproic acid is added to or deleted from a patient's pharmacotherapy. Adjustment of the barbiturate dosage may be required. If therapeutically feasible, an alternative sedative-hypnotic (i.e., a benzodiazepine) should be prescribed in order to avoid this interaction.

Benzodiazepines	*Alcohol*

—See "alcohol + sedative-hypnotics"

Benzodiazepines **(e.g., diazepam,** **midazolam, triazolam)**	**Ketoconazole**

The hepatic microsomal metabolism of benzodiazepines, such as midazolam (Versed®) and triazolam (Halcion®), is significantly inhibited by the systemic antifungals ketoconazole (Nizoral®) and itraconazole (Sporanox®). This interaction can result in severe and excessively long-lasting benzodiazepine sedative-hypnotic effects. Thus, avoid concurrent use of midazolam and other similarly metabolized benzodiazepines (e.g., triazolam [Halcion®]) among patients requiring ketoconazole or itraconazole pharmacotherapy.

Benzodiazepines	**Omeprazole**

The hepatic metabolism of diazepam (Valium®) and other benzodiazepines is inhibited in a dose-dependent manner by omeprazole (Prilosec®), an antisecretory drug used to treat hypersecreting disorders (e.g., duodenal ulcers, gastroesophageal reflex disease). Thus, this interaction can increase benzodiazepine blood levels and associated CNS depressant effects. The mechanism of this interaction appears to be a genetically mediated effect on the rate of omeprazole metabolism. Concurrent use of benzodiazepines and omeprazole among susceptible patients has resulted in CNS toxicity (e.g., ataxic gait, confusion).

When benzodiazepines are prescribed for patients concurrently receiving omeprazole pharmacotherapy, monitor carefully for early signs of CNS toxicity and reduce accordingly the benzodiazepine dosage.

| **Benzodiazepines** | **Tobacco Smoke** |

The hepatic microsomal metabolism of the benzodiazepines is increased by chronic tobacco smoking (generally, one package of 20 cigarettes or more daily). Thus, this interaction can result in decreased benzodiazepine serum levels and pharmacologic effects.

When benzodiazepine pharmacotherapy is prescribed to patients who smoke tobacco, monitor for therapeutic effect and adjust appropriately the benzodiazepine dosage. In an effort to improve health, as appropriate, encourage and/or offer to assist patients with treatment to stop smoking.

| **Benzodiazepines** | **Valproic Acid** |
| | **(divalproex sodium, sodium valproate)** |

The concurrent use of benzodiazepines (e.g., diazepam [Valium®], lorazepam [Ativan®]), and valproic acid (Depakene®, Depakote®, Epival®) has been shown to result in decreased clearance of the benzodiazepines and increased displacement from plasma protein-binding sites. The net result is a significant increase in the plasma levels of unbound benzodiazepines and a resultant potential increase in associated adverse drug reactions.

When these substances are used concurrently, patients should be carefully monitored for signs and symptoms of benzodiazepine toxicity.

| **Carbamazepine** | **Cimetidine** |

The hepatic metabolism of carbamazepine (Tegretol®) is significantly decreased by cimetidine (Tagamet®), a histamine-inhibiting antiulcer drug. Thus, this interaction can increase carbamazepine serum blood levels and pharmacologic effects.

When prescribing carbamazepine to patients who require cimetidine pharmacotherapy, monitor carbamazepine serum levels and observe for signs of toxicity, particularly when cimetidine pharmacotherapy is initiated. Observe for lowered carbamazepine serum levels and signs of decreased therapeutic efficacy when cimetidine is discontinued. Collaboration with the prescriber of cimetidine may be indicated.

| **Carbamazepine** | **Erythromycin** |

The metabolism of carbamazepine (Tegretol®) is inhibited by erythromycin (E-mycin®, Ilotycin®), a general broad-spectrum antibiotic. This interaction may result in increased carbamazepine serum concentrations and resultant toxicity.

When carbamazepine pharmacotherapy is prescribed, avoid the concurrent use of erythromycin. If this is not possible, closely monitor serum carbamazepine levels and observe patients for signs of carbamazepine toxicity (e.g., impaired consciousness, psychomotor impairment). Adjust accordingly carbamazepine dosage.

| **Carbamazepine** | **Isoniazid** |

The hepatic microsomal metabolism of carbamazepine (Tegretol®) is inhibited by isoniazid (INH®), an antitubercular. This interaction increases the serum level of carbamazepine and the risk for toxicity.

When carbamazepine pharmacotherapy is prescribed to patients who concurrently require isoniazid pharmacotherapy, monitor carbamazepine serum levels and observe patients for signs of carbamazepine toxicity, particularly when isoniazid pharmacotherapy is initiated or discontinued.

| **Carbamazepine** | **Olanzapine** |

Carbamazepine (Tegretol®) can induce the hepatic microsomal enzyme metabolism of olanzapine (Zyprexa®), resulting in a 50% increase in the total body clearance of olanzapine.

It is extremely difficult to appropriately manage patients receiving concurrent carbamazepine and olanzapine pharmacotherapy because of the lack of a clear relationship between olanzapine serum levels and clinical effect. Therefore, it is recommended that this combination of psychotropic pharmacotherapy be avoided.

| **Carbamazepine** | **Oral Contraceptives** |

Carbamazepine (Tegretol®) can induce the hepatic microsomal enzyme metabolism of estrogen. This interaction appears to be particularly clinically significant in regard to the use of estrogen-containing oral contraceptives and can result in contraception failure, particularly with the use of low-dose estrogen formulations.

High-dose estrogen formulations (e.g., those containing 50 μg ethynyl estradiol in each daily dose) are more resistant to this interaction and may provide greater protection against pregnancy. Adolescent girls and women of childbearing potential who require carbamazepine pharmacotherapy and oral contraception with estrogen formulations should be advised of this interaction. Collaboration with the prescriber of the oral contraceptive is indicated in order to consider an alternative method of contraception, particularly if seizure control has been maintained with carbamazepine.

| **Carbamazepine** | **Risperidone** |

Carbamazepine (Tegretol®) can induce the hepatic microsomal enzyme metabolism of risperidone (Risperdal®), resulting in significantly decreased plasma levels of both risperidone and its active metabolite, 9-hydroxy-risperidone.

It is extremely difficult to appropriately manage patients receiving concurrent carbamazepine and risperidone pharmacotherapy because of the lack of a clear relationship between risperidone blood levels and clinical effect. Therefore, it is recommended that this combination of psychotropic pharmacotherapy be avoided.

Chloral Hydrate   Alcohol

—See "alcohol + sedative-hypnotics"

| **Chloral Hydrate** | **Oral Anticoagulants** |
| | **(e.g., warfarin [Coumadin®])** |

Trichloroacetic acid, a major metabolite of chloral hydrate (Noctec®), can displace oral anticoagulants from their protein-binding sites. This interaction causes a transient increase in hypoprothrombinemic effect.

This interaction is not generally clinically significant for most patients; however, when chloral hydrate is prescribed to patients who require oral anticoagulants, prothrombin time should be closely monitored. Thus, collaboration with the prescriber of the anticoagulant is indicated. For patients for whom this interaction poses increased risk, an alternative sedative-hypnotic (e.g., a benzodiazepine) should be selected.

Chloramphenicol   Phenytoin

—See "phenytoin + chloramphenicol"

Chlordiazepoxide

—See "benzodiazepines"

Chlorothiazide

—See "thiazide diuretics"

| **Chlorpromazine** | **Guanethidine** |

Chlorpromazine (Thorazine®), like other phenothiazine antipsychotics, possesses an intrinsic hypotensive effect. When prescribed concurrently, chlorpromazine can antagonize the antihypertensive effect of guanethidine (Ismelin®) by competitively inhibiting its uptake and that of norepinephrine into the adrenergic neuron. This effect is generally delayed, occurring 1 week after the initiation of concurrent chlorpromazine and guanethidine pharmacotherapy, and may persist for up to 10 days following discontinuation of the chlorpromazine.

Concurrent use of chlorpromazine and guanethidine should be avoided. Thus, collaboration with the prescriber of guanethidine is required. If an antihypertensive is needed for patients stabilized on chlorpromazine, it is recommended that an antihypertensive (e.g., methyldopa) be used that does not significantly interact with chlorpromazine.

| **Chlorpromazine** | **Tobacco Smoke** |

The hepatic microsomal enzyme metabolism of chlorpromazine (Thorazine®) and similarly metabolized phenothiazine antipsychotics can be induced by chronic tobacco smoking (generally reported as a minimum of one package of 20 cigarettes daily). Patients who are smokers generally require a significantly higher dosage of phenothiazine pharmacotherapy than do matched cohorts of nonsmokers. The effects of smoking on phenothiazine metabolism may persist for a month or longer after smoking is discontinued.

In an effort to improve health, as appropriate, encourage and/or offer to assist patients with treatment to stop smoking.

Chlorpropamide   Alcohol

—See "alcohol + chlorpropamide"

Cimetidine   Alcohol

—See "alcohol + cimetidine"

Cimetidine   Carbamazepine

—See "carbamazepine + cimetidine"

Cimetidine   Moclobemide

—See "moclobemide + cimetidine"

Cimetidine   Paroxetine

—See "paroxetine + cimetidine"

Cimetidine   Phenytoin

—See "phenytoin + cimetidine"

Cimetidine   Tricyclic Antidepressants

—See "tricyclic antidepressants + cimetidine"

Citalopram   Moclobemide

—See "monoamine oxidase inhibitors + selective serotonin reuptake inhibitors"

Clomipramine

—See "tricyclic antidepressants"

Clonazepam

—See "benzodiazepines"

Clonidine   Tricyclic Antidepressants

—See "tricyclic antidepressants + clonidine"

Clorazepate

—See "benzodiazepines"

Corticosteroids   Barbiturates

—See "barbiturates + corticosteroids"

Corticosteroids   Phenytoin

—See "phenytoin + corticosteroids"

Cyclosporine   Phenytoin

—See "phenytoin + cyclosporine"

Desipramine

—See "tricyclic antidepressants"

Dexamphetamine

—See "dextroamphetamine"

Dexfenfluramine   Monoamine Oxidase Inhibitors

—See "monoamine oxidase inhibitors + selective serotonin reuptake inhibitors"

Dextroamphetamine

—See "amphetamines"

Diazepam

—See "benzodiazepines"

Digoxin   Nefazodone

—See "nefazodone + digoxin"

Diphenylhydantoin

—See "phenytoin"

Disulfiram   Alcohol

—See "alcohol + disulfiram"

Disulfiram   **Oral Anticoagulants**
                              (e.g., warfarin [Coumadin®])

Disulfiram (Antabuse®) increases the plasma levels and hypoprothrombinemic effects of the oral anticoagulants. Although the exact mechanism of this drug interaction has not yet been fully determined, decreased hepatic metabolism of the oral anticoagulants by disulfiram appears to play a significant role.

Concurrent prescription of disulfiram for patients requiring oral anticoagulants should be avoided. When concurrent pharmacotherapy with these drugs cannot be avoided, collaboration with the prescriber of the oral anticoagulant is essential so that patients can be observed for signs of bleeding and their prothrombin times carefully monitored. The anticoagulant dosage should be adjusted accordingly.

Disulfiram   **Phenytoin**

Disulfiram (Antabuse®) increases phenytoin (Dilantin®) blood levels (up to several-fold) by inhibiting phenytoin's hepatic microsomal enzyme metabolism. This interaction may occur within several hours of initiating disulfiram and phenytoin pharmacotherapy and commonly results in phenytoin toxicity if not anticipated and dealt with appropriately.

When disulfiram pharmacotherapy is initiated, monitor blood phenytoin levels and observe for signs of phenytoin toxicity (e.g., ataxia, mental impairment, nystagmus) until a new steady state is achieved (i.e., after a time period equivalent to five half-lives) (see Chapter 3, "Pharmacokinetics and Pharmacodynamics," for details). Adjust the phenytoin dosage accordingly.

Divalproex Sodium

—See "valproic acid"

Dopamine

—See "sympathomimetics"

Doxepin

—See "tricyclic antidepressants"

Ephedrine

—See "sympathomimetics"

Epinephrine

—See "sympathomimetics"

Erythromycin   Carbamazepine

—See "carbamazepine + erythromycin"

Ethanol

—See "alcohol"

Fluoxetine   Monoamine Oxidase Inhibitors

—See "monoamine oxidase inhibitors + selective serotonin reuptake inhibitors"

Fluoxetine   **Phenytoin**

Fluoxetine (Prozac®) can inhibit the hepatic metabolism of phenytoin (Dilantin®). Patients stabilized on doses of phenytoin have developed elevated blood phenytoin concentrations and clinical phenytoin toxicity following the initiation of fluoxetine pharmacotherapy.

Avoid, when possible, this combination of pharmacotherapy. When concurrent pharmacotherapy cannot be avoided, carefully monitor phenytoin plasma levels whenever the fluoxetine dosage is modified.

Fluoxetine   Risperidone

—See "risperidone + selective serotonin reuptake inhibitors"

Fluoxetine   Sympathomimetics

—See "selective serotonin reuptake inhibitors + sympathomimetics"

Fluoxetine   Tricyclic Antidepressants

—See "selective serotonin reuptake inhibitors + tricyclic antidepressants"

Fluvoxamine

—See "selective serotonin reuptake inhibitors"

Glutethimide   **Oral Anticoagulants**
                                                        (e.g., warfarin [Coumadin®)

Glutethimide (Doriden®) decreases the hypoprothrombinemic effects of the oral anticoagulants by inducing their hepatic microsomal enzyme metabolism. This interaction, which may require up to 1 week to reach maximum effect, is similar to that observed when barbiturates are prescribed concurrently with the oral anticoagulants.

When possible, a noninteracting sedative-hypnotic (e.g., benzodiazepine) should be prescribed as an alternative to glutethimide pharmacotherapy for patients who require oral anticoagulants. If this is not possible, collaboration with the prescriber of the anticoagulant is required so that prothrombin times can be carefully monitored and patients observed for any signs of bleeding. The dosage of the anticoagulant should be adjusted accordingly.

Guanethidine   Chlorpromazine

—See "chlorpromazine + guanethidine"

Haloperidol   **Tricyclic Antidepressants (TCAs)**
                                                        (e.g., amitriptyline [Elavil®], imipramine
                                                        [Tofranil®], nortriptyline [Aventyl®,
                                                        Pamelor®])

Haloperidol (Haldol®) inhibits the metabolism of TCAs. The resulting increase in TCA serum concentrations may cause a corresponding increase in TCA adverse drug reactions (ADRs), particularly anticholinergic effects (e.g., blurred vision, dry mouth, confusion, constipation, postural hypotension, tachycardia, and urinary retention).

Monitor the patient for an increased incidence of ADRs when TCAs are used concurrently with haloperidol. The TCA dosage may need to be decreased when haloperidol is started or increased when it is discontinued.

Hydrocortisone

—See "corticosteroids"

Imipramine

—See "tricyclic antidepressants"

Insulin   Alcohol

—See "alcohol + insulin"

Isoniazid   Carbamazepine

—See "carbamazepine + isoniazid"

Isoniazid   Phenytoin

—See "phenytoin + isoniazid"

Isocarboxazid

—See "monoamine oxidase inhibitors"

Itraconazole

—See "ketoconazole"

Ketoconazole   Benzodiazepines

—See "benzodiazepines + ketoconazole"

Levodopa   **Monoamine Oxidase Inhibitors (MAOIs) (e.g., phenelzine [Nardil®], tranylcypromine [Parnate®])**

Levodopa (Dopar®) is a precursor of dopamine, which, in turn, is converted in vivo into norepinephrine. The MAOIs decrease the metabolism of both dopamine and norepinephrine. This interaction can increase the blood levels of these biologically active amines, resulting in flushing, hypertension, and palpitations.

Whenever possible, a different class of antidepressant (e.g., selective serotonin reuptake inhibitor, tricyclic antidepressant) should be prescribed instead of MAOIs for patients who are receiving pharmacotherapy with levodopa. If this is not possible, the addition to the levodopa regimen of a peripheral decarboxylase inhibitor (e.g., carbidopa) is recommended. The peripheral decarboxylase inhibitor will generally significantly reduce the metabolism (decarboxylation) of levodopa to dopamine and, thus, suppress the hypertensive reaction associated with concurrent MAOI therapy.

Levodopa   **Pyridoxine (See Chapter 6, "Drug Interactions," Table 6-9)**

Pyridoxine (vitamin B_6), particularly in daily doses of 5 mg or more, increases the peripheral decarboxylation (metabolism) of levodopa (Dopar®) in the gastrointestinal tract. This interaction may decrease the anti-Parkinsonian effects of levodopa.

Concurrent use of a peripheral decarboxylase inhibitor (e.g, carbidopa), which is available in the combination product Sinemet®, can prevent the pyridoxine-induced increased metabolism of levodopa. As a result, lower total dosages of levodopa are required to achieve the same therapeutic effect. Consequently, dose-related adverse drug reactions of levodopa also are decreased.

Levothyroxine

—See "thyroid hormones"

Lithium Carbonate

—See "lithium salts"

Lithium Citrate

—See "lithium salts"

Lithium Salts	**Nonsteroidal Anti-Inflammatory**
(lithium carbonate,	**Drugs (NSAIDs)**
lithium citrate)	**(e.g., ibuprofen [Motrin®], indomethacin [Indocid®, Indocin®], naproxen [Naprosyn®])**

The renal excretion of lithium is reduced by the concurrent use of NSAIDS, presumably as a result of NSAID-mediated renal prostaglandin inhibition. The effect, although variable (depending on NSAID used, dosage, and individual patient response), can be significant and result in lithium toxicity.

Monitor serum lithium concentrations and adjust the dosage accordingly. Collaboration with the prescriber of the NSAID (e.g., family physician, rheumatologist) may be indicated. In addition, because several NSAIDS (e.g., aspirin, ibuprofen) are available without a prescription, proper patient education will be required for all patients prescribed lithium.

Lithium Salts	**Thiazide Diuretics**
	(e.g., chlorothiazide [Diuril®], hydrochlorothiazide [HydroDiuril®])

Lithium (Eskalith®, Lithane®) serum levels are inversely related to sodium levels. Thus, any drug or food that affects sodium levels also will affect lithium levels. The renal excretion of lithium is significantly decreased by thiazide diuretics. This interaction may result in toxic lithium serum levels.

When possible, patients who require lithium pharmacotherapy should not receive thiazide diuretics. The potassium-sparing diuretics have been suggested as possible suitable alternatives. Collaboration with the prescriber of the thiazide diuretic is required. Monitor carefully lithium serum levels when diuretic or other pharmacotherapy-affecting sodium levels cannot be avoided. Adjust the lithium dosage accordingly. Advise patients to avoid significant changes in their diets, including eating foods high in sodium (e.g., canned vegetables and soups, potato chips, salted nuts).

Lorazepam

—See "benzodiazepines"

Meperidine	**Monoamine Oxidase**
[pethidine]	**Inhibitors (MAOIs)**
(Demerol®)	**(e.g., phenelzine [Nardil®], tranylcypromine [Parnate®])**

A number of cases of severe, generally immediate, reactions (e.g., coma, delirium, excitation, fever, hypertension, hypotension) have been reported among patients receiving meperidine (Demerol®) and a MAOI. The exact mechanism of this drug interaction has not yet been fully determined.

Avoid the use of meperidine among patients receiving pharmacotherapy with an MAOI. When such patients require an opiate analgesic, morphine can be prescribed as an alternative because it does not appear to undergo the same drug interaction. When morphine is prescribed, initiate pharmacotherapy with a low dosage and carefully monitor patient response.

Methamphetamine

—See "amphetamines"

Midazolam   Ketoconazole

—See "benzodiazepines + ketoconazole"

Moclobemide	**Cimetidine**

The hepatic microsomal enzyme mediated metabolism of moclobemide (Manerix®) is inhibited by cimetidine (Tagamet®), a histamine-inhibiting antiulcer drug. This interaction results in significantly increased moclobemide blood levels and possible toxicity. When moclobemide is concurrently prescribed for patients who require cimetidine pharmacotherapy, initiate moclobemide therapy at the lowest therapeutic dosage (up to a 50% reduction in the dosage of moclobemide may be necessary). Monitor carefully patient response and adjust dosage as required.

Moclobemide   *Selective Serotonin Reuptake Inhibitors*

—See "monoamine oxidase inhibitors + selective serotonin reuptake inhibitors"

Moclobemide   *Citalopram*

—See "monoamine oxidase inhibitors + selective serotonin reuptake inhibitors"

Moclobemide   *Clomipramine*

—See "monamine oxidase inhibitors + tricyclic antidepressants"

Monoamine Oxidase   **Amines in Foods and Beverages**
Inhibitors (MAOIs)   **(see Chapter 6, "Drug Interactions," Table**
(e.g., moclobemide [Manerix®],   **6-7)**
phenelzine [Nardil®],
tranylcypromine [Parnate®])

Monoamine oxidase inhibitors impair the normal metabolism of tyramine and other biologically active amines present in some foods (see Table 6-7). These amines possess a pressor effect. Thus, they can significantly increase blood pressure to the point of hypertensive crisis or hemorrhagic stroke among patients receiving MAOI pharmacotherapy.

Advise patients receiving pharmacotherapy with monoamine oxidase inhibitors to avoid foods high in amine content. If dietary management is not possible, a change to a different class of antidepressant (e.g., selective serotonin reuptake inhibitor, tricyclic antidepressant) is recommended. Note that the clinical significance of this interaction is significantly reduced among patients who are receiving the MAOI moclobemide (Manerix®). See Table 6-7 for further discussion.

Monoamine Oxidase Inhibitors   *Amphetamines*

—See "amphetamines + monoamine oxidase inhibitors"

Monoamine Oxidase Inhibitors   *Dexfenfluramine*

—See "monoamine oxidase inhibitors + selective serotonin reuptake inhibitors

Monoamine Oxidase Inhibitors   *Levodopa*

—See "levodopa + monoamine oxidase inhibitors"

Monoamine Oxidase Inhibitors   *Meperidine*

—See "meperidine + monoamine oxidase inhibitors"

Monoamine Oxidase   **Selective Serotonin Reuptake**
Inhibitors (MAOIs)   **Inhibitors (SSRIs)**

Several cases of a serious, sometimes fatal, drug interaction involving MAOIs and SSRIs (i.e., fluoxetine [Prozac®], sertraline [Zoloft®]) have been reported. Signs of this interaction, which have been referred to collectively as the "serotonin syndrome," include agitation, chills, confusion, diaphoresis, impaired gait, loss of coordination, and memory impairment. Fatal cases of the serotonin syndrome also have been reported with the more recently marketed MAOIs (e.g., moclobemide) and other SSRIs (e.g., citalopram). The exact mechanism(s) of this interaction has not yet been clearly established. However, it is thought to involve an increase in serotonin levels. Although similar drug interactions involving MAOIs and dexfenfluramine have not yet been reported in the clinical literature, the official prescription monograph for dexfenfluramine (Redux®) cautions against the use of this drug combination based on the action of dexfenfluramine (i.e., stimulation of serotonin release and prevention of its reuptake).

The concurrent use of an MAOI and an SSRI for the treatment of refractory cases of depression is not generally recommended because of the potential mortality associated with this interaction. In general, in order to avoid this potentially fatal interaction, a "washout" period equivalent to five half-lives is recommended before changing the patient from an MAOI to an SSRI, or vice versa. If this combination of therapy cannot be avoided, carefully monitor patients, preferably under hospitalization. Immediately discontinue the SSRI if signs and symptoms of the "serotonin syndrome" are noted (see Chapter 5, "Adverse Drug Reactions").

| Monoamine Oxidase | Sympathomimetics |
| Inhibitors (MAOIs) | (e.g., dopamine [Intropin®], ephedrine, phenylpropanolamine, pseudoephedrine [Sudafed®]) |

Concurrent use of MAOIs and sympathomimetics possessing indirect or mixed activity may result in hypertensive crisis and hemorrhagic stroke. This interaction appears to result from the accumulation and release of large amounts of norepinephrine in the CNS. Monoamine oxidase inhibitors impair the major route of metabolism of norepinephrine, resulting in its accumulation. Indirect-acting sympathomimetics cause catecholamine (e.g., norepinephrine) release. Phentolamine (Regitine®, Rogitine®), an alpha-adrenergic blocker, has generally been used to block the major effects associated with excess norepinephrine release.

Patients receiving pharmacotherapy with MAOIs should not generally receive pharmacotherapy with indirect- or mixed-acting sympathomimetics. When unavoidable, collaboration with the prescriber of the sympathomimetic is required because impaired metabolism may persist for up to 2 weeks following the discontinuation of MAOI pharmacotherapy.

| Monoamine Oxidase | Tricyclic Antidepressants (TCAs) |
| Inhibitors (MAOIs) | (e.g., amitriptyline [Elavil®], imipramine [Tofranil®], nortriptyline [Aventyl®, Pamelor®]) |

The combination of an MAOI and a TCA, if initiated carefully with close patient monitoring, may be beneficial in treating some refractory cases of depression. However, this combination of pharmacotherapy may produce severe toxic and potentially fatal reactions (e.g., agitated delirium, dyspnea, hyperpyrexia, hyperthermia, hypertonicity, and seizures, including status epilepticus). The exact mechanism of this drug interaction has not yet been fully determined; however, it has been putatively related to the serotonin syndrome (see "monoamine oxidase inhibitors + selective serotonin reuptake inhibitors").

Combined MAOI and TCA pharmacotherapy should be reserved for patients who are refractory to conventional treatment for depression and should be supervised by experienced clinical psychologists. When combined pharmacotherapy is prescribed, monitor patients closely. If toxicity is noted, discontinue the interacting drugs and refer for supportive medical care as needed.

Monoamine Oxidase Inhibitors   Tyramine (in diet)

—See "monoamine oxidase inhibitors + amines in foods and beverages"

Nefazodone   **Digoxin**

Nefazodone (Serzone®) increases the bioavailability and serum concentrations of digoxin (Lanoxin®), a cardiac glycoside with positive chronotropic effects. The exact mechanism of this interaction has not yet been clearly established.

Patients who are receiving concurrent pharmacotherapy with nefazodone and digoxin should have their serum digoxin levels closely monitored because of the narrow therapeutic index of digoxin. Adjust digoxin dosage accordingly. Collaboration with the prescriber of the digoxin is required. When possible, an alternative antidepressant that does not interact with digoxin should be selected.

Nicotine

—See "tobacco smoke"

Nicoumalone

—See "acenocoumarol"

Nilutamide   *Alcohol*

—See "alcohol + nilutamide"

Nonsteroidal Anti-Inflammatory Drugs   Lithium
—See "lithium + nonsteroidal anti-inflammatory drugs"

Norepinephrine

　　—See "sympathomimetics"

Nortriptyline

　　—See "tricyclic antidepressants"

Olanzapine　　　*Carbamazepine*

　　—See "carbamazepine + olanzapine"

Omeprazole　　　*Benzodiazepines*

　　—See "benzodiazepines + omeprazole"

Omeprazole　　　*Phenytoin*

　　—See "phenytoin + omeprazole"

Opiate Analgesics

　　—See "individual drugs"

Oral Anticoagulants　　　*Barbiturates*

　　—See "barbiturates + oral anticoagulants"

Oral Anticoagulants　　　*Chloral Hydrate*

　　—See "chloral hydrate + oral anticoagulants"

Oral Anticoagulants　　　*Disulfiram*

　　—See "disulfiram + oral anticoagulants"

Oral Anticoagulants　　　*Glutethimide*

　　—See "glutethimide + oral anticoagulants"

Oral Anticoagulants　　　*Phenytoin*

　　—See "phenytoin + oral anticoagulants"

Oral Contraceptives　　　*Carbamazepine*

　　—See "carbamazepine + oral contraceptives"

Oral Contraceptives　　　*Phenobarbital*

　　—See "barbiturates + oral contraceptives"

Oral Contraceptives　　　*Phenytoin*

　　—See "phenytoin + oral contraceptives"

Oxazepam

　　—See "benzodiazepines"

Paracetamol

　　—See "acetaminophen"

Paroxetine　　　　　　　　　　　　　　**Cimetidine**

　The first-pass metabolism of paroxetine (Paxil®) is inhibited by cimetidine (Tagamet®), a histamine-inhibiting antiulcer drug. This interaction results in an increase in paroxetine blood concentrations.

　Monitor patients who are receiving concurrent paraxetine and cimetidine pharmacotherapy for symptoms of paroxetine toxicity (i.e., dilated pupils, dry mouth, irritability, nausea, tremors, and vomiting). Adjust appropriately paroxetine dosage.

Paroxetine

—See "selective serotonin reuptake inhibitors"

Pentobarbital

—See "barbiturates"

Pethidine

—See "meperidine"

Phenelzine

—See "monoamine oxidase inhibitors"

Phenindione

—See "oral anticoagulants"

Phenobarbital

—See "barbiturates"

Phenothiazines

—See "chlorpromazine"

Phenylephrine

—See "sympathomimetics"

Phenylpropanolamine

—See "sympathomimetics"

Phenytoin	**Chloramphenicol**
(diphenylhydantoin)	

The hepatic metabolism of phenytoin (Dilantin®) is inhibited by chloramphenicol (Chloromycetin®), a broad-spectrum general antibiotic. Thus, concurrent use of phenytoin and chloramphenicol may result in phenytoin toxicity.

Patients who are receiving phenytoin pharmacotherapy should generally avoid concurrent chloramphenicol pharmacotherapy if possible. Collaboration with the prescriber of the chloramphenicol may be required. If concurrent therapy cannot be avoided, monitor phenytoin blood levels and observe patients for signs of phenytoin toxicity (i.e., ataxia, mental impairment, nystagmus). Decrease phenytoin dosage if required.

Phenytoin   **Cimetidine**

The hepatic microsomal enzyme-mediated metabolism of phenytoin (Dilantin®) is inhibited by cimetidine (Tagamet®), a histamine-inhibiting antiulcer drug. This interaction results in increased phenytoin serum levels and possible phenytoin toxicity.

Collaboration with the prescriber of cimetidine is required. When possible, a histamine antagonist (e.g., ranitidine [Zantac®]) that does not significantly inhibit hepatic microsomal enzymes should be selected. If the use of this alternative pharmacotherapy is not possible, monitor phenytoin blood levels and carefully observe the patient for signs of phenytoin toxicity (e.g., ataxia, nystagmus). Adjust accordingly phenytoin dosage.

Phenytoin   **Corticosteroids**
                                                                (**e.g., dexamethasone [Decadron®], prednisone
                                                                [Deltasone®]**)

Concurrent use of phenytoin (Dilantin®) and corticosteroids may result in decreased corticosteroid blood levels and pharmacologic effects. This interaction appears to be primarily related to the induction by the phenytoin of hepatic microsomal enzymes.

Collaboration with the prescriber of the corticosteroid pharmacotherapy may be required. Patients who require concurrent phenytoin and corticosteroid pharmacotherapy require monitoring in regard to corticosteroid pharmacotherapy and an increase in corticosteroid dosage if necessary.

Phenytoin   **Cyclosporine**

Phenytoin (Dilantin®) may decrease the absorption of cyclosporine (Sandimmune®), an immunosuppressant used in organ transplantations, and induce its metabolism, resulting in lower cyclosporine blood levels and possible therapeutic failure (i.e., rejection of the transplanted organ). The exact mechanism of this drug interaction has not been fully determined.

When patients who are receiving phenytoin pharmacotherapy require concurrent cyclosporine pharmacotherapy, collaboration with the prescriber of cyclosporine is required so that cyclosporine blood levels can be closely monitored. Patients who are stabilized on phenytoin and who are being considered for organ transplantation require particular attention.

Phenytoin   Disulfiram

—See "disulfiram + phenytoin"

Phenytoin   Fluoxetine

—See "fluoxetine + phenytoin"

Phenytoin   **Isoniazid**

The hepatic microsomal metabolism of phenytoin (Dilantin®) is inhibited by isoniazid (INH®), an antitubercular. This interaction increases phenytoin blood levels and the potential for phenytoin toxicity. This interaction is generally more significant for patients who are slow acetylators (metabolizers) of isoniazid.

When patients who are receiving phenytoin pharmacotherapy require concurrent isoniazid pharmacotherapy, monitor serum phenytoin levels, particularly when isoniazid therapy is initiated, changed, or discontinued. Adjust accordingly phenytoin dosage.

Phenytoin   **Omeprazole**

The hepatic metabolism of phenytoin (Dilantin®) is inhibited in a dose-dependent manner by omeprazole (Prilosec®), an antisecretory drug used to treat hypersecreting disorders (e.g., duodenal ulcers, gastroesophageal reflex disease). Thus, omeprazole increases phenytoin blood levels. This interaction appears to be genetically mediated. Concurrent phenytoin and omeprazole pharmacotherapy among susceptible patients has resulted in phenytoin toxicity (e.g., ataxic gait, confusion, nystagmus, slurred speech).

Monitor carefully patients concurrently receiving phenytoin and omeprazole pharmacotherapy for signs of phenytoin toxicity. Reduce accordingly the phenytoin dosage.

Phenytoin   **Oral Anticoagulants**
                                                         (e.g., warfarin [Coumadin®])

Concurrent use of phenytoin (Dilantin®) and oral anticoagulants may result in variable effects. Initially, during the first week of concurrent therapy, phenytoin may cause an increase in the effect of the oral anticoagulant due to displacement from protein-binding sites. As concurrent therapy continues, phenytoin may cause a decrease in the effect of the oral anticoagulant as a result of the induction of hepatic microsomal enzymes.

Monitor the prothrombin time (PT) or international normalized ratio (INR) and adjust accordingly the oral anticoagulant dosage whenever initiating or discontinuing phenytoin pharmacotherapy in patients who are also receiving oral anticoagulants. Collaboration with the prescriber of the oral anticoagulant is indicated.

Phenytoin   **Oral Contraceptives**

Phenytoin (Dilantin®) can induce the hepatic microsomal enzyme metabolism of estrogen. This interaction appears to be particularly clinically significant with the use of oral contraceptives and can result in oral contraceptive failure, particularly with the use of low-dose estrogen formulations.

High-dose estrogen oral contraceptives (e.g., those containing 50 μg ethynyl estradiol in each daily dose) are more resistant to this interaction and may provide greater protection against pregnancy. Collaboration with the prescriber of the oral contraceptive is indicated so that an alternative method of contraception can be considered for adolescent girls and women of childbearing potential whose seizure control is maintained with phenytoin.

Prednisolone

  —See "corticosteroids"

Prednisone

  —See "corticosteroids"

Primidone

  —See "phenobarbital"

Protriptyline

  —See "tricyclic antidepressants"

Pseudoephedrine

  —See "sympathomimetics"

Pyridoxine   Levodopa

  —See "levodopa + pyridoxine"

Risperidone   Carbamazepine

  —See "carbamazepine + risperidone"

Risperidone   **Selective Serotonin
                                                    Reuptake Inhibitors (SSRIs)
                                                    (e.g., fluoxetine [Prozac®], paroxetine [Paxil®],
                                                    sertraline [Zoloft®])**

   Concurrent use of risperidone (Risperdal®) and the selective serotonin reuptake inhibitors (SSRIs) can result in a significant increase in the plasma levels of both drugs. The exact mechanism of this interaction has not yet been determined; however, it is believed to involve the hepatic cytochrome P_{450} system that is responsible for the metabolism of both risperidone and the SSRIs.

   Avoid concurrent use of risperidone and the SSRIs whenever possible. If risperidone and SSRIs are used concurrently, carefully monitor patients for signs and symptoms of excessive dosage.

Quinidine   Barbiturates

  —See "barbiturates + quinidine"

Ranitidine   Alcohol

  —See "alcohol + cimetidine"

Secobarbital

  —See "barbiturates"

Sedative-Hypnotics   Alcohol

  —See "alcohol + sedative-hypnotics"
  (see also individual drugs)

Selective Serotonin Reuptake Inhibitors   Monoamine Oxidase Inhibitors

  —See "monoamine oxidase inhibitors + selective serotonin reuptake inhibitors"
  (see also individual drugs)

Selective Serotonin Reuptake Inhibitors   Risperidone

  —See "risperidone + selective serotonin reuptake inhibitors"

| Selective Serotonin Reuptake Inhibitors (SSRIs) (e.g., fluoxetine [Prozac®], paroxetine [Paxil®], sertraline [Zoloft®]) | Sympathomimetics (e.g., dopamine [Intropin®], ephedrine, phenylpropanolamine, pseudoephedrine [Sudafed®]) |

Concurrent pharmacotherapy with SSRIs and sympathomimetics, or other drugs that increase serotonin levels, can result in the "serotonin syndrome." Signs and symptoms of this syndrome may include agitation, confusion, increased blood pressure, high fever, muscle rigidity, and seizures.

It is recommended that a "drug-free" interval of five half-lives (see Chapter 3, "Pharmacokinetics and Pharmacodynamics") be used between discontinuing one serotonergic drug and initiating pharmacotherapy with another, because this reaction can be fatal. If not practical or therapeutically feasible, pharmacotherapy should be initiated with the lowest effective dose, and patients should be closely monitored.

| Selective Serotonin Reuptake Inhibitors (SSRIs) | Tricyclic Antidepressants (TCAs) (e.g., desipramine [Norpramin®], imipramine [Tofranil®], nortriptyline [Aventyl®, Pamelor®]) |

All of the clinically available SSRIs can increase the blood concentration of the TCAs. This interaction sometimes results in serious adverse drug reactions, including seizures. The primary mechanism of the interaction appears to involve inhibition by the SSRIs of the hepatic microsomal enzyme metabolism of the TCAs.

The SSRIs should not be prescribed concurrently with TCAs for the treatment of depression unless TCA blood levels are closely monitored (preferably in an inpatient setting). Caution also must be used when replacing SSRI pharmacotherapy with TCA pharmacotherapy, and vice versa. Close clinical monitoring and attention to an adequate "washout" period are recommended.

Sertraline

—See "selective serotonin reuptake inhibitors"

Smoking

—See "tobacco smoke"

Sodium Bicarbonate

—See "urinary alkalinizers"

Sodium Valproate

—See "valproic acid"

Sympathomimetics   *Beta-Adrenergic Blockers*

—See "epinephrine + beta-adrenergic blockers"

Sympathomimetics   *Fluoxetine*

—See "selective serotonin reuptake inhibitors + sympathomimetics"

Sympathomimetics   *Monoamine Oxidase Inhibitors*

—See "monoamine oxidase inhibitors + sympathomimetics"

Sympathomimetics   *Selective Serotonin Reuptake Inhibitors*

—See "selective serotonin reuptake inhibitors + sympathomimetics"

Sympathomimetics   *Tricyclic Antidepressants*

—See "tricyclic antidepressants + sympathomimetics"

Temazepam

—See "benzodiazepines"

Theophylline   Barbiturates

   —See "barbiturates + theophylline"

Theophylline   Tobacco Smoke

   —See "tobacco smoke + theophylline"

Thiazide Diuretics   Lithium Salts

   —See "lithium salts + thiazide diuretics"

Tobacco Smoke   Benzodiazepines

   —See "benzodiazepines + tobacco smoke"

Tobacco Smoke   Chlorpromazine

   —See "chlorpromazine + tobacco smoke"

Tobacco Smoke   **Theophylline**

   Tobacco smoke stimulates the hepatic microsomal enzyme metabolism of the bronchodilator theophylline (Theolair®). This interaction has been documented in both tobacco smokers and nonsmokers who have long-term exposure to passive ("second-hand") tobacco smoke.

   Patients who begin or quit tobacco smoking and who are receiving theophylline pharmacotherapy should be advised to have their serum theophylline levels monitored and their theophylline dosage accordingly adjusted. Collaboration with the prescriber of the theophylline may be required.

Tobacco Smoke   **Tricyclic Antidepressants (TCAs)**
                                                         (e.g., amitriptyline [Elavil®], imipramine
                                                         [Tofranil®], nortriptyline [Aventyl®,
                                                         Pamelor®])

   Chronic tobacco smoking (generally one package daily of 20 cigarettes or more) increases the hepatic microsomal enzymes responsible for the metabolism of the TCAs. This interaction may reduce the serum concentration of the TCAs by up to 50%, with resultant decreased pharmacologic effectiveness.

   When prescribing TCAs, monitor TCA blood levels, particularly when patients begin, resume, or quit smoking. Adjust appropriately TCA dosage.

Tranylcypromine

   —See "monoamine oxidase inhibitors"

Triazolam

   —See "benzodiazepines"

Tricyclic Antidepressants (TCAs)   **Cimetidine**
(e.g., amitriptyline [Elavil®], imipramine
[Tofranil®], nortriptyline [Aventyl®, Pamelor®])

   The hepatic microsomal enzyme metabolism of the TCAs is inhibited by cimetidine (Tagamet®), a histamine-inhibiting antiulcer drug. The resulting increase in TCA blood concentrations may cause a corresponding increase in adverse drug reactions (ADRs), particularly anticholinergic effects (e.g., blurred vision, dry mouth, confusion, constipation, postural hypotension, tachycardia, and urinary retention).

   Monitor patients for increased incidence of ADRs when TCAs are used concurrently with cimetidine. The TCA dosage may need to be decreased when cimetidine is started or increased when it is discontinued. Alternatively, the patient's antiulcer pharmacotherapy may be changed to an alternative histamine-inhibiting antiulcer drug, such as ranitidine (Zantac®) or famotidine (Pepsid®), that does not appear to significantly interact with the TCAs. Collaboration with the prescriber of the cimetidine is required.

Tricyclic Antidepressants (TCAs)   **Clonidine**

Concurrent use of TCAs and clonidine (Catapres®) may result in the loss of clonidine's antihypertensive effects and possible hypertensive crisis. An exact mechanism for this drug interaction has not been clearly established; however, it appears to involve inhibition by the TCAs of central alpha-2 adrenergic receptors.

Avoid concurrent TCAs and clonidine pharmacotherapy. When TCA pharmacotherapy cannot be avoided among patients receiving clonidine pharmacotherapy, collaboration with the prescriber of clonidine may be indicated.

Tricyclic Antidepressants (TCAs)   **Guanethidine**

Tricyclic antidepressants inhibit the transport and subsequent uptake of guanethidine (Ismelin®) in the adrenergic neuron. This interaction inhibits the antihypertensive effects of guanethidine. Several days following the discontinuation of the TCA may be required before the antihypertensive effect of guanethidine reappears.

Avoid the concurrent use of TCAs and guanethidine. Collaboration with the prescriber of the guanethidine may be required.

Tricyclic Antidepressants   *Haloperidol*

—See "haloperidol + tricyclic antidepressants"

Tricyclic Antidepressants   *Monoamine Oxidase Inhibitors*

—See "monoamine oxidase inhibitors + tricyclic antidepressants"

Tricyclic Antidepressants (TCAs)   **Sympathomimetics
(e.g., dobutamine [Intropin®], epinephrine,
phenylephrine [Neo-Synephrine®],
pseudoephedrine [Sudafed®])**

Tricyclic antidepressants block the reuptake of norepinephrine into the adrenergic neuron. This interaction increases the effects of the direct-acting sympathomimetics (i.e., dobutamine, epinephrine, norepinephrine, and phenylephrine). Toxicity (e.g., dysrhythmias, hypertension, tachycardia) may occur.

Avoid, whenever possible, concurrent pharmacotherapy with TCAs and sympathomimetics. When concurrent pharmacotherapy is necessary, collaboration with the prescriber of the sympathomimetic is required. Patients require careful monitoring for any signs of cardiovascular toxicity, with appropriate adjustments of the dosage of the sympathomimetic.

Tricyclic Antidepressants   *Tobacco Smoke*

—See "tobacco smoke + tricyclic antidepressants"

Trimipramine

—See "tricyclic antidepressants"

Tyramine (in diet)   *Monoamine Oxidase Inhibitors*

—See "monoamine oxidase inhibitors + tyramine"

Urinary Alkalinizers   *Amphetamines*

—See "amphetamines + urinary alkalinizers"

**Valproic Acid (divalproex sodium,
sodium valproate)**   **Aspirin
(acetylsalicylic acid)**

The free fraction of valproic acid (Depakene®, Depakote®, Epival®) can be increased twofold to fourfold by the concurrent use of aspirin. Although the mechanism of action is not completely understood, aspirin appears to both decrease the protein binding of valproic acid and inhibit its metabolism.

Concurrent use of valproic acid and aspirin should be avoided. Patients should be informed and educated about this interaction, because aspirin can be purchased without a prescription to self-medicate fever or minor aches and pains. In situations in which this combination cannot be avoided (e.g., a cardiac patient who is receiving a constant prophylactic dose of aspirin daily or a rheumatoid arthritis patient who is stabilized on an anti-arthritis dosage of aspirin), valproic acid blood levels must be carefully monitored and the dosage adjusted accordingly (see Chapter 3, "Pharmacokinetics and Pharmacodynamics," for additional related discussion).

Valproic Acid   Barbiturates

   —See "barbiturates + valproic acid"

Valproic Acid   Benzodiazepines

   —See "benzodiazepines + valproic acid"

Warfarin

   —See "oral anticoagulants"

Index